AT THE
ELEVENTH
HOUR

AT THE
ELEVENTH
HOUR

THE BIOGRAPHY OF SWAMI RAMA

By Pandit Rajmani Tigunait, Ph.D.

Himalayan Institute Press
Honesdale, Pennsylvania

© 2001 by The Himalayan Institute

Published by:
The Himalayan Institute Press
RR 1, Box 1129
Honesdale, Pennsylvania 18431

9 8 7 6 5 4 3 2

Creative direction and design by Jeanette Robertson
Electronic design and production by Julia A. Valenza

The paper used in this publication meets the minimum requirements of American National Standard for Information Sciences—Permanence of Paper for Printed Library Materials, ANSI Z39.48-1984.

Library of Congress Cataloging-in-Publication Data

Tigunait, Rajmani, 1953-
   At the eleventh hour : the biography of Swami Rama / Rajmani Tigunait.
      p. cm
   Includes index.
   ISBN 0-89389-211-4 (hardcover : alk. paper)
   ISBN 0-89389-212-2 (softcover : alk. paper)
   1. Rama, Swami, 1925-1996. 2. Himalayan International Institute of Yoga Science & Philosophy – Biography. 3. Yogis – India – Biography. I. Title

   BL1175.R28 T55 2001
   294.5'092–dc21
   [B]   2001024494

contents

POLITICAL MAP

PHYSICAL MAP

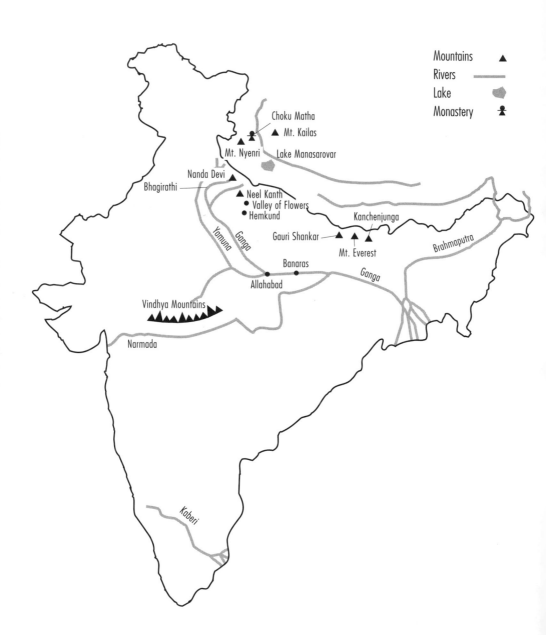

UTTAR PRADESH

introduction

I HAD BEEN HEARING STORIES about Swami Rama since I was a child. They usually centered around his intense austerities, his association with the prince of Bhawal (who had returned from the dead), and his yogic powers. In all the stories, he seemed more like a hero in a fairy tale than a real person. For example, Agamachari, a great Sanskrit scholar from Banaras, once told me that when Swami Rama was a young man he did an intense meditation practice on the bank of the Ganga just across the river from Banaras, and a highly educated dwarf who had died ninety years earlier brought him milk and sweets every night. I found the story thrilling, but it seemed like a fantasy. Agamachari also told me that in those days Swami Rama was known as Bhole or Bhole Baba.

When I repeated this story to my father he dismissed it outright. He told me that, like his master, Baba Dharam Das, Bhole Baba had been a great yogi who left his body voluntarily. He had done this in the 1950s near a shrine in the Vindhya Mountains. Once he decided that the time had come, he dug a pit in front of his guru's cottage, seated himself in it, and asked his companions to fill it with dirt up to his throat. When they had done so, he pulled his consciousness to his head, and using his yogic power, he cracked his skull open. Then, as is customary, his fellow yogis filled the pit completely and built a monument over it in his memory. "That monument is still there," my father added. I was a teenager at the time and was more impressed with my father's knowledge of such things than with the story itself, which seemed like just another marvelous tale.

Then in 1972, when I enrolled in the University of Allahabad, I met a great saint, Swami Sadananda, who taught me some of the esoteric aspects of yoga. But whenever I asked him to teach me the science of Sri Vidya, he either ignored me or told me that I should seek Bhole Baba's guidance. He called him "Yogeshvara," the lord of the yogis, and described him as a sage who enjoys solitude. He is hard to find, Swami Sadananda said, because he never stays in one place for long. I wished that I could meet him, but even though Swami Sadananda spoke of Bhole Baba as if he were very much alive, according to my father he was dead.

Then later, my thesis adviser, Dr. Lakhera, told me that Swami Rama was now living in the United States, and had started an organization called the Himalayan Institute. My first reaction was that this Swami Rama must not be the same person as the Swami Rama I had been hearing about all my life. Why would a real sage go to the West? In fact, taken together, all the stories I had heard about Swami Rama were so full of confusion and paradox that I didn't know whether to seek him out or not. But it turned out that destiny had its own plan.

The year was 1976 and the place was New Delhi's five-star Akbar Hotel—an unlikely place to encounter a sage. And it turned out to be not simply a meeting, but the beginning of a mysterious journey into uncharted territory. It took me two hours to figure out who he was, and when it dawned on me that the person I was talking to was the sage I had been hearing about all my life, I was flooded with a mixture of elation and embarrassment. A moment before I had been chatting with him comfortably; suddenly I was speechless. I did not know how to act. My whole being seemed to become an eye, and in a split second I saw him from top to toe, from inside out and outside in. I was sitting next to him and my head dropped into his lap. His large, piercing eyes were an ocean of compassion, and the love I received in this instant was beyond anything I had ever experienced. He knew that I was overwhelmed. Thought, speech, and action were suspended.

Swamiji said, "I have been waiting for you. When are you coming to the States? You have to help me." Then he began talking of mundane matters, and after a while he told me to leave and come back the next day.

I thought about him the rest of the afternoon and throughout the night, remembering what other saints and yogis, even my own father, had told me about him. In the next twenty hours, millions of thoughts passed through my mind: From now on I will live with this sage who is so loving, kind, and knowledgeable . . . Now that I have met him all my problems are over . . . He will take me to America and I won't have to face the corruption that is choking the life out of Indian society . . . . I was overcome with gratitude toward those who had inspired me to search and find Swamiji. I felt especially grateful to Mr. Anand Pratap Singh, who in an odd and mysterious way had been instrumental in bringing me to Swamiji. Anxiety and excitement made sleep impossible.

The next morning I went to the hotel. Swamiji kept me waiting in the lobby for an hour before he called me up to his room. When I got there his door was open, so I quietly walked in and found him dressed in a two-piece Western suit. I was about to touch his feet in a gesture of respect when he said, "Come with me. We have to do some shopping." In contrast with his calm demeanor the day before, he was now commanding and quite imposing. But still I gathered my courage and touched his feet to receive his blessing. His response was to roar, "What is this feet-touching business? Okay, let's go!" He handed me his bag and strode out of the room.

When we got to the car, he sat in the front seat and put me in the back, which made me uncomfortable because in India it is customary for subordinates to sit in the front—the back seat is meant for the person with status. We drove to Connaught Place, one of Delhi's major shopping districts, and as soon as the car stopped, Swamiji got out and began walking swiftly toward the shops. In my own easy way I opened the door, got out, and then checked to make sure we were leaving nothing behind. By the time I began following him, Swamiji was already fifty yards away and had stopped to wait for me. As I approached him, I saw his face: it was red, and it seemed as if flames were about to shoot out of his eyes and reduce me to ashes. The moment I was within arm's length he exploded, "A slow person himself gets late and makes others late too! Don't be a slowpoke if you wish to

3

be with me!" I got the lesson, and at the same time I saw an aspect of him that nothing I had heard had prepared me for.

The rest of the week was intense. For a while Swamiji was loving, kind, giving, and reassuring. He built my expectations beyond the heights my mind could create. I began to imagine that I was his most beloved disciple. Everything that he had, worldly or spiritual, would be mine, I thought. He would initiate me into the higher forms of spiritual practice, transmit his spiritual energy to me, and very soon yogic accomplishments *(siddhis)* would be at my disposal. Through his grace I would be free of the charms and temptations of the world. Through his grace I would not fall victim to my accomplishments. Three or four days passed while he fueled my spiritual ambitions.

Then the chairman of the University Grant Commission of India visited Swamiji and suddenly the tone changed. I did not know that Swamiji had asked him to offer me a position as a lecturer at Delhi University, and I was bewildered when Swamiji set out to convince me that becoming a lecturer at such a young age would be the best thing for me: I would soon become a professor, he told me; I could stay close to my parents and other members of my family. Furthermore, he said, a swami should not be counted on, for he has renounced everything and doesn't belong to anybody—today he is here, the next day somewhere else.

I was shocked. "What about your promise to take me under your wing?" I asked.

"Don't be emotional," he replied. "Only a fool ignores such opportunities." I became quiet.

Swamiji continued poking at me, but I did not respond. "Why are you not saying anything?" he demanded. "I'm a busy man. Either you listen to me or get out of here."

I said, "I'm trying not to be a fool. I don't want to refuse the opportunity you presented to me the first day—that is, to be with you."

Swamiji became stern and said emphatically, "I never expected you to be so stubborn and arrogant. Now go; we will talk tomorrow."

The next day when I visited him he was loving and kind. He asked sweetly why I had rejected the teaching position, and I said, "Swamiji, because I want to be with you."

At this, he became serious. His big bright eyes seemed to roll inward and he said in a deep, heavy voice, "The life of a swami is constant torture. If you are ready to be happy with pain, only then think of being with me." I didn't know what he meant, and assumed he was trying to get rid of me.

"All I want is to be with you," I pleaded. "After leading me to the summit of my imagination and fantasies, please don't toss me down."

"Is it what you really want?" he asked softly.

I said, "Yes."

"Then give up all your desires," he said. "I will make sure that you get what you need and keep what you have achieved."

I placed my head at his feet, and he put his hand on my head, saying, "Rise and promise that you will not involve yourself in astrology, politics, or petty sectarian religions." I did not understand the full implication of this promise, but I gave it anyway.

From that time on, I grabbed every opportunity to be in Delhi so I could spend time with Swamiji. Often it was impossible to see him for even two minutes, but at other times he allowed me to be with him for hours, and on those occasions there was usually no one else around. Swamiji seemed to enjoy discussing my doctoral dissertation, which was related to philosophy and spiritual practice, but to me the most exciting thing was knowing about Swamiji himself. Yet when I tried to ask him about his life he skillfully ignored my questions. It seemed that he had no past.

Luckily for me one of my father's friends, Mr. Anand Pratap Singh, had known Swamiji for a long time and was the personal assistant and family friend of His Highness Raja Dinesh Singh, the son-in-law of the king of Tihri Garhwal. Swamiji was born in this kingdom and had lived there with his master, and the royal family of Garhwal knew them both well. Within a few months Mr. Singh had told me so many stories about Swamiji's life that one day, driven by a childish impulse and unable to contain my excitement, I asked Swamiji's permission to write his biography. With a sweet smile he said in a gentle yet emphatic tone, "Yes. Twenty-one years from today you will write it." I felt a flash of embarrassment at my immaturity and presumption, as well as a burst of elation at the conviction with which

5

he spoke. Swamiji immediately changed the subject and then dismissed me. I did not see him again for almost ten months.

I was fortunate to have two other people in my life at the time who further enriched my understanding of Swamiji. The first was Mr. Singh's mother, a pious lady who had spent much time with Swamiji from 1962 through 1964, when he was living in the city of Allahabad. She was a walking encyclopedia not only on Swamiji but also on hundreds of saints and yogis from different traditions, and the moment she heard that I would be working for Swamiji she generously extended her counsel. "Don't be mistaken by his external appearance," she said. "He belongs to no one but his master. He lives in the world, but he is not of the world. He appears to be cool, but he is the living fire. Being with him means sitting in the *kunda* [the sacrificial fireplace]. He is like the wind—don't try to bind him, for your efforts will go in vain." She took me to Shiva Kuti in Allahabad, where Swamiji had lived, and shared a number of her experiences with me. What she told me helped me gain an insight into Swamiji's esoteric side. It was she who first traced for me Swamiji's life from his present identity as Swami Rama back to his identity as Bhole Baba. She also told me about Bhole Baba's master, Bengali Baba, who was also known as Baba Dharam Das (a name he was commonly known by at the beginning of the last century). She described Swamiji's ability to die at will and remain dead for several hours before coming back to life—an ability Swamiji had demonstrated to a group of eminent professors from the University of Allahabad.

My second source of information at this time was Dr. M. P. Lakhera, my thesis adviser at the University of Allahabad, who came from the village where Swamiji was born. His understanding of Swamiji was entirely different from that of Mr. Singh and his mother. According to him Swamiji was merely the son of a learned pandit from the Garhwal Himalayas. He had inherited a large sum of money from his uncle, and was the handsomest man Dr. Lakhera had ever seen. Swamiji was a brilliant student with incredible retentive power, Dr. Lakhera said, but he had wasted himself by becoming a monk. Had he joined the faculty at a university, Dr. Lakhera believed, Swamiji could have carried on the legacy of Professor R. D. Ranade, India's most learned philosopher. During Swamiji's student days Professor Ranade had demonstrated a special love for this young man and had spent much of his private time with him, but to everyone's dismay Swamiji deserted the academic world to wander aimlessly. He mastered hatha yoga and cultivated psychic powers at the cost (in Dr. Lakhera's view) of stunting his intellectual growth. But Dr. Lakhera did admit that Swamiji was a remarkable hatha yogi.

From the time that I met him in 1976 until I moved to the United States in the fall of 1979, I saw Swamiji in New Delhi whenever possible. Following his instructions, I also visited such places as Banaras and the shrine of Kamakhya. Then in the fall of 1979 I came to the United States—where I heard people talking about Swamiji in completely new ways; it was as if they were describing a different Swami Rama from the one I knew. I lived in Minneapolis for the first seven months and during that time I met a number of people who held a variety of strong opinions about him. To some he was a Himalayan adept with miraculous powers to transform a person's life; to others he was a mystic scientist of some sort who displayed remarkable control over his autonomic nervous system; and of course there were those who simply saw him as a charismatic leader to follow around. All three personae were strange to me, because in India I had seen him as an unpredictable and loving sage whose inner and outer worlds were saturated with the presence of his master and the Divine Mother. In India stories about him told of how he studied at the feet of various masters, undertook intense practices at holy shrines and remote places throughout India, and occasionally made mistakes, which were corrected by his master and other sages. Once in a while people had miraculous experiences in his presence, but unlike some of his followers in Minneapolis, no one I knew in India ever thought of him as a magician—a maker of miracles.

In the summer of 1980 Swamiji called me to the headquarters of the Himalayan Institute in Pennsylvania, where he lived most of the year. Now I saw another aspect of Swamiji. Here, he was acting the part of a CEO of a large organization. I had never imagined him adhering to a schedule, particularly a hectic one, yet here he was, traveling and lecturing all over the country. In administrative matters he was like a military commander, keeping everyone on their toes, and whenever he was at the Institute he was constantly holding meetings, giving lectures, writing books, or supervising construction and landscaping projects. In the midst of all these activities he found time to cook his own lunch. (I was lucky enough to be his assistant.) He had trained the residents so well that, unlike when he was in India, no one bothered him with spiritual or business questions when he was out and about: taking a walk, planting trees, having his meals, or playing with the children. In India I had seen him only in five-star hotels, and it often took weeks or months for even VIPs to get an appointment with him. Here Swamiji was readily available to all. In public he appeared as imposing and charismatic as he had seemed in India, but in private he lived simply.

It was amazing to see how hard he worked and how little he slept. Normally his day began at seven a.m. and continued until two a.m. Then in the early morning hours, after dismissing the late-night crew working with him, he would take a bath and begin his real work: meditation. But no matter what time it was, I always found him fully present in the moment. He enjoyed everything he did: meditating, watching TV, writing books, making children giggle, attending to important guests, and playing tennis with the residents. To him cooking, practicing music, painting, gardening, teaching, traveling, conducting business, and discussing spiritual matters were simply different modes of worshipping God. He was nice to almost everyone, but hard on those who worked closely with him: with them he was gentle in private but harsh, even merciless, in public. And because of this, students often abandoned him.

In 1983 he asked me to translate his book *Living with the Himalayan Masters* into Hindi. I worked on the translation during the day and read it to him at night. Hearing what had been written seemed to refresh his memory, and he often interrupted my reading to tell about experiences he had not mentioned in the book. These were both fascinating and enriching. I had no time to write them down then, but I tucked them away in my heart for safekeeping. It was during these sessions that Swamiji told me about his master—his birthplace, his favorite places hidden away in the Himalaya and Vindhya Mountains, and his other disciples, including Bhawal Sanyasi, the famous prince swami. At that time Swamiji also told me about his grandmaster, who lived in Tibet most of the time, and about the ancient monastery known as Choku Gompa, situated in the Lhachu Valley on the western side of Mount Kailas. But he never mentioned his own life with his master. It was only in 1985, when I accompanied him to Tikam Garh and Khajuraho in central India, that I came to know about the time Swamiji lived with his master.

During this trip Swamiji introduced me to members of his family and other relatives. I also met people who were his friends before he was ordained as Swami Rama. It was interesting and often bewildering to interact with this mixed crowd: some were Swamiji's devout students, some were merely admirers and followers, and still others treated him like a relative or an old friend. I watched him play many different roles at once. Dressed in a two-piece suit and silk shirt, he was perfectly at home with those who treated him like a relative, discussing family matters with them and demonstrating full interest in their worldly business affairs. To his students he was the beloved teacher—and in the midst of all this he managed to take short trips to meditate in nearby places where one of his "guru brothers" *(gurubhai),* the prince of Tikam Garh, had done his *sadhana* (spiritual practices) and where Swamiji's master had visited often.

Now for the first time Swamiji told me about roaming these hills and forests with his master—how his master helped him overcome his fear of snakes, and how the cluster of temples and ruins at Khajuraho was his master's favorite dwelling place. There, looking toward the distant Temple of Sixty-four Yoginis, he seemed to enter a trance, becoming speechless for a time. A week later he told me of an extraordinary spiritual experience his master had given him at that place when he was seven years old.

Ever since I first met Swamiji I had been interested in discovering how he carried his Himalayan caves into our chaotic world. I had been vigilant in observing how he taught me, how he taught others, how he kept the mundane world and the spiritual world together—and once again I was brimming with excitement. I was convinced that by now I

9

knew a great deal about him, and I wanted to write his biography right away. But when I again asked his permission he replied, "Does anyone allow anything to be written about himself in his own lifetime?" So I postponed the book, but the idea never stopped brewing, and I continued to spend as much time in Swamiji's presence as he allowed.

In 1987 Swamiji gradually started to channel his energy into building a fully equipped medical complex in northern India, just outside the town of Dehra Dun. His students from all over the world joined him in this endeavor, and by 1990 the project had taken off. The area that this medical complex was designed to serve is one of the poorest in India, and the sudden infusion of money, job opportunities, and publicity—both in India and in the United States—attracted a swarm of opportunists. It was then that an amazing number of tales about Swamiji, both positive and negative, began to circulate in both countries. Swamiji was at the center of it all. He was put on a pedestal by some, and vilified by others. A host of people in India—officials and prominent citizens as well as ordinary people—honored him as a great humanitarian, while others accused him of being a CIA agent. Many Westerners revered him for his spiritual wisdom and charitable work, while others sought every chance to prove him a scoundrel. In the midst of all this commotion I found him as calm and tranquil as an elephant immersed in a lake on a hot summer day.

Swamiji left this world late in the evening of November 13, 1996. During the last phase of his life he remained involved in supervising large construction projects, raising funds, and handling all kinds of administrative matters in India. Yet as he neared the end of his life, the sage within him became more and more apparent. No one who came to see him went away empty-handed. People from all over the world visited him or wrote or telephoned during this period, and all had one experience in common: whether they saw him, talked to him, or received an answer to their inquiries by other means, they all found that the specific concern they laid at his feet dissolved. For example, I personally know of many whose cancer was cured immediately after their condition came to Swamiji's attention. I saw those who sought Swamiji's help because they were headed for divorce find their marriages infused with new life, while those whose children were slipping into drug and alcohol abuse saw them make miraculous recoveries. Although he did not tell me the exact date it would happen, he hinted that he would soon leave this world.

By May of 1996 Swamiji's body had become a bundle of bones, but his mind was as transparent as crystal. Still living in this world, he seemed beyond time and space. Past, present, and future merged. The aura that surrounded him did not seem to have a boundary. But even in this state he held meetings, made decisions, and issued directives. He was living on water and juices, but the light in his eyes was brighter than ever and his countenance was as relaxed and cheerful as if he were resting in the lap of the Divine Mother. Even on the morning of his last day he was making jokes. He called Sri Roshan Lal Kanodia, one of his beloved students, and said, "*Haridwar le chalo* [Take me to Haridwar]." Roshan Lal got up instantly and stood for a second, thinking. Then he said, "Sir, should I bring the Tatta Sumo or the Tatta Estate [the SUV or the sedan]?" Swamiji was having a hard time speaking, but replied with a gentle smile, "Foolish man. Does anyone transport a corpse in a Tatta Estate?" That evening around eleven o'clock he left his body.

I had been around Swamiji since early September, and everything that took place during this time confirmed my conviction that Swamiji was the master of all the yogic practices he speaks of in *Living with the Himalayan Masters*. In the words of the sages, he used to say, "You have a body, but you are not the body. You are in the body, yet you are beyond the body. Birth and death are like two commas in the poem of life. For a yogi there is nothing like death. Just as an ordinary person takes off an old tattered garment and puts on a new one, so does a yogi cast off his worn-out body and assume a new one." That is how he himself left his body.

People all over the world have different reasons for believing that Swamiji was a great master. In most cases it is because of the miracles he performed. He took someone's chickenpox on himself, for example, or brought down a fever simply by sprinkling water on the patient. Or it was through his blessings that a businessman prospered or someone's father survived what should have been a fatal accident. Or through his simple touch or gaze he would sometimes transmit such incredible spiritual energy that a student would go into a trance, remaining in that state for hours. Or he would create a tumor in his own thigh, later dissolving it at will, or make a blister on someone's hand disappear in a flash.

To me such events are not valid grounds for considering someone a master. Before meeting Swamiji I had known yogis who could walk on water, play two flutes at once (one through each nostril), kill a rooster by slicing a lemon, materialize a crystal Shiva lingam from thin air, or predict future events well in advance. But I had also found that many such "accomplished" people had little or no interest in spirituality and were as miserable as those who were totally immersed in worldly affairs.

In Swamiji I saw the perfect sage, brimming with love and compassion—as well as a disciplinarian who tolerated no nonsense. He was a person of unmatched generosity—when involved in an act of charity, he saw no limit—but as the head of a charitable organization, he negotiated down to the last penny. More than once I saw him set in motion the wild dance of the forces of construction and destruction and then simply witness it from a distance. Institutions grew around him—and fell apart. Followers flocked to him with gifts and garlands—and abandoned him in disappointment and anger. In all situations I saw him cheerfully embracing gain and loss, honor and insult, with perfect equanimity. Every aspect of his life was full of extremes and contrasts, and yet to those who knew him intimately he was a simple man.

To me Swamiji is a master not because he had lots of students and followers but because he was master of himself and his surroundings. During the last forty years of his life he did not sleep for more than two hours a day, and yet he was so energetic that no one could keep up with him for long. The people who worked with him worked in shifts. A peaceful yet forceful energy filled the space around him; sloth and inertia could not withstand it. Fully grounded within, he could attend to ten tasks at a time with perfect precision and mastery. While he was dictating a book, he could shout at a contractor on the telephone and sip his tea with no sign of disturbance on his face. He was a master because he lived in the world and yet remained above it. He was always in charge of himself and the world around him. He was at once cool like the moon and hot like fire. He was exceedingly kind to those who studied with him and practiced under his supervision but kept their distance, but very hard on those who wished to be close to him and carry on his mission. He was a cyclone making everything swirl around him as he sat quietly in the eye of the storm, watching to see who had the strength and insight to face the tempest.

Yet when he lived in the Himalayas and secluded places in other parts of India, hardly anyone saw him. He was a hermit who spent his nights meditating in the Himalayan caves; villagers came to him with milk and food, seeking nothing other than the unspoken name of God that naturally filled the space around him. Swamiji had a masterly way of hiding himself. As soon as he began his work in the world he drew such a thick veil around his true identity that only a few could see who he was. He lived in the bustling cities of New Delhi, Tokyo, and Chicago, surrounded by politicians and businessmen. Villagers could no longer reach him. People came with garlands, fruit baskets, and bundles of money. Some sought his blessings to win elections, others to ensure their prosperity and progeny. Spiritual seekers who had heard of him but did not know where to find him could now ring him in the hotel and schedule an audience.

Yet even while playing the role of a five-star-hotel swami he always attended the Lord of Life Within. At midnight he took off his worldly mask and assumed his true identity: the sleepless Himalayan master. When he lived in the West he kept an extremely busy schedule, but deep down he remained the sleepless envoy of the Himalayan sages.

There have been many great masters who shine brilliantly. Swami Rama stands out among them not because he had more knowledge or spiritual power than others but because the saga of his life is similar to our own. He was a lively and curious child—he made mischief and got into trouble, just as all youngsters do. As a spiritual seeker he fought with his master, ignored his instructions, and thought of running away. There were times when he was so entangled in the world that no one but his master could rescue him. And like all of us, he had rough periods in his life. He became an orphan while still a young child, for example, and was discarded by his own brother and looked after by a saint who owned nothing. Still he managed to go to school, find time for spiritual practices, cultivate self-respect, conquer adverse conditions, and prove that through persistent practice one can become perfect.

Swamiji's life tells us that once you offer yourself to the Almighty Lord, the world naturally prostrates at your feet. Once you conquer your mind, you have conquered the world. Once you have found joy and beauty within, the whole world becomes infused with joy and beauty. Once you are successful inside, external success is yours. Once you surrender your desires to the Almighty, you are free of your personal whims and ambitions. Then the Divine Will itself becomes your desire. Swamiji's life story shows us how to discover the connection between ourselves and the Divine; how to surrender our personal desire to Divine Will; how to unfold our potential to its fullest; how to be successful in the world without losing sight of the higher purpose and meaning of life.

Swamiji's life was his message: "You are a child of the Divine and you have infinite potential to become and to be anything you wish." He knew—as all sages know—that for those who understand this message, there is no fear left on the Earth.

in the BEGINNING

SWAMI RAMA HAD PARENTS and was part of a biological family, but he had a greater affinity with the place where he was born than with the people who raised him. Spiritually speaking, the Himalayas were his parents. "Living there was like living in the lap of a mother," he writes in *Living with the Himalayan Masters*. "She brought me up in her natural environment and inspired me to lead a particular style of life." A few pages later he adds, "These mountains were my playgrounds. They were like large lawns spread as though Mother Nature had personally looked after them so that her children who live in the valleys would remain happy, joyous, and aware of the purpose of life. It is there that one can come to understand that from the smallest blade of grass to the highest of mountain peaks, there is no place for sorrow in life."

When an aspirant becomes a swami he renounces his family and stops associating with his past. No longer belonging to anyone, he is beyond all sentiments and emotional ties. But Swamiji did not renounce his true family, the Himalayan peaks, nor did he dissociate himself from the memories related to them. Instead, he nurtured those ties throughout his life. In *Living with the Himalayan Masters* he spares less than three pages for his father and mother, and even those pages are mostly taken up with how his parents met his master and what happened afterwards. He often said that what he received from the mountains, glacial streams, and flower-filled valleys could not be obtained from biological parents or other relatives. Worldly love, he said, is tainted with attachment and expectation, but traveling to Himalayan shrines infuses the heart with pure love, a love that gave him the power to roam those mountains without fear. From them he learned the gospel of nature. Living among them, he realized that everything is alive. In everything—from lily blossoms to cactus thorns, from a blade of grass to the tallest cedar, from the smallest pebble to the towering peaks—he heard the song of the life-force. Those memories occupied more room in Swamiji's mind than the memories of the parents who were instrumental in bringing him to this world.

His parents lived in that part of the Himalayas known as Deva Bhumi, the land of gods, a large portion of which is in the area now known as Garhwal. Famous shrines such as Badrinath, Kedarnath, Gangotri, and Jamunotri, and holy peaks such as Nanda Devi, Chaukhamba, and Neel Kanth are located here in the Garhwal Himalayas. These are pilgrimage sites that every Indian longs to visit at least once in a lifetime.

Villagers in this region observe the time-honored tradition of serving the saints and sages and other pilgrims traveling to the shrines. The high peaks and deep valleys, cut by untamed rivers and torrential streams, have allowed these people to remain relatively isolated from the rest of the world. They live a simple life. Nature has afforded them neither the opportunity to accumulate many worldly possessions nor the occasion to develop a distracted mind. Here, unlike the modern world, the past is never lost. Formal education rarely goes beyond the level of elementary school, yet these people have preserved their traditional knowledge intact: their knowledge of herbs and astrology is unparalleled. They are generally intelligent, and given the opportunity, Garhwalis demonstrate their abilities and earn prestigious posts in the universities and competition-based branches of the civil service.

Until the nineteenth century Garhwal maintained its sovereignty and remained an independent kingdom. Then in 1803 the Nepalese Gurkhas, a people renowned for their fighting ability, began to encroach on the region. Realizing that it would be difficult, if not impossible, to defeat the Gurkhas without help, the king of Garhwal enlisted the aid of the British, agreeing to divide his kingdom equally with the British when the Gurkhas were defeated. Accordingly, when peace was restored to the region Garhwal was divided into two parts: British Garhwal and Princely Garhwal. Swamiji's family lived in British Garhwal, near the town of Landsdowne, and because of British influence the people in this region became relatively affluent and progressive. The brahmins, already renowned for their knowledge of the scriptures, the Sanskrit language, astrology, and religious matters, had the opportunity to study English, and many secured influential positions within the British administration.

While other members of the family joined the race for modernization, Swamiji's father, Buddhi Vallabh Dhasmana, preserved tradition by studying Sanskrit, astrology, and religious sacraments. He was known as Panditji, a title for an accomplished scholar of the Vedas who has dedicated his life to spiritual practice. The Dhasmana family owned a large tract of farmland, but because they were brahmin and followed the old customs of Hindu society, they did not farm the land themselves. Villagers from other castes worked the fields and did the rest of the manual labor, leaving Buddhi Vallabh free to further his knowledge of the scriptures and intensify his spiritual practices. He was a married man with grown children, all of whom were well-educated and happily settled in government jobs before Swamiji entered the picture.

17

Seeking a quiet place to do their sadhana, aspirants and adepts from all over India frequently visited Garhwal, and the area around the village where the Dhasmana family lived was a stronghold of saints and yogis, such as Bengali Baba, Gudari Baba, Sombari Baba, and Boorhe Baba. Buddhi Vallabh was famous for his generosity as well as his scholarship, and the saints and yogis found great pleasure in visiting him, often staying at his home. One day a saint stopped by who said he had come from the holy shrine Amar Kantak in central India. Buddhi Vallabh and his wife greeted him with their customary love and respect, and soon host and guest fell into a conversation. Their talk took a startling turn when the saint suddenly asked, "Tell me, why is your family name 'Dhasmana'?" Buddhi Vallabh had no idea, so the saint explained, "Actually your family was known as 'Bhasmana,' which means 'born from ash.' Later the word got distorted and you people came to be known as 'Dhasmana.'"

Then the saint went on to tell this story: Long ago a wandering sadhu stopped in a village to ask for alms, as was the custom, and one day when a housewife came to her door to put food into his begging bowl he saw that she was unhappy. He accepted the food and sat under a tree to eat his meal. Then, determined to find an opportunity to help the woman, he built his *dhuni* (fire) a little distance from the house, and spent a few days sitting beside it. The housewife and other women from the neighborhood brought him food and other necessities, and after a few days, when the woman he wanted to help was comfortable with him, he asked her why she was so sad. She told him that she was barren and was thus thought to be inauspicious. She was shunned by everyone, she said, including her husband—no one wanted to see her face. She had thought about ending her life and overcoming her misery once and for all.

18

When he heard this the sadhu got up from his seat, and after reciting the name of the Lord, said in an authoritative voice, "Take some ash from this dhuni, smear it on your body, and put some in your mouth. You will have a child, a radiant boy who will bring joy to you and be a light to the whole world." With these words the sadhu left.

Unable to contain her excitement, the housewife told the other women in the neighborhood, but they mocked her foolishness. "What a great way of having a baby!" they scoffed. "Just rub ash! Does a baby come from ash? If your husband finds out that you are crazy, he will kick you out." Embarrassed, the woman collected all the ash and threw it in the compost pit.

Twelve years passed before the sadhu returned to see how the boy was doing, and when he discovered that the woman had no son, he was baffled. "What did you do with the ash?" he asked. "I threw it in the compost pit," she replied.

The sadhu went to the compost pit and called, "*Alakh Niranjan* [Come forth, untainted, unseen one]"—and a radiant twelve-year-old boy emerged. Because he was born from the ash of cow dung, he came to be known as Gorakha Natha (the adept who emerged from the ash of cow dung) and became a famous yogi in the Himalayan tradition. The sadhu was the great master Matseyendra Natha, Gorakha Natha's guru. The local people called Gorakha Natha "Bhasmana" and his children were also called Bhasmana. The events in this story took place near Landsdowne, and even today there is a shrine in the area dedicated to Gorakha Natha.

When he had finished telling this story the sadhu reminded Buddhi Vallabh that there had always been yogis in his family and asked him, "When are you going to wake up and uphold your family legacy?"

The next day the sadhu was gone, but his visit left a deep impression on Buddhi Vallabh. He began to reflect on his life—what had he done so far, what was he doing now, and where would it lead him? Had he done anything other than keep himself alive and support those who were dependent on him? If he died at that instant, he wondered, what would go with him? Who would accompany him? Do life's gains and losses, successes and failures, honors and insults have any real value?

Buddhi Vallabh began to reevaluate the knowledge he had gained from his teachers and from the scriptures, and he realized that he had been repeating mantras and reciting scriptures simply because that is the job of a pandit. He had thought that he knew everything there was to be known, and thus he had never felt the need for a guru. Yet all the scriptures say that unless you are initiated by a competent master, mantra and scripture recitation are of little value, and he saw that even though he had been reciting his favorite scripture, *Durga Saptashati*, for the past thirty or forty years, he had not gained the direct vision of the Divine Mother, which the scripture promises to those who recite it faithfully.

The fire the saint had kindled in Buddhi Vallabh kept burning brighter until he could no longer contain it. He yearned to leave home to commit himself one-pointedly to an intense *tapas* (austerity) and meditation. His knowledge of the scriptures convinced him that if he could fuel his intense desire, a *sat guru* (genuine master) would come into his life to guide him, and he would reach his goal. But he knew that his family would not allow him to just walk away and leave the world behind. He also knew that if he stayed at home and tried to intensify his practice there, it would be hard to avoid all the perfunctory tasks of a pandit that he had been performing for years.

19

He was convinced that to transform himself from a professional pandit to a genuine *sadhaka* (seeker) he must move to a place where no one knew him. So one night he gathered his courage, withdrew his attachment to his family, and walked away.

Buddhi Vallabh was already a great devotee of the Divine Mother Durga, so living near a shrine dedicated to that goddess was a natural choice. There were several such places in Garhwal, but all were too close to his village to give him the anonymity he sought. So he went to a shrine dedicated to Manasa Devi in the forest near Haridwar and built his dwelling in the hills nearby. He began his meditation with the intention of finding a master who could initiate him and put him on the path.

Manasa Devi is a compassionate goddess. According to popular belief, she fulfills the desires of those who pray to her for help and brings peace and happiness to the human mind *(manas)*. Her shrine is now a central pilgrimage site in Haridwar and can be reached by cable car, but seventy-five years ago it was only a small temple on top of a steep hill surrounded by a thick forest. It could be reached only by foot. Elephants and tigers roamed the area, and the scarcity of even the barest necessities prevented all but the most courageous and austere *sadhakas* from doing their practices there.

Buddhi Vallabh's family was bewildered by his sudden disappearance. The villagers were full of speculation. Some thought he might have become a monk, and others were sure that he was dead. They looked for him at the nearby shrine of Tarkeshwar, to no avail. No one had the time or the inclination to undertake a more extensive search. His wife was distraught—all she could do was cry and hope for his safe return. But after a few months of waiting, she gave up hope and undertook intense austerities herself—fasting, and worshipping the gods and goddesses who, according to her faith and family tradition, resided at nearby shrines.

Six months passed. Buddhi Vallabh continued to meditate on the Divine Mother at the shrine of Manasa Devi. He had undertaken a very special practice known as Shata Chandi, which required that he observe many austerities, such as eating only once a day, bathing in the Ganga, worshipping the Divine Mother at the temple, and reciting the entire scripture, *Durga Saptashati,* every day. He spent his remaining time doing *japa* of the *navarna* mantra, and on the day he finished the practice, the great Himalayan adept Bengali Baba visited Manasa Devi. Buddhi Vallabh was thrilled to see the sage and was certain that the Divine Mother had brought this great master on the last day of his practice. He was also certain that Bengali Baba was the master who would guide him on the path. Still holding his mala, he placed his head at the master's feet, and Bengali Baba blessed him, saying, "Your practice at Manasa Devi's shrine is complete. Now let us go to Chandi Devi, the shrine across the river."

Following Bengali Baba (who was also known as Babaji), Buddhi Vallabh set off to Chandi Devi. Master and student bathed in the Ganga and filled their vessels with water before climbing to the small temple, perched at the summit of another steep hill. Here Bengali Baba formally initiated Buddhi Vallabh and gave him precise instructions on how to meditate on the *navarna* mantra while focusing at the navel center. Buddhi Vallabh had been practicing this mantra for the past thirty or forty years, but he had learned it from the scriptures. Now he experienced how it felt to receive the mantra from a realized master.

In 1983, when I showed him the Hindi translation of *Living with the Himalayan Masters,* Swamiji began to speak about his master and his father. Sensing that he was in an unveiling mood, I asked, "Swamiji, I wonder: What was the exact nature of the practice pertaining to the *navarna* mantra that Babaji taught to your respected father? Was it a particular variation of that mantra, or were some of the syllables different from the mantra as it is written in the scriptures?"

Swamiji replied, "The practice, which is associated with Ganesha, is a precursor to the *navarna* mantra. When the time comes, you too will learn this practice." With these words he closed the subject, but during the more than six months it took me to translate the book, Swamiji told me how the practices described are to be done, and the results that one can expect. He also told me more about Babaji's interaction with his father.

Babaji and Buddhi Vallabh remained at Chandi Devi for a week, and during that time Babaji answered questions that had long been brewing in Buddhi Vallabh's mind. Babaji reminded him that the purpose of his life was not simply to be born, grow old, and die—he had already completed his personal duty toward his family, and now he must commit himself to fulfilling the wishes of a long line of sages.

Babaji then instructed Buddhi Vallabh to return home to his wife and have another child, promising that raising this child would not be an obstacle to his own spiritual growth. He told Buddhi Vallabh to always remember that the child was not his, that he was only the instrument for bringing it into the world. This child, he said, would be his *guru dakshina* (the love offering a student makes to the teacher upon receiving initiation). Buddhi Vallabh was amazed, but he knew that his master would tell him to do only that which was right, so he willingly agreed to return home.

When he reached the village his wife was overjoyed to see him again, but others were bewildered, dismayed, and chagrined. When Buddhi Vallabh disappeared, they had been worried about him and concerned about his wife. So they had searched a bit and waited for a while before concluding that he was dead. The family held a funeral for him in absentia, followed by the traditional thirteen-day ritual. His wife, however, had not accepted this and was still wearing the clothes and ornaments of a married woman. Her refusal to follow the customs of a traditional Hindu widow had created a stir in the community and embarrassed the family.

That was not all. Had the villagers known that Buddhi Vallabh was alive and involved in intense spiritual practice, some would have regarded him as a spiritual hero and others as an irresponsible escapist. But when he returned unexpectedly after so long, it caused a different kind of commotion. Many wondered whether he had taken *sannyasa*, the formal vows of renunciation, when he was away, for according to Hindu custom the greatest sin imaginable is to reenter a householder's life after becoming a renunciate. The village wanted to make sure it was not sheltering a sinner who would bring misfortune to the community, so they busied themselves trying to find out where Buddhi Vallabh had spent his time, what he had done during his absence, and where the saint was who may have initiated him.

Buddhi Vallabh learned an important lesson about love and fear. As soon as he returned he told everyone about the mental state that had caused him to leave, that he had gone to the shrine of Manasa Devi, that he had been visited by the great master Bengali Baba, who initiated him, and that he had returned home at Babaji's behest. He assured the villagers that Babaji had not ordained him as a monk—he was still the same old Buddhi Vallabh. He told them that Babaji had instructed him to continue following the householder's path, and had even blessed him and his wife so that they would have another son. The commotion subsided somewhat, but suspicion lingered.

Buddhi Vallabh was in his late sixties and his wife was in her late fifties; considering the life span in the mountainous regions of India they were quite old. But even though his wife was skeptical that they would have another child, the miracle happened as predicted: within a year or so she conceived, and in due course a son was born.

On the very day that the baby was born, Babaji arrived at Buddhi Vallabh's home and demanded to see the child. According to custom, however, the mother and child were to remain in seclusion for twelve days, so the mother and other family members hesitated to take the baby outside the room. But Buddhi Vallabh reminded his wife that this child was the fruit of Babaji's blessings and convinced her that it was all right. When the infant was placed in Babaji's hands, the saint held the baby for a few minutes, looking at him deeply. He then gave the baby back, saying, "Remember, he belongs to me. Raise him with love, and when the time comes I will take him with me." Buddhi Vallabh asked Babaji to have lunch in his home, but Babaji refused, saying, "I came only to see the child and to remind you that he belongs to no one but God. Do not be attached to him." With these words, Babaji left.

At the naming ceremony the infant was given the name Brij Kishor Kumar, and the people in the village affectionately called him Kishori. His parents called him Puttu (slang for *putra,* son). From the beginning, this baby was unusual. He was born with holes in his earlobes, for example, and the fearful villagers saw this as an inauspicious omen. It confirmed their belief that Buddhi Vallabh should not have reentered the life of a householder. They were afraid, and prayed that whatever misery the child brought would not affect anyone other

23

than his parents. Yet these same holes in Kishori's earlobes were what convinced Buddhi Vallabh that this baby was indeed an extraordinary gift from his master and the Divine Mother. The sadhu who had told him how his family name came to be Dhasmana had also told him that the saints in this tradition pierced their ears as part of their spiritual initiation, and Buddhi Vallabh saw the holes in the child's ears as living proof that this soul belonged to the tradition of Guru Gorakha Natha. He shared this conviction with his wife so that she would care for the baby lovingly but without becoming attached to him.

Because of her advanced age the mother was unable to nurse the infant, but fortunately the wife of her twenty-eight-year-old son had recently given birth, and nursed the baby willingly. As was usual in an Indian household, Buddhi Vallabh had little to do with the day-to-day aspects of raising his son, but he was fully aware of his spiritual responsibility toward the boy and he knew that he could fulfill this duty only by committing himself exclusively to sadhana. So he devoted his time to the practices into which his master had initiated him. In worldly matters he was not as useful to his family as he had been before; he was no longer interested in such things.

Buddhi Vallabh's older sons were grown, educated, and settled in government jobs. In economic terms the family was middle class, but their British education and their connections with officials high in the government gave his sons a sense of superiority. Their father's withdrawal from social contacts in favor of meditating and reciting ancient scripture was beneath these modern English-educated men. And if this were not enough, their father was also exhibiting a love for Kishori that was so one-pointed it prevented him from giving his grandchildren the kind of attention they deserved. As Swamiji told me, "Definitely there was a feeling of discomfort, especially in the heart of the brother whose children were my age." Even so, that brother's wife, the one who nursed Kishori in place of his mother, was generous, loving, and kind, and always treated him as her own child.

Kishori was the most handsome boy anyone had ever seen. Active and energetic, he was also moody and unpredictable. At times he slept sixteen to twenty hours straight; at other times he woke up frequently, crying or saying things that made no sense. He was healthy physically, but on occasion he seemed abnormal mentally. Yet for some indescribable reason, even though they feared he might bring them harm, people in the neighborhood were drawn to him. After Kishori was born, sadhus began to visit the village more frequently, and the curious villagers would talk to them about the child. Some villagers would say that he was specially blessed; others would say he was possessed, and ask the sadhus to free him from evil spirits through their blessings.

Buddhi Vallabh had adopted a strict routine. He would get up early, take his bath, and begin his practice. A big part of this consisted of lengthy rituals to propitiate Ganesha and the Divine Mother. He worshipped them with ritual ingredients such as water, sandalwood paste, flowers, milk, yogurt, honey, turmeric, rice, vermilion powder, incense, a ghee lamp, fruits, and sweets. Then he recited the entire *Durga Saptashati*, followed by *japa* of his guru mantra. He concluded the practice by giving the sweets from the offering to his beloved son.

One day when Kishori was almost three years old, his oldest brother invited some friends for lunch and ordered special sweets in their honor. It was around noontime, but the guests had not yet arrived. Buddhi Vallabh had just finished his practice and had given the graced sweets to Puttu as usual. He remained in his meditation room while the child came out, happily clutching a sweet in his hand. Seeing this, the brother assumed that the spoiled kid had stolen a sweet reserved for his guests, and asked him sternly where he had gotten it. With a mischievous look, the boy crammed it into his mouth and tried to run away. But his brother caught hold of him and demanded an explanation. Kishori's mouth was so full he could not speak—he was trying to swallow quickly, but he was having a hard time moving his tongue. Furious, his brother slapped him on the cheek. Despite the pain, Kishori could not cry out. All he could manage was a muffled sob. So his brother began to beat him, all the while shouting, "You stubborn boy! This is what you are learning?"

Kishori spat out part of the sweet and swallowed the rest. Now he was able to cry, and did so at the top his lungs. His brother continued to beat him, trying to force him to admit that he had stolen the sweet.

25

Hearing the commotion, Buddhi Vallabh came out of his meditation room, and the boy pulled himself free and ran to him. Shocked, Buddhi Vallabh wrapped his arms around the child and asked why his eldest son was treating him so cruelly. "You have spoiled him!" his son replied angrily. "He has no manners! He steals things and won't admit it when he's caught!"

Overwhelmed, Buddhi Vallabh told his son where the sweet had come from and said to him with profound sorrow, "Misery will befall you and you will have no peace." Then he carried Puttu to his meditation room, where he hugged the child and wept. After this incident he became increasingly introverted. He rarely spoke to anyone, and died a short time later.

His wife was devastated. Already weak from childbearing and caring for her youngest son, she grew even weaker. Eventually she became blind and was no longer able to do much for Kishori. His brother's wife remained steadfast in her love for him, but with his mother suffering from grief and declining health, the superstition that Kishori's existence would bring misery grew. Many members of the family were beginning to believe this as well, even though Bengali Baba had assured them that the boy was special and would bring joy to everyone.

Soon after his father's death, dreams began to wake Kishori up during the night—sometimes they made him happy, and at other times they frightened him. When he described what he saw in these dreams, he said that in some he was led by bizarre-looking people to dense forests and dark caves, where people with red eyes and matted hair were doing something that scared him; in other dreams, he and Bengali Baba went to the place where his father lived, and his father gave him sweets, and he was very happy. He also had dreams about beings that did not look human.

Even when he was awake, Kishori would get lost in the world of his imagination. These symptoms had been apparent when his father was alive, but now they were getting worse. His family consulted doctors and priests. Exorcists performed their esoteric rituals—to no effect. One day Kishori was eavesdropping as a group of astrologers discussed his horoscope, and he heard them say that he had special astrological factors *(markesha dasha)* and would die at the age of twenty-eight. Bengali Baba arrived at that moment and shouted at the astrologers, "You all will die, but nothing will happen to my son! He is an innocent boy *[bhola bhala]* and you people are creating fear in his mind. I will make sure that your stars are useless." Then, patting Kishori's shoulder, Babaji said, "I love you the most. You are my son, and soon I will take you with me." With these words he departed.

During my talks with Swamiji in 1983 he mentioned his master on several occasions, but he could never say more than a sentence or two before drifting off into his private world. His eyes would focus in the far distance without blinking and he would remain quiet for a few moments. Then very gently he would say to me, "Now you go." His long gaze and serious countenance enabled me to hear his unspoken words, and I knew that the more he valued something, the less he talked about it. That was the case with his master, his father, the practices he undertook, and the experiences he gained from them.

27

After his father departed from this world Kishori was basically an orphan, but the joint family system enabled him to grow up with his nieces and nephews, and when the time came he was enrolled in the nearby elementary school. He was not fond of school, however, preferring to sit quietly and contemplate the mysteries of life. People thought he had become an introvert as a result of his father's death. His childhood habit of waking up from bizarre dreams had subsided, but his habit of remaining aloof grew stronger. He had all the symptoms of depression. He went to school only because the other children his age went, the school was nearby, and the teachers loved him. But he was always preoccupied by his own innate questions: Why was I born? Why in this family? What is my relationship to these people who are taking care of me? Who are those people who come so often in my dreams? Babaji is my real father and mother: When will he come to get me? Why should I bother to study in this school if I'm not going to be part of this world?

In *Living with the Himalayan Masters* Swamiji wrote that when he was young he remembered his past life very clearly, and it felt strange to find himself with this particular family. But as he grew up, the memories began to fade. He tried to hold on to them through contemplation and conscious effort, but the more involved he became in the world around him the more he forgot, and the gradual loss of his true identity made him anxious and sad. When he was little he had expressed his thoughts and feelings without hesitation and was considered abnormal. Now he was old enough to understand that such feelings should not be shared with everyone.

Yet Kishori was not completely isolated. There were two old women in the village who, in Swamiji's words, "were very holy," and with them he could sit and talk about anything. They were kind and their words were consoling. They told him stories of saints and yogis and the miraculous powers of the gods and goddesses. And what they told him about reincarnation helped the boy demystify his own dreams and visions. These women were not educated, but they knew the value of an education, and they encouraged Kishori to go to school and study hard so that one day he could become as learned and respected as his father.

After he completed primary school, no one except for the elderly members of the family called him Kishori any more. They used his full name, Brij Kishor Kumar, and during his junior high school years (grades six through eight) he began spending more time with Bengali Baba and other sadhus. By now the bond between Brij Kishor and the saint had become so strong that whenever Babaji was in the vicinity, the boy lost interest in everything else. Babaji spent most of the summer and early winter in the Garhwal Himalayas, so the boy could spend his summer vacation with him. But once summer was over, being with Babaji usually meant missing school, and so his attendance was poor. Still, he always scored the highest marks in the class.

Bengali Baba himself was highly educated, and he made sure that his blessed child paid attention to his studies. Under Babaji's direction a host of sadhus frequently visited Landsdowne and the nearby villages. They called Brij Kishor "Bhole," which means "innocent boy," and they all had one purpose in visiting him: to inspire him to learn worldly skills and become familiar with the world without falling victim to it. They helped him overcome his indifference to his studies by convincing him that he would get the best of the best from Babaji only after he completed his schooling. By this time the villagers of awakened mind realized that Brij Kishor was actually the Bhole these sadhus spoke of, and that sooner or later he would walk away from the confines of their little community.

Although Bengali Baba never drew a crowd, he was a well-known master among the circle of sadhus. His followers were prominent people in society, high government officials, and heads of state in northern and eastern India. He was a wanderer and never built a permanent dwelling, yet whenever he wished, wealth in unimaginable quantities was at his feet. The king of Amar Gargh in north India, for example, donated hundreds of acres of land and built a monastery for Babaji and his students, and then endowed it heavily both with money and farmland. So Bengali Baba, this mysteriously capable mendicant, now took charge of Bhole's education and made him go to the best schools in north India.

29

After eighth grade Bhole's life is extremely hard to trace in its entirety. For decades I have tried to follow his movements and develop a chronology of his activities, but with little success. For example, of the many people I talked to who came from the same region of Garhwal, there is not a single one who can remember more than a few facts about those days. The information furnished by Garhwalis such as the Purohits, Dhasmanas, Saklanis, and Khanduris gives the impression that Swamiji was born and raised in Garhwal, vanished from people's memories after junior high school, and then reemerged in the mid-1950s. They said that sixteen years of his life, between the ages of approximately fourteen and thirty, are obscure. I found this puzzling, and pondering it gradually convinced me that this must have been a period of intense inner growth for Bhole. So I began to look outside the known circle of his friends and family for information.

With the exception of the last few pages, *Living with the Himalayan Masters* tells of Swamiji's experiences during those sixteen years, and in 1981 a powerful thought swept through my mind: If I read this book a thousand times, one way or another I will actually experience the company of the saints and sages and the places described there. So I began reading, and the more I read the more I could hear the unspoken parts of the stories. Then, just as I was close to completing my thousand repetitions, Swamiji asked me to translate the book into Hindi. And as I read the translation to him in the evenings, he began to answer my questions even before I asked them.

One of my questions was how had he gone to college if he was staying with his master in the cave monasteries. Like anyone else who has read *Living with the Himalayan Masters* I was under the impression that Swamiji lived with his master from early childhood and that he also graduated from the University of Allahabad in India. During one of our sessions I asked Swamiji how it was possible to do both, but he only told me how spiritually enriching those days had been.

So one day I asked Swamiji directly: "After your father died, when Babaji came and took you with him, nobody at home said anything? They just let you go?"

Swamiji replied, "My mother had full faith in Babaji. She knew he was capable of providing me with anything I needed. She knew he would take care of me better than anyone else."

"So you stayed with him and never came back?" I asked him. "Then how did you go to school?"

"I stayed with him sometimes for a few days, a week, or sometimes even months. 'Living with him' does not mean to be with him in a cave. Usually he did not stay in one place for a long time, and when he stayed for a while, there were other sadhus with him. I knew he loved me very much, and I loved him too. But in those days I was a child and my problem was that I wanted to be active—running, talking, playing—but he was too quiet. I enjoyed being with him more when there were other sadhus around him.

"Traveling with him was full of excitement," he continued. "Walking in the mountains, crossing the streams, sitting under a protruding rock during a storm, sitting around a fire in the nighttime, helping him and other sadhus cook a meal in the middle of nowhere thrilled me. But by the time my vacations with them were over I was excited to go back to school. Not that I liked school, but during the next vacation they promised to take me to more beautiful places than before. And each time I came back home I felt that everything was stale—same family, same friends, same schoolmates. They looked strange to me; I looked strange to them. That is how I continued living in both worlds."

The summer Bhole was fourteen his life reached a turning point. He was in high school; peer pressure was taking its toll and he was gradually getting sucked into the world. An old sadhu visited his home and handed him a note written on a piece of birch bark. It read, "Bhole, my blessings. Turn your face from the world. Set out on your spiritual journey. Avadhoota, Gangotri, 1939." Bhole had never seen this sadhu before, nor did he know who had sent the note, but it had a powerful effect on him; jolted by this note, he drifted back into his inner world. Deep contemplation brought back flashes of his past, and once again he thought seriously of quitting school. Finally, unable to manage his conflicting emotions, he visited his master, who was staying at a shrine in the region. At that time Babaji was accompanied by his senior disciple, Swami Shivananda of Gangotri, and at Babaji's behest Swami Shivananda talked Bhole into remaining in school.

Because the school in the village ran only up to eighth grade, Bhole had to leave the village for places like Mussoorie, Dehra Dun, and Allahabad for higher education. Life became more intense for him in both the worldly and the spiritual sense. He was precocious, and the freedom from home coupled with the opportunities at school and the company of sadhus allowed his spiritual genius to express itself. But he was also a teenager, high-spirited and full of mischief. He began to enjoy shopping and playing music, and he tried to impress his master and other sadhus with his fancy clothes and his transistor radio. This didn't work, but it never undermined their love for him.

Once Bhole carried three gramophones and dozens of records to his master, who was staying with five other sadhus on the outskirts of Narendra Nagar, a town beyond Rishikesh. Once there, he played music day and night while the others were doing their meditation. His music became louder and louder, until finally the sadhus complained to his master. With a smile Babaji said, "He's a young boy looking for attention. Let us go and listen to his music." So Babaji went to Bhole, admired his taste in music, and enthusiastically asked him how many gramophones he had. Bhole told him that he had three, and more than

31

two dozen records, in addition to a battery-operated radio so that he could keep up with the news and remain informed about the top musicians. His master smiled and said, "I am glad you are growing to be a person of refined taste. Let me hear your music." So Bhole turned on one of the gramophones. But his master was not impressed, and asked him to turn on the others too. Bhole told him that you cannot play more than one gramophone at a time, and his master asked, "Why not?"

Puzzled, Bhole said, "Because it becomes noisy and you can't hear anything." Looking disappointed, Babaji said, "Oh, I thought the more the better." Bhole was embarrassed, but he still played his gramophones, becoming less mischievous only when he realized that the sadhus were not reacting to the disturbance. By the end of his stay Bengali Baba had made Bhole understand that hearing someone else's music makes you dependent on that music. You don't enjoy it—you become addicted to it. The pleasure derived from this music addiction is nothing compared to the pleasure of hearing yourself sing.

Now Bhole really got into music. Every day, as soon as his academic classes were over, he practiced—he sang and played the tabla, the harmonium, the sitar, and the vina. Even his friends grew tired of his songs and his instruments. He performed for a radio station in Lucknow and was proud of his performance. The next time he visited Babaji he took his vina and became so absorbed in his music that he did not want to do anything else. When he was with his master, however, he was expected to gather the firewood, clean the rice and beans, and wash the dishes, at the very least. So he was always looking for ways to escape from his duties.

One day when he was cleaning the beans a mischievous thought came into Bhole's mind: "If these sadhus realize that I'm sloppy and not good at separating the pebbles from the beans, they will stop asking me to do it." So instead of removing the pebbles from the beans, he added a few tiny ones. The beans were cooked and served, and suddenly there was a loud cracking sound: an old sadhu had broken his tooth. Everyone knew what Bhole had done, and his master, feigning ignorance, decided to teach the boy a lesson. He told the other sadhus that Bhole was getting out of hand and needed to be disciplined. So they made a plan.

The next morning at dawn, when all the sadhus were in meditation, Bhole began playing his vina as usual, and singing a love song. With this, the sadhus rose as one, marched over to the young musician, broke his vina, and beat him up. And when he ran to his master, who was sitting quietly in the cave, meditating, and told him what had happened, Bhole complained that it was Babaji himself who had told him to practice music. His master replied, "I told you to practice that music which doesn't disturb others. Do you know the law of karma? If you break someone's tooth, you are bound to have broken bones. From now on listen to the inner music. No more of this noisy music for forty years."

For the next few hours Babaji and the sadhus remained distant. Then a great adept, Gudari Baba, who had not participated in the beating, took Bhole to his own little hut, and with his kind and loving touch healed the boy's injuries, both physical and emotional. He reminded Bhole of how much Babaji and the other sadhus loved him. "It is good to have the best of the best, but be humble and kind," he told him. "Ask Babaji how to listen and enjoy the inner music. He will tell you how to entertain the Lord of Life with that inner music. And when you entertain the Lord of Life, you will be able to entertain yourself and others naturally. Don't forget the purpose of life."

33

Soon Babaji came to Gudari Baba's hut and was embraced by a tearful Bhole. Babaji hugged him and, looking at Gudari Baba, said, "He doesn't know how painful it is to me when I see him sad." That day Babaji systematically taught Bhole how to sit, how to breathe, and how to meditate. He also gave him lessons on how to lead a healthy and happy life and how to be with friends yet remain unaffected by their company.

Years later, Swamiji still remembered that incident vividly. It took place at a Shiva temple near Sombari Baba's ashram, at the confluence of the Koshi and Siraut Rivers, approximately fifteen miles outside of Almora. Bengali Baba, Sombari Baba, Hariakhan Baba, and Gudari Baba used to meet in this area quite often. Swamiji had told me several stories about the greatness of these masters, and I had heard from other sources that they were like living gods and that it was only through God's grace and good karma that one could be in their company. So after I heard how mischievous Bhole was and how he misbehaved with them, I wondered: How was it possible to be so naughty in the company of such great masters? In such a rarefied environment, how could his conscience permit him to play music while these holy men cooked and washed the dishes? One day, when an opportunity presented itself, I asked Swamiji these questions.

"Self-transformation requires more than just being in a sanctified atmosphere," he replied. "Habits ingrained in the unconscious mind are very powerful. Intellectual understanding and periodic inspiration from the sages bear fruit only when one commits to transforming oneself. I was a tough kid. My master worked hard to transform my stubbornness into willpower, my mischief into creativity.

34

"When I was only seven years old he had given me a vision of the Divine Mother by throwing me at her feet, and that experience helped me to understand that she is my mother. I am always under her protection. My master is always with her and she is with my master. After I received that vision I was filled with boundless gratitude toward my master and other sages. I thought that I would never misbehave with them again, that I would love them and serve them. But within a week or so I went back to my old self—the same mischief, the same negligence. Once in a while I felt sorry for my misbehavior and confessed it to my master. But he would say lovingly, 'It's not you. It's childhood. I will throw you at her feet a few more times and you will be all right.'"

I had not yet received a complete answer to my questions, so I asked, "Swamiji, when did you have that vision? Where did it happen and how?"

"It happened in Khajuraho," Swamiji said. "Only a few years after my father's death my master took me there with five other sadhus. In those days the area was still wooded and there was no town around it, only a few villages in the distance. Khajuraho itself consisted of a cluster of sixty or seventy temples, and most of them had fallen apart. Everybody in our group stayed in the Temple of Sixty-four Yoginis. My master stayed in the temple most of the time and kept his eyes closed, meditating. Other sadhus either meditated in one place or offered their worship at different temples in the area.

"For a few days I was excited. I accompanied the sadhus and played around while they did their worship and meditation. And when asked, I bowed my head to the idols in those run-down temples and closed my eyes, pretending that I was meditating because I knew the sadhus liked that. But within a few days I was bored. It was wintertime. In the night it was cold. In the morning everybody was meditating and I wanted to have a fire to warm myself, and also I was hungry. So one morning I ran all around the temple noisily, hoping to catch the attention of the sadhus meditating there. But with no success.

"I finally came to my master's chamber, where I coughed and dropped things and made all sorts of noises, but my master remained motionless. I even pulled his hair. Finally I opened his eyelids with my fingers. With that he got up, enraged, picked me up with both hands, raised me above his head, strode to the main shrine in the temple, and swinging me in the air, shouted to the Divine Mother, 'Make him learn how to behave or take him back!'

"Just as my master was about to hurl me at the statue of the goddess, the Divine Mother appeared in her full glory. She was the embodiment of beauty and bliss as she took me from my master's hands and held me lovingly in her lap. I still remember the rays of compassion that emerged from the corner of her eyes and the wave of love from her countenance. With an indescribable smile she looked at my master and blessed me, saying, 'From now on he will be a good boy.' I was filled with both joy and terror as she handed me over to my master and disappeared. The memory of the Most Beautiful One stays always in my heart.

"Unable to contain myself, I wanted to talk about this to the other sadhus. But my master stopped me: 'Lay your hand on your mouth and do not allow the secret to come out of the chamber of your heart.'"

Then, looking at me, Swamiji said, "One day I will take you there."

I felt that he did not want to talk more about her, yet he seemed interested in saying more. So I asked him, "Swamiji, after you had her vision and received her blessings, were you no longer driven by your childish behaviors?"

"No, no," said Swamiji. "Even after that I sometimes behaved

35

foolishly, but the memory of the vision and the blessing of the goddess helped me remain free from guilt and self-condemnation. The experience convinced me that she and my master knew everything about me and were always helping, guiding, and protecting me. And I knew that if I did something foolish on the spur of the moment it wasn't a sin for which I would be punished. The vision also gave me the strength to remain open to my master and to discuss my weaknesses with him.

"Whenever I talked about my problems and weaknesses to my master," Swamiji went on, "he would simply say, 'It's okay. Be nice to yourself. Be honest to your feelings. Do not be the slave of your mind and senses, but don't work against your natural inclinations.' This advice left me on my own to decide when to restrain myself and when to flow along the natural currents of my thoughts and emotions.

"Many times I thought I was right, but it turned out that I was wrong. My master always stressed that I must discover the truth from my own experience. The truth received from sources other than direct experience, he told me, is mere information—opinion that does not stand the fire of trial and test. Furthermore, looking back, I realize that my master wanted me to be a normal person. He did not want to spoil my childhood. So he imposed "dos and don'ts" on me very rarely. When discipline was absolutely necessary he handed me over to my *gurubhai* [guru brother], Swami Shivananda, whom I lovingly called Bhai Shiva."

Even though Swamiji lived in the company of Babaji and other great masters, he rode the roller coaster of youthful emotions just as we all do, and as a college student he was distracted by the charms and temptations of the world. At the University of Allahabad—a prestigious university—he was surrounded by well-to-do friends, and in their company he wanted to be like them: have a car, attend parties, and spend money shopping and traveling. During vacations, instead of facing the hardship of walking through the mountains with his master, he wanted to visit Bombay with his friends.

Babaji knew that these desires had to be conquered through fulfillment rather than repression, so he gave Bhole opportunities to do this through the generosity of Aghori Baba, an adept who lived in a cave near the shrine of Dhari Devi, on the outskirts of Sri Nagar. Aghori Baba was an adept of the esoteric science *surya vijñana*. He was full of miracles, and with his unlimited financial help Bhole could have all the material goods he wanted. Trips to Europe in those days were for rajas or wealthy aristocrats, but Aghori Baba made it possible for Bhole to have the best of the best in both the worldly and the spiritual realms, to taste everything, and then to discern for himself what is fulfilling and what is worthless.

At the University of Allahabad Bhole's professors and friends knew him as an outstanding student. Few people knew him as Bhole; here he was Brij Kishor Kumar, a brilliant scholar of philosophy as well as English and Hindi literature. His friends marveled at his genius and his revolutionary ideas. To his fellow students he was always a puzzle— he was carefree, he frequently skipped classes, and yet he scored the highest marks. Professors regarded him with respect and awe because Professor R. D. Ranade, the most renowned philosopher in India, had taken him under his wing and treated him as his most beloved disciple. Professor Ranade was unmatched as a scholar of every school and every aspect of Indian philosophy, but he was most honored for his profound spiritual wisdom. He was the rare combination of mystic and academician. Those with open minds and clear insight easily sensed that Brij Kishor was blessed with inner light and that it was in honor of that light that Professor Ranade had extended special love and attention to this young man.

Among those who also detected this light in Brij Kishor was the eminent poet and revolutionary, Nirala. His full name was Surya Kant Tripathi, but "Nirala"—which means "unique, strange, mysterious"— was a title that had been conferred on him in recognition of the mystical quality of his poetry and its multilayered meaning.

Nirala was a giant in body as well as in spirit. Healthy and strong, he consumed mounds of food at a sitting, and as he approached old age he became more and more strange. Most of the time he remained in a state of non-dualistic awareness in which he saw no difference between himself and others, so he was acutely sensitive to the pain and pleasure of those who happened to be right in front of him. He was so attuned

37

to universal consciousness, in fact, that he had lost the sense of "mine and thine." Nothing stayed with him for long. If someone covered him with an expensive shawl to protect him from the cold, it wouldn't be long before he had given it away to someone in poverty. Everyone who knew him was aware of his exalted state and treated him as a member of their own family.

Nirala was also temperamental. It was impossible to predict when he would lose his temper and at whom—and once he was in a fury, it was hard to control him. People noticed, however, that in Brij Kishor's presence he **was** invariably gentle, kind, and open to whatever discussion this young man initiated. Nirala often called him "Bhole Prabhu."

One hot summer night Nirala walked into Company Garden, a park reserved for British officers and their families, where he took off his clothes, and fell asleep on a bench. At dawn the guards, seeing a naked man, hit him with their sticks to get him up so they could throw him out—but when Nirala woke up, he beat all of them. Soon a truck full of policemen arrived, including the police inspector—who realized that the offender was Nirala. At once the inspector apologized and respectfully asked him to leave the park, explaining it was not open to the public. But Nirala roared, "This is where I live! Who is here to throw me out from my home?" The British authorities knew that using force on Nirala would be like adding a spark to a sulfur mine—the whole city would go up in flames. But the time for the British ladies to go for their morning walk was drawing near and it was unthinkable that they should see a nude man lying there in the park.

Nirala's connection to Bhole Prabhu was well-known, so someone sent for him, and as soon as he arrived Nirala chuckled, "Bhole Prabhu, come. See how foolish people are, that they want me to leave my own place."

"How can they, your own self, fight with you?" Bhole Prabhu asked. "They want you to come and have your breakfast."

Like a child, Nirala said, "Oh? Then let's go."

Handing him his clothes, Bhole said, "Put on the veil of maya, Maharaj [great lord]," and while Nirala was dressing, Bhole Prabhu turned to the inspector and said, "Before he reaches the police station, you'd better get some breakfast there. And make sure there is plenty of food."

The distinguished scholar and writer Rahul Sankrityayan had also detected the light in Brij Kishor's eyes. Rahul and Nirala were friends, even though both men had strong opinions and were often at odds philosophically. Rahul was a Buddhist convert but his knowledge of all aspects of Indian philosophy and literature was vast. Rahul was also a wrestler. Intellectually he wrestled with Sanskrit, Pali, Prakrit, Tibetan, and Chinese texts; he debated and defeated Hindu, Buddhist, Christian, and Islamic ideas at will. And on the physical level, he was so strong that he had a hard time finding anyone strong enough to wrestle with him. So to give exercise to his mighty shoulders, he would run with all his might and hit trees with his shoulders. At breakfast he would consume a stack of *puris* (deep-fried, unleavened bread) that reached from his navel to his chin, chasing it with a dozen bananas and a liter of milk. But figuratively speaking, his brain was a thousand times larger than his stomach. The contents of the top libraries in India, China, and Tibet occupied just a corner of it.

Shortly after the incident in Company Garden, Nirala and Bhole paid a visit to Rahul in Lucknow. Bhole was getting tired of living an uneventful life, so in his mischievous way he set out to embroil these two dynamic men in a contest of strength and wits. He knew exactly how to spark Nirala, but he needed to figure out how to incite Rahul. He knew that Rahul was particularly proud of his knowledge of Chinese and Tibetan, and that deep down Rahul was convinced that no one could have restored the ancient Sanskrit Buddhist texts (which had been lost) had he not retranslated them from Chinese back into Sanskrit. Bhole also knew that Nirala was blessed with genius beyond imagination and that his mind could penetrate where the rays of the sun could not. So one evening Bhole managed to maneuver these two bulls into a fight by remarking, "What a charismatic person Shankaracharya was, to have single-handedly wiped out Buddhism in India and established the dominance of the Vedic dharma. And he accomplished it all before the age of sixteen! It took twelve hundred years for someone like Rahul to incarnate and revive the knowledge that Shankaracharya so mercilessly destroyed."

39

Nirala shot back, "Knowledge is not an object that can be manufactured, destroyed, or recycled. Knowledge is eternal. It has its own way of coming to light and disappearing again. Only an ignoramus thinks he has discovered or rediscovered knowledge."

Rahul remained quiet, but Bhole could see that he was fast becoming incensed. So Bhole added fuel to the fire by saying, "Hindus revere Shankaracharya for freeing India from Buddhism, but they don't realize that in doing so he did irreparable damage to the Indian heritage. That was not very saintly of him."

The lion within Nirala woke up with a roar. "Big words from a small mouth! Shankaracharya is knowledge walking in the flesh. Before you dare to criticize this light, better you shape yourself up! Do you know that by the time he was sixteen he had completed his studies, found his master, completed his sadhana, defeated the scholars and philosophers of all faiths, written the commentaries on the Upanishads, restored the knowledge of the Vedas, established monasteries in all four corners of India, transformed the lives of millions, and given his body back to nature—at that age many of us have not even learned how to wash our bottoms!"

At this, Bhole made a gesture of humility and submission, as if he were trying to prevent the conversation from taking an ugly turn—thus cleverly seeking protection in Rahul.

Rahul jumped into the fray. "If a young boy with a shaven head, followed by a bunch of groupies, walks among ignoramuses, what do you expect? Religion is like opium—the majority in any society are addicts. To become a hero in such a society, all you have to do is convince them that your opium is the best. That's what Shankaracharya did. He was a confused man. He had no clear stance in his philosophy and religious practices. Befitting his personality, he taught the philosophy of confusion—maya—and all confused people loved it. Ignorant Hindus were so blind they did not notice that Shankaracharya advocated the nameless, formless Brahman on one hand, but ran into every single temple he passed—the more run-down the better—and worshipped all the gods and goddesses, hoping to accumulate their grace. Sanskrit pandits put him on a pedestal and capitalized on his desire for name and fame. And trying to please local people—local rulers, pandits, and peasants—he demonstrated his dedication to local shrines, be they associated with Vishnu, Shiva, or any other form of the Divine. Just like his grandguru, he plagiarized Buddhist ideas—and at the same time he led the public against Buddhism and Buddhist monks. He was more a shrewd politician than a philosopher and spiritual leader."

The battle was joined, and it grew more and more heated as the night wore on. Bhole cunningly assumed the role of referee. The voices of the disputants got louder; they rolled up their sleeves and pounded their thighs for emphasis and thumped the furniture. It was early morning before they went to bed.

The next day, they had been invited for breakfast at the home of Acharya Narendra Deva, and there they resumed their dispute, dragging this civilized and very learned gentleman into the melee in the role of judge. And while pretending to act as a referee, Bhole skillfully continued to fuel the fire, saying that Rahul represented Buddha and Nirala represented Shankaracharya, and since the argument did not seem to be winding down, he decreed that whoever consumed the most food would be declared the winner. Nirala said, "This first pile of potatoes on Rahul's plate is for his knowledge of *Vishuddhi Magga*" [a prominent Buddhist text].

41

"A few more bananas, Nirala, for sustaining your Shankaracharya's commentary on the *Brahma Sutra*," Rahul mocked. With such remarks flashing from both sides, the two men consumed a huge amount of food, and it was impossible for the acharya to determine who had eaten the most. Eventually the contest between these two great men ended in a draw.

In the company of such scholars and his friends at the university, Bhole was growing into adulthood. He was fully involved in the world around him. He experienced the stress of exams and felt pressure from his peers to participate in their social life, but at the same time he was constantly being reminded of the higher purpose and meaning of life. Bhole had been welcomed into Professor R. D. Ranade's inner circle, and had an opportunity to observe him closely. He found that, intellectually stimulating as it was, Professor Ranade's company was even more spiritually stimulating. He was a living example of how to live in the world and yet remain above it. Ranade was always busy writing books, giving lectures at the University of Allahabad and other universities, and overseeing his ashram in Maharashtra, but despite all this activity Bhole saw in him a mystic who transcended the realm of intellect. Ranade possessed a startling clairvoyance—Bhole often saw him reply to a stack of letters without opening them. And one day, on the spur of the moment, he started to talk about a very private aspect of Bhole's life: his relationship with Babaji, how much Babaji loved him, and what Babaji expected of him. Professor Ranade spoke of some of Bhole's experiences with Babaji as though he had been right there when they happened. And when Bhole asked how he knew about those things, Ranade replied, "Why not? I am him and he is me. We are in each other."

When Bhole asked, "Will I be able to experience the same, and will people and events become as transparent to me as they are to you?" Ranade replied, "That great master does not want you to waste your time with fortune-tellers. Riding the wave of my own inner joy I uttered those words—and perhaps it was due to the wish of that great one who made the arrangements for you to be with me."

Being with Professor Ranade helped Bhole remain aware of the higher goal of life despite all the attractions and distractions the world had to offer. By watching this great man, Bhole was finally convinced that it is possible to be both a scholar and mystic, to be successful in the world and yet maintain a spiritual life.

Later when Bhole mentioned Ranade to his master and asked how he had reached such a height of realization, Babaji said simply, "Practice."

"Can you teach me what to practice and how to practice?" Bhole asked.

"I was waiting for the day when you would ask me about practice," his master replied. "Go to Darjeeling. Outside the city there is a stream, and on the bank of that stream is a cremation ground. No matter what happens, for forty-one days you should do a particular practice, which I am going to teach you. No matter how much your mind attempts to dissuade you from completing the practice, you should not leave that place."

Bhole found this exciting. Darjeeling is one of the most beautiful places in the eastern Himalayas. What a great way to spend his vacation: doing practice in such a place. Furthermore, that cremation ground on the outskirts of the city is where Bhole Baba's brother disciple, the prince swami, popularly known as Bhawal Sanyasi, was supposed to have been cremated but where Babaji brought him back to life instead.

Bhole went to Darjeeling and began his practice at the cremation ground. Following all the disciplines and observances as prescribed by his master, he undertook the practice and continued it for thirty-eight days. But he did not see any result. On the thirty-ninth day, a powerful thought came into his mind: "What a waste of time! I have disconnected myself from the world and am living here in this lonely place. My master has told me that when I have completed the practice I will see a marked growth in myself, and that I must not give it up before the forty-first day. And he warned me not to be swayed by the suggestions of my mind. But I wonder: If nothing has happened in thirty-nine days, why expect anything to happen in the next two?"

Bhole pondered this awhile and decided it was better not to waste any more time with this practice. So he poured a bucket of water on the *kunda* (the sacred fireplace) and destroyed the little thatched hut where he had been living. Wrapped in a woolen shawl, he walked to the city and wandered through the streets. Suddenly he heard a woman singing from an upper window: "There is very little oil in the vessel of life, and the night is vast." The drummer accompanying her kept the beat, "dhak dhik," a sound which resembles the Sanskrit word that means "shame on you." Bhole was overwhelmed, sure that this sweet and meaningful song was coming from the Divine Mother, whom he had seen years ago in the Temple of Sixty-four Yoginis. He felt as though the "dhak dhik" of the tabla was coming from his master, Professor Ranade, and all the sages who had bestowed their blessings on him so selflessly and lovingly. He was profoundly ashamed, and went back to the cremation ground, completed his practice, and was

43

blessed with the outcome as predicted by his master.

This experience showed Bhole how tricky the mind is and how cleverly it convinces our reason and conscience to surrender to the charms and temptations of the world. It was also a lesson in patience: tend the plant with faith and it will mature and bear fruit. And through it Bhole learned to exercise his power of will and determination: once embarked on a journey, do not turn aside until you reach your destination. Later his master would ask him from time to time, "Bholia, what was that mother singing?"

"There is very little oil in the vessel of life, and the night is vast," Bhole would reply.

His master would say, "Hmm. Well said."

The woman's song had acted like dynamite. Through its agency, Swamiji later realized, the teacher within him woke up and put him back on the right path. Contemplating the words of the song, he realized that there is indeed very little oil in the vessel of life—life is short and the journey is long. He saw that before the body falls apart we must reach the goal or suffer a great loss—and his logical mind surrendered to the power of faith. He surveyed his past, assessed his present, and understood how fortunate he was to be raised by his great master, Babaji.

This and hundreds of similar experiences enabled Bhole to understand the true meaning of love and its transformative effect on our overall development. And after seeing his master as an embodiment of selfless love, he no longer had the desire to see God in a personified form. He always proclaimed, through his lectures and writing, that "Love is the Lord of Life." And as an embodiment of this love, Babaji was the lord of Swamiji's life. Whenever anyone asked him about his master, all he would say was, "He is my mother, father, friend, guide, and guru. Whatever I am is because of him. He gave me everything, but did not ask for even a glass of water from me. I did not find any appropriate word for addressing him, so I called him 'my master.'" Swamiji was by no means an emotional man, yet even in the normal course of conversation, if someone reminded him of his master he could hardly say more than a sentence or two before drifting off into the realm of memory.

In 1993, during his last visit to the United States, Swamiji said, "All I have is the gift of love, which I received from my master and other sages. That same gift I offer to you." There is no way we can begin to understand or appreciate the gift that Swamiji offered to the world unless we know the source of this love—his master—and how his master bestowed this love on Swamiji.

45

the SAGE FROM THE HIGHEST PEAK

FOR ALL INTENTS AND PURPOSES Bhole was raised by his master—he grew up in his company; traveled with him throughout India, Nepal, Tibet, Sikkim, Bhutan, and Bangladesh; studied with him; and did spiritual practices under his supervision. Yet Bhole was not drawn to Babaji because of his great knowledge and spiritual powers, but because the love he received from him was so extraordinary that the world and worldly love seemed pale in comparison. But after he received the vision of the Divine Mother in the Temple of Sixty-four Yoginis at Khajuraho, Bhole realized that his master was far more than an old sadhu who gave him sweets. He wondered who Babaji really was, but he was a child, and not yet able to comprehend Babaji's spiritual magnitude.

As he grew to adolescence, however, Bhole observed in his master powers so extraordinary as to be almost inconceivable to the human mind. One day, for example, when Bhole and Babaji were walking in the mountains, an avalanche roared down the slope directly above them. "Run!" Bhole cried.

"Why?" Babaji asked.

"Don't you hear the thunder and see the rolling rocks?" cried Bhole. "We are going to die!"

"Don't worry," his master replied calmly. "Death has not yet come. How can this sliding mountain hurt us?" With these words he raised his hand and said, "Stop." The avalanche froze in midair, and Babaji and Bhole continued along the trail. On the other side of the avalanche's path, his master turned and said, "Now you may continue your work." And as the two watched, the avalanche thundered down the mountain, obliterating the path where they had been walking only moments before.

From this and similar experiences Bhole realized that the forces of nature were his master's friends, that Babaji was literally one with the Divine. Bhole's heart was already filled with gratitude for the selfless love his master had been showering on him from childhood; now he was brimming with reverence for the spiritual light this great man embodied.

Bhole was eager to know more about this mysterious soul—where he was born, who his parents were, who his own master was, and how he had attained such a high level of self-mastery. But sadhus do not associate themselves with their past. After taking the vows of *sannyasa* (renunciation) they no longer belong to the family or the place where they were born; they deliberately expunge the past from their memories and thus clean the slate of the mind. Bhole knew this, but so strong was his desire to know this great man that he asked his master about his birthplace and parents anyway. The only answer he got—and that only after persistent requests—was that his master was born to a brahmin family in the village of Medini Pur in west Bengal.

But Bhole was determined to solve the puzzle of his master's origins, and from 1982 to 1985 Swamiji told me in installments how he did it. In addition to the tidbits he gleaned from Babaji himself, Bhole had three main sources of information: Swami Shivananda, Pagal Baba, and the prince swami, also known as Bhawal Sanyasi.

Swami Shivananda was Bhole's older brother disciple. A great yogi in his own right, he had known of Babaji long before meeting him in person because, like Babaji, he had been born in Medini Pur and his family knew Babaji's family well. When he was a teenager Bhole's curiosity led him to visit Babaji's birthplace, and Swami Shivananda was able to guide him to the right location even though Medini Pur had grown from a village into a small town. Bhole found no trace of the house Babaji grew up in, but he did meet two ladies in their eighties who remembered the day he left with a sadhu from the Himalayas. Bhole spent several days with them and other families who knew Babaji's parents. They had been learned and well-to-do Bengalis, Bhole discovered, religious people who were devout worshippers of the Divine Mother Kali. Babaji's parents had been initiated by a sage from the Himalayas and Babaji had also been initiated by that same Himalayan adept at an early age.

Bengali Baba was highly educated and had once held a prestigious position in the British administration. He had been married and had children. But at some point in his life he renounced the world and offered himself at his master's feet, and his master took him to the shrine of the goddess Chinnamasta. Neither the two elderly ladies nor anyone else in Medini Pur knew what had happened to him after that.

Then, as he attempted to further unravel the mystery of his master's life, Bhole remembered that when he had been with Babaji in the jungles of Assam he had noticed that his master had a special affinity for the Divine Mother Chinnamasta. He felt that if he could know more about his master's association with the goddess, especially at her shrine in what is now the state of Bihar, it might help him. So at the earliest opportunity Bhole spoke of this to his guru brother, Swami Shivananda, who was living at Gangotri at the time. And Swami Shivananda told Bhole that the goddess Chinnamasta at the shrine in Bihar was the family deity *(kula devi)* of Babaji's parents. In those days the shrine was in the middle of a dense forest, where tigers and other wild animals roamed at night, but in spite of this the family used to visit the shrine often. Babaji's master, the Himalayan adept, had also spent a considerable time there.

Chinnamasta is an amazing goddess. According to the tradition, she stands on the bosom of Shiva, holding a sword in one hand and her own severed head in the other, flanked by two goddesses, one on each side, drinking the blood gushing from her neck. To her devotees Chinnamasta is a living embodiment of non-attachment and victory over the ego: she stands on the firm ground of Shiva, Supreme Consciousness, and with the sword of knowledge she severs her head, the storehouse of reason and logic. She subdues the ego by holding her head below the level of her heart, thus enabling faith to attain victory over intellect. The two goddesses by her side are the forces of worldly enjoyment and spiritual freedom, and she nourishes both of them with

49

an ever-flowing stream of vitality and wisdom, which is represented by her gushing blood.

For centuries her shrine in Bihar has been a magnet for yogis and mystics. It was there that Babaji was ordained a monk, and through this ritual he severed himself from his past and became Baba Dharam Das. Babaji then spent several years living and traveling with his master, often visiting his master's favorite place, Mount Kailas in Tibet. In winter they came down to Darjeeling and, using it as a base, they traveled in the Himalayan kingdoms of Nepal, Sikkhim, and Bhutan.

When Bhole asked Swami Shivananda if he had ever met Babaji's master, his guru brother replied simply, "This thing you have to find out on your own." Because Bhole knew that his master would not say anything about himself directly, he asked him about the goddess Chinnamasta. "I recently visited Medini Pur and learned that Mother Chinnamasta is our family deity," Bhole said. "I don't know anything about her. Will you tell me who she is? How can I win her grace so that I too can walk in the footsteps of the sages?"

"When the time comes, I will teach you," his master replied. "Chinnamasta is the guardian of the yogis. She grants the boon of *yoga siddhi* [yogic accomplishments] but demands that you offer her your head. If you then offer your body and blood to her attendants, she will offer you the gift of immortality. It takes two lifetimes to complete this practice."

Bhole was startled. His mind was awhirl. Was Babaji still doing the practice? Had he died halfway through the practice and been reborn? In that case he could not be the same person who was born in Medini Pur. How is it possible to continue a practice from one life to the next? As the result of this half-done practice would you remember your past and pick it up in the next lifetime exactly where you had stopped? What kind of experience, knowledge, or *siddhis* do you gain once you complete this practice? Bhole tried to ask these questions but could not penetrate the wall of silence surrounding his master.

Then one day, out of the blue, Babaji told Bhole to visit a great sage who lived on a mound of pebbles on the bank of the Falgu River at the holy site known as Gaya. According to the Hindu faith this river is sacred and so is its water, but except during the rainy season the riverbed is dry. If you dig a pit in the sand, however, it will fill with clean, drinkable water within a few minutes.

No one around Gaya knew where the great sage had come from—he had arrived one day with nothing, not even a water pot or a loincloth. At a distance from the temples and the pilgrims who visited them, he collected some pebbles and fragments of brick, piled them on the riverbank, and sat on them, gazing into emptiness. At first the priests and others who saw him thought he was a madman, so no one bothered him. But soon they realized they were wrong. The sadhu was calm and tranquil and kept to a definite schedule. Every day at midday he went to the riverbed, dug a pit in the sand with his hands, and when it filled with water, he drank and then returned to his mound. If anyone offered him food before he had dug his pit, he placed it on the ground and made no effort to protect it. If dogs, crows, or other creatures claimed it, he paid no attention, so people realized that the best time to give the sadhu food was when the pit was filling with water. He was always in silence except when someone tried to force him to talk, and on those rare occasions, he would make the sound, "Du, du, du, du, du . . ." Because he always sat on this mound of pebbles, local people called him Kankaria Baba (Pebble Baba) and children often addressed him as Pagal Baba (Crazy Baba).

51

Bhole approached this sadhu and bowed his head respectfully, but he got no response. He sat down and waited. Finally at midnight the sage called, "Come, my son." Then, referring to Babaji, the sage asked, "Which part of the land is being blessed with Sri Maharaj-ji's presence these days?"

Surprised, Bhole asked, "Do you know my gurudeva?"

"Of course," the sage replied. "Who here on the Earth with opened eyes does not know him?"

Bhole got the message: It is through this sage that my master wants me to know something about him. So Bhole told the sage humbly that he had been asking his master and his guru brothers about Babaji, but all he had discovered was that his master was born in Medini Pur, left with his own master for the Himalayas, and stopped at the shrine of the goddess Chinnamasta on the way. "I want to know who my grandmaster is and where he lives," Bhole told the sage. "And what is the mystery of the goddess Chinnamasta? Ultimately, I want to know about my master."

"When the time comes," the sage replied, "Babaji himself will tell you about your grandmaster and guide you to him. Tonight I will tell you about the goddess Chinnamasta and your master.

"Chinnamasta is one of the ten *mahavidyas* [the exalted paths of tantra sadhana]. Only the most advanced yogis dare to undertake the practice that reveals this supreme knowledge, and only those who have conquered the fear of death are fit to follow this path. Death is not an obstacle to this practice; rather, it becomes a doorway to the inner chamber of the Divine Mother Chinnamasta, wherein she stands on the pedestal of Shiva.

"During this practice there are three different ways to pass through the corridor of death and still continue the practice. First, you can cast off your body voluntarily before death approaches and enter another body, bypassing the process of birth. In the yogic tradition this method is known as *para-kaya pravesha*.

"Another way is to die a normal death; the accomplished master accompanies you spiritually during this transition, and pushing the forces of nature aside, he takes charge of your destiny and decides when, where, and how you are going to be reborn. During the pregnancy he prevents you from being affected by the nine-month slumber. He preserves the knowledge you gained before you died and gradually deposits it as the brain matures in the new body, and throughout all this the master continues the practice on your behalf. When the time comes, he initiates you and you pick up the practice.

"The third way is to go through the experience of death and yet remain physically alive. For one who is ignorant, social death is even more painful than physical death. When your reputation is ruined, when you are socially humiliated and abandoned by those you love, when people suddenly change their perception of you and identify you as something you are not—that is death: the disappearance of the old persona and the appearance of the new.

"Babaji is one of the rare adepts who has become one with the Divine Mother," the sage went on. "He has become immortal. He is capable of bringing the dead back to life, as he did with your guru brother, the prince swami, Bhawal Sanyasi."

Bhole spent the whole night with this sage, learning that Babaji had been halfway through the Chinnamasta practice when his master ordained him a monk at the Chinnamasta shrine, at which point Babaji's master had burned Babaji's past in the fire of yoga. As part of the process of renunciation he had performed the funeral and post-funeral rites and named this totally transformed person Baba Dharam Das. From that point on Babaji did not look back. He spent some time in Darjeeling in the company of his master, and from there he moved on to Sikkim and finally to Tibet, where he lived with his master for several years.

When Bhole returned to Babaji, Bhole immediately asked, "Who is this Pebble Baba? Is he my own grandmaster playing tricks on me?"

Babaji replied that the Pebble Baba was like his grandmaster. He was the famous sage Sri Tota Puri, who had initiated Ramakrishna Paramahansa long before. When Babaji had been ordained at the Chinnamasta shrine Tota Puri had been present, and during the initiation he stood next to Babaji's master and showered blessings on the newly ordained Baba Dharam Das.

Babaji also told Bhole that after the initiation Tota Puri stayed with his master in Tibet, along with three or four other sadhus, for almost seven years. And at the end of this period, at his master's order, Babaji accompanied Tota Puri as he traveled to hundreds of shrines in various parts of India.

Babaji lived a mysterious life. Although the Himalayas were his favorite place, he often spent the winters in the plains of India, but he avoided crowds and it was extremely rare for him to stay with house-holders: run-down temples, lonely riverbanks, and natural shelters, such as trees and caves, were his first preference. He was well-known among adepts throughout India and the Himalayan kingdoms, but many kings and owners of large estates were also among his disciples and followers. Some of his wealthy students built huts and monasteries away from settled areas, hoping he would live there during his visits, and the king of Amar Garh in north India even built a monastery for him when he was known as Baba Dharam Das. The king tried his best

53

to create a natural setting in accordance with Babaji's taste—a large body of water, a hill, a forest, and wildlife—and so this monastery, known as Sadhu Ki Kutia, is beside a man-made lake surrounded by a high berm on which the monastery, complete with several underground caves, was constructed. It is still there. The monastery covered approximately three hundred acres, and was heavily endowed with acres of farmland. And whether or not Baba Dharam Das was there, the monastery held an annual *bhandara* (feast) in his honor.

Over time the monastery became a sanctuary for wandering sadhus and other spiritual seekers. Baba Dharam Das appointed one of his disciples, Baba Karam Das, as caretaker; Baba Karam Das was succeeded by Baba Fular Das, who, before taking monastic vows, had lived in the nearby village. No one in the monastery knew who Baba Dharam Das was, where he was born, or where he lived when he was not in residence there. Because he bore "Das" as a last name, even to this day people in the area believe that Baba Dharam Das and his successors belong to the order of Saint Kabir Das, who lived in the fifteenth century. Those who are better informed, however, believe that he was a *naga* sadhu and belonged to the *vairagi* order because sadhus of this tradition also have "Das" as their last name. They substantiate this belief with the fact that Baba Dharam Das did not encourage rituals, rarely wore clothes, and spent a great deal of time in Ayodhya, the stronghold of *naga* sadhus.

For generations my family had been associated with the royal family of Amar Garh. My father was *raja purohit,* the family priest and spiritual guide of this family, and Baba Fular Das, the grand-disciple of Baba Dharam Das, was my father's childhood friend and colleague before he joined the monastery. I remember my father and Baba Fular Das arguing heatedly with each other about Babaji's true identity. My father would say, "Fular Das, you are foolish. You know nothing about Baba Dharam Das. He did not belong to any order, any tradition. He was a tradition in himself. Do you remember what our Sanskrit teacher, Pandit Bhola Datta, who became my guru, used to say about him? Babaji's real name was Swami Madhvananda Bharati, and he was clearly a saint. He belonged to the order of Shankaracharya."

In response, Baba Fular Das would shout, "I am his grand-disciple!

Who will know better than me about him? I am a Kabir Panthi, a sadhu associated with the tradition of Saint Kabir. So was my guru, Baba Karam Das, and his guru, Baba Dharam Das. Neither my guru nor grandguru ever cared for your Sanskrit scriptures."

"Babaji did not care for scriptures because he was an embodiment of the scriptures!" my father shot back. "Furthermore, he was dealing with illiterates like you. No wise man throws pearls to swine. I don't say that he was not a Kabir Panthi sadhu. All I say is he was more than that—more than what you, me, or anyone else could possibly conceive. Kabir Panthi sadhus wear white clothes, for example, but Babaji didn't care for such clothes. Babaji sat in front of the *dhuni* [fire] and his body was smeared with ashes. Kabir Panthi sadhus never do that practice.

"What is more, Fular Das, Babaji had another name. Several years ago I visited Vindhychal [a famous Shakti temple in the Mirzapur district of Uttar Pradesh]. There with my own eyes I saw a two-room building—one room was a temple dedicated to Krishna and Kali, and the other was for Babaji. And on a plaque above the door leading to Babaji's room there was an inscription that read:

THIS KRISHNA KUTI WAS ERECTED BY RAI K. K. CHANDRA, HONORARY MAGISTRATE AND ZAMINDAR SARHAHRI ESTATE DT GORAKHPORE FOR SWAMI PURNANAND BENGALI BRIDHA BABA IN 1917.

"This puzzled me," my father continued. "So far I had known Babaji as Madhvananda, never as Purnananda, as this inscription said. But when I asked our teacher, Pandit Bhola Datta, which was his real name—Madhvananda or Purnananda—he dismissed me, saying, 'God has a thousand names. Can't Babaji have a dozen?'"

Babaji was a constant traveler. Even though several places had been built just for him, he spent very little time in one location, and those who knew him in one place knew nothing of his connection with other places. Babaji never built a network and never involved himself in social or religious projects. He did not allow a following to coalesce around him. He worked only with fully prepared students, guiding those who had already found the world tasteless. In different times and at different places he assumed different names, five of which I know: Bengali Baba, Babaji, Baba Dharam Das, Swami Madhvananda, and Swami Purnananda. There were no doubt many more, and because of this Babaji could conveniently hide himself. Yet the time came when he became a public figure.

That time was the first quarter of the twentieth century, and the occasion: the Bhawal Sanyasi case. To this day it is still referred to as "the great trial that rocked India." It was the most sensational case ever brought to trial. Recapping it in a series of articles in 1993, the prestigious weekly magazine *Blitz* reported:

> Justice Sir L. W. J. Costello, who was one of the three judges of the Calcutta High Court who heard the Bhawal Sanyasi case, remarked in his judgment: "The suit beyond doubt is one of the most interesting and remarkable that ever came before a court of law in this country or indeed in any other. It is no exaggeration to say that it is unique in legal annals." D. N. Pritt, who appeared for the sannyasi in the Privy Council, avowed that it was the queerest case he had ever argued in a long and successful career at the bar. "It could have happened only in India," said Pritt.

Bhawal Sanyasi, the prince swami, was a disciple of Baba Dharam Das; he was Bhole's guru brother. He left the world and became a monk under the most unusual circumstances. *Blitz* summarized the case as follows:

> An heir to one of the richest zamindaris [kingdoms] of Bengal is declared dead and properly cremated toward the close of the first decade of the century. Twelve years later, he makes a dramatic reappearance and is recognized by his sister and grandmother but is rejected by his wife as an imposter. He files a case toward the end of the third decade for the restitution of his rights to his property and the suit is finally decreed in his favor by the Privy Council in July 1946. This is the fantastic

Bhawal Sanyasi case, which has no parallel in the legal annals of the world.

Since Babaji was the one who had brought this dead prince back to life, he was the subject of wild talk and speculation throughout the case: Are such miracles really possible? Are such masters still in the world? How do you recognize them? Baba Darsan Das and a few other disciples gave their testimony and stood up under the relentless cross-examination of the attorneys. The story of how Bhawal Sanyasi was found, how he was revived, how he was initiated, how he received his training as a monk, under what circumstances he was sent back to his home—and, years later, of his sudden death two days after the case was finally resolved—gives us a glimpse of what Babaji truly was.

57

According to *Blitz*, Bhawal Sanyasi had been a prince of one of the richest kingdoms in east Bengal, Bhawal Raj, before becoming a monk. His name was Ramendra Narayan Roy Chowdhury, and he was the king's second son. People affectionately called him Mejo Kumar, "the second Kumar." He lived with his parents and an older and a younger brother in a luxurious palace at Jaydebpur, twenty miles from Dacca, the capital city of modern Bangladesh. The palace was furnished with regal splendor: dance halls, music rooms, stables for elephants and horses, and even a miniature zoo. There was a host of servants, and a doctor was available around the clock. The princes were surrounded by sycophants who fed their vanity and inflated their sense of self-importance. In this indulgent atmosphere they ran through a series of tutors, one after the other, learning only enough Bengali and English to sign their names. When the king died in 1901, Ramendra was only seventeen, and with his father's death the few restraints on the prince were lifted. He plunged into a life of utter indulgence, spending his nights drinking and consorting with prostitutes and his mornings riding and hunting.

At the age of eighteen Ramendra married a beautiful thirteen-year-old girl, but this did not stop him from running after women of easy virtue. Eventually he contracted a venereal disease and his health began to decline. He went to Calcutta for treatment, accompanied by the palace doctor, Das Gupta, and his wife's brother, Satyendra Nath Banerjee. Then, following his brother-in-law's advice, they went to Darjeeling in the eastern Himalayas to improve his health. The prince's brother-in-law, Satyendra, made all the arrangements. The prince stayed at the famous bungalow Step Aside (which later became the residence of one of India's greatest personalities, D. B. Chittaranjan Das; it was at this house that Mahatma Gandhi and Dr. Annie Besant stayed while visiting Darjeeling).

The prince's health continued to deteriorate, and he began to have bloody diarrhea. Within three weeks he was pronounced dead at midnight, May 8, 1909, by both the family physician, Das Gupta, and the Civil Surgeon of Darjeeling, Lt. Col. Calvert. The cremation was scheduled for the morning of May 9, and the funeral pyre was prepared on the bank of a stream. The body was placed on the pyre and more sticks were piled above the corpse—but the moment the pyre was lit, a torrential downpour began to fall. The prince's brother-in-law, the doctor, and other relatives and friends ran for shelter, leaving a few attendants to restart the fire after the rain passed—but it rained so hard that the stream swelled and washed away the pyre and the bamboo cot to which the corpse was still tied. The attendants, seeing the corpse floating away, frantically ran after it, but they failed to retrieve it. And when they told the prince's brother-in-law what had happened, Satyendra ignored their information and declared the cremation complete.

The body floated several miles downstream and washed up at a spot near the cave where Babaji was living in the company of four disciples. In the evening they heard a strange sound coming from the riverbank and Babaji sent two of his disciples, Baba Darsan Das and Baba Lok Das, to investigate. They came back to report that a funeral cot had washed up near the river and that there was a body tied to it. Babaji told them the man was his student and they should get him, so the sadhus untied the knots and carried him to the cave, removing his wet clothes and covering him with dry ones. Then they moved him to the house of a villager who lived nearby, and there Babaji had the man's head shaved and applied some herbal paste to his scalp. The man began to breathe. Soon news of the rescue spread through the village, and to avoid the crowd that was beginning to gather, Babaji and his disciples moved the unconscious man further downhill to another village. Within three days he regained consciousness, but he suffered from total amnesia. In a few more days, when he was strong enough to walk with them, the small band of sadhus left the area.

The resurrected prince of Bhawal, now the child of Baba Dharam Das, was like a newborn baby. Babaji and other sadhus taught him from scratch—beginning with the basic skills of life and moving on to the Hindi alphabet. He was a fast learner, and in a few years he mastered hatha yoga and became proficient in the knowledge of alchemy and Ayurveda, the system of medicine indigenous to India. Applying this knowledge, the now-disciplined prince became healthy and as strong as a bull. In Babaji's company he ranged across the vastness of the Himalayas and wandered through the Vindhya Mountains and across northern India. By the time they reached the holy shrine of Amarnath in Kashmir almost four years had passed, and there Babaji finally initiated him into a formal practice. Soon after receiving the mantra, he began to wonder where he had been born and who his parents were, and he asked Babaji on several occasions. But the only answer he got was, "I shall send you home when the proper time comes."

59

A few more years passed. Babaji was staying at Brahchhatra in Nepal along with several sadhus, including the prince swami, when suddenly the sadhu remembered that his home was in east Bengal, somewhere near Dacca. As soon as Babaji heard this, he said to him, "Go. Your time has come." As he was leaving, however, Babaji told him that if he could tear off maya (the veil of illusion) he could come back and rejoin them.

By now the "prince" was a *naga* sadhu with matted hair and a long beard, dressed only in a loincloth and smeared with ashes from head to toe. He still did not know who he was, who his relatives were, or the exact location of his home—he knew only that it was somewhere near Dacca. Finally, after wandering a few years, he reached Dacca in December of 1920. He built his *dhuni* (fire) under a tree on the outskirts of the city and sat in *padmasana* (the lotus pose) for four months, day and night, facing the fire. He had a tattoo on his arm that read, "Baba Dharam Das ka chela naga [Naga disciple of Baba

Dharam Das]," but people immediately noticed a striking resemblance between this sadhu and prince Ramendra. They were sure this man was actually the prince of Bhawal.

The news spread like wildfire. Among those who recognized him was prince Ramendra's old friend, the raja of Kasimpur, a small state just a few miles to the northwest of the Jaydebpur palace where the prince had grown up. The raja took the sadhu to his own palace, and after five or six days sent him to Jaydebpur on an elephant. When he arrived, however, the sadhu dismounted and seated himself near a temple close to the palace. He was still not clear about who he was or what his relationship with this place was, but in no time relatives, servants, and hundreds of other citizens recognized him.

The prince's older sister heard the news, and out of curiosity she sent her son to bring the sadhu into the palace. Once there, he recognized his sister and grandmother instantly. He began to sob when he saw the photo of his younger brother, who had died during his twelve-year absence, and was further grieved to hear that his older brother had also died. The palace now contained only widows, and the kingdom was controlled by the Court of Wards. As reported in *Blitz*, "On being asked why he, an ascetic, was weeping, the sannyasi remarked cryptically, 'Maya makes me weep.' When asked whether he was Kumar Ramendra Narayan, the sannyasi replied, 'No. I am nothing to you.'"

Meeting with his family and other residents of the palace churned up a storm of emotions. His past and present collided, and he was caught in the middle. He knew he was a sadhu, the disciple of Baba Dharam Das, but he also realized that he was the prince of Bhawal. Summoning his courage, he said again, "I am nothing to you," and walked out of the palace, returned to Dacca, and resumed his life beside his *dhuni*. But people would not leave him alone. His sister followed him and eventually managed to bring him back to the palace, where he was not allowed to smear his body with ashes. Instead, he was bathed in the traditional royal fashion, and after careful scrutiny his sister found the mark left by a carriage wheel when Ramendra was young. She was free of all doubt—the sadhu was her brother.

The sadhu, however, did not want to be confined to the palace; the

60

joyful memories of being with Babaji rendered the royal life tasteless. Furthermore, he suspected that his wife and brother-in-law had plotted to murder him in 1909, and the prince within him was demanding time in private to contemplate the question of what to do about those who had hatched this plot. The sadhu within him demanded that he forgive and contemplate these events only to nurture *vairagya* (non-attachment). But the princely sadhu within him said, "Don't be a coward. It is your duty to get up and fight for your rights. After regaining what rightfully belongs to you, then you can renounce it." He was so surrounded by people that he did not have time to resolve these issues, but throughout it all he kept hearing Babaji's last words: "If you tear off maya, come back and rejoin us." He lost sleep pondering what it really meant to tear off the veil of maya. Should he live in the world and remain above it? Should he refuse to return to worldly life and thus remain above it? By now the sadhu's memory had returned completely, and his intellect was much sharper than it had been before he "died." He saw clearly that he had two dharmas—the duty of a sadhu, and the duty of a prince—and he had to choose between them. And he was under enormous pressure to declare his identity. Somehow he must decide on the most appropriate course of action—to live in the world, or to turn his back on it and walk away.

61

One day the prince's sister, tired of waiting for his decision, demanded that he declare his identity in the presence of a group of people that had gathered in front of the palace. If he refused, she said, she would starve herself to death. She argued that even though he had become a sadhu, he must speak the truth. So on the evening of May 4, 1921, the man who had come to be known as the Bhawal Sanyasi appeared in front of the crowd, and when someone asked him his name, he replied, "Ramendra Narayan Roy Chowdhury."

"Who nursed you?"

"Aloka," he replied. (This was the name of the wet nurse in the palace during his infancy.)

Instantly the air was filled with thousands of voices crying, "*Mejo Kumar ki jay* [Hail to the second prince]."

Overjoyed to have their king restored to them, the citizens of the kingdom of Bhawal brought gifts in his honor and began to pay taxes to him. His wife, however, had never once come to see him since his arrival at the palace. She and her brother had been denouncing him as an imposter, and they were enraged to hear that this *naga* sadhu was actually claiming the kingdom. Her brother, Satyendra, immediately contacted Mr. H. B. Lethbridge, the secretary of the Board of Revenue, which controlled the Court of Wards, and showed him the prince's death certificate signed by the doctor, Das Gupta; the Civil Surgeon of Darjeeling, Lt. Col. Calvert; and the Deputy Commissioner of Darjeeling, Mr. Crawford. He also presented papers showing that he had collected the death benefit from the Scottish Union Insurance Company on behalf of his sister, the wife of the late prince. Then, at the suggestion of the revenue commissioner of the Governor's Executive Council, Satyendra wrote a letter to the editor of *The Englishman,* a British-owned daily newspaper circulating in east Bengal, in which he gave his full account of the death of Ramendra, the second Kumar.

The Bhawal Sanyasi's identity now became the center of a hotly debated controversy. Evidence was offered both in his favor and against him, and finally on June 3, 1921, the Board of Revenue declared the sadhu an imposter and issued the following notice: "Notice is hereby given that the Board of Revenue has gotten conclusive proof that the dead body of the second Kumar of Bhawal was burnt to ashes twelve years ago at Darjeeling town. It follows, therefore, that the sadhu who is calling himself the second Kumar is an imposter. Whoever will pay him rent or chanda [contribution] will do so at his own risk." As this notice was read to the beat of a drum in the local bazaar a riot erupted, and the police opened fire, killing one person and injuring several others. Formal charges were filed against those supporting the sannyasi, but when the case came to trial the defendants were acquitted. Then, in August of 1921, at the request of the king of the neighboring state of Burdwan, Babaji came to Dacca and gave a succinct account of how he had found his disciple and revived him, how he had trained him, and finally how he had sent him back to his homeland.

Meanwhile the prince's cause was being actively promoted by his sister and grandmother. In July of 1922 the grandmother wrote to

Bibhabati, the prince's wife, asking her to come and "see things with your own eyes and save the honor and fame of the family of my distinguished husband by doing what you conceive to be your duty according to justice and religion." The prince's wife refused to accept delivery of this letter. The grandmother was now convinced that she and her brother had plotted to murder the prince and would do their utmost to prove him an imposter. So she approached Mr. J. G. Drummond, who was then the Collector, the highest officer in the administration of Dacca, with a request that this matter be examined by six eminent lawyers, "if possible, one lawyer from each of the six different high courts of India." She offered to bear the cost of such an examination from her own private funds.

The Bhawal Sanyasi too had made up his mind: he chose the path of conquest; he would renounce the world, but only after victory was his. For practical reasons he stationed himself in Calcutta, and with the exception of two short visits to Dacca he remained there from 1924 to 1929. These were the days when the Indian independence movement had the whole nation in an uproar. But even though he was the greatest celebrity in Bengal, he took no part in politics. (His sympathies were with the nationalist movement; Satyendra, his wife's brother, was a British loyalist.) He did keep himself in the limelight, however, and gathered a large following outside the political realm.

63

In October of 1929 the Bhawal Sanyasi moved back to Dacca and began living with his sister and collecting the rents and taxes that were due to the king of Bhawal. Satyendra, however, managed to convince the court to serve the sadhu with an order under section 144 of the criminal code, prohibiting him from entering the town of Jaydebpur. Later this prohibition was extended to the entire state of Bhawal. Finally, in the beginning of 1930 the prince consulted with several top lawyers and filed a case in the Dacca Sessions Court to regain his rights to the kingdom.

The leading counsel for the prince was B. C. Chatterjee, a lawyer renowned for his spectacular victories in political trials. The case went to court on April 24, 1930, and continued for six years. There were 1,609 witnesses and 2,000 exhibits. As reported in *Blitz:*

The ages of the witnesses ranged from 21 to 100: they came from all castes and creeds. They were Hindus, Muslims, Sikhs, Parsis, Christians, Buddhists, animists, naga sannyasis, and bhutias [Tibetans]; there were quite a few Englishmen too. There were doctors and lawyers, sculptors and photographers, zamindars, ryots, moneylenders, professors and pandits, fishermen and coachmen, mahouts and grooms. Quite a few pimps and prostitutes rendered evidence and the testimony of some of the latter related to intimate sexual pleasures.

The case was so complicated that Scotland Yard was called in to investigate the facts provided by both sides. Medical advisers with the Scottish Union Insurance Company, which had insured the prince's life in 1905, confirmed that the identifying marks described in the policy were present on the sadhu's body.

64

The statements that Babaji had made during his five-day stay in Dacca in 1921 were produced and read into the record. The Bhawal Sanyasi described how the sadhus had rescued and revived him, and how his master, Baba Dharam Das, had sent him back to Bengal. This testimony was further substantiated by many of Babaji's disciples, such as Baba Darsan Das, Baba Lok Das, and Baba Pritam Das. The sadhu's identity as the prince was established by the testimony of the prince's grandmother, the wife of his older brother, his sister, members of the royal families of neighboring states, hundreds of servants, and other people from his kingdom.

On August 24, 1936, the court ruled that the sadhu was indeed the prince, that he had been poisoned and the body taken to the cremation ground, but that heavy rainfall had extinguished the flames. His brother-in-law, Satyendra, was found to have plotted the murder. The citizens of Dacca and Jaydebpur celebrated the victory of the prince swami for three days, and the prince was officially enthroned as Raja Ramendra Narayan Roy Chowdhury. His wife, under the influence of her brother, still refused to recognize him as her husband.

On October 5, 1936, Raja Ramendra's wife, the wife of his younger brother, her adopted son, and the Court of Wards filed an appeal in the Calcutta High Court in which their attorneys ridiculed the earlier verdict, arguing, "If the head of a dead body is shaved and some primitive ointment is applied to it by a half-naked naga sadhu, do the dead come back to life according to the learned Sessions Judge?" After four years of argument and counter-argument, the original verdict was upheld on November 25, 1940. But the raja's wife and brother-in-law refused to give up, challenging the verdict of the High Court and appealing the case to the Privy Council in London. There, after studying twenty-eight massive volumes of printed court records and seven hundred photographs, the Privy Council dismissed the appeal on July 30, 1946.

The news of this final victory reached Raja Ramendra via cable from his solicitors on August 1. By that time it was also making headlines in newspapers in Calcutta and Dacca, and everyone expected him to celebrate his triumph. But he seemed to have no enthusiasm for it. Even though the court had recognized him as the king of Bhawal and the people were hailing him as their raja, deep within he knew he was a naga sadhu, the privileged disciple of Baba Dharam Das. Visitors thronged his residence in Calcutta and thousands of congratulatory telegrams poured in, but he was absorbed in profound contemplation: Is the dance of maya over? Did I play my role properly? Is there a final touch I have yet to give to this performance? Those around him attributed his apparent indifference to his age (he was sixty-two) and the strain of this ordeal, which spanned more than thirty-six years. But the truth, which Swamiji shared with me, is that he was in direct communication with Babaji, who was in Darjeeling at the time, staying at almost the exact spot where more than thirty-six years before he had re-placed the soul of his beloved disciple in the body of the prince of Bhawal.

At the time the court case reached its final resolution there were five sadhus with Babaji in Darjeeling, including Swamiji and some of those who had rescued the prince's body and testified for him in court. Babaji had become completely quiet. Once in a while he opened his eyes, and it seemed as though he was looking into the far distance. Swamiji and the sadhus wondered whether Babaji was looking into the past or the future through his penetrating eyes, or into some other place where an ordinary mind cannot reach. While he was telling me this story in 1983, Swamiji himself seemed to be slipping out of his body.

The same thing was happening with Raja Ramendra. His sec-
retaries and assistants were concerned; he was not in the mood to be
entertained or even served—he simply wanted to be left alone. At long
intervals he came out of his room wearing the mask of worldly
glamour, shook hands with his friends, waved to well-wishers, and
then reentered his private world. For a quarter of a century, while he
had been living in the world, he had spent his days planning legal
strategies, ruling the kingdom, looking after business affairs, attending
parties, and discharging his duties toward his relatives and friends. No
one, not even his sister, knew that he spent his nights in meditation.
He gave his days to the world, and his nights to the Lord of Life.
When surrounded by people he was the Bhawal prince (and later
king), but in private he was Bhawal Sanyasi.

66   The cable from his solicitors in London had come to the king of
Bhawal, Raja Ramendra. But no one knew that the sadhu within him had
also received a message—this one from the creator of his destiny, Baba
Dharam Das. This message too said, "You have won the battle." But it
also said, "Now decide what to do with the fruit of your victory." It
was exactly thirty-three years since he had been initiated by Babaji at
Amarnath, and the practice he had undertaken at that time had just come
to an end. At the conclusion, it required a *purna ahuti* (final offering).

The sadhu made the decision: he would tear off the most interior
layer of the veil of maya. Going beyond the world created by Brahma,
the creator, he would make his final offering into the divine fire and
return the fruit of his victory to those he had defeated. So he withdrew
his perception of duality—honor and insult, success and failure, gain
and loss, birth and death—and prepared himself to enter the world
that shines through its own inherent effulgence.

More than thirty-six years before, Babaji had brought the prince
back to life. This time the royal mendicant, the disciple of Babaji, cast
off his body voluntarily. As reported in *Blitz:*

Two days after receiving the cable from London, even as
congratulatory telegrams and messages were pouring in, the
Bhawal Sanyasi died suddenly on Saturday the 3rd August
1946. His cremation was to take place the next morning at

9 a.m. Throughout the night the belief gained credence in the city that there would be a miracle and that the sannyasi would rise from the pyre as a young man of eighteen.

On the morning of August 4 there was a strong wind and heavy rain, just as there had been in Darjeeling in 1909, and thousands of people were gathered around the pyre under a sea of umbrellas to witness the second coming of the Bhawal Sanyasi. This time the fire consumed the body within a few hours.

During the time I was translating *Living with the Himalayan Masters* into Hindi, Swamiji said more than once that his master was an impenetrable mystery. Babaji advised his casual devotees to follow the middle path, but he himself lived as an extreme ascetic. He was kind and gentle with those who sought his blessings, but strict with those who wished to walk in his footsteps. He never said directly whether students were or were not fully prepared to study with him. Instead, by creating a situation in which each student must either cross the chasm of fire or turn away, Babaji helped them come to an understanding of how well-prepared they were. For example, he gave a new life to the prince. He raised him like a mother would raise her child. He uplifted his consciousness and led him all the way to the point at which his spiritual journey had come to its end in his previous life. Babaji made him see both worlds—spiritual and mundane, the everlasting and the short-lived—leaving it totally up to the prince to decide which way he wanted to go. Babaji's guiding and protecting arms were always with him, but he wanted the prince to be honest with himself and come back to him as a conqueror rather than an escapist.

I asked Swamiji who this prince had been in his previous life, what point he had reached in his spiritual journey, why he had to go through such an extreme experience in this lifetime, and what practice Babaji had initiated him into at the Amarnath shrine in Kashmir. Swamiji told me that the prince had been an ascetic in his last life and in many other lifetimes. But despite the fact that he had committed himself to the rigors of spiritual life, he was always struggling with an inner conflict. On the surface he knew the dangers of money and women,

67

but deep down he lusted after both. To conquer this lust he resorted to austerities and penances, keeping himself in isolation. He fasted frequently, and constantly surrounded himself with the fivefold fire (fire on all four sides, and the scorching sun above) in the hope that his weakened body and senses would not disturb his spiritual practices. He had full faith in guru and God. He was a disciplined aspirant and a person of unmatched willpower, but his attitude toward money and women was an obstacle—he had to transform it. He had to acknowledge the fact that he had these desires. Instead of repressing them, he must free himself from them either by fulfilling them or by renouncing them completely. Thus he was born a prince. Providence led him through a period of utter indulgence. He saw the world as it is when his wife, his brother-in-law, and the family doctor plotted to

kill him for money, power, and pleasure. His master rescued him not only from the funeral pyre but also from drowning in the confusion of worldliness. But to become the custodian of the sages' tradition he had to demonstrate that he was free from all the charms and temptations of the world, that he had torn away the final veil of maya—the most subtle attachment toward family and children, power and prestige, money and worldly glamour.

Swamiji had still not answered my question about the exact practice the prince had undertaken at the time of his initiation, so I asked him once again. In a deep voice he responded, "It was the practice of Chinnamasta," and from the expression on his face I knew he did not want to talk about it. However, Swamiji had told me about the goddess Chinnamasta on several previous occasions, and I had read about the practice in prominent tantric scriptures such as *Shakti Sangama Tantra*.

Knowing that both Babaji and the Bhawal Sanyasi plunged into deep contemplation when the final court victory was announced and that the Bhawal Sanyasi died suddenly two days later enabled me to construct my own hypothesis as to what had happened: thirty-three years before his death Babaji initiated the Bhawal Sanyasi into the practice of Chinnamasta, which he continued to his last breath. Once he was recognized as the prince he was free to either run away from the world or drown in it. He decided to conquer his desires by first acknowledging that they existed and then throwing them into the fire of knowledge, thus attaining freedom from them once and for all. As he maintained discipline over his body, breath, mind, and senses, Babaji watched him from a distance. And by the time victory was his, both externally and internally, he had completed the practice.

This was the same practice that his own master had given Babaji when he was still a young man. Babaji had completed it at the shrine of Chinnamasta in the state of Bihar and went through the process of rebirth when his master performed his funeral rites and ordained him Baba Dharam Das. Bhawal Sanyasi did the same thing. He left his body in the way of the yogis. In the eyes of those who thronged to the cremation of Raja Ramendra Narayan, he did not rise from the dead. But in Swamiji's own words, "He still wanders in the Himalayas and has been assigned by the tradition to guide aspirants stranded along the path."

69

In the chapter "My Master and the Prince Swami" in *Living with the Himalayan Masters* Swamiji makes a striking comment: "He [Babaji] predicted that this prince swami would meet his sister and would recall his past. My master said, 'There are going to be a lot of problems for us, so I had better leave for higher altitudes.' He went to our ancestral cave in the Himalayas and stayed there for several years."

One evening, when the opportunity presented itself, I asked Swamiji the location of this ancestral cave, and Swamiji replied that it is at Mount Kailas, near the Ganga. It is the cave that Sage Angira built at the behest of Bhagwan Sanatkumara, and it lies at the foot of Mount Nyenri, located in the valley just west of Mount Kailas.

For the next sixteen years I contemplated Swamiji's description of this ancestral cave. My fantasies took me all over Tibet. I would imagine an opening to the cave, a narrow passage leading to the interior. Deep inside the cave were several chambers, some naga sadhus sitting there in front of a dhuni . . . I wondered where the smoke went. At other times I imagined it as a non-physical cave, a celestial one. Following the wishes of the masters residing there, this cave would become visible to some and remain invisible to others. However, Swamiji's description indicated that it was a real cave and that it was located on the bank of the Ganga. I studied maps but I could not find the Ganga anywhere at or around Mount Kailas, and I knew from my own experience that Swamiji was good at dismissing a question he did not want to answer. But I also knew he did not lie. And he had been assertive when he said the cave was at the bank of the Ganga.

One night, when I had almost finished translating the book, I read him the chapter "My Grandmaster in Sacred Tibet." Once again he remarked, "Our ancestral cave is in the Himalayas."

I said, "Isn't it in Tibet near Lhasa, Swamiji?"

"No, no," he replied. "The place I visited is where my grandmaster was residing, but the ancestral cave is on Mount Kailas, and one day I will take you there."

Babaji left his body in 1982 on the Himalayan peak of Tungnath, but even after that Swamiji never used the past tense when he talked about his master. During the translation of the chapter "My Master Casts Off His Body," I asked him, "So, Swamiji, where is Babaji now?" "In our ancestral cave," he replied, and said again, "One day I will take you there."

In 1996 Swamiji left his body, but I remembered his promise, "I will take you there." One night in 1998, in the first week of December, I was overcome by memories of Swamiji. Generally I fall asleep doing *japa* of my guru mantra, but that night I kept thinking of him and don't remember falling asleep at all. Very early in the morning I dreamed that Swamiji, along with another sage whom I know well, walked into my living room. I got up, touched his feet, and as Swamiji held me in his arms I said, "Swamiji, I know you are always with me, but still I miss you." He said, "Then come." In my dream I assumed that he meant that I should die and join him, but to make sure that I was correct in my interpretation I asked, "Where?" He said, "Nachiketa Tal."

I was happy. I calculated the travel time—it would take one day to reach Delhi and another day from Delhi to Uttar Kashi, and one more day to trek from Uttar Kashi to Nachiketa Tal. I was elated.

Meanwhile Swamiji looked at my wife and said, "Meera Bete, can you make super tilk?" "Yes, Swamiji," Meera replied, and began to prepare it. The sage next to Swamiji asked, "What is tilk?" Swamiji laughed and said, "You will enjoy it. You can't get it in the Himalayas.

This is very special. I lived on tilk for several years. When you boil tea in milk, it's called tilk; when you spice it with saffron and cardamom, it's called super tilk." And they both laughed.

Then, after drinking the tilk and talking about all kinds of spiritual and mundane matters, they got up to leave, and Swamiji said, "It gets too cold at Nachiketa Tal in the winter. Also you have lots of work to do. Come and see me in the summer at Mount Kailas." Then, with a mischievous look in his eyes, he continued, "I have to take you to our ancestral cave. And it is on the bank of the Ganga. I have made all the arrangements for you and Meera. Bring Ishan [my son] too."

It so happened that for several days before this Bonnie Albert, an architect from Buffalo, New York, had been trying to phone me, but had not been available when I returned her calls. So early the next morning, as soon as I completed my meditation practice, I called her at home. The first thing she said was, "So when are we going to Mount Kailas?" She told me that when she was with Swamiji at Gangotri many years before, he promised that he would take her to Mount Kailas. I told her about my dream the night before, and after a few minutes' conversation we decided that we must go to Kailas the next summer, that Swamiji was waiting for us.

I kept our plans as secret as I could, but here at the Himalayan Institute nothing can be hidden for long. Momentum kept gathering, and eventually twenty people joined me on this pilgrimage. Shelly Craigo, head of the Institute's Voice of the Himalayas tours, took charge of the trip and completed the formal paperwork with the Nepalese and Tibetan governments, and finally, on June 10, we were on our way. We arrived in Nepal on June 12 and on the 15th we caught a flight from Kathmandu to Lhasa. After visiting ancient monasteries and the Potala Palace of the Dalai Lama, on June 18 we began the seven-day journey by car from Lhasa to Mount Kailas, arriving at the holy lake Manasarovar on June 23. We camped at the lake for two days and at last arrived at the foot of Mount Kailas on June 25. We camped at Darchan, a small settlement from which pilgrims set out on the traditional three-day trek around the holy mountain.

The circumambulation was the group's main objective, but my mind was set on our ancestral cave. From Lhasa all the way to Mount

Kailas, whenever I saw a river or stream of any kind I tried to learn its Tibetan name. I asked about the origin of every stream and tried to find out which river it flowed into. I knew that geographically there is no Ganga River in the vicinity of Mount Kailas, but still I wished to see it there so I could find our ancestral cave. I was confident that the Ganga was there, the cave was there, and Swamiji and his master were there: Swamiji had told me to come and see him there, and he had told me quite clearly that he had made all the arrangements.

On the morning of June 26 we loaded our gear onto twenty yaks, and accompanied by a Tibetan guide, ten sherpas, and a group of yak-men, we set out on the outer *kora* (circumambulation route). Darchan, the starting point of this journey, is at an elevation of about 16,000 feet. Lhasa sits at 12,000 feet, and we had become somewhat acclimated to the altitude since arriving there eleven days earlier. Even so, the smallest exertion left us breathless. We had to walk very slowly, carrying only the barest necessities in our packs—the most important of which was water. After three hours, we entered the Lhachu Valley on the western side of Mount Kailas. It was a beautiful day: a clear sky with a few bright clouds hanging like crowns over the surrounding peaks. Some of our companions had gone on ahead and others were lagging behind, but by this time the sherpas had assessed the stamina of each member of our group and had distributed themselves accordingly. Thinlay, the leader of the sherpas, and Bhuchung, the Tibetan guide, had been on this trip more than a dozen times. They spoke Hindi, English, Tibetan, and Nepalese. To them, walking in these mountains was like playing in their own courtyard; they ran back and forth to make sure that everyone was safe and sound.

As we trekked through the Lhachu Valley I was absorbed in my own world of desires and imaginings. I thought, "This is the western valley. Our ancestral cave must be somewhere near here, but what about the Ganga? I wonder what the name of the river flowing through this valley is? This is only the first day. I might see it tomorrow or the day after . . ." With these thoughts I continued walking—when suddenly I saw a small structure tucked away on the mountain slope on the western bank of the river about a mile in the distance. My heart began to pound—Perhaps this is the entrance to the ancestral cave?

About this time our Tibetan guide, Bhuchung, came by to see how we were doing. I asked him the name of the river. "The Lhachu River," he replied.

"Why is it called 'Lhachu'?" I inquired. "What does it mean?"

"*Lha* means 'God' and *chu* means 'water'; thus it means 'water of the gods,' 'river of the gods,' or 'divine river.' And this valley too is called Lhachu Valley."

"What is that structure?" I asked, pointing across the river.

"It is Choku Gompa [the Choku monastery]," he replied.

"What is the name of the mountain?"

"The Palace of the Son of God. In Tibetan it is known as Nyenri Mountain."

"Do you know who founded that monastery and whether anybody still lives there?" I asked him.

73

Bhuchung replied, "I don't know, but the yak-men live in the area, and they know these mountains very well. They might tell us something."

The yak-men were approaching with their yaks and dogs, and so, with Bhuchung acting as translator, I put this question to the eldest. His eyes glittered as if he were finally getting the chance to share his treasure with someone who understood its value.

"Yes, this mountain is the Palace of the Son of God," he said. "Accompanied by thousands of gods and goddesses, he lives here. His name is Sanagpa. Demchok is his father and Parvati is his mother. This Lhachu is also his mother.

"He is very gentle but very powerful and an unmatched warrior. Once he got angry at one of the mountains and shot thousands of arrows into it with so much force that it looked like a sieve. There are numerous caves in Nyenri Mountain, where divine beings live as the guests of Sanagpa. All of them are very kind. They protect our yaks and sheep and heal us when we get sick."

Pointing at the monastery, I asked him, "What about that place? It doesn't seem to be just a cave. Who built it? Does anybody live there?"

"Yes," he replied. "A long, long time ago, before humans reached here, a lama, a man of god, came to this valley. His name was Nyen. He was very wise; he glowed like fire. The son of God liked him very much and told him he could make a *gompa* [monastery] in his palace.

That is how, with the permission and blessings of Sanagpa, in the beginning of time, Nyen built this *gompa*, which enshrines the statue of Lord Amitabha, the god of limitless light."

By this time his yaks had almost disappeared from view and he had to rush to catch up with them, and Bhuchung had to leave to check on the people walking ahead. Several members of the group had caught up with us by now, but the beauty and grandeur of the mountains, valley, river, sky, and clouds was so awesome that no one was inclined to talk.

My mind was spinning: "Who is this son of God, who according to the Tibetans is gentle yet powerful and an unmatched warrior? Tibetan legend says that Demchok is his father, that Parvati is his mother, and that the Lhachu River is also his mother. The yak-man said that once this son of God got angry at one of the mountains and shot thousands of arrows into it with so much force that it resembled a sieve—well, the scriptures belonging to the Vedic tradition also describe how the son of Shiva once got angry and shot his arrows into a mountain, known as Kraunch. The name of this Tibetan son of God is Sanagpa; in the Vedic tradition, the sage Sanatkumara is said to have been born as the son of Shiva, and Parvati is his mother. Just as the Lhachu River is his mother in the Tibetan tradition, the Ganga is his mother in the Vedic tradition. Definitely this Sanagpa is Sanatkumara, because another name for Sanatkumara is Sanakpada, and it is a standard practice in the languages spoken in the eastern part of India, Bhutan, and Tibet to drop the last letter, which would make Sanakpada, Sanakpa. In Tibetan, Sanagpa is also known as Korpa, which is equivalent to the Sanskrit "Kumar Pada" (Sanatkumara). In 1983, Swamiji had told me that Sanatkumara is the immortal sage who was the founder of our tradition. So the Lhachu River is the divine river, Ganga, and this mountain is the palace of her son, Sanagpa.

"Sanagpa is Sanatkumara, the son of God. Then who is this man of God, Nyen? He must be the sage Angira whom Swamiji has mentioned, because according to the local yak-man, Nyen is a man of God who glowed like fire—that is how the scriptures describe the sage Angira. Through his *tapas* he glowed like fire, which is why he came to be known as Angira, 'shining like fire.' Furthermore the Upanishads and the Puranas describe how the sage Angira studied with Sanat-kumara. Beyond doubt this is the location of our ancestral cave."

Overcome with emotion, I said to my wife in Hindi, "Meera, how beautiful and peaceful is this place. How wonderful it would be to spend some time here and do some sadhana."

She replied, "What else is there in the world for us to do? Complete the basic steps and then come and conclude the practice here."

While we were talking, I looked at the main peak of Mount Kailas on our right—and could not believe my eyes: there I saw an arched gate. I told Meera and the others with us to look at the peak. They were awestruck. Someone asked, "Is it appropriate to take a picture?" I said, "Why not?" My son Ishan and a few of the younger members of the group had gone ahead and were resting near the monastery. I called them to come back and witness this celestial manifestation.

I said, "This vision means that the door is open. Our job is to do our practice, and access to eternity is guaranteed."

While we were discussing its symbolism, the gate became even more vivid and we saw someone clad in white standing on the left-hand side of the entrance. We wondered who it could be: Swamiji, or his master? What difference does it make? This image was appearing on the peak at least 5,000 feet above us, and the mountain was at least a mile away. The vision was not a physical phenomenon, and it was not a hallucination, either, because everyone present was seeing it. We bowed our heads in gratitude.

Once again I said, "The one who called us has now given his *darshana* [vision] and, as promised, he has shown us his ancestral cave. The goal has already been reached. If he wants us to complete the rest of the pilgrimage, that is fine: if not, that is fine too."

Suddenly one of the group members, Sandy Anderson, shouted, "Look here!" as she picked up a beautiful piece of rock with an inscription in Hindi. It read "Ishan." While traveling from Lhasa to Mount Kailas we had seen thousands of inscribed mani stones. Most of them carried the mantra "Om Mani Padme Hum," and all were in Tibetan, never in Sanskrit or Hindi, as this was. This further confirmed my conviction that we had found the place where Babaji, his

75

master, and Swamiji himself live. Among the eight aspects of Shiva, the Ishan aspect refers to Surya (the Sun), the source of light, which in the Tibetan Buddhist tradition is known as Amitabha, the Lord of Limitless Light that the yak-man had spoken of.

We had not yet assimilated the vision of the gate, the yogi standing at the threshold, and the inscription "Ishan" on the stone when we were jolted by a final vision: Mount Kailas turned into three eyes. So penetrating were they that it felt as if we were sucked into them. We stood there dumbstruck, thinking: "How is this possible? But why not? Is there anything not possible for almighty God? We are not the first to have the vision of three eyes—thousands of scriptures talk about the three eyes of Shiva throughout Nepal, Sikkim, Bhutan, and Tibet. We have seen the three eyes depicted in the monasteries and in Tibetan paintings. Art has to have an origin somewhere in reality, and that reality is Mount Kailas."

No one had the courage to turn their cameras toward the three eyes. A thought flashed in my mind: If this vision is given to all of us, then it means that the sages living on this mountain want to bless the seekers by giving their *darshana* through photographs; if my understanding is tainted, then this vision cannot be captured by camera. So I asked everyone to take photographs, and when they were developed all the visions—the gate, the sage inside the doorway, and the three eyes—were clearly visible.

Before visiting Mount Kailas and the nearby holy lake, Manasa-rovar, I had only a limited understanding of the content and intent of the stories which Swamiji had told about his master and grand-master. But once I was in the region of Mount Kailas, Swamiji's words turned into a living reality. When I saw the Lhachu River in the western valley I understood Swamiji's intention when he called it the Ganga. According to the scriptures, the Ganga is a celestial river and flows from the matted hair of Shiva, who lives on Mount Kailas. Just as the glacial streams flowing from these peaks water the lands of Tibet, Nepal, and India, finally merging with the ocean, the knowledge flowing from the sages of these peaks nurtures people of all faiths. Today the Choku monastery and the cave at that spot is affiliated with the Buddhist tradition—so was Babaji a Buddhist? Mount Kailas, according to Hindus, is the abode of Shiva, and Babaji lived and undertook his spiritual disciplines here—so was he a Shaivite Hindu? While living at Gangotri he spent most of his time at the shrine of Bhairava in the valley known as Bhairava Ghati—and since Bhairava is the purely tantric form of Shiva, was Babaji a tantric yogi? It is also evident from Swamiji's writings that Babaji was a direct link in a long chain of the lineage of the Vedic sages, and was an initiate in a monastic order established by Shankaracharya—so was he a monk with a clear affiliation with Shankaracharya's tradition?

The answer to these questions can be found in Swamiji's oft-repeated observation, "Sages do not belong to any culture, religion, caste, or creed. They belong to God. They move like the wind and cannot be captured by anyone. Their religion is the religion of love. They converse among themselves in the language known as *sandhya bhasha,* the twilight language."

77

The only thing we can say with certainty is that Babaji is a Himalayan adept—a sage from "the highest peak." His soul is as pure and white as the Himalayan snows. He is immortal. Seated at the summit of spiritual ecstasy, he occasionally walks among us in the flesh and guides fully prepared aspirants such as the Bhawal Sanyasi, Swami Rama Tirtha, Swami Sivananda, Sir John Woodroffe, and Swami Rama.

Several times, beginning in 1976, Swamiji had promised that he would take me to his master. I felt disappointed and betrayed when in 1982 I heard that Babaji had left his body at Tungnath, a peak in the Garhwal region. But I began to get a sense of the immortality of these masters and the illusory nature of birth and death in relation to them when, during the translation sessions in 1983, Swamiji continued to promise that he would take me to his master. Then in November 1996 Swamiji himself left his body, and once again I wondered how he would fulfill his promise. Two years later he restated this promise, this time in a dream in which he asked me to come to Mount Kailas. And when I did, the sage stood in the arched gateway to the main peak. Whether I met Swamiji or his master, Babaji, at Mount Kailas is a question that I myself have to digest and assimilate . . . and perhaps I will never know.

But I do know that there is a permanent resident of Mount Kailas who reared Swamiji and led him across the endless terrain of worldly and spiritual experiences, enabling him to learn the art of joyful living in all situations and circumstances of life.

Once in my ignorance I said to Swamiji, "You spent so much time with Babaji!" Swamiji looked at me with disapproval and said, "How can you spend time with someone who has no time for anyone but God?" Babaji too did not entertain useless questions and did not teach until the student was fully committed to practicing what he taught, and he often made Swamiji visit other sages, study while sitting at their feet, and learn the basic principles of humility, sincerity, self-motivation, and commitment. Babaji never forced Swamiji to have faith in him or in anyone or anything else, including God; instead, he allowed him to cultivate faith in a higher reality on his own. He created circumstances in which Swamiji had to bake his faith in the fire of logic and reason and make it firm by validating it through his own direct experience. Babaji gave him the option to choose any way of life he wanted. He sent him to live with saints (both genuine and bogus), politicians, businessmen, scholars, artists, and orators. He led Swamiji to experience the hardships of monastic life and the luxuries of wealth.

Babaji's philosophy was that the world and its pleasures should be renounced only when you realize through your direct experience that they are empty and tasteless. Resorting to spirituality as an escape from the world is embracing misery in another form. Switching from one lifestyle to another—worldly to spiritual—and hoping that doing so will put an end to all your problems is like running after a mirage to quench your thirst. Similarly, you don't become happy and peaceful just by knowing that your guru is great and your God is almighty. You gain peace and happiness by discovering the mystery of mind and its relation to the charms and temptations of the world, on the one hand, and to spiritual yearning, on the other. You don't unveil this mystery by living in isolation or by simply being around someone who seems to possess great spiritual wisdom and power. Rather, you must train your mind and transform your habit patterns so that you can live in the world and yet remain unaffected by it.

Babaji understood spirituality as a journey of self-transformation and inner conquest—a journey all of us must embark on sooner or later. He taught Swamiji how to navigate the tumultuous river of life and not get caught in the whirlpool of sorrow and joy. He taught him to be happy and peaceful while trekking among the lofty peaks of Mount Kailas—or while walking through the noisy streets of Tokyo or New York. Babaji trained Swamiji in the art of enjoying the divine music not only while he was receiving the unconditional love of the sages but also while he was being deceived by people who pretended to love him.

The memory of Babaji's teachings and training led Swamiji to write in his own hand one day, "Who has, like Thou, mingled the strains of joy and sorrow into the song of my life, enabling me to realize 'the joy that sits still on the lotus of pain and the joy that throws everything it has upon the dust and knows not a word'? To those who understand thy message there shall be no fear left on the Earth. Therefore today the flower of undying gratitude offers its petals at thy lotus feet."

LIVING *with the* MASTERS

IN LECTURE AFTER LECTURE Swamiji would say, "You are already divine. All you have to do is become human." I pondered this for twenty years, and several times I thought I knew what he meant, only to realize that my understanding was as yet incomplete. Then, as I watched Swamiji during the last days of his life, the revelation dawned. I saw in him a man so skilled in granting protection to the divine within him (so that it was not engulfed by the force of maya) that he was free to bask in its inherent effulgence and bliss.

Nine years before he left his body Swamiji engaged in a mammoth undertaking: building a hospital, medical college, and nursing school in the foothills of the Himalayas, as well as establishing a rural development project. This project reached its climax in 1994–96. In those days VIPs, such as cabinet ministers in the Indian government and governors of Uttar Pradesh and other states, visited Swamiji and garlanded him for his wisdom and selfless service to humanity. But during that same period Swamiji was also forced by local street politicians to appear in front of groups of villagers and prove that he was not an agent of the CIA or that, by bringing money from the West and embracing Western scientific influence, he was not damaging the pride and dignity of Mother India. As I watched him handle both ends of this spectrum with the same equanimity, I finally understood the truth of his maxim, "Only one who remains unaffected by honor and insult can keep the divine flame alive."

In all cultures there are legends about a war between demons and divine beings, and often the forces of light lose the battle. In Indian mythology the defeated bright souls either run to higher powers for protection or hide in remote regions, often on isolated mountain peaks, and commit themselves to intense spiritual practices. Only after they have gained the grace of God and attained inner strength do they challenge their opponents again and reclaim their rightful status. During these "divine calamities" the sages come forward and help the defeated souls gain self-mastery by gathering up the virtues of fearlessness, self-confidence, unwavering faith, and the indomitable power of will and determination. Self-mastery entails cultivating all of these qualities collectively. It enables us to conquer our subhuman tendencies and allows us to become fully human. But achieving mastery over ourselves is a gradual process which keeps unfolding as we continue to walk on the path of self-transformation. The purpose of life, as Swamiji often said, is not to know God as an external being, but to transform ourselves so that we are constantly aware of the divine within—which is our essential nature.

As I learned more of Swamiji's early life I saw that Babaji made sure his beloved Bhole became a complete human being and learned to light and protect the divine flame within. But this was not an easy task, because Bhole had not come to him as a seeker nor was the relationship between the two strictly that of guru and disciple: Babaji was also Bhole's father and friend. Furthermore, Babaji did not want to spoil Bhole's childhood. To experience life in its fullness he needed to grow as a normal child, become a teenager, learn from his folly, and choose the direction in life that made the most sense to him. That is why Babaji created an environment for him that would evoke all his hidden tendencies—from mischievousness, impatience, and rebelliousness to compassion, patience, and obedience.

Knowing that Bhole was often trying to fool him, Babaji sometimes let himself be fooled. On one such occasion he was staying on the outskirts of Narendra Nagar, a town near Rishikesh, when in the middle of the night he said, "Bholia, let's go." Bhole knew that once the thought of leaving had come into Babaji's mind no one could convince him to stay, but on this bitter-cold night Bhole did not want to leave the warmth of the campfire. Nevertheless he wrapped Babaji in a blanket and fastened it with thorns, and they began walking along the road until they reached a traffic circle in the town. Bhole knew that Babaji's mind was hardly in his body, so he led him around the circle several times and then started walking back the way they had come. And when they reached the campfire again, he exclaimed, "Look! Here's a fire. Let's rest." Babaji sat down. In the morning he opened his eyes and said, "Bholia, how come we walked the whole night and still we are at the same place?"

"Because I tricked you," Bhole replied. Babaji just laughed.

But on other occasions Babaji would remain firm. For example, one morning in Rishikesh Babaji set off to take a bath in the Ganga, and Bhole followed him as usual. On the way they passed a sweetshop where the shopkeeper was making *jalebi* (a deep-fried Indian sweet filled with syrup), and as soon as Bhole saw them he shouted, "Jalebi! I want to have jalebi!" "After you have taken your bath and offered water to the Lord Sun, then you can have jalebi," his master responded. But Bhole didn't want to wait. He rolled on the ground, crying for sweets. Babaji said firmly, "I said no, and it is no. Learn to behave." Out of pity, the shopkeeper offered the sweet to the boy, but Babaji intervened. "No, he can't have it," he said. "I don't want you to have a loose palate," he said to Bhole, "and I won't let you become pitiful by eating jalebi given to you out of pity. Come, take your bath. And after that you can have anything you want." But Bhole refused to get up; he kept rolling in the dust in the middle of the road. Babaji sat on the roadside and watched him cry. A truck came along and stopped in front of the boy, honking. Bhole thought that if he stayed on the road and kept crying he would win, but instead Babaji said to the driver, "Drive right through this silly boy." So the driver, honking madly, began to edge his truck toward Bhole. At the last moment, Bhole got up and ran. Babaji said, "If you are done crying, then come take your bath." Bhole did, and finally got his jalebi.

Babaji very rarely taught or disciplined Bhole directly. He gave him love and affection, but discipline was mostly the job of an older disciple, Swami Shivananda, who lived in Gangotri most of the time. A learned scholar and devout practitioner, Swami Shivananda was

83

well-versed in Sanskrit, spoke Hindi, and wrote in Bengali. His famous work *Sugam Sadhana Pantha,* which has been translated into Hindi, gives us an idea of his high standards in philosophy as well as his non-attachment.

From time to time Babaji sent Bhole to Gangotri to learn Sanskrit and the principles of spiritual discipline from Swami Shivananda, but in the beginning Bhole could not withstand the rigors and austerities of life there. For his part, Swami Shivananda complained that Bhole was spoiled, and often sent him back to Babaji. As he matured, however, Bhole realized the value of discipline as well as the subtle love that Swami Shivananda had for him, and in the introduction to the Hindi translation of *Sugam Sadhana Pantha,* published under Swamiji's supervision in 1965, Swamiji wrote of how grateful he was for all that Swami Shivananda had taught him.

84

Swami Shivananda had many students, most of whom were in the Punjab, especially the part now in Pakistan, and he visited them in the winter when it was too cold to remain at Gangotri. In those days (under the influence of Swami Dayananda Saraswati, the founder of the Arya Samaj, and his students) the Punjab was a cradle of Vedic scholars. The Punjab, as well as Kashmir, and especially the area then known as Sindh, had also been the land of Sufi saints and Muslim fakirs. Traveling with Swami Shivananda to this part of India was an eye-opening experience for Bhole—he saw firsthand how true saints from every tradition are not confined by religious, social, or academic boundaries. For example, Swamiji once told me about a Sufi saint in Agra known as Shahanshah ("the king of kings"), who got his name because he often dressed like an emperor. He was a mystery to everyone. He had no fixed residence, and those who sought him out— merchants and teachers, attorneys and doctors, saints and government officials—usually searched for him in vain. He had the power to remain invisible at will and could be found only if he wanted to be found. But at times he would be seen walking in the streets like an ordinary person. Once while returning from Lahore (a city in what is now Pakistan) by train, Swami Shivananda and Bhole got off in Agra, and after walking about half a mile Swami Shivananda paused and said, "I wonder where Shahanshah is now?"

With that, a voice came from under a nearby tree: "Shiva, I am here!"—and suddenly there was Shahanshah, reclining on his side, just as Lord Krishna is pictured in Indian mythology. After they had greeted and honored each other, Shahanshah said, "So you just arrived? Young Bhole must be hungry. See, Bhole, just a few moments ago someone brought a packet of sweets. They are *rasgullas*, one of your favorites." Without getting up, he reached around the tree trunk and pulled out a packet. Bhole knew that there are mysterious adepts, like Babaji and other masters, in whose presence mind-boggling things happen. So he accepted the sweets respectfully. They spent a few hours with Shahanshah, and then boarded the train for Tundala. From there they walked to join Babaji, who at that time was residing with other sadhus at Garh Mukteshwar on the bank of the Ganga.

Most of the time while living with Babaji at Garh Mukteshwar, Bhole was trying to understand the dynamics of *siddhis* (the extraordinary abilities of yogis). During his travels with Babaji and other adepts he had seen all kinds of mysterious happenings—Shahanshah's appearance and disappearance was only one. Some sadhus, for example, did not care for anything, but got everything they needed, while others used every stratagem possible just to get some food, yet still remained chronically underfed. Bhole never saw any trace of anxiety in Babaji; he never seemed to have a plan for where he wanted to be or when, and yet unfailingly at the end of the day he would somehow have reached a place where someone was waiting for him. At night there would be a *dhuni* (fire) for him, and people would bring him food. Once, when they were walking through Bhairava Ghati, a valley several miles from Gangotri, Bhole saw bears and mountain lions come up to Babaji as though they wanted to have his *darshana*, then depart.

One afternoon when they were staying at Sonprayag, Babaji suddenly decided to visit Kedarnath, but by the time they reached Chirbasa it was almost ten o'clock and freezing cold, and the crescent moon was setting. On the side of the trail they managed to see the tiny temple of Chir Bhairava, not more than five feet square. When they reached it Babaji said, "Bholia, he's the gatekeeper of Kedarnath. Bow your head to him. If he wants, we'll continue; otherwise we'll rest here tonight."

Babaji lowered his head and spoke in his unique Bengali-accented Hindi, as though he was conversing with the presiding force of the shrine. And as he talked, a fire appeared suddenly on the other side of the trail. At that, Babaji thanked Chir Bhairava for making arrangements for their stay.

When the two were seated by the fire, Bhole asked who had made this fire for them, and Babaji replied, "The immortal sage of our tradition, Bhagwan Sanatkumara, has lighted 108 dhunis throughout the Himalayas. These dhunis are eternal. Chir Bhairava is the custodian of this one. It is an ever-blazing fire, but it becomes visible only when Chir Bhairava wishes. Do you see? It is smokeless. This is the fire that the monks in our tradition carry on their heads."

In the morning they departed for Kedarnath, arriving there at noon, and joined Gudari Baba, an adept. This great sage treated Bhole as his own child, and Bhole could talk to him without hesitation, just as he could talk to Babaji. So one evening, when the opportunity presented itself, Bhole asked Gudari Baba why adepts like him and Babaji were so well taken care of by everybody. "Why do people love Babaji? Why do they have so much trust in him? And why do necessities spontaneously manifest to him and not to others?"

Gudari Baba replied, "Babaji has become one with nature, our all-pervading, compassionate mother. To those who are ignorant, nature does not seem to be a conscious living force, but to those who have eyes to see, she is divine and filled with all tangible and intangible gifts. Once you live in harmony with nature, you will begin to cultivate sensitivity toward her. You will see that she cares for you and makes sure that you get what you need and retain what you have already achieved. If you adjust to your surroundings without disturbing her, nature will nurture you, and you will receive all that is needed for your growth and well-being."

This made perfect sense to Bhole. He knew that Babaji never plucked a flower except on those rare occasions when he offered flowers to God; when he needed a twig to brush his teeth, he always mumbled something first.

Out of curiosity Bhole asked Babaji one day, "What do you say to the plant? Do you talk to it? Should I do the same?"

Babaji replied, "Go and fetch a twig so we can brush our teeth. But before breaking it from the branch, hold the twig lovingly in your hand and say, '*Ishe twa urje twa.*'"

"What does it mean?" Bhole asked.

"'May I take you for cleansing and strength.'"

The words Babaji told Bhole to utter when he separated the twig from the branch are the two mantras from the *Yajur Veda* that are to be recited when fetching twigs for any ceremonial purpose. But Babaji lived such a simple life that no one could guess he had any knowledge of the scriptures at all. He carried no books, and when he taught he quoted no scriptures—but the scriptures came to life in his every thought, speech, and action. He was the Vedas in flesh. To Babaji life was one grand ceremony which the Lord of Life performs in the vast courtyard of nature. Everything—from seemingly insignificant acts to the most magnificent worldly tasks or spiritual practices—has its rightful place in this grand ritual.

One day as he and Bhole were walking on a mountain path, Babaji saw a fledgling which seemed to have lost its mother; it was so weak it was not able to lift its head. The instant he saw it, the words *"Vishnor bahubhyam"* spontaneously issued from his mouth. He picked up the bird, held it in his palm, looked at it again, and then threw it into the air. The bird flew away! When Bhole told this story to Gudari Baba he asked how the dying bird had suddenly become healthy enough to fly, even though it was still a fledgling. Gudari Baba explained that when Babaji saw the bird in such a helpless condition the thought of Lord Vishnu, the god of protection and nourishment, flashed in his mind. Through this spontaneous absorption in Lord Vishnu, Babaji became Vishnu, and in that state of awareness the words *"Vishnor bahubhyam"* came forward. It is a mantra from the Vedas; it means "with the arms of Vishnu." As he uttered those words, Babaji became a conduit for the energy of the protecting and nourishing arms of Lord Vishnu, and thus the bird's life was restored. Instantly it became healthy and strong.

Gudari Baba was one of the greatest adepts of the Himalayas. He too was in perfect harmony with nature. Like Babaji, he was free from hunger and thirst, heat and cold; tiredness approached him only with his permission. He had an amazing quilt, a composite of hundreds of patches. Any discarded piece of usable woolen or cotton cloth he found made its way into this quilt, and over the years it became so thick and heavy that eventually only he could carry it. Those close to him knew that his quilt was a living entity. Wherever he went the quilt went too—which is why people called him Gudari Baba ("Quilt Baba").

Gudari Baba and Babaji often traveled in the mountains together, and the joy of being with them was beyond description. Swamiji once told me, "Living with my master and Gudari Baba at Kedarnath was one of the most memorable times in my life. Both of them used the other as a means to unveil their own mysteries, and in the process they taught me the gospel of love for nature." After a week in the enchanting valley of Kedarnath, Babaji departed for his favorite place, Tungnath, while Gudari Baba and Bhole moved on to the Valley of Flowers.

For untold ages the Valley of Flowers has been the abode of adepts. It is an extraordinary place. The mountain towering over this valley is known as Gandha Madana, "the peak of intoxicating aroma," and the area is a place of spiritual ecstasy. According to both scripture and local legend the peaks beyond the Valley of Flowers are forbidden to humans; they are protected and guarded by invisible forces. Long before reaching the valley, however, one has to pass through a special place, now known as Hemkund, where the tenth guru of the Sikh tradition, Guru Gobind Singh, did his *tapas* (austerities), and for this reason the Sikhs regard it as a holy shrine.

Gudari Baba and Bhole reached Hemkund after traveling several days. Then, as they were departing for the Valley of Flowers, a journey of several more days, they met a Japanese monk who was also setting out for the valley. So Gudari Baba, Bhole, the monk, and a couple of people carrying the monk's supplies and equipment began their journey together. The monk was proud of his mountaineering skills and was confident that he was well-equipped for the journey, but he thought Gudari Baba's quilt was too cumbersome for traveling at such altitudes—it was heavy and difficult to carry. And he was disturbed to see that whenever Bhole looked tired, Gudari Baba put the quilt around the boy's shoulders and told him to carry it—which seemed inconsiderate, even abusive. Once, in an effort to be nice, he even said that he could have hired an extra porter for the quilt. He had not noticed that after carrying the quilt for a few minutes Bhole was refreshed and Gudari Baba took it back.

They were still a day's walk from their destination in the Valley of Flowers when the monk came down with chills and a high fever. He was afraid he had contracted malaria in the plains of India, and tried all the medicines he had, with no result. He did not want to die in the Himalayan wilderness, so he burrowed into his sleeping bag and covered it with all the blankets he had. And when he continued to shiver, he asked Gudari Baba if he would add his heavy quilt to the pile. Gudari Baba told him that his quilt was sewn by Mother Nature and that the forces of healing and nourishment resided in it. If the monk would remove his sleeping bag and blankets, he said, and cover himself with only the quilt, it would take away his illness. That's what happened. Gudari Baba covered the monk with the quilt, and within a few minutes his fever vanished and he was full of vitality.

89

The next morning the group set out for their final destination. But after walking for a few hours the scent became so intense that the porters refused to go any further. The monk pointed at the shepherds accompanying herds of sheep grazing in the distance, and asked the porters why they couldn't walk in the valley, since the shepherds obviously could. The porters told him that the sheep and the shepherds were part of these mountains, but they were outsiders. "If we trespass," they explained, "we will lose our minds and possibly our lives; we can only rejoice in the beauty of this celestial valley from a distance." Gudari Baba told the monk that if he wanted to go beyond this point, it would be better to first spend some time here in meditation and then ask the custodians of this valley and the surrounding mountains for permission to go further.

The monk ignored this advice. His goal was to cross the valley and camp on the other side, and from there he wanted to explore the interior of the mountains until he found the place where Bhima, a legendary character of the *Mahabharata,* had met the mighty god Hanuman. His proposed camping spot was less than an hour's walk away and the monk started off, still accompanied by Gudari Baba and

Bhole, who was carrying the quilt around his shoulders. But before he got very far the monk began to feel disoriented and started to lose his memory. He did not become frightened, however, until he realized that he was also losing his sense of direction. And his fear turned to terror when he noticed that he was feeling euphoria for no reason. He did not want to lose his mind and wander forever in these mountains, so he told Gudari Baba what was happening, and the adept told him to go back immediately and join the porters, who were waiting for him. At once terrified and euphoric, the monk returned to Hemkund. Gudari Baba and Bhole went on alone. They crossed the Valley of Flowers and continued into the mountains.

Swamiji once told me that only through the grace of an adept like Gudari Baba could a human ever travel beyond the Valley of Flowers. There, he said, the distinction between Earth and heaven disappears and past, present, and future lose their separate identities. After experiencing places like these, one begins to understand that divine beings actually do exist and that it is possible to be in their company. Here Bhole finally realized that the adepts are truly citizens of two worlds—they are simultaneously here as well as there, and through their eyes one can see celestial sights while still on Earth. In our familiar sense, there were no ashrams and no people in that place, yet everything was there.

Somewhere deep in the mountains Gudari Baba sat on a rock and told Bhole, "This is the ancient ashram where the sage Arshtishena lived long ago. At the juncture of the full moon and the following day the great sages who live only on water and air visit this place, and at that time nature plays her celestial music in their honor. Through the ears of meditation you can hear it—but do not try to reach the source of that music."

When I asked Swamiji exactly where that place is and whether he himself heard the music, he did not reply. I watched as he lost himself in the realm of memory, and by looking at his distant gaze I could sense how profound his experience there had been.

Descending from the mountains, Gudari Baba and Bhole once again had to cross the Valley of Flowers, but before entering it Gudari Baba said, "Young man, this time I hope you will not need help from this quilt when you cross the valley." But to Bhole's surprise, he began to lose his memory almost as soon as they set out. His reason and linear thinking almost stopped functioning. He did not want to talk, and when he did, it did not make sense. Gudari Baba made fun of him but kindly returned the quilt to Bhole's shoulders and thus helped him reorient himself.

Once back to normal, Bhole asked why he had been affected by the strong scent of the flowers when Gudari Baba was not, and Gudari Baba replied that it happened because Bhole had a flimsy body and a weak mind. "See, on one hand," Gudari Baba said, "you are experiencing great joy, but at the same time you are afraid of losing your memory and sense of direction. This kind of joy, induced by these wildflowers, leads you nowhere. It is like taking drugs. When people in the world take drugs like marijuana and hashish they get intoxicated and think they are in meditation. But such a state is induced by the chemistry of the body, which momentarily becomes excited by the external stimuli of the flowers. That is what happened to you. Once you are out of this valley you will feel terrible because the mind will demand the same joy, but lacking the stimuli, the body will not be able to produce it. However, if you learn to preserve and enhance the infinite wealth of joy which is already buried in your body, you can be happy all the time without the help of these wildflowers."

They stayed in the Valley of Flowers a week, and during that time Gudari Baba taught Bhole how to be strong in body and mind, how to discover the hidden wealth of joy within the beautiful vessel of the body, and how to keep himself fully alert through meditation and not be affected by external stimuli and the charms and temptations of the world.

Above all, he taught Bhole that the human body is a living shrine of the Divine, but that through carelessness and bad habits we turn this beautiful shrine into a landfill. Perennial joy stored in the body is buried, and we suffer because we have no peace and happiness. The physical structure of the body, he told Bhole, is supported by invisible but powerful beams of prana (the life-force), but through our unwholesome activities we weaken these beams. Then, lacking the support of vital energy, the body caves in and we lose energy and stamina.

And when our energy level drops, any small excuse—germs, bacteria, viruses, the change of seasons, drugs—can become the cause of physical illness and mental instability.

To enjoy life you have to be healthy and strong, Gudari Baba told Bhole, for it is only in a healthy body that there can be a sound mind. No matter how spiritual you are, he said, when you are not well a great deal of your mental and spiritual energy is wasted in managing the complaints of the body. And when you spend so much energy complying with the demands of your body, where do you have the time and energy to discover the higher purpose and meaning of life? Therefore, first take care of your body.

Gudari Baba made Bhole work hard. Laziness, he felt, is the greatest evil a human being can ever embrace. He had no time or respect for slowpokes. To be with him meant walking fast, thinking fast, and getting your work done fast. He liked Bhole because he was not slow, but even so Bhole did not measure up to Gudari Baba's standards.

That week, while they were in the Valley of Flowers, Gudari Baba did not give Bhole his quilt unless he was in desperate need. To help him remain unaffected by the powerful scent, the sage made him do vigorous exercises and sweat profusely. He also made him bathe in the icy water of the mountain streams. According to modern science sweating profusely at such altitudes and bathing in icy water is not healthy, but that's what Gudari Baba made Bhole do. When I asked Swamiji why Gudari Baba forced him to do such things, Swamiji replied, "This way he was helping me overcome the normal limits of the body and mind. And I knew everything would be all right because he was there and his mysterious quilt was there."

At this time Gudari Baba was in his nineties, and still his stamina was beyond our ken. At an elevation of 20,000 feet he would stroll, make jokes, and laugh with no sign of strain. He was a master of walking. At this age he did not do any yoga *asana* or *pranayama*, but he regularly practiced *agni sara*, a yogic technique to fan the fire at the navel center. He taught Bhole the advanced disciplines of *pranayama*, *mudra*, and *bandha*, and told him that he must exercise vigorously every day.

Gudari Baba was also an expert alchemist. He knew plants and minerals just as we know our family and friends, and during this journey he explained the qualities and healing properties of hundreds of plants that grow in the Himalayas. He taught Bhole how to take specific herbs to detoxify and rejuvenate the body. He also taught him the subtle mysteries of hatha yoga, pranayama, and meditation, which are combined with the esoteric practices of alchemy.

But Bhole had not seen Gudari Baba doing these practices himself, so he wondered if they were the true source of the sage's strength and wisdom. He knew that it is through tapas that yogis achieve extraordinary powers, and he was convinced that Gudari Baba must have done some kind of tapas—and must still be doing something of the sort—in order to be able to walk through the valley and into the mountains where humans cannot go, converse with divine beings who cannot be perceived through the senses, and remain unaffected by hunger, thirst, tiredness, and sleep. His quilt must be the result of a boon from God, Bhole thought. So one day he said, "Practices bear fruit only when an aspirant is also committed to austerities. What kind of austerity can I practice so that what you have taught me can bear fruit?"

When Gudari Baba finished making fun of Bhole's speculations he told him that taking care of oneself is the first and most important step in practicing austerity. He explained that the Sanskrit word *tapas* literally means "heat" or "glow." The practices that help you shine are called tapas, he said. Unhealthy living smothers the fire within us. To blow off the ashes of sloth and inertia and allow the fire to become active is tapas. Keeping the body cleansed and nourished is the way to practice tapas. "If you overcome your resistance and practice what I have taught you regularly," Gudari Baba told Bhole, "you will be practicing tapas."

Bhole traveled with Gudari Baba for more than a month, and then returned to his master, who was staying at the shrine of Tungnath ("Tungnath" means "the lord of the peaks," and like the famous shrine of Kedarnath, it is a mysterious site in the land of the gods). Here, a little above 12,000 feet, is an ancient temple that can hardly accommodate ten people (if they are sitting down). And near this temple

93

are a dozen or so small structures housing shrines that are associated with various gods. According to local legend (and the oral tradition of the sages) the main temple stands at the opening of a cave, which in our current dark age has been closed and is no longer visible to human eyes. The back part of the temple is built into the mountain itself, and here people worship a sacred rock, which probably also serves to cover the opening into the cave. Few pilgrims visit this shrine, and when they do it is only in summer. For more than six months out of the year the place is inaccessible to all but a few adepts, who leave in the summer to avoid visitors. These days one can reach the nearest settlement, Chopta, by car, but the trail to Tungnath, which is five kilometers uphill, is accessible only by foot. Even Chopta is deserted during the winter. A short distance above Tungnath is Chandra Shila, the famous peak of the Divine Mother, where Lord Rama did his meditation. And on a mountain nearby is Ravana Shila, the place where Ravana, the famous king of Sri Lanka, resided while meditating on Shiva, the lord of the peaks. Even today in the midst of the breathtaking beauty that pervades this area, the mind of the meditator can hear the music of silence without any effort.

Only a few adepts knew that Tungnath, and its surrounding mountains, was one of Babaji's favorite hideouts in the Himalayas, and after leaving Gudari Baba in the Valley of Flowers, Bhole joined Babaji here. His experiences with Gudari Baba were still fresh, and the desire to practice austerity that had awakened in Gudari Baba's company was becoming more intense every day. Bhole's understanding, based on the knowledge he had gained before going to the Valley of Flowers, was that austerity entailed strict fasting, sitting in front of a dhuni, and refraining from associating with others. But Gudari Baba had shaken this understanding, so Bhole waited for the right time to clarify the matter with his master. When that time came he asked Babaji about the mystery of Gudari Baba's strength and stamina. As was Babaji's style, the reply was short. "It is austerity," he said and closed his eyes.

This answer led Bhole nowhere. Luckily Babaji's senior disciple, Swami Shivananda, was present, and he was willing to answer Bhole's questions.

Bhole asked him, "How can you be healthy and strong if you dry up your body through fasting and sitting in front of a fire all the time?"

"Such austerities simply weaken the body and senses so that they can't comply with the nasty demands of a wild mind," Swami Shivananda replied. "But a weak body and senses fail to comply with the mind's uplifting thoughts and impulses. For those endowed with the power of will and determination, wisdom, and self-surrender, that kind of austerity is of little value. In fact, adopting a healthy way of living is true austerity, or tapas. By eating too much or too little, by sleeping too much or sleeping very little, by exercising too strenuously or not taking any exercise at all, by thinking too much or not using the mind at all, one disturbs the pranic forces, which support and sustain both body and mind. But due to bad habits and carelessness, that's what people usually do.

"Breaking such a habit and overcoming negligence requires self-discipline. But discipline becomes torture if you do not understand its value and if you are not motivated to help yourself. It is self-motivation that prepares the ground for self-commitment. Only then do you enjoy the disciplines you undertake. Such discipline is called austerity. If you don't enjoy it, it is torture."

95

Then Bhole asked Swami Shivananda, "What is the exact nature of self-discipline? Who do you discipline, and how? What do you mean by self-commitment? How do you enjoy exercising when you don't like to exercise? How can you walk for hours in the mountains when you hate to be tired? How can you enjoy practicing restraint in eating when the food is tasty and plentiful?"

"Only when you contemplate on the higher meaning and purpose of life can you begin to understand the value of the precious moments of your life," Swami Shivananda explained. "When you do, you no longer wish to waste your time and energy on trivial things and meaningless experiences. Death is a definite fact of life. So, while you are healthy and strong, imagine you are dying and no one can prevent it, and in that situation try to think of what is going with you and what is staying behind. In the face of death do you find yourself happy? If not, what do you have other than misery to take with you? Is that all you have earned through your hard work? Is it the purpose of life to be born, work hard, and leave the world carrying the burden of misery on the journey after death? Creating an environment in which you can ponder on these issues with the least distractions is called living a spiritual life. Training the body, breath, senses, and mind to discover the answers to these questions is called sadhana, or spiritual practice. Because the charms and temptations of the world as well as our own bad habits force us to run after sensory pleasures, commitment to a spiritual practice is a tough job. That is why it is called austerity—you don't want to do it, and yet you convince yourself to do it."

"Then my next question is," Bhole said, "what do you discipline first? How do you begin a spiritual practice that can answer our inherent questions?"

This was not a simple question. However, both Babaji and Swami Shivananda knew that Gudari Baba and many other sages had kindled a fire in Bhole and he was ready to learn and practice. So they imparted the knowledge gradually, step by step, which Swamiji summarized in *Living with the Himalayan Masters* and later taught his own students through lectures and practical demonstrations. The essence of these teachings can be gleaned in quotes from his lectures and writings:

"For a genuine and everlasting transformation you must practice a systematic method of self-discipline and self-training. Mere philosophy and intellectual knowledge cannot stand in time of need.

"For the sake of curiosity you may study and entertain yourself with a variety of philosophical doctrines, but those theories work only when you learn to apply them to yourself. Applying theoretical knowledge and living with it in daily life is called 'practice.'

"People have formed a habit of leaning on others. They want others to help them and tell them what to do and what not to do. You are a human being. Take charge of yourself. By becoming dependent on others you suppress your self-motivation. Without it you cannot accomplish anything. Summon your willpower and throw aside the fear of failure. Soon you will notice success kissing your feet."

"As part of a systematic practice, first learn to sit with your head, neck, and trunk straight. It is the healthiest and most comfortable way of sitting. The pressure at the base of the spine creates heat, and as heat increases, the pranic forces expand and rise upward. Because the spine is straight and the nervous system is relaxed the pranic energy flows freely upward along the spinal column toward the head. In this pose you are free from sloth and inertia. Without a proper posture you will face numberless obstacles in your practice.

"Remember, for any practice you need a strong, healthy body. When you practice regularly in one sitting posture for a long time the body will become still, the breath serene, and the mind tranquil. Then you will realize that you have a body, but you are not the body. You will also understand that the body is a wonderful instrument and you should take care of it properly.

"An unhealthy body dissipates the mind—you will have no time to work with other aspects of yourself. That is why maintaining physical health is an integral part of spiritual practice."

"To start and complete any practice, first you must have a strong, burning desire. Such a desire leads to commitment. Commitment needs to be nourished by the power of determination. When you are determined that today you will sit in meditation, no one has the power to disturb you.

"Do not expect too much in the beginning. There is no instant method of meditation. Expectation will force you to fantasize, imagine, and hallucinate. Expectation will lead you to anxiety, and anxiety will not allow you to meditate. As a result you will be frustrated and you will stop doing your sadhana.

"As far as technique is concerned, first relax your body and mind. Calm your breath. Detach yourself from the external world and watch your breath.

"Have faith in yourself, in your practice, in the master who taught you, and in grace, which accompanies you all the time. The combined force of your burning desire, the actual practice, and God's grace will guide you. And whenever you are about to make a mistake, that same force will protect you."

Aghori Baba, another great sage who played a pivotal role in Bhole's growth, lived in a cave at Dhari Devi, a shrine outside Sri Nagar in the Garhwal Himalayas. Rumor had it that he ate the flesh of human corpses and consumed his own feces, even though no one had seen him doing such things. Rumor also had it that he was a powerful saint with a boundless capacity to heal. Some even believed that he had mastered a special *vidya* (spiritual science) and that he could use that knowledge to summon the forces of nature to function as he wished.

Bhole had known Aghori Baba from early childhood, and because he always gave Bhole any amount of money for whatever he wanted, in the early days all Bhole knew about Aghori Baba was that he was kind and generous. When he grew up, however, Bhole was puzzled to learn there were conflicting views about the sage. According to the local residents he was an evil, powerful man who worshipped devils, but according to Babaji and other sadhus Aghori Baba was an adept, a sage who always helped others. And Bhole knew he was a sage as great and mysterious as Babaji.

After he had stayed with his master and his brother disciple awhile, Bhole visited Aghori Baba, seeking answers to the burning questions that still nagged him. What Bhole had learned thus far from Babaji, Gudari Baba, Swami Shivananda, and other masters can collectively be termed "yoga," but he felt that there must be more to it. He wanted to know the core of yoga. Earlier when he had asked his master about the source of Gudari Baba's strength and stamina, Babaji had simply replied, "Austerities." Elaborating further, Swami Shivananda talked about discipline and the importance of taking care of one's body. The answer certainly made sense, but it was not fully satisfying. In all traditions aspirants and adepts alike seemed to subscribe to the notion "No pain, no gain"; this seemed to be the very spirit of austerity. Still, Bhole wondered why the scriptures identify austerities with self-imposed hardship.

All the masters Bhole had met so far placed some restriction on what they taught, but Aghori Baba's generosity was limitless, and Bhole intuitively felt that anything he asked would be given. So he said, "Lately I feel that I have been wasting the time of sages like Babaji, Gudari Baba, yourself, and others. I don't want to do this anymore. I know that practice is the key to yoga sadhana, but I do not know what should be the focus of yoga sadhana. I know that expectations lead to anxiety, and anxiety creates an obstacle in the practice. But I must expect something from the practice, otherwise it becomes aimless. If I don't look forward to anything then how can I keep myself motivated to do the practice?"

Aghori Baba replied, "The practice that makes your body healthy and energetic and your senses balanced and self-contained qualifies as yoga practice. Such practice alone can help you overcome your negligence toward striving to know and find the purpose and meaning of life. Such practice also can help you gain mastery over your body, senses, and mind, and eventually enable you to create or destroy your personal karmic world at will. But no practice can ever bear fruit unless it is nurtured by tapas."

"My master told me the same thing," Bhole replied, "but when I asked my guru brother to elaborate, in essence he said that the practices that help you maintain a healthy body and improve your energy and stamina are tapas. Practices that help you shake off sloth and inertia and help you shine with indomitable will, enthusiasm, and self-motivation are tapas. So what is tapas exactly? And how do you nurture the practice with tapas?"

"Tapas means to practice *brahmacharya*," said Aghori Baba. "There is so much fuss about brahmacharya. Generally people think it means celibacy. That is only partially true. Brahmacharya means to delight in supreme consciousness. Driven by the primitive urges of hunger, sleep, sex, and self-preservation, consciousness slides to its lowest rung, and it is no longer able to experience its divine nature. But still the longing is there. It manifests in the form of sense cravings, which human beings drain a great deal of energy to fulfill, and there comes a time when both body and mind become weak and eventually empty. A weak body and mind cannot withstand the storms of disease, old age, and death. Brahmacharya means to conquer the cravings of the senses and mind, to preserve energy, to become strong in body and mind. Only then, by using the body and mind as a tool, is it possible to rediscover the highest level of consciousness, which is the finest aspect of yourself."

"This practice of brahmacharya, which you consider to be the core of tapas," said Bhole, "clearly requires that I undertake some sort of discipline. But nobody tells me exactly how I should do it. I know I should not indulge my senses—but should I simply withdraw from everything and everyone, lock myself in a cave, survive on a minimum

99

amount of food and water, and by constantly seeing and thinking of fire, for example, ward off all other thoughts? Is this enough to preserve my energy and rediscover the highest level of consciousness?"

Aghori Baba remarked, "Yes, you are right: there is more to it," and ended the conversation for the day.

A few days later Aghori Baba gave Bhole money, and asked him to get some groceries and ritual ingredients for his fire offering. So Bhole set off for the nearby town of Sri Nagar. On the way he met a pandit, one of those who believed that Aghori Baba ate human flesh and was an evil person even though he was spiritually powerful. This pandit did the morning and evening worship at the shrine of Dhari Devi, but he had seen Aghori Baba only from a distance because whenever he saw Aghori Baba approaching he hid behind the statue of the goddess.

The pandit had known Bhole's father, and so he was concerned when he realized that Bhole was spending time with Aghori Baba. He told Bhole that he should not live in bad company. Bhole replied that Aghori Baba was Bengali Baba's friend and a gentle and loving sage— it was simply a rumor that he lived a dirty life. "Aghori Baba is a pure vegetarian," Bhole said, "and he never takes drugs of any sort. He is a worshipper of the God Sun and the fire." The pandit accompanied Bhole all the way to the market, and each tried to convince the other that his impression of Aghori Baba was the correct one. Because he was under the impression that Aghori Baba met his needs through magic powers—that he materialized food and other necessities from thin air—the pandit was surprised to see Bhole buying butter, sugar, and grain, as well as ritual objects that were pure and quite benign. So Bhole, trying to convince him that he was mistaken about Aghori Baba, asked the pandit to come with him to the sage and see things through his own eyes. The pandit agreed because he knew Bhole and had known his father, and therefore trusted that Aghori Baba would not harm him.

When they came up to Aghori Baba in his cave, Bhole said to the sage, "It was getting late, so I asked the pandit to help me. He is the one who performs the worship at the temple, Baba. He is a very good person."

The pandit prostrated at Aghori Baba's feet. "You *pandat!*" Aghori

Baba roared in fury. "When at my cave you touch my feet, but behind my back you say bad, bad things about me. Get up! Pick up that ax!"

The pandit began to tremble, but he picked up the ax as ordered. "Go to the river and fetch that corpse from the water," Aghori Baba demanded. "Slice some meat from its thighs and bring it here."

The river was right below his cave, and Bhole had never before seen a corpse at that place—but he stood with Aghori Baba at the cave's entrance and watched the pandit drag a corpse out of the river. The pandit was so frightened that he tripped and fell on the corpse. Terrified, he sliced off a few pieces of flesh and brought them to Aghori Baba, who ordered him to put them in the pot with some water, cover it, and boil it.

Bhole had never seen Aghori Baba treat anyone this way. The pandit seemed to be totally disoriented. He had cut his own finger and it was bleeding profusely. Aghori Baba shouted at the man again, "Why this blood? Show me your finger!" The pandit was too frightened to speak. He was trembling so violently that when he tried to extend his hand toward Aghori Baba his knees buckled and he fell. Aghori Baba looked down at him and said, "We don't eat dirty brahmin meat, do we, Bhole?" Then he gently took the pandit's hand in his palm—and the cut closed and healed. He told the pandit lovingly, "From now on, don't think negative thoughts about me. Do you think I eat meat? Do you agree with the people here that I am dirty? I too am a pure vegetarian."

At this the pandit calmed down a bit, but he still could not understand this "vegetarian diet" he had been forced to cook for Aghori Baba. Ten minutes later, however, when Babaji asked him to serve the food from the pot, both Bhole and the pandit were surprised to find that it was not flesh but *rasgulla,* an Indian sweet made of cheese and sugar. Aghori Baba laughed and said, "This sweet has no meat in it."

They all ate their fill, but still there were more rasgullas than the pot could possibly have contained, so Aghori Baba gave the remaining sweets to the pandit to share with others, and as the man was leaving he said, "I told you not to think negative thoughts about me, but I have not asked you to tell others that I am a good person. Once in a while you can visit me, but no need for bringing friends."

After the pandit had gone Bhole asked, "Why did you do all that? Was the corpse real? If so, how did the flesh turn into sweets? And why do you live the way you do?"

Aghori Baba replied, "Why do you call it a dead body? It is no longer human. It is just matter that is not being used. You are associating it with human beings. No one else will use that body, so I will. I am a scientist doing experiments, trying to discover the underlying principles of matter and energy. I'm changing one form of matter to another. My teacher is Mother Nature; she makes many forms, and I'm following her law when I change the forms around. This time I did it for that pandit. He himself will be transformed, but he will warn others to stay away from me. I've been living in this cave for thirteen years and no one has visited me. That is how I want it. My outer appearance makes people afraid of me. They think I'm dirty and I live on fish and dead bodies. I throw pebbles at them but I make sure no one gets hurt. I want to do my work in peace."

Swamiji described part of this episode in *Living with the Himalayan Masters,* to clarify the specific path that Aghori Baba followed. As Swamiji indicated there, Aghori Baba was a tantric master with a vast knowledge of the scriptures. Extremely intelligent, he was a spiritual scientist who constantly experimented with the dynamics of matter and energy, their interchangeability, and how they relate to pure consciousness. The scriptures pertaining to the *aghora* path describe the way matter and energy in numberless forms have evolved from consciousness, how this whole universe has been created by consciousness, and how consciousness uses matter and energy as a stage for its divine play. One who knows this truth is learned, and one who has gained a direct experience of it is enlightened.

I had always noticed Swamiji's special love for Aghori Baba and the cave where he lived. And even after this sage had left his body, Swamiji frequently visited this cave, often taking select students with him. Then in 1983 Swamiji spoke of this saint in the context of the aghora tradition and the esoteric knowledge of solar science *(surya vijñana),* and I got a glimpse of Swamiji's relationship with this master.

By now I was certain that Aghori Baba was one of Swamiji's main sources of knowledge about solar science. From conversations with him and from the writings of a great scholar, G. N. Kaviraj, I had learned that masters of this esoteric science possess extraordinary healing powers and can transform matter into energy, and vice versa, at will. And in my heart I had a feeling that Swamiji himself was a master of this science, for both in India and in the United States I had heard dozens of tales about him healing others and materializing objects—such as a Shiva lingam, yantras, and different kinds of flowers—out of thin air.

One such story revolved around the Tandon family in Kanpur, whose members had been Swamiji's students for a long time. As the family was preparing to celebrate a wedding, one of the children fell ill. The doctors could do nothing, and it appeared that the boy would die. Swamiji stopped by, and when he heard of the condition of the child, he asked for and received a glass of water. He then walked around the boy's bed with the glass in his hand, drank the water, and left the house. Instantly the child's fever disappeared and he made a complete recovery. As we will see later, there are similar accounts of Swamiji healing people here in the United States.

I had no doubt about the truth of these stories, but I did not know the specific practice that enables a yogi to gain the extraordinary ability to heal others or to transform one form of matter into another. Then late one night, after I had read aloud some pages of my Hindi translation of *Living with the Himalayan Masters* to Swamiji, he dismissed me with instructions to come again in the morning. I went to see him at 6:30 a.m. Normally he slept in a corner of his small dining room, but that night he had made his bed in the adjacent conference room, and I found him sitting on the blanket he used for a bed, which was unusual at so late an hour. Soon after I entered the room I noticed that the big rubber tree growing in the western corner seemed to have shrunk. The tree had grown so tall that the top was bent against the ceiling, and we had been planning to move it to the solarium, where the ceiling is higher. But now its top was at least two feet below the ceiling. At first I thought someone must have put it in a smaller pot or maybe even pruned it, but when I looked more closely I saw that the pot was the same and the top of the tree was intact. So I asked, "Swamiji, what happened to this plant? Why is it so short?"

"I was making an experiment on how to make a big object become smaller," he replied.

"How did you do that?"

"It is simple: remove some of its mass by transforming it into energy and transport it to another place."

"How did you transform the plant's matter into energy?" I asked him. "And where did you transport it?"

"Do you want to see how I did it? I'll show you."

With that, he pointed his index finger at the plant and asked me to put my hand between the plant and his finger, which was approximately three feet away from the plant. I felt an incredible current of energy passing from his finger toward the plant. It was unbearable—I could not keep my hand there. Then, asking me to keep my eyes on the plant, Swamiji explained that he was transferring some of the matter from his body into the plant. Within minutes small lumps appeared all over the plant; the largest were on the trunk. Swamiji said that although the rubber tree is fast-growing, it could not assimilate the amount of matter he was transferring into it so quickly, which was why the lumps had appeared.

Dropping his finger, he said, "Now the plant is a couple of pounds heavier and I'm a couple of pounds lighter."

Then he raised his finger again and reversed the procedure. This time, when I put my hand between his finger and the plant, I felt a strong energy current coming from the rubber tree. Within five minutes all the lumps on the plant had vanished.

I was curious to know how the human body could assimilate such a mass of matter in minutes, so I asked, "Are there lumps in your body now?" He said, "No."

"So where are you depositing the matter? And how are you assimilating it?"

"I'm depositing it in my abdomen," he replied. "I'm giving it to the fire, who will digest and properly distribute it throughout the body in the course of time."

At this moment Swamiji's secretary, Kamal, came into the room. Swamiji looked at her and said with a chuckle, "Hey, tall girl! Do you want me to make you short?"

With her customary disciplined smile, she replied, "No, thank you," and proceeded with her morning tasks.

From previous discussions with Swamiji and from reading the scriptures I knew that fire is the basis for all transformation. So as soon as he said, "I'm giving it to the fire, who will digest and properly distribute it throughout the body," I grabbed the opportunity to hear more about fire. Swamiji was in a generous mood, so I asked, "Swamiji, what is this fire? Where does it reside? What are its functions? Is it the fire or is it the yogi with the help of fire who transforms matter into energy and vice versa? Is it through our practice that we gain mastery over the fire or is it through the practice that we receive the grace of the fire? And ultimately, what is the exact practice for unraveling the mystery of fire?"

Swamiji said, "Aghori Baba was the master of this science, and he always reminded me that fire is the core of yoga practice. It is the action of fire that enables a yogi to cultivate and maintain a radiant body and a brilliant mind. Yogis meditate on fire at the navel center, but in our tradition adepts meditate on fire at the pelvic center, known as *svadhishthana*. Here fire is called *samvarta agni*. It is this particular aspect of fire that transforms matter into energy; inseparable from it is *samaya agni*, which transforms energy into matter. All forms of change—physical, mental, and spiritual; internal and external—are totally dependent on these two inseparable aspects of fire. Some meditate on this fire by following the path of yoga, and others worship it by performing ritual offerings and mantra recitation."

I urged, "May I learn and practice this science?"

"Why not?" he replied. "In fact we should offer an intensive course on this subject. It will help people. The course will be called 'The Path of Fire and Light.'"

That is how Swamiji started his annual retreat and intensive that came to be known by this name. Later the lectures were compiled and published in book form under the same title.

Another sage Swamiji remembered gratefully was Sombari Baba, who lived fifteen miles outside Almora, a district in the Kumayun Himalayas, and who was known for his austerity and generosity. No one knew his birthplace or his original name, so people began to call him Sombari Baba because he held a public feast in his ashram every Monday (*Sombar* in Hindi dialects). Sombari Baba was extremely austere. In the early days of his spiritual practice he had committed himself to *panchagni sadhana,* a practice that entailed completely surrounding himself with fire—the fire in all four directions around him, and the Sun above—and while surrounded by these five fires, he meditated on the inner fire, *kundalini shakti.*

As part of his daily routine he got up well before dawn, bathed in the nearby river, and after several hours of meditation, began a fire offering that ended at noon. Then he would walk up to the samadhi shrine of Gudari Baba (the monument in his honor at his burial place, which was also the place where he had left his body voluntarily). According to Sombari Baba, Gudari Baba remains here, absorbed in a thousand-year-long meditation. Only after paying homage to him at his samadhi shrine would Sombari Baba tend to his own physical needs.

Sombari Baba was particular about his diet. In the late afternoon he drank his tea, and in the evening he cooked his meal. He made just enough for one person, but he split it into thirds: one portion he gave to the fish, another portion was put aside (no one knew for whom or what), and the third portion he ate. He spent his nights in solitude— the first time anyone could catch a glimpse of him was in the morning as he was preparing his fire offering.

Sombari Baba was famous for his healing powers, and every afternoon he was surrounded by those in need of medical attention. The medicines he gave were free. They usually consisted of spices and herbs growing in the region, although sometimes he gave ash from his dhuni. Without exception, everyone who came to him was cured. But doctors in the nearby towns of Almora and Nainital regarded Sombari Baba as their enemy—his selfless service was ruining their business. He had no medical degree, so they accused him of practicing medicine illegally and persecuted him relentlessly, eventually badgering him to the point that he had to stop helping people with his herbs and spices.

But still he continued healing—he simply changed his method. He began giving *bhandara* (a feast) every Monday that was open to all. Each week he fed between three hundred and five hundred people, and the food from his kitchen served as medicine—it was a vehicle for transmitting his loving energy to those in need of it.

In the early part of Swamiji's life, when he was known as Bhole, he visited Sombari Baba frequently, often in the company of his master or other sages, but in those days he did not have sufficient understanding of the sage to discuss spiritual matters with him, nor was it appropriate to do so in the presence of his master or other great adepts.

While he lived with Aghori Baba, however, Bhole had become convinced that fire was the core of yoga practice. Through observation and personal experience he knew that sages like Babaji, Gudari Baba, and Aghori Baba meditated on the internal fire of kundalini but only rarely performed external fire rituals. Bhole was grateful to Aghori Baba for teaching him how to awaken and meditate on this inner fire, but he also felt that Aghori Baba had imparted only half the mystery. He knew that the knowledge of external fire also has its value, and from observing the profound reverence Aghori Baba and Sombari Baba had for one another, Bhole sensed that Sombari Baba was the adept who held the key to this knowledge. Thus, after leaving Aghori Baba's cave, Bhole went to Sombari Baba—this time alone.

There are hundreds of stories in the Himalayan villages near Almora regarding Sombari Baba's ability to know in advance who was going to visit him and with what intention. And so it was that several days before Bhole arrived, Sombari Baba began to perform an even more elaborate fire offering than was his custom—it now lasted from four to five hours each morning. When Bhole arrived, Sombari Baba allowed the young sadhu to assist him in collecting wood, preparing the ingredients, and arranging the sticks in the *kunda* (sacred firepit), and he also asked Bhole to remain nearby in case anything was needed. This gave Bhole an opportunity to witness the amazing phenomena that spontaneously manifested around Sombari Baba during his fire ritual. The flames often grew so big that Sombari Baba was completely surrounded by them, yet he was not harmed. Sometimes the wood exploded and a glowing coal would land in his lap, yet the adept continued his practice undisturbed, picking up the coal with his fingers and putting it back in the fire only when his hands were free from offering oblations. Bhole also noticed that from time to time the flames would change their color, that sometimes the flames emerging from different parts of the firepit emitted different hues.

So one afternoon Bhole expressed his astonishment to Sombari Baba, and asked him how it was that the fire didn't burn him. "How can fire burn itself?" Sombari Baba replied. "Fire is me and I am fire. The whole universe is pervaded by fire, but is anything being destroyed by fire? Fire is that which sustains life. Only those who do not know the divine nature of fire are afraid of it."

Bhole did not understand all the implications of Sombari Baba's explanation, but he understood that fire is divine energy and embodies intelligence, just as we do. He also knew, intellectually at least, that the whole universe is pervaded by fire in the form of heat and light, but he had a hard time grasping Sombari Baba's statement, "Fire is me and I am fire."

Hoping to eventually understand what this meant, Bhole posed another question: "Why do the colors of the flame change from time to time?"

"Flames are the tongues of fire. They are seven in number, and each tongue has its own color. These tongues have their specific functions. Before you start the fire ritual, you invoke the fire with all its tongues. Only then do you begin your offerings to the fire. Depending on the intention behind the offerings and the characteristics of the objects being offered, specific tongues come forward to accept them. Although all the oblations I offer into the fire contain the same ingredients, at various times I offer them to nurture different forces of nature. That is why the flames change color from time to time."

"I thought that fire rituals help us strengthen our spiritual practice—that the ingredients for the offering symbolize our karmas, and that by putting the oblations into the fire we symbolically burn our karmas in the fire of knowledge. I never thought that through the fire offering we can nurture the forces of nature. I don't understand. They are more pervasive and powerful than we are. Are they dependent on us for nurturance?"

Sombari Baba replied, "Everything in this web of life is interconnected. Our health and happiness are not separate from the health and happiness of others. Our inner strength and spiritual wisdom affect the world outside us, and vice versa. For all practical purposes we are totally dependent on the forces of nature. These forces, such as water, air, and light, are constantly supplying the nourishment we need. If these forces are weak, we cannot be healthy. Similarly, there is a collective intelligence. If this collective pool of intelligence is undernourished, then our individual intelligence becomes confused and disoriented. The best way to help yourself is to keep nature healthy and strong, for you are an integral part of it.

"You modern children have become slaves to your intellect. Instead of experiencing the truth directly, you look for a symbolic meaning in it. Fire is a living truth. It is a link between Earth and heaven. It is divine and resides in everything and everyone. Seated in every single cell of our bodies, it witnesses our every act. Fire is the source of our thought, speech, and action. The same fire resides outside our bodies. It is fire that initiates and maintains the process of change in everything that exists in creation. You burn your psychological trash in the fire of knowledge, but you can burn your tangible, physical trash only in a living, blazing fire—a fire that is not a symbol of something else but rather is a self-evident reality. Similarly, you provide nourishment to your soul by offering your love to God, who is beyond names and forms. But you provide nourishment to your body, mind, and senses by expressing your love through oblations offered into fire, the manifest form of God on Earth.

"Gaining direct experience of the divine nature of fire that pervades the universe and maintains the law of change is God-realization. Gaining direct experience of that same fire in the form of the kundalini shakti within us is self-realization. Attending the fire within and rejoicing in the consummate bliss that spontaneously emerges from its brilliance is yoga sadhana. Attending the fire outside and nursing nature's forces by offering oblations into its mouth is *yajña* [sacrifice]. For your personal fulfillment, practice yoga, but for the pleasure of the higher self who is both within and without, practice yajña. That's what God has been doing eternally. In the form of Yogi

Shiva he is always meditating on Mount Kailas, and in the form of Indra he is always performing yajña in the three worlds—Earth, heaven, and the space in between. If you wish to be with God, join him in the practice of both meditation and yajña."

Bhole was startled, and in the days that followed he turned what Sombari Baba had said over and over in his mind. He had read about Shiva, who according to legend lives on Mount Kailas, but he had assumed that the tales were myths—expressions of yogic experiences in the form of stories. Similarly, he knew that Indra was the king of gods in the complex polytheistic mythology of the Vedic pantheon. Indra presides over the phenomenon of rain, he rides a chariot of clouds, and he wields a lightning bolt. Bhole's comparative study of Indian and Greek mythology had led him to identify Indra with the Greek god Zeus, and until now he had been happy in his conviction that Indra symbolizes the collective mind of all living beings and thus rules over all the other gods, who represent the forces of the senses. It was incomprehensible to Bhole that Indra would be continually performing yajña in the three worlds.

At the earliest opportunity Bhole asked Sombari Baba, "What is yajña? Who is Indra? How is he performing yajña? And how is it affecting the creation of which we are a part?"

"Selfless giving is yajña," Sombari Baba replied. "Performing actions for the welfare of others is yajña. There are numberless ways of serving others through kind and selfless deeds, but best are those that serve creation on the largest scale and whose effects are long-lasting. Helping nature maintain its harmonious balance is the best way to serve creation, for when the natural ecology is imbalanced, all forms of life suffer. According to the scriptures those who bring suffering to the world by disturbing the ecological balance are demons; those who serve nature and thereby relieve this suffering are *devas* [divine beings].

"All life depends on food," Sombari Baba continued. "The entire food chain is in turn dependent on rain. The vitality of rain depends on the vitality of the clouds. The vitality of the clouds depends on nourishing elements in the atmosphere. Elements of nourishment in the atmosphere depend on fire, both within us and outside us. Ultimately, the health and well-being of all forms of life depends on fire. That is why fire is the center of yajña."

Bhole had encountered the concept of yajña in scriptures like the *Bhagavad Gita* and the Upanishads, but he was always inclined to interpret such descriptions symbolically. His preference was to meditate on the fire of kundalini and gain mystical experiences from such meditative practices. In fact, he had considered all ritual practices, including the fire practice, to be mere ceremonies—priestly business devoid of spiritual significance.

During these conversations Sombari Baba dismantled Bhole's preconceived notions, and in his heart Bhole had faith in Sombari Baba. He believed what he said, but his intellect demanded more explanation. Bhole wanted to know exactly how one can nourish the atmosphere and thereby nourish the entire food chain through a fire practice. So one day he said, "Still, I don't understand why a fire offering is the best way to serve creation. Why not give the grains and herbs offered to the fire to those who need them? Why not spend time planting trees and serving people in the hospitals rather than spending hours and hours making offerings to the fire? How can a fire offering be more effective in restoring the balance of nature than educating people about the importance of protecting the natural world?"

Sombari Baba explained, "Humans are intelligent but self-destructive. Like the other animals, they are driven by reward and punishment. In addition, they are selfish. They are so blinded by the desire for pleasure that they don't see how momentary pleasures bring unending suffering. That is why their ears are deaf to good advice.

"I hear that some cities are so polluted that people have no clean air to breathe. Those who are away from those cities don't care, because they believe they are not affected. But the planet is a single living organism. Those pollutants are being deposited in the atmosphere, and the wind and clouds are the first elements to be contaminated. They suffocate; their vitality declines. All forms of life—plants, minerals, and animals—that depend on these elements also suffer. The wind and clouds encircle the globe and thus affect the entire planet, not just a tiny part of it. Even here in the Himalayas, where there is no visible disturbance in the balance of nature, the vitality of the grains and herbs is beginning to decline. The clouds that bring rain to the plains of

India and the Himalayas, for example, come from the Bay of Bengal. In addition to the pollution rising from cities like Calcutta, the clouds are laden with the vibrations of the inner poverty of the people who live between the Bay of Bengal and the Himalayas. The quality of that rain alters the subtle properties of the soil here in the mountains. The vegetation growing in that soil is affected, and so are those who eat it.

"How can you tell the whole world not to pollute the air and the clouds with chemical and mental toxins? Who will listen to you? How can you convince the world that you are not a fool? The best way to restore balance is to come up with a system to detoxify and revitalize the forces of nature—soil, water, fire, air, and space. The ancient sages discovered this system. They called it yajña.

"As part of yajña, we offer ingredients that are detoxifying and nourishing. Fire transforms them into subtle energy, and the power of mantra carries that subtle energy to the intended realm. The action of fire, the willful determination of the sages, the intelligent energy generated by mantra, and the intention of the person performing the yajña—together all these bring fresh life to nature's forces. The energy generated by the yajña is like a tonic to the clouds. In turn those clouds bring a healthy rain; a healthy rain brings a healthy harvest; a healthy harvest brings good health to those who consume it. Healthy individuals create a healthy society. And while living in a healthy society you will face fewer obstacles to achieving the highest goal of life. Remember what the *Gita* says: 'One who does not perform his actions in conformity with the principle of yajña lives in vain. His actions are blind, and so are the fruits of his actions.'"

Bhole stayed with Sombari Baba for a month, and during that time he learned why Indra is said to be the king of the gods: Indra presides over the phenomenon of rain, and life on the planet is totally dependent on rain. He is the collective consciousness of all the forces that bring rain to the planet, and he is the presiding god of all those forces that shower us with inner fulfillment. Indra is also known as Rudra, which means "one who showers tears of pain and happiness." When pleased by the performance of yajña, he brings tears of joy; when people become lazy and careless and harm nature, he bathes them in tears of pain. That is why some regard Indra as kind, and others find him terrifying.

His stay with Sombari Baba made Bhole realize that social custom, superstition, and dogma have even crept into the sublime science of the fire practice, and he saw that yajña as taught by the Vedic sages is virtually extinct. Vanity-ridden brahmins, not knowing a single Vedic practice, have disconnected the practice of fire from its roots in the Vedas. Hinduism is simply carrying its corpse. Otherwise how could the children of the Vedic sages suffer from such extreme internal and external poverty?

Sombari Baba was an embodiment of the Vedas, Bhole realized: he did not teach—he simply served. Most of his visitors were laymen—farmers, merchants, and craftsmen—with the occasional poet, writer, or teacher. There wasn't a single book in his ashram, and he held no discourses. Not a single student ever came to study with him.

On the day Bhole departed, Sombari Baba blessed him, saying, "Gather the fire within and serve the fire outside."

Bowing in gratitude, Bhole asked, "May I personally perform yajña and inspire others to do so?"

Sombari Baba replied, "First awaken the fire within and transform yourself. Learn from the Upanishads how a sadhu carries the fire on his head. Babaji will give you the spark to awaken your dormant fire. He will also tell you how to carry that fire from cave to cave. Millions of caves—human hearts—have sunk into darkness. May you carry fire and light to those damp, dark caves."

With this profound blessing, Bhole returned to his master, joining Babaji at the famous Shakti shrine Chandra Badani in the Garhwal Himalayas.

When the right time came, Bhole told Babaji about his experiences with Sombari Baba, and with a smile Babaji expressed his satisfaction with Bhole's progress. He told Bhole that now he should go and practice what he had learned. Bhole's dilemma was: Where to start? He had learned so much in bits and pieces from Babaji and other sages: the system of hatha yoga, including advanced breathing exercises, from Gudari Baba; the Vedantic method of self-reflection from his guru brother, Swami Shivananda; meditation on the navel center from Aghori Baba; and the fire ritual from Sombari Baba. How could he practice them all?

So Bhole asked Babaji what to do, and his master told him to meditate on the navel center. He instructed him to live in a cave at Sitabani, a place near Haldwani in the Kumayun Himalayas, until the practice he would give him was complete, and gave him clear instructions: "Don't carry many belongings—take two sets of clothes, a blanket, a water pot, a begging bowl, and an ax. Make a dhuni in the cave. Don't socialize with anyone. Wake up in the morning and sit for meditation while focusing at the navel center: within the body, that is the center of fire. When the awareness of the fire at the navel center begins to fade, open your eyes, look at the fire in the dhuni, then gently close your eyes and bring the image of that fire to the navel center. This is the mantra: . . . Remember it all the time during your meditation. Once a day, at noon, you should go to the nearby village with your begging bowl, and whatever you get as alms, be happy with that. Throughout the practice make sure that you don't become dependent on anyone or anything." With these instructions, Babaji sent Bhole to the cave at Sitabani.

When he arrived, Bhole found the cave empty. It looked as if no one had lived there for years. He cleaned it and lit his dhuni, but it was not a comfortable cave and it took several days for the fire to remove the dampness. Furthermore, it took many hours every day to collect sticks and logs, and even those were so damp that the cave filled with smoke. He remembered Babaji's instructions not to socialize and not to be dependent, yet it seemed to Bhole that the only way to obtain wood dry enough to burn well was to accept the offerings of the villagers, who had collected an ample supply.

Finally, after a week or so Bhole established his routine. In the beginning he collected as many sticks from the forest as he could and accepted as little from the villagers as possible. But gradually he became comfortable with the villagers' generosity and stopped gathering sticks for himself. Now the only thing he had to do to support himself was to go to the village every day with his begging bowl. Within two weeks his practice was going smoothly.

Then one day when he was about to leave the cave, he heard a voice. "We are pleased with your sincerity," it said. "You don't have to beg for food. Eat as much as you wish right here." With that, a platter of food appeared. Bhole was thrilled at this supernatural phenomenon. He was proud of himself for being such a sincere *sadhaka* (seeker) that he had won the favor of divine beings inhabiting the cave. He was also flooded with gratitude for his master, who had sent him to this special place. He accepted the food gladly, and from that time on he no longer went to the village to beg for alms. He lived in the cave for six months, and after the first two weeks he did his practice in comfort. The villagers supplied the wood for his dhuni, and his food came without any effort as well.

When the practice was complete Bhole returned to his master, sure that Babaji would be proud of him. But to his dismay, the moment Babaji saw him he began to shout. "You lazy boy! Go and live in that cave! You don't need to be with me. I expected you to be a human, not a parasite."

Later, as he contemplated on this incident, Bhole realized what the sages meant when they said that the path of sadhana is not for dull and lazy people. An aspirant must reflect on the teachings of a realized master with care and be vigilant not to distort them for his own comfort and convenience. The experience in the cave had made Bhole acutely aware that there is a higher reality, one beyond the reach of the mind and senses. He knew without doubt that the immortal sages do exist regardless of whether we perceive them or not, that life extends beyond the boundaries of birth and death, and that the purpose of life is to recognize the immortal self, not to busy oneself solely with meeting the demands of the body and senses.

Once again Bhole surveyed his life. He refreshed the memories of his childhood, reminding himself of the emptiness of worldly relationships—how his father had died, how his mother had become blind, how no one other than his brother's wife had cared for him, how he was now disconnected from his biological family. In contrast were the memories of how Babaji and other sadhus raised him, the vision he was granted of the Divine Mother at Khajuraho while he was still a child, his many experiences with the masters who bestowed their blessings so lovingly. This contemplation confirmed the conviction that had been growing in him that the world is tasteless. He did not want to associate himself with it. He decided, once and for all, to follow the path of the sages, the path that leads to perfect freedom.

Bhole still did not understand when and how to honor the grace of the Divine and when to remain indifferent to it. If a platter of food coming to him out of thin air in the cave at Sitabani was not the grace of the Divine, then what was it? I did not ask for it, he thought, and I did not have the capacity to stop it. It is true that I became dependent on that food and that I disobeyed my master by not asking for alms at different doors every day. In future, how can I handle such situations so that I obey my master without committing an offense against divine grace?

One day Babaji explained that such situations call for discrimination, and reminded Bhole that brooding on the past is a waste of time. "To honor the sages living in that cave in their subtle bodies," he said, "you could have accepted the food humbly on the first day. The second day, you could have explained that because of the instructions I had given you it was not appropriate for you to accept their generosity every day. Furthermore, you could have added, 'Since I have been blessed by your presence I will get anything I need for my survival. Therefore I seek not food but your blessings so that I may complete my practice successfully.'"

Bhole then asked Babaji how he could cultivate the power of discrimination so that he wouldn't make such mistakes again. Babaji's reply was that through the practice of the *gayatri* mantra one can illuminate the mind and sharpen the intellect. And in the tradition of the Vedic sages, he said, aspirants are required to undertake its practice. Only after that does the door to higher practices open.

"But if I take the vows of *sannyasa* [renunciation]," Bhole argued, "won't I be free from the charms and temptations of the world? That will enable me to do the practices successfully, for then I will have no distractions."

Babaji laughed. "There are thousands of renunciates. Are they less miserable than other people? If a ceremony performed by priests can free you from all problems and make you a swami—a master of yourself—you don't need a teacher, nor do you need to do any practice.

There are many people deluded by this swami business. In an attempt to escape the soul's call for self-discovery, the ignorant go to priests, who promise instant salvation through their rituals and ceremonies. Similarly, in an attempt to escape their past the ignorant run to those gurus who promise instant transformation through renunciation ceremonies—as if a shaved head, different clothes, and a new name make a man holy.

"Instead of denying that you have problems, face yourself. For that, you have to do sadhana. And as you grow spiritually, you become a swami—a master of yourself. Overcome the illusion that swamihood is something that can be passed on to you by someone else. Come with me to Banaras. There I will teach you where and how to do your *gayatri* practice. It will help you to see yourself face to face. Then you can decide what part of yourself you need to renounce and what part needs further nurturing."

Bhole reached Banaras in Babaji's company, and after they paid homage to Shiva, Babaji took him to the other side of the Ganga and arranged for a hut to be built for him. He then lit a dhuni for Bhole under the overhang outside the door and drew a line around the hut, telling him that, except to relieve himself, he was to stay inside the circle until he had completed the practice. Babaji appointed a pandit from the city to bring him food once a day, as well as other necessities such as lamp oil and wood for the dhuni.

Then before leaving, Babaji gave Bhole these instructions: "In the presence of fire and the Ganga, complete the practice of 2.4 million repetitions of the *gayatri* mantra. Maintain your equilibrium. Pay no attention to the world outside the circle I have drawn."

Bhole started his practice. Very soon people in the city began to talk about him: "The young sadhu on the other side of the Ganga is austere and radiant. He is quite advanced for one so young. I wonder whose incarnation he is?" And so on. Gradually a crowd began to gather around his hut. Bhole did not socialize with the crowd, but it was hard to keep his concentration on the practice. And the less he spoke, the more they praised him. But soon ugly rumors began: "He is a fake; he knows nothing, that is why he doesn't talk; he's a young and handsome man, nothing more; he's clever: he's trying to attract

117

rich people from the city—once he collects enough money from them, he will vanish."

One day a group of pandits approached and challenged him to a philosophical debate. For a while Bhole was quiet, simply acknowledging their questions with a smile. By focusing his mind on the mantra and the fire, he tried not to be disturbed by their behavior. But the pandits responded to his silence by becoming more aggressive. They ridiculed his practice and accused him of being a hypocrite until, all of a sudden, Bhole lost his temper. He crossed the line Babaji had drawn, which by now was no longer visible, and, shouting, caught one of the pandits by the neck and shoved him toward the river. The other visitors also shouted at the pandits: "What business do you have to challenge someone who is not interested in debating you? Leave him alone!" Without a word, Bhole walked into his hut, and the crowd dispersed. A few hours later the pandit who brought him food and other supplies arrived with a telegram from Babaji that read: "Bhole, you have ruined your practice. Start again."

Bhole contemplated the origin of his anger and remembered that anger comes from unfulfilled desires. He realized that somewhere deep within he was attached to honor and had an aversion to public humiliation. In his heart he prayed to his master to help him overcome these subtle tendencies. Then he started his practice again.

Several months passed, and the practice was going well. Bhole had proven that he was not as peaceful a sage as people expected, so there were fewer visitors. Gradually, however, an unusual guest began to arrive at an odd hour. The man was a dwarf, and the first few times he showed up at noon. Bhole paid no attention to him. Then the dwarf came at midnight. From outside the invisible circle, he made a gesture of respect and then left without a word. This became his daily routine. Since he seemed gentle and peaceful, Bhole invited him to come and sit near the dhuni one night. The dwarf entered the circle and sat down, keeping his distance from the fire. Bhole talked to him briefly, asking his name, where he lived, and what he did. Without prolonging the conversation, the dwarf answered the questions and left after a few minutes. The following night at exactly the same hour he came again, and sat near the dhuni. Bhole expressed his desire for milk and jalebi, and asked the dwarf if he could bring some when he came the next night. The man jumped up, saying he would get them right away. Bhole protested: it was the middle of the night, the shops would be closed, and furthermore there would be no boats available at this hour to cross the Ganga. The dwarf insisted, explaining that he had been living in the city for ages—the boatmen knew him, and he himself knew exactly how to get milk and jalebi. Then without giving Bhole a chance to stop him, he left. An hour later he was back, and Bhole was able to enjoy his favorite treat.

This became routine—every midnight the dwarf brought Bhole jalebi and milk, spent a few hours with him, and left. Soon the pandit who brought Bhole food every day noticed that Bhole was eating less, and asked why. Bhole told the pandit about the dwarf, and the pandit asked for the dwarf's name and address so he could pay him for the food. So when the dwarf came the following night, Bhole asked him to get reimbursed by the pandit for the money he was spending. The dwarf refused. Bhole then asked for his address, and after a brief hesitation the dwarf gave it to him. The next day the pandit went there, but found no trace of the dwarf. In the process of scouring the neighborhood, however, he learned that about ninety years before, a dwarf had lived in the spot corresponding to that address and that this dwarf had been a learned Sanskrit scholar.

The pandit was annoyed, and the next time he saw Bhole he said sarcastically, "Brahmachariji Maharaj [great celibate saint], tell me what's going on with you? Why have you lost your appetite?"

"I told you," Bhole replied. "A dwarf brings me jalebi and milk every night."

"You are trying to create trouble for me, but I'm telling you: you are going to be in trouble if you don't tell me the truth," the pandit said. "I wasted my whole day looking for your dwarf. The one I found at the address you gave me died ninety years ago. If a dead dwarf feeds you jalebi and milk, that's fine with me. But I can't pay him."

Bhole was puzzled. So when the dwarf arrived with the jalebi and milk at midnight, Bhole demanded that he reveal his identity and the purpose of his midnight visits.

"I have told you," the dwarf said. "You are doing your job; I am doing mine. I never disturb you, and by serving you I do my work the way I am instructed to."

"Who can he be?" Bhole wondered. "Why does he visit me exactly at midnight? Is he truly helping me, or is he trying to disturb me? Is he human, or not? Is he a projection of my own deluded mind, or is he real? Have I been eating real jalebi and drinking real milk, or something materialized by him?"

Suddenly another thought flashed into his mind: Nobody makes jalebi in the middle of the night. In Banaras and throughout north India jalebi are prepared in the morning and consumed then and there. The jalebi the dwarf brings are warm and fresh. Even if someone were making them in the city at night, they would be cold by the time he brought them across the river. This dwarf is not who he pretends to be.

Enraged, Bhole poured some water into his right palm, and holding his hand in midair, shouted, "Tell me who you are and why you come here every night! Otherwise I will destroy you!"

The dwarf remained quiet and motionless, and Bhole lost control over himself. Repeating the *gayatri* mantra mentally, he flung the water on the dwarf, who vanished. In the spot where he had been sitting, Bhole saw a piece of bone.

In his heart Bhole knew he had made a mistake once again—and sure enough, the next day the pandit came with another telegram from Babaji: "Bhole, you ruined it again. Be strong. Follow the instructions I gave you carefully."

The pandit was surprised to see the jalebi and milk still sitting there from the previous night and was totally confused when he saw the piece of bone near the fire. But when he asked where it came from, all Bhole said was, "It doesn't matter. Take me to Manikarnika Ghat" [the famous burning ghat in Banaras].

With the help of the pandit, Bhole cremated the bone at Manikarnika, but he never explained why he did so. He resumed his practice at the end of the day, and this time he completed it successfully.

When they met again, Babaji said to Bhole, "What you need to renounce is the unwanted part of yourself, not the world. I am glad you completed the practice. I hope you will remember the lessons and not brood on the incidents themselves. A failure is more rewarding than success, provided you learn something from it. See how subtle are the causes of emotion? Ultimately they stem from ego—the awareness within you that does not want its image to be disfigured. From this ego comes attachment, aversion, desire, and anger, all of which create delusion; delusion is damaging to memory and the power of discrimination. Attachment, aversion, desire, anger, delusion, loss of memory, and loss of discrimination are children of the ego. They eclipse the intrinsic wisdom of the soul. Now I want to see you walking on the path of renunciation."

With that, Babaji ordained Bhole as a monk and named him Sadashiva, but people lovingly called him "Bhole Baba."

the ROAD TO SELF-MASTERY

BEFORE HIS ORDINATION as a monk, Bhole had been filled with anticipation, his hopes running high: *Babaji will tear the veil of maya and I will delight in the supreme knowledge forever; Babaji will throw all of my karmas into the fire as part of the ceremony, thus bringing my past to an end; Babaji will help me perform my own funeral and I will emerge as a new person—a clean slate without the slightest trace of fear, anxiety, desire, or attachment.*

The ceremony went as planned. As was the rule, he had fasted the day before the ceremony and further purified his body and senses by bathing in the Ganga and drinking only Ganga water. He had purified his *nadis* (energy channels) with pranayama and his mind with meditation. Then came the ritualistic part of the ceremony, the major components of which are: cutting the hair, to symbolize disconnection from the past; bathing, to symbolize cleansing; putting on ochre robes, to symbolize non-attachment; receiving the staff, the symbol of discipline; donning wooden sandals, the symbol of austerity; receiving a new name, the symbol of a new identity; and placing a sacred rock on the head, to symbolize holding the sacred fire as the highest goal of life.

On the day of the ceremony Babaji cut the first lock of hair while pandits recited mantras; the rest was shaved by a barber. Then, after Bhole took his ceremonial dip in the Ganga, Aghori Baba gave him a beautiful ochre robe made of silk. Bhole's guru brother, Swami Shivananda, who had come down from Gangotri, gave him the staff.

Gudari Baba came from the Valley of Flowers to present Bhole with the wooden sandals. Babaji gave Bhole a mantra and pronounced his new name: Sadashiva. Nirvanji, a gentle sage from Rishikesh, tied a garland of flowers on Bhole's head. And Babaji secured the *shaligram* (sacred rock) on the garland.

By the time the ceremony was over it was almost evening. The sadhus showered their blessings on the young swami and called him Bhole Baba, and as a token of his blessing, Babaji gave the young monk leaves of holy basil in a bowl of Ganga water. Then he sent him to do the *brahma jagarana* practice.

"Brahma jagarana" means "to stay awake in the night while contemplating the highest truth," and as part of this practice the newly ordained monk spends his first night in a lonely place, preferably on a hilltop, on a riverbank, or at a cremation ground. Because the ceremony had taken place outside Aghori Baba's cave, Bhole Baba spent the night on the bank of the Ganga.

The next morning, however, Bhole Baba saw a marked change in the attitude of Babaji and the other sages, who had always given him unconditional love. He had not eaten for several days in preparation for his ordination, and when he returned to the cave the next morning he was very hungry. All the visitors were gone. Only Babaji and Aghori Baba remained, and they kept their eyes closed in meditation until late morning. At the earliest opportunity, Bhole Baba asked about lunch.

Babaji replied, "Now you are a swami, master of yourself and creator of your own destiny. Design your life, your routine, how you want to manage your urges and to comply with your needs, and to what extent you want to interact with the world."

"You are the creator of my destiny," Bhole Baba replied. "Please give me definite guidelines so I can follow the path without deviation."

"There are many kinds of renunciates," Babaji said. "Some live in an ashram and do their sadhana while following the rules of the ashram. They work for the ashram, and the ashram provides them with the bare necessities: food, clothing, and shelter. They beg alms only if the ashram requires it, and what they get goes to the ashram. Another kind of renunciate travels constantly, stopping briefly wherever they are welcome. They may stay in an ashram or temple from time to time, yet they bear no responsibility for that place. They beg and content themselves with what is given to them. Yet another group has strict rules for begging. They will make only three stops to ask for alms, for example, or they will accept only enough food for eight bites. Some renunciates do not ask for alms at all; they accept only what comes to them without asking. Some renounce even the begging bowl, using their palms instead. You may choose any of these ways, but remember: self-realization is the goal, not a particular way of living."

Bhole Baba said, "Please be more precise about which of these approaches I should adopt."

"Stop at only one door, and be happy with what comes to you from that door," Babaji replied in an authoritative tone. "Start your practice today."

So Bhole Baba picked up his begging bowl and walked to the nearby village, still clad in the beautiful silk robe. Stopping at a villager's door, he uttered the customary "Narayan Hari." A woman had been milking her cow when Bhole Baba approached, and the sudden "Narayan Hari" spooked the animal, causing the woman to lose her grip on the milking pot. "You useless swami! Get away from here!" she screamed. "You have money to wear a silk garment, and yet you are begging! You destroyed my precious milk pot!" When Bhole Baba tried to appease her, she shouted, "This was an antique pot, given to me by my mother-in-law! You parasite! Get out of my sight!"

Bhole Baba returned to his master empty-handed, and the two sadhus passed the rest of the day in silence. In the evening Bhole Baba said, "Today you did not ask me if I have taken food."

"You are a swami now," Babaji said, and reminded him that he had taken a vow to stop at only one door and that he had to adhere to the vow. "The path of renunciation is not for the weak or faint of heart," he added.

At this a compelling thought came into Bhole Baba's mind: Everyone in the world is a beggar. Can anyone breathe and think without the grace of a higher force? Why stop at a different door each day? Why not stop at only one door, once and for all—the door of the Divine Mother, who provides for the whole world?

Knowing that Babaji's blessings were with him and that Babaji always chose the challenging paths and avoided the easy ones, Bhole

125

Baba did not ask for his master's permission to follow this course. He simply bowed his head in homage and went to the bank of the Ganga and sat down, fully resolved to beg sustenance only from the Divine Mother—no one else. For the first few days no one paid any attention to him, and when people did begin to notice, they brought flowers and garlands, not food. For thirteen days nobody asked him if he had eaten. He became so weak he could hardly walk.

One night in 1983 when I was translating this episode, "My First Days as a Swami," in *Living with the Himalayan Masters,* I asked Swamiji how he managed to go without food for almost two weeks. How did it affect him mentally?

"I was drinking Ganga water," Swamiji replied. "The first week was hard. My whole consciousness was occupied by hunger. Every moment was filled with prayer for food. All kinds of fantasies and imaginings were passing through my mind: I thought that a stranger, inspired by the Divine Mother, would come with food and ask me to eat. When I saw visitors coming with garlands I would imagine them to be the Divine Mother in disguise—I fancied that she would free me from hunger by placing a garland around my neck. I remembered how the platter of food had come to me while I lived in the cave at Sitabani, and this memory led me to imagine a plate filled with food coming from the sky or appearing out of the rocks nearby.

"Then I crossed the boundary of hunger. My awareness shifted from stomach to forehead, and I lost my appetite even for water. Visitors appeared to be mere reflections in a mirror. My mind was absorbed either in my guru mantra or in a spontaneous prayer to the Divine Mother to accept me at her feet so that I might attain freedom from all forms of hunger—hunger for name, fame, popularity, money, power, prestige, and the pleasures of the senses. Without any effort on my part this prayer was arising from my heart as mist arises from a valley. I knew my master was residing nearby, but I was constantly feeling him within me and around me. There were times when I was brimming with the joy of understanding that he had no pity for me, only boundless compassion."

After thirteen days, something amazing happened. As Swamiji writes in *Living with the Himalayan Masters,* "Suddenly I saw a hand

126

coming out of the water—only a hand, holding a bowl filled with food. It started coming toward me, and I heard a woman's voice saying, 'Here, this is for you.' I took the bowl and ate. No matter how much I ate, the bowl did not empty."

Bhole Baba kept this bowl for three years, and during that time he fed thousands from it. No one could fill it—people would bring gallons of milk to pour in it and yet the bowl never overflowed. But not a single person came to learn anything from him; they came only to see this miraculous bowl. Even more amazing, people were less interested in eating from the bowl than in seeing how much it could contain. They even borrowed money to buy sweets, fruits, and milk to put in the bowl to test its capacity. People began to call the young monk Katori Wale Baba ("Bowl Baba"). Then one day Babaji told his disciple to give the bowl back to the Ganga, and without a second thought Bhole placed the bowl in the water and it disappeared.

127

"Now you have firsthand experience of divine grace," Babaji explained. "This bowl, embodying that grace, will always stay with you in one form or another. You may not remember this, but a long time ago, when you were a child, you gave your lunch to a hungry sage, and he blessed you, saying, 'You will never feel hunger unless food comes before you.' This whole circumstance of hunger and starvation was created by me," Babaji continued, "and through this train of events you have been blessed to receive all that you need, not just food. You must now learn to live in such a manner that you do not attract a crowd. Don't bind yourself with the external trappings of a swami.

"Now you should travel. You will digest your knowledge and experience through traveling and interacting with others. The principle of equanimity is the core of spirituality. Maintain a serene state of mind while you interact with rich and poor, learned and illiterate, genuine saints and hoodwinkers. To live with and learn from people in every stratum of society, don't hesitate to throw away these swami clothes if necessary. You should also spend some time with those great souls who live a lifestyle that is different from ours, and even those involved in humanitarian work and politics."

With these instructions, the two parted: Babaji for the high mountains, and Bhole Baba for Rishikesh.

Bhole Baba's reputation as the swami with the magic bowl was still fresh in people's minds. He did not go hungry, but it was not easy to find solitude. He lived in a thatched hut on the bank of the Ganga five miles from Rishikesh, and people came to see him all day long, bringing food, flowers, and money. His visitors would sit around him, chanting; to do his practice, he covered himself with a blanket. There were times when he was irritated and told them to go away, but the followers took his annoyance as a blessing, convinced that whatever Bhole Baba did to them would bring fortune into their lives. They would say, "He is the blessed son of Mother Ganga. He cannot really be angry, he can only pretend." If he called them bad names to get rid of them, they would say, "Sir, your bad names are like flowers for us; they are blessings."

"A swami's life is a constant persecution," Swamiji wrote in *Living with the Himalayan Masters*. "People believe he is high above any ordinary human being. In India 'swami' means one who is all-powerful, a healer, a preacher, a doctor, and much more. A swami is put in such a difficult situation that it would drive an ordinary person crazy. People do not realize that some swamis are still beginners on the path, that others have trodden the path a bit, and that only a very few have attained the goal. This lack of differentiation creates expectations which confuse both the people and the swamis.

"It is not easy to extricate oneself from this confusion. Whenever I was truthful in telling people, 'I am still practicing; there is nothing to share. Please leave me alone,' they would interpret these words in whatever way suited them and come to me more and more. . . . Sometimes I became fed up with this swamihood.

"It is not necessary for one to wear the garb of a renunciate to attain enlightenment. What actually matters is the constant spiritual sadhana of disciplining mind, action, and speech. How wonderful it is to be a swami—but how difficult it is to be a real one."

After spending a few weeks in Rishikesh, Bhole Baba moved on to one of Babaji's favorite places: Vindhyachal in the Vindhya Mountains, in a place known as Gerua Talab, near the famous shrine of Vindhya Vasini. (This two-room structure built in 1917 for Babaji by the honorary magistrate and zamindar of Gorakhpur still exists.)

Bhole Baba had not been to Gerua Talab for several years and was hoping to have a normal life there, and to some extent he succeeded. To those few who knew him he was simply Bhole, the young man who used to accompany Babaji. However, a famous saint, known as Siddha Baba, who lived in Chitrakut, some distance away, had come to know that Bhole Baba was in the vicinity. He knew Babaji and Bhole Baba quite well. He also knew about the magic bowl.

Every year Siddha Baba held a huge festival at his ashram, during which he fed thousands. People believed that he was blessed by the Divine Mother Annapurna, the goddess of food, and this was why he could feed so many from his kitchen. So when he heard that Bhole Baba was staying in the region of the Vindhya Vasini shrine, Siddha Baba paid him a visit and invited him to be the guest of honor at his feast. He also invited him to bring anyone he wished.

A few days before Bhole Baba planned to leave for Siddha Baba's ashram, a young sadhu from Bengal, a stronghold of tantric practices, visited him, and Bhole Baba asked him if he would like to accompany him to the feast. The Bengali sadhu accepted, and the two set out for Chitrakut. As they neared the ashram Siddha Baba went out to greet his guest, followed by a crowd playing drums, cymbals, conches, and other musical instruments, and when the group reached the gate of the ashram a still larger crowd emerged and converged on Bhole Baba, shouting, *"Bhole Baba ki jaya."* All of them wanted to touch his feet. In the commotion the Bengali sadhu got separated from Bhole Baba and was swallowed by the crowd.

When the devotional chaos subsided, Siddha Baba and some senior sadhus took Bhole Baba to a private chamber, where he made himself comfortable, assuming that the Bengali sadhu would be accommodated with the other guests. But once Bhole Baba was out of sight, the crowd dissolved and the ashramites resumed their duties. No one realized that the Bengali sadhu was with their honored guest, so instead of being offered food and water, the sadhu was assigned to watch over the shoes that the guests were leaving at the gate. His job was to make sure that the thousands of shoes, slippers, and wooden sandals were not stolen or dragged away by wandering dogs. It was late morning. The stream of arriving guests was greeted with sweets and

129

fruits. But when the young sadhu, who had walked with Bhole Baba for miles without breakfast, asked for food and water, no one paid any attention.

The main meal would be served at four in the afternoon, and some ashramites began sprinkling water on the ground to settle the dust, and others were sweeping and arranging banana leaves on which the food would be served. By now the Bengali sadhu was parched and famished, so he approached the ashram manager, explaining that he hadn't eaten since the previous day and asking that someone else be appointed to watch the shoes so he could have a meal. The manager scolded him: "Shame on you! If you don't have patience, why did you become a sadhu? Where did you borrow those sadhu clothes?"

"Please don't make fun of me," the Bengali sadhu said. "I've come with Bhole Baba, who is inside with Siddha Baba."

Not believing that he was really with Bhole Baba, the people nearby laughed, and the manager quipped, "These days people become sadhus so that they can live a comfortable life." At this, the young man lost his temper. He walked over to the Mandakani River, which flowed in front of the ashram, caught a small fish, returned to the gate, sat down on the fish, closed his eyes, and began to do a tantric practice.

Inside the ashram Bhole Baba, Siddha Baba, and other VIPs were already seated. According to the rule of the ashram, a large portion of food had been brought to Siddha Baba, who first blessed it and then, after serving the dignitaries sitting with him, returned the remainder to the main kitchen. They were about to begin their meal when the Bengali sadhu completed his tantric practice, and instantly the food began to smell like rotten fish. All the swamis looked at each other, and after a few moments of bewildered silence Bhole Baba suddenly exclaimed, "Oh my god! Where is the Bengali sadhu?"

"Maharaj," they responded, "we did not know you had anyone with you."

"Yes, the person walking with me was with me. Did he get any food?" No one knew.

Bhole Baba got up and went outside, the others close behind him. They found the young sadhu at the gate, still sitting with his eyes closed in meditation. Bhole Baba kicked him. "Get up, you rascal!" he shouted. "See what you have done! Why did you do it?"

The Bengali sadhu got up. "I'm hungry and no one listened to me."

"You would not have died," Bhole Baba replied. "I should beat you up. Now tell me, what will happen to all these sadhus who have come such a long way for their meal? All the food in the ashram is spoiled because of you."

The sadhu realized he had made a mistake. He had misused his power. (As part of his penance, he lived on leaves for the next eleven months.) But meanwhile, the foul smell was becoming unbearable. Siddha Baba went to the kitchen and recited all the prayers to the goddess Annapurna, but to no avail. Then he put his head on Bhole Baba's chest and cried, "Maharaj, the Bengali sadhu also ruined my *siddhi!* I can't do anything unless you help me. He has cursed me to starve in my remaining years. All these sadhus too will curse me if they go away hungry. They are my guests. Help me, please. I surrender this all at your feet."

"Have faith in God," Bhole Baba consoled. "I will pray to the Mother to remedy this." So he closed his eyes and, cupping his palms at his heart, bent his head in prayer. Instantly a bowl filled with food appeared in his hands. He gave a small amount to Siddha Baba, who mixed it with the spoiled food in the kitchen, and in a flash the food regained its original freshness, the foul smell vanished, and the feast went on as planned.

This incident caused such excitement among the Chitrakut sadhus who were present at the feast that they invited Bhole Baba to stay for three days and give discourses on the Upanishads. Normally Bhole Baba declined such invitations, but this time he agreed to participate, and there are still a few who remember those three enlightening days when Bhole Baba spoke, entertained their questions, and demonstrated yogic practices.

For ages Chitrakut has been a stronghold of *vairagi* sadhus (Vaishnavite sadhus who meditate on Lord Rama). The practice of *brahmacharya* (celibacy) is the core of their sadhana—they practice little else. Some of the vairagi sadhus had not been present when the bowl appeared, and others, intent on preserving their own popularity and honor, discounted the episode and attempted to discredit Bhole Baba by challenging him in philosophical debates (traditionally known as *shastrartha*). During the first two days, however, he did not quote scripture during his presentations, and the adversarial sadhus concluded that he was not familiar with them. So on the third day they brought their scriptures with them, most of which were in manuscript form. The sadhus were aggressive. Instead of posing straightforward questions, they used the logician's most famous tool—wrangling—and quoted scriptures to prove their points. This went on for four hours, as they tried to demonstrate the vastness of their knowledge. Bhole Baba listened quietly. Then, at the end of the lengthy and complicated harangue, he responded with a few simple sentences: "Knowledge without direct experience is like being married to someone who lives in a picture. For direct experience, you need to do the practices. First learn to sit properly, breathe properly, and meditate properly. Those who practice what is written in the scriptures enjoy silence; those who simply worship the scriptures become defensive and prone to argument. Ask any question regarding any practice described in these manuscripts of yours and I will answer. But there is one condition: that you sit in one posture, without moving, while you ask your questions and I answer them."

At this, a gentle sadhu, who had been sitting next to Bhole Baba, remarked to the gathering, "Have you noticed that for the last four hours Bhole Baba has been sitting in the lotus pose without making any movement? Don't you realize that, like a lotus, he is above the earthly mud?"

Looking toward him, Bhole Baba said, "Maharaj, I wish they would hand over the burden of their scriptures to me and let their minds and souls bask in the divine light radiating from every speck of dust in this holy land. How fortunate they are to be living here in this region, which has been blessed with the living energy of the great sages, as well as that of Lord Rama and Mother Sita—the land where great masters such as Bhagwan Dattatreya, Parashurama, Gorakha Natha, and Hanuman still meditate in their subtle form."

With this, the sadhus who had been arguing with Bhole Baba humbly surrendered the manuscripts to him. In return, Bhole Baba gave them practical lessons in how to sit, breathe, and meditate. He taught them the gospel of love, humility, and selfless service. And the next day he loaded the manuscripts on ponies and took them to Allahabad.

I heard this story in 1987 when I met Dr. Shyam Sundar Shukla, a retired professor of Sanskrit at Kanpur University. Dr. Shukla had been present at the three-day debate, and as a Sanskrit scholar, he was concerned about the preservation of those rare and precious manuscripts. After telling me the story, he asked if I knew where they were and whether or not they had been recopied. I did not, but I asked Swamiji at the earliest opportunity, and he told me that some of them might still be in Allahabad, at Beni Babu's place. Then, several years later, Swamiji handed me a pile of the manuscripts stacked between two boards. One was beautifully illuminated, with a border around each page and miniature paintings at the end of each chapter. The top board was coated with a layer of sandalwood paste and stained with traces of saffron and turmeric, which indicated that it had been worshipped. Swamiji explained that the sadhus in Chitrakut worshipped manuscripts without doing the practices that revealed their inner meaning. "I gave them freedom from the bondage of these manuscripts when I took them," he added with a twinkle in his eye.

133

After he became a monk Bhole Baba lived the life of a wanderer. During this period he stayed with people like Mahatma Gandhi, Sri Aurobindo, Ramana Maharshi, Rabindranath Tagore, Anandamayi Ma, Mataji (the woman sage at the Kamakhya shrine in Assam), and Brahmananda Sarasvati, the Shankaracharya in north India. Swamiji shares some of his experiences with these giants in *Living with the Himalayan Masters,* and he told me later that his experiences with Mahatma Gandhi and Tagore, especially, made such a strong impression on him that their influence would be reflected in the work he planned to undertake near the end of his life.

Many years earlier, before Bhole had been ordained a monk, Babaji had said, "Whenever you have an opportunity to be with Mahatma Gandhi, watch how he walks and try to understand how his convictions are reflected in his speech and action. When you are with Tagore, observe how he sits, walks, talks, and sleeps. Observe his attitude toward every action he takes and try to understand his relationship with others and all aspects of nature."

When he went to the ashram of Mahatma Gandhi, Bhole Baba did not wear the garb of a swami or simply sit and meditate, as was customary. The whole ashram was vibrating with such a strong spirit of karma yoga (selfless action) that his traditional lifestyle would have been inappropriate. Everyone—young and old, poor and rich, women and men, educated and illiterate—worked hard. No work was inferior or superior: cleaning the toilets, feeding the goats, writing books, and attending meetings to resolve national issues were all of equal value. Hindus, Muslims, Sikhs, and Christians attended the group prayers. In addition to household chores, Bhole Baba was assigned to be an assistant copy editor for the ashram magazine, *Harijan*.

134

Mahatma Gandhi was so straightforward and unpretentious that everyone felt he had a special love for them and were comfortable expressing themselves freely to this great soul. For example, one day when Gandhi visited the magazine's editorial staff, Bhole Baba was startled to hear the great man say to him, "Hey, *chhore* [young man], when did you come?" Bhole Baba told him and began to tell him his name, but Gandhi interrupted, "Yes, yes, I know. *Tu Baba Dharam Das ka Bholia hai* [You are Baba Dharam Das' Bhole]."

Bhole Baba was speechless. Gandhi had met Babaji briefly many years earlier in Tagore's ashram, and Bhole had been present. Now, years later, Gandhi not only recognized the man who had emerged from that young boy, he even remembered his name.

After this meeting, Gandhi took Bhole Baba under his wing, as he had done with thousands of others, and during his three-month stay at the ashram Bhole Baba had several opportunities to discuss the issues of the day with him. Many of these issues centered around religion and politics, but there were some questions Bhole Baba hesitated to ask because they seemed to be insulting. For example, during his wanderings he had heard several sadhus and scholars criticizing Mahatma Gandhi for not giving appropriate recognition to Hinduism, and Gandhi's son, Ram Das, and Bhole Baba often discussed these matters without resolving them. Gandhi sensed what was going on in the minds of these two young men, so one day he said to Bhole Baba, "How do you classify the different kinds of swamis living today in India?"

Bhole Baba replied, "I would say there are four kinds of swamis. First, there are the anti-British freedom fighters who are loyal to you. They simply wear the clothes of a swami; they have nothing to do with sadhana—they have no teachers, and their goal is external freedom rather than spiritual freedom. Then there are the swamis who dislike both the British and you, but are active in the freedom movement. They too have nothing to do with sadhana—their only goal is to find freedom in the external world. The men in these two categories have assumed the name and appearance of swamis to take advantage of Hindu sentiments and to more easily accomplish their political goals.

"A third category of swamis comprise those whose sole intention is to attain self-mastery. They have already been convinced that true freedom comes from within and that only one who has achieved this can create an environment of freedom in the outside world. Their goal is to walk the path of self-discovery—to realize who they are and what their relationship is with the rest of the world and with God. The fourth category is made up of swamis who, out of frustration, run away from the world and roam aimlessly. For them, swamihood is a livelihood."

Hearing this answer, Gandhi said, "Hmm."

Bhole Baba waited a few moments; when Gandhi remained silent, he added, "But Bapu, you do not fit in any of these categories, yet the great masters honor you as Mahatma."

At this Gandhi asked, "In which particular category do you fall?" Bhole Baba was dismayed. He had not presented himself in Gandhi's ashram as a swami and had assumed that no one there would identify him as one. "I hope I am in the third category," he answered.

"Even the desire to be a swami of that category is a great thing," Gandhi said. "It is not so bad to become a swami out of frustration if you then live a simple life of non-possessiveness and non-violence. But swamis from the first two categories are trouble. Their ulterior motives force them to be dishonest and deceitful, and often they are judgmental and harbor hatred in their hearts. Even if they practice non-violence in their external lives, they plant the seed of violence at the subtle level. Such seekers of freedom perpetuate both external and

135

internal slavery. You are fortunate to have Baba Dharam Das as your guide. Gather the best of the gifts from that great soul and share them with the world."

Bhole Baba realized that Gandhi was in the mood to clarify some of the questions that would have been inappropriate on other occasions, so he said, "Bapu, I understand that according to your philosophy, religion and politics don't go together. But anyone can see that the freedom movement, which is a political matter, clearly stands on spiritual ground the way you are leading it. People know that you have no hatred for the British, but they also accuse you of being passive toward Hinduism. You are a Hindu, yet you are supporting other religions."

"Because I am a human being, I have the privilege of being Hindu or anything else," Gandhi answered. "Religions come out of our humanness; they flourish only as long as they are nourished by that humanness. Humanness is the soil, and religion is the tree that grows in that soil. Some take care of the soil, others tend the tree—and some fight for possession of the fruit.

"I happened to be born under the tree of Hinduism, and when I came to understand that this tree and its fruit must remain connected to the soil for nourishment, I began working for the soil. If the same soil also nurtures other kinds of trees, such as Christianity, Islam, and Sikhism, is that bad?"

"The British empire is misusing its power by supporting the efforts of Christian missionaries to convert Hindus," Bhole Baba replied. "You have not included this issue in your agenda, so some religious leaders believe you support Christianity."

"I do not endorse or oppose any religion," Gandhi answered. "It is the fundamental right of all human beings to choose and practice their religious beliefs. The British were the first people in Europe to bring about a separation between church and state. Throughout their empire they have given their subjects complete freedom to teach and preach as they wish. Today people like you and other sadhus have the courage to speak out loudly only because of the religious freedom granted by the British. Remember history and remember the circumstances here in India four or five hundred years ago. People were oppressed: rulers forced their own religion on their subjects. The British have given the world a court system that ensures justice, so today you can challenge the government in the courts—this concept did not exist before the British."

"Do the Christians have the right to convert others?" Bhole Baba asked.

"Christians have the right to convert those who wish to be converted, but they have no right to attempt to convert those who do not wish it. This whole issue of conversion requires education, but the majority of those being converted are living in poverty. They do not know who they are and what they are becoming. Food, clothes, and medicine are basic necessities of life, and once provided with these, the poor can work toward raising their consciousness and begin to understand the subtle principles of religion and spirituality. Worldly incentives, such as food, clothes, and medicine, motivate them to take an English name; by doing so they think they are now Christian and this will bring them good fortune. Converts living in poverty deserve your love and compassion, not your criticism."

137

Bhole Baba was beginning to understand the source of Gandhi's strength. He saw that there was perfect harmony in Gandhi's thought, speech, and action: his speech was a reflection of his thoughts, and his action was a manifestation of his speech. He did not impose his beliefs on others, yet he conducted every aspect of his life in accordance with his beliefs. He had no enemies—he fought only for principles. By watching Gandhi, Bhole Baba saw that the path of selfless service (karma yoga) is as great as the path of sannyasa (renunciation). And more than that, he realized that the only difference between one who is on the path of selfless service and one who is a true renunciate lies in their priorities: the karma yogi focuses on serving others and uses any time left over to contemplate on the inner self, while the sannyasin focuses on inner contemplation and devotes his remaining time to serving others.

When the time came for Bhole Baba to depart, Gandhi's son joined him, and the two young men traveled to the Himalayas, where they passed a few weeks in a beautiful place called Kausani in the Kumayun Himalayas. From there Ram Das Gandhi left for Almora and Bhole Baba joined his guru brother, Swami Shivananda, at Gangotri.

Babaji and Swami Shivananda were both from Bengal; both were friends of Rabindranath Tagore, who was also from Bengal. One day Swami Shivananda began to tell Bhole Baba about Tagore's lofty ideals and inner experiences. He was convinced that Tagore was a Vedic sage born in our time to reintroduce Vedic wisdom. The Vedic sages did not erect a wall between spirituality and life in the world, he said. They saw the world as the manifestation of the Divine, and they felt no need to isolate themselves in order to experience the Divine. They were interested in self-realization only as a means to understanding who they were and what their relationship was with a world filled with beauty and joy. Shivananda explained to Bhole Baba that the idea of *moksha* (liberation) is a much later development in the spiritual history of India.

138

"You have learned much from Gandhi," said Swami Shivananda. "Now, to further refine your understanding of renunciation, as well as to enrich your understanding of selfless service, you must go and live in the company of the great Vedic sage Tagore."

As a boy, Bhole Baba had been to Tagore's ashram, Shanti Niketan, with his master, but he had simply hung around the grounds while Tagore spent his time with Babaji and Swami Shivananda. In those days Bhole did not yet have enough insight to appreciate Tagore's wisdom or his multifaceted talents. But now he saw him with different eyes. He came to Shanti Niketan with a definite purpose: to learn from this sage, who was also a matchless poet, musician, dancer, painter, playwright, and teacher of all forms of the fine arts. And because nothing was hidden from the eyes of this Vedic seer, Tagore knew why the young swami had come, and welcomed him with love and respect.

Swamiji did not often speak about his past, but once in a while he expressed his gratitude and special love for Tagore. The powerful role that Tagore played in the formation of Swamiji's philosophy of life is beyond words—a fact that Swamiji pointed out to me more than once. One day, for example, while leafing through *The Golden Book of Tagore*, Swamiji said, "He is a depthless ocean. Depending on where and how you dive, you will find different gems."

Swamiji did not say more about Tagore, and so for years I had been hoping to meet someone who had been at Shanti Niketan when Swamiji was staying there. Finally in the summer of 1993 my wish came true. In the third week of August, Swamiji left the United States for India. The day after his plane departed from New York an elderly Indian gentleman walked into the Himalayan Institute and asked to see Swami Rama. When he was told that Swamiji had just gone to India, he expressed disappointment and then went across the hall to the Institute's bookstore to browse. I happened to be passing by, and introduced myself. We fell into conversation and the gentleman told me his name was Har Rai Desai. Then, as if he were weighing every word, Mr. Desai said that he had known "him" during his college years. When I asked where, he said, "In Shanti Niketan." His eyes were filling with tears and his words were threatening to stick in his throat. In his manner I began to feel Swamiji's presence, an experience I rarely have, and I knew that he must have some precious memories of Swamiji.

I took Mr. Desai to Swamiji's special guest room to rest, for he was now so overwhelmed with emotion that he was not able to complete even one sentence. I realized from this that his understanding of Swamiji was profound and that the relationship had been an intimate one, but it was not appropriate to question him further under those circumstances. So I asked instead how he came to know about the Institute, and he replied that while visiting his son-in-law, who lived in New Jersey, he had happened across a copy of *Living with the Himalayan Masters*. He began to read, and when he reached the chapter "My Grandmaster in Sacred Tibet" he realized that he was reading an account of his own adventures and that the author was his own beloved Bhole Baba, who had lived in the room next to his at Shanti Niketan. Mr. Desai had not seen Swamiji since 1946 and had no idea where he was or how to find him until he read about the Himalayan Institute in the back of the book. He immediately asked his daughter to drive him to the Institute. During our conversation he said very little about his time with Swamiji at Shanti Niketan, but just before he left he said, "After such a long time I heard about him—and look at the game of Providence, that he left just the day before I found my way here."

139

Three years later, in November, Swamiji left his body, and about six weeks after that we held a New Year's celebration in his honor here at the Institute. Har Rai Desai was again in this country, so I asked him to attend as our honored guest and say a few words about Swamiji during the opening ceremony. He came, but when I asked if he would address those who were participating in the celebration, he was once again overcome by a flood of memories, and expressed his inability to talk about this great soul in public—his memories were too precious to be shared publicly. But he most graciously agreed to talk about some of his experiences with Swamiji in private.

When later in the day we had our private conversation, it was very hard for him to get the words out of his mouth, and he said, by way of explanation, "How can one talk about someone who is beyond words?" But finally we began conversing in a mixture of Hindi and English, and most of the information that follows was gleaned from that conversation.

As soon as Bhole Baba arrived at Shanti Niketan, Tagore granted him an audience, and during that brief meeting he introduced the young sadhu to Sri Malikji, a devout and learned man who was instrumental in running the ashram. At Tagore's behest, Malikji took a special interest in making sure Bhole Baba was comfortable and that his educational and spiritual needs were seen to. Although Tagore's time was largely taken up with his personal practice, writing, or painting, he was still able to give Bhole Baba special attention.

One day, when I was reading the Hindi translation of the chapter in *Living with the Himalayan Masters* entitled "'Not Sacrifice but Conquest'—Tagore," Swamiji remarked, "What Tagore taught me just by keeping me in his presence far exceeds what he taught me in lectures and discourses. He worked hard and remained ever-happy. He slept only a few hours and never rested in the daytime. Old age could not make the slightest difference in his habit of working hard and being cheerful. He was totally different from all the saints and sages I had seen so far in my life, and by observing Tagore's life I began to understand my master better. Like my master, he was surrounded by a vibrant tranquility rather than the inert peace that characterizes so many swamis."

By this time Bhole Baba had been in the company of hundreds of swamis and saints from different traditions, many of whom were highly respected for their asceticism and pious life. But one thing had always bothered him about some of these holy men: they seemed to spend a great deal of their mental energy protecting their heavy load of peace. Some made it part of their practice to walk slowly, talk slowly, even to slow down their every gesture, as if weighed down by ecstasy. And some books on monasticism prohibited laughing, singing, and painting, not to mention dancing. Tagore was different: he was full of active joy. He participated in the celebration of life. He sang, painted, wrote, and directed plays; he was a dance teacher as well as a performer. And yet he was a conduit for revealed knowledge, as surely as the Vedic seers had been conduits for the mantras.

One day Bhole Baba asked Tagore whether there was something that could be achieved only by detaching oneself from the world. Tagore replied, "Yes. You can attain freedom from the unwanted part of yourself by detaching yourself from it. Nothing more. Liberation by detachment from the world is not my way. Higher than detachment is transforming what you want to get rid of." 141

Swami Rama wrote in *Living with the Himalayan Masters*, "According to him [Tagore], the evolution of man is the evolution of creative personality. Man alone has the courage of standing against the biological laws. Behind all great nations and noble works done in the world there have been noble ideas. An idea is that something which is the very basis of creativity. It is true that life is full of misfortunes, but fortunate is he who knows how to utilize the ideas which can make him creative. Time is the greatest of all filters, and ideas are the best of all wealth. Fortune is that rare opportunity which helps one to express his ideas and abilities at the proper time."

After only a few days in the joyful atmosphere at Shanti Niketan, Bhole Baba began to think about the nature of creativity. He realized that just as religious ideas and practices are mixed with customs, dogma, and superstition, so is the world of renunciation mixed with these same elements. Whether we live in the world or renounce the world, the goal is the same: inner fulfillment. He pondered: How can books on renunciation advocate killing human creativity? Creativity is the basic force behind the process of evolution. How is it that meaningless man-made rules and laws have crept into monastic life? Could anyone be a better renunciate than Shiva, who, accompanied by Shakti, teaches all the arts and sciences of the sages? Did Shiva fall from his inherent glory when he performed his exuberant dance with Shakti to the beat of Ganesha's drum? True renunciation, he concluded, involves more than isolating oneself from others and from the unwanted part of one's own personality. Renunciation, at least in part, establishes guidelines on how to avoid wasting time in useless tasks and how to channel all potentials and creativity to explore the unknown dimensions of reality. Bhole Baba did not want to make his life a barren desert, as some ascetics had done, and when he expressed these feelings to Tagore, the sage encouraged him to explore different aspects of the fine arts while he was at Shanti Niketan.

142

Mr. Desai told me that people at Shanti Niketan were astonished at how fast Bhole Baba mastered anything he studied. In a matter of weeks he was one of the best music students and accompanied the top musicians in the ashram. Then he moved on to painting, and soon his expertise in abstract painting was the talk of the ashram. Similarly, one day he joined the dance classes and quickly became the most accomplished dancer. But in spite of his one-pointed dedication, he was a jolly young man with plenty of time to talk and joke with the ashramites.

Mr. Desai lived in the room next to Bhole Baba, so he had many opportunities to be in his company. But he had a unique and odd problem: he was afraid of cold baths. Bhole Baba knew this, so one day he called on his neighbor and said, "Har Rai, I have a gift for you. Come with me." They walked to the well near their rooms, and he told Desai to close his eyes and sit quietly without moving. Then he fetched a bucket of water and poured it over his head. While Desai was still soaking wet, Bhole Baba then asked him to fetch seven more buckets of water and bathe him in return. When it was done, Desai discovered that his fear of cold baths had vanished. The rest of the time they were at Shanti Niketan, Mr. Desai bathed every day and then bathed Bhole Baba with seven buckets of water.

Gradually those in the ashram were coming to realize that Bhole

Baba was not an ordinary student, and it was rumored that he was a disciple of the famous sage Baba Dharam Das, who had brought the dead prince of Bhawal back to life. Then one day the Bhawal Sanyasi—Bhole Baba's guru brother and now the king of the state of Bhawal—visited Tagore, throwing the ashram into a fever of excitement. People watched with amazement as the young Bhole Baba and the elderly king of Bhawal embraced. They were even more amazed when they saw Tagore greeting the king with the honor due a sage. And they were flabbergasted when Bhole Baba accepted the seat of honor next to the king and let Tagore treat him as a sage rather than a student.

By this time many in the ashram were no longer fooled by Bhole Baba's humility and youth, and they attempted to find out more about him and his master. They found the young sadhu mute on this subject, but he did seem willing to talk—at least to some extent—about his grandmaster, who lived in Tibet. Hearing these stories, a group of his friends, including Har Rai Desai, expressed their desire to visit this sage. To their delight, Bhole Baba agreed to take them.

While the group was making plans for the trip, a mysterious telegram arrived from his master: "Bhole, come soon. The time has come." Without revealing the telegram's contents to any of his friends, Bhole Baba announced that he must leave at once. He then went to Tagore and explained what had happened. "Before you give me your permission to leave," he asked, "please bless me with the gift of a lesson, which I may treasure here and hereafter."

Bhole Baba sat humbly on the ground, and Tagore reminded him that the whole universe is one living consciousness and that everything that exists in it is a manifestation of this consciousness. *Satyam, Shivam,* and *Sundaram* (truth, goodness, and beauty) are its intrinsic attributes. In the language of religion, this consciousness is known as God, the core of all that exists. Those who seek God "out there" live in vain, while those who seek God within soon experience God as their own soul. The soul is but a wave of the truth, goodness, and beauty of God. The relationship between God and the soul is like that of the ocean and the waves arising from it and subsiding in it. Once this realization comes, people stop searching for God, for they know that

143

they and God are one and the same, just as the waves and the ocean are one and the same. Only through this experience can a person overcome the fear of death, because to such a person birth and death are natural phenomena, the appearance and disappearance of the waves in the oceanic pool of consciousness.

Tagore also reminded Bhole Baba that those who seek God only outside themselves find this world a prison. To them the Earth is a foreign land, and they themselves are aliens in it. The outward approach to God blinds their vision and thus they fail to see the truth, goodness, and beauty which are at once intrinsic to God's creation and to themselves. Those who seek God within are blessed with divine creativity long before they experience their oneness with God.

And finally, Tagore reminded Bhole Baba that the evolution of matter is exactly like the formation of an island in an ocean. As waves wash this island, infusing it with the life-force, it begins to pulsate with consciousness. This is called "birth." When the waves recede and become one with the ocean, it is called "death." But the ocean, in essence, always remains the same. Through the ceaseless rhythm of birth and death, the unchanging ocean of consciousness delights in the constantly changing form of her own creative energy.

"May you see her through your direct experience—both the eternal and the eternally changing face—and partake of the intoxicating music and dance of her creativity," Tagore said. Having received this blessing, Bhole Baba prepared to join Babaji in Darjeeling.

Now began the most mysterious and adventure-filled of the many journeys in Bhole Baba's life. He left Shanti Niketan in the company of ten friends, Har Rai Desai among them. They did not know Bhole Baba was planning to meet his master; for them, Darjeeling was merely the first stop on an exciting journey to Tibet and a meeting with Bhole Baba's grandmaster. Meanwhile, Bhole Baba was absorbed in solving his own puzzle.

At the time, Bhole Baba had not seen anything mysterious about the visit of his guru brother, the king of Bhawal, to Shanti Niketan. The way Tagore treated him also seemed normal. But a few weeks later, when the telegram with its cryptic summons came from Babaji,

144

Bhole Baba began to wonder if there was a connection between the telegram and his guru brother's recent visit: Had the king come to visit Tagore, or to see Bhole? Normally the king would have invited his beloved Bhole to Calcutta for a visit, but this time there had been no such invitation. And when they parted, his elder brother, who usually gave him a handsome sum of money, offered him only a loving embrace and then gazed intensely into his eyes for a long moment before turning away.

When Tagore in his blessing had explained the reality behind birth and death, Bhole Baba's curiosity could hardly be contained. He knew that Tagore never spoke a single word that did not have a profound reason, and wondered if Tagore was signaling his own imminent departure from this world, or that of the king of Bhawal, or perhaps even that of Babaji. He remembered that just a year ago Babaji had expressed his wish to cast off his body, and Bhole Baba had argued with him, saying, "It is written in the scriptures that the master who leaves a foolish disciple in the world is committing a sin and goes to perdition." At this, Babaji had replied, "Okay, then I will not cast off my body, because you are still a fool and ignorant."

The message in the telegram, "The time has come," pounded in his head—it was almost unbearable, especially because he could not share his thoughts with any of his friends. So as soon as the group arrived in Darjeeling, Bhole Baba took them to a guesthouse and set out to meet Babaji.

Bhole Baba knew exactly where his master would be staying: a mile downriver from the cremation ground, at the spot where thirty-six years before, Babaji had recovered the body of the prince of Bhawal. And sure enough, Babaji was there in the cave. Outside were five other sadhus, including some who had testified for the prince in court. They told him that for the last few days Babaji had been silent, opening his eyes only occasionally. Bhole Baba knew it was not appropriate to approach his master without being called, but a few minutes after his arrival Babaji's voice came from the cave: "Bholia, come in." And as soon as he approached, Babaji asked, "How is sadhu Bhawal?"

"He seemed fine when I saw him, but only you know how he really is," Bhole Baba replied.

He sat down in front of Babaji, and after several hours of silence, Babaji opened his eyes and said, "He emerged victorious."

"Is there any way that I can understand this mystery a little better?" Bhole entreated.

"Yes," said Babaji. "That's why I called you. He has gone back to his real abode, and is engaged in meditation under the supervision of my master. Now is the time to visit your grandmaster. He is waiting for you. He will teach you anything you want to learn."

"Should I go to Mount Kailas? Is that where he is staying?"

"No. By the time you reach Tibet it will be winter, and in the wintertime he moves to one of our monasteries in central Tibet, near Lhasa."

Then Bhole Baba told Babaji that there were ten people from Shanti Niketan with him, who wanted to have *darshana* of the grandmaster. Babaji simply said, "Hmm." This response was typical—if someone asked a question when he was in a meditative mood, Babaji would say "hmm" whether the answer was "no" or "yes." Bhole Baba knew how to decipher the meaning, and this time he interpreted "hmm" as somewhere between "yes" and "no."

So accompanied by his friends, Bhole Baba left for Tibet, stopping in Kalingpong on the way. When he was young, Bhole had learned kung fu here from a master, who was blind, and now the group stayed with this master for a few days before moving on to Sikkim. The British authorities in Sikkim, suspecting the group of spying for the Congress Party (which was fighting for India's independence from the British), searched their luggage and frisked them. The officers found two letters: one from Pandit Jawaharlal Nehru, and the other from Mahatma Gandhi—and arrested the travelers on the spot. Although their contents were not political, these letters from India's key leaders proved that the group was linked with the Congress Party. But it also established them as important people, so the officers decided it would be prudent to treat them as VIPs. Thus they were housed in a government guesthouse, under guard. They had every comfort except freedom.

The officers conducted an investigation, sending inquiries to their counterparts in Calcutta and Ahmadabad, and requesting letters of clarification from Pandit Nehru and Mahatma Gandhi. Weeks passed, and the group being detained became impatient. Bhole Baba used the delay to brush up on his Tibetan, but after being confined for two months he risked buying an old and dirty coat from one of the guards. It was long and it made an effective disguise, and one night, when the guards, who had been drinking, had fallen asleep, he put on the coat and escaped, leaving a note for his friends that said he was going to Delhi. Instead, he headed for Tibet. After walking three days, he arrived at the Sikkim-Tibetan border, and when the Gurkha soldiers there asked for identification, he spoke to them in fluent Nepalese. The soldiers allowed him to pass.

As Swamiji recounts in *Living with the Himalayan Masters,* the journey through Tibet was long and strenuous. It was hard to find food other than meat and fish, and he avoided eating most dairy products because they were dirty and had a foul smell. Once in a while he forced himself to drink milk freshly drawn by shepherds and yak herders, even though the milking vessels were always dirty. His knowledge of astrology and palmistry came in handy, because Tibetan nomads love astrologers and fortune-tellers. And so, even though telling fortunes bothered Bhole Baba's conscience, it helped him make friends with the local people, who then gladly provided his necessities.

During the long journey through Tibet to Lhasa, Bhole Baba saw thousands of flat rocks along the trails, and especially in the higher passes, on which the famous mantra *Om mani padme hum* had been inscribed. Even though with very few exceptions the Tibetan peasantry did not know how to read, at each mountain pass they prostrated themselves in respect to the piles of rocks inscribed with the mantra. When Bhole Baba asked them why, they would reply, "Mani, mani," with the sweetest smiles imaginable. They were innocent and trusting. They had heard the word "Buddha" but knew nothing about Buddhism or its sublime practices.

The life of Tibetan peasants was harder than the lives of the farmers, herders, tribal people, and nomads in India and Nepal or any of the other countries Bhole Baba had visited. They lacked anything but the barest necessities, but they were blessed with the wealth that contentment brings. Even when hungry, they would share their yak-butter tea; they ate their *sampa* (dough made with roasted barley flour)

147

only after offering it to whatever guest happened to be traveling with them. In this world, time lost its meaning. People rarely knew the name of the month, let alone the exact date, and while living and traveling with them, even Bhole Baba forgot to keep track of the days. But imbued with a burning desire to see his grandmaster, he pressed on—crossing glaciers, fording mountain streams, and traversing high passes. Finally he reached Lhasa.

Bhole Baba had never been to this part of Tibet, although he was familiar with the western part, where his master and grandmaster spent most of their time. He had roamed in the region of the Himalayas now known as the Indo-Tibetan zone, and from there he had roamed the Tibetan plateau, especially in the region of Lake Manasarovar and Mount Kailas. In both India and western Tibet he had heard extraordinary stories about Lhasa, "the city of the gods," and the spiritual wisdom it embodied, and so he approached it with great expectations.

Once there, however, he found that Lhasa consisted mainly of monasteries and of village-like settlements that supplied the monasteries. Two different worlds existed side by side—the religious and the mundane—and except for a few high lamas, who also held influential government positions, there was no link between the two. Administrative affairs focused on collecting revenue and making sure that foreigners did not enter the country. The world outside the monasteries was a sea of poverty, illiteracy, and ignorance. Spiritual practices centered around the worship of ghosts, demons, and serpent gods who lived beneath the mountains and in the lakes and rivers. Like everywhere else in Tibet, all forms of suffering—even if caused by hunger, dehydration, or unsanitary conditions—were attributed either to the wrath of the gods or to the wrath of demons or ancestors.

The life inside the monasteries, however, was totally different. Here there was comfort and security. Because of the lamas who held high governmental posts, the monasteries were centers of political power as well as religious activity. Monks had the privilege of going to school—in fact the only way to get any schooling in Tibet was to join a monastery and become a monk. Admission depended on family status. Once accepted, the monks were taught to read and write

Tibetan so they could study the scriptures. Then as part of their higher education they studied Pali, the language of the ancient Buddhist texts, or they specialized in secular administrative matters.

Although Bhole Baba was himself a monk and had a basic knowledge of Tibetan, he did not belong to the tradition of the lamas and therefore had no access to the monasteries. But after a few days of wandering through Lhasa he met a Christian missionary who offered him food and shelter. With the missionary's help Bhole Baba met one of the lamas and convinced him that he was a spiritual man from India, that he had studied in Saranath and Gaya (Buddhism's most sacred sites in India), and that he knew Sanskrit and Pali. This lama, in turn, helped Bhole Baba find his way into the monasteries in Lhasa, and thus he was able to visit Tibet's grandest and most ancient places: the Jokhang monastery, situated near the Potala Palace of the Dalai Lama, and the Drupong monastery a few miles away.

The monasteries housed thousands of monks—Bhole Baba was surprised to learn that there were six or seven thousand living in the Jokhang monastery alone. Every available space—chambers of all sizes as well as every hall—was filled with statues of gods, goddesses, angels, demons, different incarnations of Buddha, and renowned lamas, including Dalai Lamas. There was barely room to sit down and meditate. Everywhere ritual butter lamps burned constantly, and the floors were so slippery with yak butter that walking was a challenge. Furthermore, the big monasteries held thousands of unbound manuscripts wrapped in cloth and stored in a honeycomb of floor-to-ceiling compartments, one manuscript per compartment. They were dusty and it looked as if no one had opened them for years.

In addition to the large monasteries, Bhole Baba visited a small monastery outside Lhasa because he had heard that the head lama there was a great tantric yogi. Swamiji writes in *Living with the Himalayan Masters:*

"When I met this lama he was seated in a wooden room surrounded by seven women, who were chanting mantras with him. After a few mantras they would pick up and eat a piece of raw meat which was mixed with certain spices, including chilies, and then continue chanting again.

"After fifteen minutes the lama stopped chanting and asked me the purpose of my visit. I smiled and said I had come to see him. He said, 'No, no, that's not true. Your name is such and such and you are in disguise. The Sikkim police are searching for you.' He said all this in an angry tone because he knew that I despised his way of worshipping and at the same time eating raw meat. He studied my thoughts, which terrified me. But I was not surprised that he could do this, because by this time I had already met several thought-readers and knew the whole process of reading someone's thoughts. I became humble and said I was in his country only to learn more about tantra. This yogi was a tantric and he gave me his book of worship to go through, but I had already read this scripture before."

The lama allowed Bhole Baba to spend a few days in his monastery, and here he had an amazing experience. Many of the lamas, including the head lama, worshipped a Sanskrit manuscript that was wrapped in a silk cloth and smeared with a thick crust of sandalwood paste. It was forbidden to read it, and the monks believed that anyone who did so would immediately get leprosy and die. Bhole Baba was not superstitious; he remembered the saying "The scriptures belong to those who study them, not to those fools who own them but do not know their contents," and he had a strong desire to read this text. So in the middle of the night he entered the monastery's inner chamber, which was lit by butter lamps, and unwrapped the manuscript. But after reading a few pages here and there, he realized that he already knew this scripture. It was part of the *Linga Purana,* one of the eighteen major texts of puranic literature, the one that describes heaven and hell and explains how a soul is transported to one of these realms after death. In Indian villages this text is recited as part of the thirteen days of ancestral rites that follow a funeral. Bhole Baba rewrapped the manuscript and returned it to its place on the altar.

In removing the manuscript from the altar, however, Bhole Baba had not only disturbed the position of the lamps, he had also wrapped the manuscript slightly differently from the way the lamas did, and in the morning the monks discovered that someone had opened it. An incredible commotion ensued. Bhole Baba was the main suspect, and for a few moments it seemed as if the lamas would kill him on the spot.

But as they surrounded him, Bhole Baba faced them and spoke with authority: "I have been assigned by the Himalayan masters to go through this manuscript," he said, "and if you say anything to me, it is you who will suffer, not me." This threat, along with his manner, frightened the lamas and they stepped back. They also saw that Bhole Baba showed no signs of leprosy from having opened the forbidden scripture, and so they believed he was authorized to read it.

Soon the rumor spread throughout the monastery that a young lama with great power and wisdom had come from Bodhigaya, and everyone, both lamas and laymen, began to prostrate at his feet. But Bhole Baba knew that undue respect from superstitious and sentimental people soon invites misery, so he announced that it was time for him to depart for his final destination. The lamas made arrangements for his journey, and even provided guides to take him to the monastery where his grandmaster lived. Bhole Baba summarized his experience in the Lhasa monasteries in one sentence: "Sometimes utter ignorance in the path of spirituality is accepted as secret knowledge; people do not like to examine their blind beliefs."

When Bhole Baba reached his destination, his grandmaster embraced him with these words: "You are very tired. You have gone through many problems. The path of enlightenment is the toughest path, and that seeking is the hardest task." Bhole Baba was exhausted. He had not done his practices for months. His health had declined. But with the embrace of this grandmaster, his pain and fatigue vanished.

As Swamiji describes it in *Living with the Himalayan Masters*, his grandmaster "looked very old, but very healthy. He would get up from his seat once early in the morning and once in the evening. His height was five feet nine or ten inches. He was very slim, but very energetic. He had bushy eyebrows and his face glowed and radiated deep calmness and tranquility. He had a perennial smile. He lived on yak's milk most of the time and sometimes barley soup. Occasionally a few lamas would come and study with him. He lived in a natural cave. . . . His students made a wooden portico before the entrance of his cave. It was a beautiful place, from which we could see the long mountain ranges and vast horizon."

There were five other yogis living with this venerable sage. All were loving and kind, and all spoke Hindi with a generous sprinkling of words and expressions from Nepalese and northeastern Indian dialects. But none exhibited any of the characteristics of the king of Bhawal. Bhole Baba wondered if his guru brother still had a physical locus for his consciousness, or was simply living with his grandmaster in his ethereal body.

Once in a while a few Tibetan lamas would come to study with this small group and their master. They liked to hear stories of the saints and yogis of India, but for the most part they were interested only in learning sorcery and the techniques of exorcism. Bhole Baba, however, knew that these yogis, and especially his grandmaster, were great adepts who knew the mystery of birth and death, the enigma of life here and hereafter, and could perform many more advanced techniques, including *para-kaya pravesha,* by which they could leave their bodies and enter another body without dying. And he was amazed at how simply and effortlessly these great ones brought themselves down to the level of the visiting lamas. In their company the five adepts posed merely as the makers of miracles, healers who had the capacity to drive away melancholy and protect cattle from the wrath of the gods and demons who, the lamas believed, ruled over the valleys and mountains of the Tibetan plateau. And watching these adepts teach the lamas, Bhole Baba learned many simple tantric formulas and techniques for overcoming the fear of ghosts and darkness, for curing colds and other common ailments, for calling your sheep out of a neighbor's herd, for subjugating fierce dogs, and other practices useful to nomads and farmers. In turn, these lamas and their followers provided the yogis with necessities, such as food, blankets, oil for their lamps, and wood for their dhuni.

Being in the company of his grandmaster was as delightful to Bhole Baba as being in his master's company. Like Babaji, his grandmaster often answered Bhole Baba's questions even before he asked them, but usually he spoke very little and answered questions with a sweet smile or with a simple yes or no. One day, however, he was in the mood for entertaining questions and answering them with more than a few words. He asked Bhole Baba, "Why are you not expressing your main desire?" At this, as Swamiji writes, "With trembling voice I said, 'Please let me understand the technique of para-kaya pravesha.'"

Bhole Baba had heard about this technique in childhood. When Bhole was sixteen he had met an old sage named Boorhe Baba ("Old Sadhu") who lived in the Naga hills of the eastern Himalayas and visited Babaji frequently. The two masters would talk about changing bodies, but Bhole was too young to fully understand what they were saying.

Then one day when Boorhe Baba was taking his leave after a ten-day visit, Babaji told Bhole to go with him, and after a long and strenuous journey the pair reached Assam, where they stayed in a cave in which Swami Nigamananda had once lived. There Boorhe Baba told Bhole that the next day he was going to cast off his body and enter another. Bhole was astonished. Why, he wondered, did Boorhe Baba need to die? Was it possible to get into another body so easily? And even if it was, who would volunteer to give his body to this old sadhu? When he expressed these feelings, Boorhe Baba replied, "I am over ninety years old now and my body is not a fit instrument for remaining in samadhi a long time—and the opportunity has presented itself. Tomorrow there will be a dead body in good condition. A young man will be bitten by a snake, then placed in a river thirteen miles from here." He said that they would leave the cave early the next morning so they could reach their destination before sunset.

When they arose the next morning, however, they found the entrance to the cave blocked by the body of an elephant that had inserted its trunk, head, and two front legs into the cave. At that point a scorpion had stung it and the elephant had died on the spot. Boorhe Baba found the scorpion, caught it in his bare hands, and scolded it: "Bad boy!" he said. "What a horrible thing you have done!"

Bhole shouted, "Don't do that—it will sting you!"

But Boorhe Baba said calmly, "No, it would not dare to do that." Bhole wanted to kill the scorpion with a wooden sandal, but Boorhe Baba stopped him, saying, "No one has the authority to kill any living creature. These two got even with each other. You will know what happened when you understand the cause and effect of karma." Then Boorhe Baba let the scorpion go, and he and Bhole began to push the elephant's body away from the entrance. They struggled for two hours

153

before they made enough space to crawl out. Once free, they set off and walked north to the river, where they made their camp.

In the morning Bhole took a bath and sat on the riverbank for meditation. When he opened his eyes, Boorhe Baba was gone. Bhole searched all around for the old sage and then simply waited, but when he had still not returned by the end of the day, he decided to return to his master. The nearest railway station was at Gauhati, a journey of several days by foot. Once there, he boarded a train for Haridwar, and from there he walked to Gupta Kashi, a shrine in the Garhwal Himalayas where his master was staying.

When he arrived, Swamiji writes: "My master said, 'Boorhe Baba was here last night and was inquiring about you.' A few days later a young sadhu visited our cave. He started talking to me as though he had known me for a long time. He described all the events of our journey to Assam in detail and said, 'I'm sorry you could not be with me when I changed my body.'. . . I found that his new physical instrument did not affect his previous capacities and characteristics at all. He exhibited all the intelligence, knowledge, memories, talents, and mannerisms of the old Baba."

These and other such experiences had convinced Bhole Baba that highly advanced yogis like his master and grandmaster could perform para-kaya pravesha, but no one would talk about it. Now his grandmaster was sitting before his eyes and asking him not to hesitate in expressing his prime desire. So he asked his grandmaster to explain exactly how it is done. The old sage agreed, and the next morning, in the presence of the five adepts and a few lamas, he said he was going to leave his body and then come back to it. When he heard this, a thought flashed in Bhole Baba's mind: "Perhaps he wants to cast off his body and wants us to immerse it or bury it." Instantly the sage said, "It's not that." Then he asked Bhole Baba to go inside the cave and satisfy himself that there was no outlet or hidden door. The young man had been staying in that cave for more than a month and knew very well that there was no opening other than the front one, but he followed his grandmaster's order anyway. When he returned, his grandmaster showed everyone a wooden plate and asked them if they saw it. Everyone did. He also asked if they could all see him. They could. Then he asked Bhole Baba and the lama next to him to hold the plate. They did as they were told.

As Swamiji recounts: "His body started becoming hazy, and that haziness was a human form like a cloud. That hazy cloud human form started moving toward us. Soon in a few seconds' time the cloud disappeared. We found that the wooden plate which we were holding started to become heavier. After a few minutes the wooden plate again became as light as it was before. For ten minutes the lama and I remained standing holding that plate, and finally we sat down, waiting in great suspense and awe for something to happen. After ten or fifteen minutes the voice of my grandmaster told me to get up and hold that wooden plate again. When we held the plate it started becoming heavier, and again the cloudy form reappeared in front of us. From the cloudy form, he came back to his visible body. This amazing and unbelievable experience was a confirmation. He demonstrated this *kriya* [action] once again in a similar manner."

155

In *Living with the Himalayan Masters* Swamiji brings this experience to an end when he says that there are adepts who not only have penetrated the mystery of death and birth but are also expert in transforming matter into energy, and vice versa, solely by using the power of their mind. Knowing that it was not Swamiji's nature to settle for less than the best, I was convinced that he would not have been satisfied with simply watching his grandmaster perform this miracle; he would have asked his grandmaster to teach him the technique. Then, as I was working on the book's Hindi translation, I read "His way of teaching was very practical and straightforward," and something suddenly clicked in my mind. This sentence has no relation to what comes before it or what comes after it—by all editorial standards it is out of context. But it gave me the key for opening a dialogue with Swamiji. I asked him, "Swamiji, what did he teach that was so practical and straightforward?"

As was typical, he appeared not to hear my question but to drift instead into a realm far away. For a minute or so he sat without blinking, looking as if he was seeing something existing beyond our familiar boundaries of time and space. When he returned he asked softly, "What did you say?"

At that moment the aura around him became totally different from what it had been a few minutes before. The author of *Living with the Himalayan Masters* was gone. In his place was a gentle and compassionate sage, ready to give everything he had to the world, provided the world had the capacity to receive and retain it. Without knowing whether or not I was worthy, I asked again, "What did he teach that was so practical and straightforward? How can I unravel the mystery of death, which according to what you have written and taught also seems to contain the mystery of rebirth? What should someone like me do to learn the technique of casting off the body without dying, and thereby attain freedom from the fear of death?"

"It is simple," Swamiji replied. "The first step is to overcome your identification with your body. 'This body is me' or 'I am this body' is what causes consciousness to remain bound. Free your consciousness from the identification with your body. Then you will neither find yourself the doer of your action nor be affected by the fruits of your action.

"The realization that the body and mind are motivated by the intrinsic attributes of nature to perform actions will loosen your karmic bonds. Body, breath, mind, and soul are held together by the strings of karma, and strongest among all strands of this rope is attachment to the body. That is why, despite excruciating pain, people are still not able to leave the body easily. Attachment clouds the inner vision and thus the person fails to know that even though he has a body, he is separate from the body.

"Knowing the difference between the body and the soul is called discrimination. Experiencing oneself as independent from the existence of the body is called 'self-realization.' Once you are fully established in self-realization you can choose between two paths; both will give you freedom from the fear of death. One is the path of self-surrender; the other is the path of yoga sadhana.

"On the path of surrender you are always accompanied by the conviction that God is in you and you are in God. Just as the present is taken care of by providence, life hereafter too will be taken care of by providence. Trust in providence grants you freedom from the fear of death.

"On the path of yoga sadhana you systematically learn the dynamics of your body, breath, mind, and consciousness. You learn exactly what keeps your body alive and your mind active, and what is gone when you die. The technique of para-kaya pravesha has two parts: loosening the bond that binds the soul to the body, and becoming sensitive to the pranic force through which the soul breathes life into inanimate matter.

"This technique has been described in the third chapter of the *Yoga Sutra,* and one day I will teach it to you systematically."

Trying to find some excuse to prolong the conversation, I asked, "When you saw Parama Gurudeva [the grandmaster] leave his body, where did he go? What other body did he enter? What was the purpose of you and the lama holding the wooden plate? What was that cloud?"

"He did not enter another body, because there was no vacant body available," Swamiji replied. "First he came out of his body, then he dematerialized the matter of his body except for a small portion of the water element. He then transformed that water into a cloud and used that cloud as a temporary locus for his awareness. The rest of the matter was transformed into energy, which he directed onto the plate, and that is why the plate became heavy. Later he withdrew that energy from the plate, the cloud reemerged, and gradually, as it condensed, the original body came forward. As far as para-kaya pravesha is concerned, had a suitable body been available, he could have entered and animated it, creating the illusion of resurrection."

"What is the purpose of para-kaya pravesha?" I asked.

"By leaving your body and entering another one, you come to know the dynamics of death and birth," he answered. "Then to you death is nothing more than abandoning a house that is no longer useful, and birth is nothing more than claiming occupancy of a vacant house. This gives you an opportunity to realize that you are pure consciousness and that it is totally up to you whether or not you want to live in a body. Honoring the law of karma, you may decide to live in a body for a while and discharge your duties or complete your sadhana, and then leave it. You experience no pain when you enter the body or when you leave it.

"There are other spiritual goals which you can accomplish by learning this technique," Swamiji continued. "You can suspend your prana [vital energy], senses, and body in a meditative state known as *laghu samadhi* and get out of your body. Then using your subtle body you can connect yourself with others—help them, heal them, guide them—and then return to your own body.

"You can also travel to different parts of the universe and gain the knowledge of the *virat rupa* [the cosmic form] of God bit by bit. This is a science. As a spiritual scientist you can explore the universe and see how it equates with the human body.

"The most important prerequisite for practicing this technique is that you must have the full cooperation of the forces that reside at the *muladhara* center. Yogis who have not gained access to that center become mentally imbalanced while they attempt to gain out-of-body experiences."

Swamiji was in the mood to talk about this subject, but it was still hard to pull the technique itself from him. So I asked again, "Swamiji, to walk in your footsteps, where should I start?"

"*Ganapati ki aradhana karo* [Worship Ganesha]," he replied.

"Should I worship Ganesha's statue with water, flowers, sandalwood, incense, and so forth, the way the ritual manuals prescribe?"

"That is priestly business. It helps a little bit when it is done with faith and sincerity, but in the tradition of yoga, you meditate on Ganesha in the form of the light that resides at the *muladhara* chakra. One day I will teach you how to do this properly." With that, he dismissed me for the night.

The next evening, when I had finished translating the chapter "My Grandmaster in Sacred Tibet" into Hindi, and had read Swamiji most of it, I deliberately reread the portion where his master demonstrated how to dematerialize and rematerialize the body. Swamiji seemed oblivious to the fact that we were covering the material I had read and discussed with him the night before, and to me this was a hint that he was willing to reopen the conversation. Just as had happened the night before, when I was reading this particular passage I looked into the window of his eyes and saw that he was gone to a faraway land. Although I knew he did not hear me, I continued reading aloud because stopping might have brought him back abruptly. A few minutes later he blinked and asked, "So what did you say?"

I quickly went back and began to read the whole passage again, and when I reached the perfect place at which to instigate a discussion, I stopped and said, "The *Yoga Sutra* talks about several ways of attaining such *siddhis* [yogic powers], such as mantra, herbs, tapas, or samadhi. I wonder which one Sri Maharaj [Swamiji's grandmaster] used when he dematerialized himself."

"He did it through *mantra shakti*," Swamiji replied immediately. "Before dematerializing himself, he was looking at me. I thought he was looking into my eyes to mesmerize me, so I told him, 'Please don't mesmerize me. Don't try to trick me. I'm not going to look into your eyes.' He told me he was going to demonstrate how to leave the body by using different techniques. This time he would use the power of mantra, and later he would demonstrate some other techniques.

159

"In later sessions he explained how to withdraw from one limb or organ at a time. He had such perfect mastery over his mind and pranic force that when he withdrew himself from his feet, they became totally dead; there was no sign of life in them. When he withdrew from the entire body, it was like a corpse. Although I did not have sophisticated tools to monitor his brain waves, I found no trace of heartbeat, pulse, or breath.

"Before leaving his body he had put one of the lamas in a state of suspended animation, and when he was totally out of his body he began describing the condition of the limbs and organs of his own corpse, using the lama's body as a conduit. Then he explained how he was going to initiate breathing in his own corpse and thereby create a link between body and mind. And after this demonstration, he explained the meaning of Patanjali's *sutra* that describes the technique of para-kaya pravesha.

"Just as physicists conduct their experiments in laboratories to gain experiential knowledge, yogis teach through demonstrations. You must die while remaining alive. Only then will you have real knowledge of the dynamics of death and birth."

I resumed reading my Hindi translation, until I reached the sentence, "Having met my grandmaster and having received this knowledge, my purpose for visiting Tibet was fulfilled." Here I stopped reading and asked, "Wasn't the purpose of your visit to meet your brother disciple, the king of Bhawal?"

Swamiji replied, "Yes. That was the ostensible purpose. But I see now that I was sent to my grandmaster to learn the technique of para-kaya pravesha. However, I did ask him about my brother disciple."

"So what did he say?"

"He told me that the king of Bhawal had been part of our lineage for many lifetimes," Swamiji replied. "In this lifetime he had been born into the royal house of Bhawal, murdered, revived from the dead, and initiated into the practice of the Divine Mother Chinnamasta. At the completion of his practice he had no further reason to live in the same body. So he left that body when I was sitting with my master in the cave near Darjeeling. An adept beyond birth and death, his home is our ancestral cave at Mount Kailas. Time and space pose no barrier to him. He still wanders in the Himalayas and is assigned by the tradition to guide aspirants stranded along the path."

It was during this session that Swamiji told me about our ancestral cave, the monastery established by the sage Angira where Krishna did his meditation for twelve years—a story documented in the *Harivansha Purana*. Tibetans call this cave Choku Gompa.

The sessions in which Swamiji worked with me on this chapter were the most precious moments of my life. It may take eons to practice what he taught me by telling of his own experiences with his grandmaster, but the seeds he planted on those summer evenings are self-sustaining. And whenever I remember the divine glimpse granted us as we stood near our ancestral cave in the summer of 1999, the illusion that creates a wall between heaven and Earth dissolves.

Bhole Baba stayed with his grandmaster for two and half months, and during this time his grandmaster helped him string together the advanced practices he had learned in fragments from such masters as Gudari Baba, Aghori Baba, Sombari Baba, Swami Shivananda, and his own master, Babaji. In addition to learning the technique of para-kaya pravesha, he gained a comprehensive knowledge of the solar science and Sri Vidya.

As Swamiji relates in his book, just a few days before he left for India he had one last exchange with his grandmaster. "I was sitting outside our cave thinking about the diary in which I used to record my experiences. A thought flashed in my mind: 'I wish I had my diary here so I could note down a few experiences.' My grandmaster smiled and beckoned me to come to him. He said, 'I can get your diary for you. Do you need it?' Such a possibility was not a great miracle for me anymore, for I had experienced such things before. I casually replied, 'Yes—and a few pencils too.' I had left my diary in India at a sanitorium called Bhawali near the Nainital hills in north India. Suddenly three pencils and my diary, which was quite large, containing 475 pages, were before me. I was pleased but not especially surprised. I told him that I preferred him to give me something spiritual. He laughed and said, 'I have already given you that. You should learn to retain it without resistance or carelessness.' Then he said, 'My blessings are with you. Now I want you to go to Lhasa, and from there you should return to India.'"

That is how Bhole Baba completed his journey to his grandmaster and again joined Babaji in India.

SHANKARACHARYA

BHOLE BABA REACHED INDIA in the middle of September 1947, and found his master in the Gorakhpur district in eastern Uttar Pradesh. Babaji was on his way to Muktinath in Nepal, but Bhole Baba stayed with him for a few days, telling him briefly about his recent adventures. Babaji expressed his happiness that he and his grandmaster had met, but said little else.

He noticed that his young disciple had become content—perhaps too content—and he did not want this contentment to slide into complacency. Knowing is one thing; direct experience is quite another—and Babaji's standards demanded that an aspirant should be content with nothing less than the direct experience of all that he had learned. And Babaji also knew that even after gaining direct experience, an aspirant may slip backward: it is constant practice that brings maturity and stability. Regardless of how great and profound the experience, it can be retained only in the vessel of *vairagya* (dispassion). Otherwise, even if he has reached the highest level of realization and yogic accomplishment, the aspirant may lose ground. To soar into the depthless space of spiritual freedom one must have two strong wings: methodical practice, and absolute dispassion.

So Babaji called his disciple to him and said, "Now you must commit yourself to an intense practice. Watch your mind and see where you invest the spiritual energy you have gathered from your sadhana, and how effortlessly you do it. If you are not fully established in the principle of dispassion, you will be under great pressure to cash in your spiritual wealth for name, fame, and the other trappings of worldly success. My blessings are with you. Go and live on the bank of the Narmada. Commit yourself to the practice I will give you, and visit the villages and towns occasionally so you can serve and guide others." With these instructions Babaji left for Nepal.

The Narmada River flows through central India, and on the way Bhole Baba stopped at the sacred site of Khajuraho, where he had passed several winters with Babaji and other sadhus. It was at Khajuraho, at the age of seven, that he had been graced with the appearance of the Divine Mother, and now he lingered for a few days in her courtyard: the grounds of the Temple of Sixty-four Yoginis. From there he went to Ujjain, the holy city of Maha Kala, where he again 164 interrupted his journey. When he was younger he had visited that holy city several times with Babaji and once with Aghori Baba, and he wanted to revisit some of the holy sites.

I was not aware that there was a special relationship between Ujjain and our tradition. I knew Ujjain as one of the seven holy cities and Maha Kala as one of the twelve famous shrines of Shiva, but during an unusual encounter in the summer of 1992 Swamiji told me that Durvasa, one of the immortal sages of our tradition, is closely linked to the shrine of Maha Kala and hundreds of other shrines within the region of Ujjain.

This conversation took place in Pennsylvania just after Swamiji had translated the famous epic the *Ramayana* from Sanskrit to English. In the introduction he shared some of his experiences during his pilgrimage from Ayodhya, the birthplace of Lord Rama, to Sri Lanka, and had asked the editor, Kay Gendron, to have me check the translation of the Sanskrit terms. Everything seemed in order except that I was struck with a Sanskrit word that Swamiji had translated as "foul-mouthed," and which he had used as an epithet for the sage Durvasa. According to the tradition, Durvasa was Shiva incarnate, so I circled the word with a red pencil and made a note to the editor in the margin: "This is not an appropriate epithet for a sage."

As it happened, I was in Swamiji's room when Dr. Gendron read him the edited version of the introduction. Not wanting to change Swamiji's direct translation of the term, she said, "Swamiji, Panditji says that 'foul-mouthed' is not an appropriate epithet for a sage."

Swamiji looked at me and exploded. "What is wrong with it?"

When I did not reply, he said, "No, no, tell me—what is your problem?"

I said gently, "Durvasa is a Brahma Rishi, the highest-caliber sage. So how can he be foul-mouthed?"

"What about all the stories of him getting mad for petty reasons— cursing people and upsetting the whole world?" Swamiji shot back.

"His anger was motivated by compassion, not by his personal desires. Through his actions he simply speeded up the chain of karmic events and thereby granted freedom to those whom he loved, although on the surface it seemed as if he were cursing or punishing someone. Furthermore, Swamiji, he never did such things to poor, ignorant, and helpless people. Those who embraced his wrath as a blessing were rewarded spiritually."

165

Swamiji still seemed to be in a fighting mood, although the flames shooting from his eyes were a little less fierce. "But he used to eat too much, and overeating is not a sign of a yogi," he said.

Encouraged by his relatively soft tone, I said, "Swamiji, he never willingly ate anything other than the leaves of durva grass. That's why he was known as Durvasa: the grass eater. He is an incarnation of Rudra [the fire aspect of Shiva]. Out of compassion, whenever he ate at someone's home he offered the food into the living fire that is he himself. He did it for the welfare of the host and for the welfare of all creation. This fact is well-documented in the scriptures."

Swamiji's remaining temper vanished. "Then how should we translate it?" he asked.

"Probably 'short-tempered' will do," I replied.

Turning to Dr. Gendron, Swamiji said, "Panditji insists it should be translated as 'short-tempered,' so let us do it." To me he said, "I will tell Durvasa that you are his admirer. And I'm sure he will be very happy to hear it." He then asked Dr. Gendron if I had any other comments and when she said no, he said, "Good; go and make the change and it's done."

During my sixteen years with him I had learned how to read Swamiji's moods, and it was evident that he was in the frame of mind to talk about the sage Durvasa. So I said, "Swamiji, there is something I cannot understand about Durvasa. Why was he instrumental in the death of Lord Rama and his brothers? And he was also instrumental in the death of Krishna and Krishna's whole family. Why is this?"

"Durvasa is ever-absorbed in Maha Kala. To guide aspirants, he appears as a sage. And as cosmic fire he accompanies Shiva in his act of destruction," Swamiji replied. "Durvasa is beyond the realm of time. He is immortal: the conqueror of death and the devourer of time. So were Rama and Krishna—death could not touch them. They needed an excuse to leave the body, and Durvasa supplied it. You have to understand the difference between dying and leaving the body voluntarily. Both Rama and Krishna left their bodies without dying, and in doing so they honored Durvasa's wish as though it were a command.

"Ujjain is Durvasa's main abode. Just as Narada presides as *acharya* [the spiritual preceptor] at the Badrinath shrine in the Himalayas, Durvasa is the *acharya* in the holy city of Ujjain. All the adepts and aspirants who study and practice here—those who know him and those who do not—have Durvasa as their guardian."

Then Swamiji went on to tell me that he had interrupted his journey to the Narmada River in order to linger awhile in Ujjain. He remembered that Babaji's favorite place was an underground cave on the bank of the Shipra River that King Bhartrihari had built fourteen hundred years earlier when he renounced his kingdom and became a disciple of Guru Gorakha Natha. Now it was in the possession of a group of sadhus who had their headquarters in Haridwar.

Bhole Baba stayed in this cave for a week or so to visit the yogis who lived near the prominent shrines in the area. These adepts followed the path of *aghora,* to which Aghori Baba had introduced Bhole Baba years before. These adepts spent their nights at the shrine of Vikranta Bhairava, a small temple at a cremation ground on the bank of the river, discussing the dynamics of inner fire and the esoteric knowledge of solar science. Bhole Baba joined them there.

As Swamiji explained to me, the path of *aghora* is the most mysterious among all paths of yoga and tantra. Ujjain is one of the most mysterious cities on Earth. Pilgrims flock to the temple of Maha Kala, which is now surrounded by the city; but the desolate places, like Vikranta Bhairava on the city's outskirts, come to life only at night when the adepts converge there. The topics they discuss would be considered fantasy by some, insanity by others, but a few would hear in their words the impenetrable mystery of spirituality. The adepts speak of the different realms of existence, such as hell and heaven, the condition of the soul after death, and the possibility of pulling weak-willed souls to our earthly plane and communicating with them through human or non-human mediums. Some of these sadhus could read the minds of others, but they confessed that they could not read their own minds.

It was here at the shrine of Vikranta Bhairava that Bhole Baba met a tantric who could answer any question as long as it did not pertain to spirituality. He always had alcohol with him and he often smoked marijuana. He was unkempt and almost deaf, and some found him disgusting, yet people were attracted to him because of his ability to predict the future and answer questions about worldly matters. In spite of his powers, however, he admitted that he was miserable.

The ignorant people who visited him could not understand this tantric's pain, but one night he explained that several years earlier he had fallen into the company of a low-grade tantric who taught him a practice called *karna pishachini*. In tantra, *karna pishachini* is described as a *shakti* (power) that whispers the answer to questions asked by others into the ear of the practitioner. As a result of doing this practice, this tantric came to possess that power. He did not realize he was inviting misery for himself by doing so.

In the beginning he found it exciting. People were impressed when he relayed the answers to their questions. But in order to retain that power, he had to do the practice regularly, and it required that he invoke the power in his ears and offer her alcohol and meat by consuming them himself. The power worked only when she was not hungry. And the more he used that power, the more she shared his body. In the beginning he had control over her: he could invoke and dismiss her at will. But gradually she took over until he had no choice but to comply with her demands—drinking, smoking marijuana, and consuming flesh. Furthermore, she was a restless power and she continually shouted unasked-for information about others into his ears. The constant chatter ringing in his ears made it hard for him to sleep and prevented him from hearing anything else very well. Neither he nor his teacher knew how to get rid of the power.

This unfortunate tantric begged the sadhus to help him. Feeling pity for him, they made a plan. The great tantric adept Datia Wale Maharaj, who was among them, took the lead. Early one morning they forced the tantric to shave his head, against the wishes of the power that was controlling his life. Then, still against the wishes of the power, they forced him to take a bath in the Shipra River and dragged him to the nearby shrine of Kala Bhairava. There Datia Wale Maharaj drew the power of *karna pishachini* from his body and placed her at the feet of Kala Bhairava, while Bhole Baba performed a special fire ceremony, *viraja homa* (the fire offering for all aspects of body, mind, and consciousness). When it was over, the tantric was free from his terrible accomplishment, although it took months for him to reorient himself properly.

Several days later Bhole Baba had another interesting encounter. As he visited the different shrines in and around Ujjain, he kept seeing an old sadhu everywhere he went. After noticing him at three or four different shrines, Bhole Baba asked some of the local priests and sadhus as well as the beggars and sweepers who this old man was, but no one knew. And when Bhole Baba asked the sadhu himself, all he said was, "I live and work here."

As he rested in the cave one night, Bhole Baba pondered: How can this man be everywhere? If he is a sadhu, he has to have a place where he can do his practice; if he's a beggar, he must stay within his own territory or he will be beaten by the other beggars. He seems fully familiar with all the shrines in Ujjain, but nobody knows him. He seems to be simply watching rather than involving himself in any activity at these shrines. And then a thought flashed: Perhaps he is the sage Durvasa in disguise—Babaji told me that Ujjain is his main abode. And the scriptures say these sages remain in disguise only as long as you do not recognize them. I hope I see that old sadhu tomorrow so I can acknowledge him appropriately if he is Durvasa.

Suddenly another thought flashed in Bhole Baba's mind: I have seen that old sadhu at all the shrines, except here at this cave. Perhaps this is because I visited those places with the attitude of a pilgrim but have come to think of this cave as my residence rather than as a pilgrimage point. But this cave is more than a physical structure. This is where Guru Gorakha Natha, Bhartrihari, and other adepts lived and did their practices. Legend also has it that one of the chambers in this cave has an invisible tunnel that opens on the bank of the Ganga in Haridwar, several hundred miles from here. For the sake of formality I must leave this cave and enter it again after I have sought the permission and blessings of the sage Durvasa, the principal guide of all the masters and seekers who reside here in this region.

With this resolve, he picked up his flashlight and left the cave, and as he did, he saw the old sadhu sitting under a nearby neem tree. Bhole Baba bowed his head and called out, *"Hay karuna murti atri nandan apko pranam hai* [O embodiment of compassion, son of Atri, my homage to you]." When he heard these words, the sadhu's limbs arranged themselves in a yogic sitting posture, and from his ordinary-looking countenance a divine aura suddenly emerged. The night was pitch-dark and the sky was completely enveloped with clouds, but the air was infused with a soothing light. It was indeed Durvasa. Bhole Baba was thrilled but not surprised—he had encountered such divine beings in the presence of his master and his grandmaster.

"In this circumstance," Bhole Baba said to Durvasa, "I do not know how to worship you. Kindly tell me what is the right way for me to express my respect and gratitude."

The sage Durvasa responded, "It's okay. This is what my job is: to serve those who have offered their life in the service of God. Tell me, what do you seek from me?"

"I know that great adepts such as my master and my grandmaster have the capacity to leave their bodies at will and yet continue to exist. You, on the other hand, are immortal. You know both shores of life—time and space offer no obstruction to you. I want to know more about the other shore. I have seen my master curing villagers in the Himalayas who were possessed by spirits—it barely took a minute for him to bring someone back to normal. I have also heard my master ordering

169

a spirit to stay in a pipal tree and to derive its sustenance from the sap of that tree. I want to know exactly what these spirits are. Do they feel hunger or thirst? Do they have to occupy someone else's body? But when I asked my master, he dismissed my questions by saying, 'It's all in the mind.' Yet the scriptures as well as sadhus talk about heaven and hell and those that dwell therein as though they are as real as this world we are now conversing in."

"The mind creates reality," the sage replied. "Our actions create bondage."

"But it is important to renounce actions and the fruits of actions," Bhole Baba replied. "Is there any action we must not renounce, even though we are on the path of renunciation?"

"Charity," the sage replied. "Giving is at the core of creation. Dispassion brings contentment only at the level of the intellect. It is charity—the selfless act of giving and serving—that comes forward in different forms and becomes the source of true peace and happiness. Lacking charity, even great monks and ascetics remain unfulfilled. Come with me to the ashram of sage Agastya. There you will find further clarification of your questions."

At this, Bhole Baba drifted into a reverie, and accompanied by sage Durvasa, he entered a beautiful ashram. The huts were made of bamboo and sugarcane leaves. The air was alive with the scent of flowers and the songs of birds perched in the bushes and flitting among the trees. Bhole Baba and Durvasa strolled through the grounds until they reached the dwelling of the sage Agastya. There, surrounded by students and other sages, Agastya was entertaining Lord Rama. He was insisting that Rama accept a gift and Rama was refusing, arguing that it was not appropriate for a king to accept a gift from a sage. And sage Agastya argued that since the light of God lives in a king, offering a gift to a king was his way of honoring God.

At this, Rama accepted the gift. When he opened it he was dazzled by an array of radiant ornaments, and he told the sage that he had never before seen such a display, not even in Ravana's palace in Sri Lanka. "These things seem to be made of gold and gems not found in this world," he said. "What are they? Where did they come from?"

In answer, sage Agastya told the following story:

While wandering through the dense forest of Dandaka, Agastya happened upon an ashram on the shore of a beautiful lake. When he entered, it was apparent that the ashram had been abandoned for a long time, but the day was drawing to a close and so he stayed there for the night. Just before dawn he set out for the lakeshore to bathe, but before reaching it he came upon the corpse of a large, healthy-looking man. He examined it, but saw no sign of disease, injury, or poison.

Then, as he was trying to unravel this mystery, he saw a golden chariot descending from the sky. It landed on the lakeshore, and while sage Agastya watched, a handsome, celestial-looking man came out of the chariot, bathed in the lake, walked straight to the corpse, tore it open, and began to eat it. Then, as soon as the man finished and turned to walk away, the corpse reconstituted itself. Within seconds, it was as if it had never been touched. The man once again bathed in the lake.

Just as the man was about to get into his chariot, sage Agastya addressed him, saying, "Please wait a few moments and tell me who you are. You don't seem to have a physical body. The aura around you tells me you are a celestial being, but your actions are strange and your diet barbaric. Who are you? Why must you live like this?"

"You do not seem to be an ordinary person, either," the man replied calmly. "No ordinary creatures—human or animal—can reach here. I am a celestial being with a sad history.

"While living in that body," he went on, pointing to the corpse, "I was king of Vidarbha, until one day I appointed my younger brother king and dedicated my life to spiritual pursuits. I mastered the science of longevity and then became absorbed in an intense meditation practice. At the end of my life I left my body in a yogic manner, and due to the knowledge and purity I had gained through my spiritual practices, I went to heaven.

"There I was surprised to find myself suffering from hunger and thirst. When I asked the Lord of Heaven why this was so, he explained that in my life both as a king and as an ascetic I never shared anything with anyone; I was interested only in my own health and happiness. Even my renunciation of the crown was motivated by personal pleasure: freedom from the headache of ruling a kingdom and fulfillment of my desire not to be bothered by anyone. The Lord of Heaven told me that for this reason the only food I was entitled to was the body on which I had lavished such care. He assured me that it would not decay but would remain an inexhaustible source of nourishment. I was also told that it would be the great sage Agastya who would bring me deliverance. Years have passed while I have been living on my own corpse and waiting for him."

"I am Agastya," the sage said. "Please tell me how I can help you."

The celestial being fell at Agastya's feet and asked the sage to accept the ornaments that adorned his body. And as soon as he placed them on Agastya's outstretched palms, the corpse vanished and the celestial being ascended to heaven.

At this, Bhole Baba came out of his reverie to find himself sitting in front of sage Durvasa under the neem tree. Once again the sage stressed the importance of selfless service, explaining that love for God is expressed by serving others selflessly. "Worshipping God with ritual paraphernalia is like children building castles in the sand," he said. "The Divine is all-pervading, residing in its full brilliance in every heart. You connect yourself with the Divine with relative ease by doing your sadhana at shrines and holy sites, but if you get attached to these places your consciousness will contract. These shrines are doorways, not destinations. Move on to the next holy site and see where that doorway leads you."

In the morning Bhole Baba departed for his final destination, the Narmada River, which is second only to the Ganga in terms of sanctity. It originates from Amar Kantak, and its banks are lined with shrines, most of them dedicated to Lord Shiva. The most famous is Omkareshwar. Beautiful and remote, this shrine is situated on an island at the confluence of the Narmada and Kaberi Rivers, and can be reached only by boat or footbridge. Bhole Baba set out for this island.

When he arrived at Omkareshwar, Bhole Baba searched for a spot where he could practice austerities without being disturbed, but the main shrine, as well as the other temples on the island, attracted pilgrims and so was not suitable for his purposes. This was also true of the hundreds of other temples along the banks of the Narmada. A few miles downstream from the island, however, he found a secluded spot on the western bank, and that is where he built his hut. The nearest village was six miles away, so before beginning his practice Bhole Baba made arrangements with the villagers to supply him with milk and bread once a day. Except for a water pot, a blanket, and two loincloths, he was free of all possessions. As Swamiji writes in *Living with the Himalayan Masters*, "Those six months of intense physical and mental austerities were a high period in my life."

When he built his hut Bhole Baba had not noticed that the river was full of crocodiles. He had arrived in the month of September, when the midday sun is still quite hot, and so the crocodiles sunned themselves on the bank only in early morning and late afternoon, when Bhole Baba was doing his practices inside the hut. He was happy that the villagers respected his privacy; even the herders, with their cows and goats, did not venture into this part of the forest. For their part, the villagers thought that if this was a fake sadhu, he would soon be eaten by the crocodiles; if he was genuine, he would be protected and would complete his practice.

173

According to Indian mythology the crocodile is the vehicle of the goddess Ganga. And so, some weeks later, when Bhole Baba noticed the crocodiles lying in the sun outside his hut, a spiritual interpretation came immediately to mind: Mother Ganga had come to see her son. He was elated, for this meant that no matter where he went, Mother Ganga was there to offer him her nourishment and protection. The presence of the crocodiles convinced him that he would be successful in the practice he had undertaken here.

As winter began, the young sadhu began doing his practice outside to take advantage of the sun's warmth, and he made his seat on the riverbank—a perfect spot, sunny and protected from the wind. The crocodiles found it perfect too, and once he had closed his eyes in meditation they would crawl onto the bank beside him and sun themselves.

One day while Bhole Baba was meditating, a group of big-game hunters happened by and were astonished to see a young sadhu sitting on the riverbank, surrounded by crocodiles. Without his noticing, they took pictures, which soon appeared in the regional newspapers, then larger papers, and before long the story was everywhere. It even reached the Shankaracharya of Karvirpitham, Jagadguru Kurtkoti, hundreds of miles away in the state of Maharashtra. This learned scholar had held this position for a long time, and was now in search of a qualified successor. So he appointed a group of pandits to watch Bhole Baba's daily routine and gather information about him. Some stayed in the nearby village, while others journeyed to Rishikesh to find out what they could about this young sadhu. By the time Bhole Baba had completed his six-month practice, Jagadguru Shankaracharya was convinced that the young man was his perfect replacement.

So Jagadguru sent Bhole Baba an invitation to visit him at Karvirpitham, and after a long discussion asked the young sadhu to succeed him. Bhole Baba felt that accepting this post would give him both the opportunity and the means to serve humanity, but he would not agree to fill the position without Babaji's permission. When he asked Babaji by telegram, however, all his master said in his reply was, "Do as you wish. My blessings are always with you." Taking this response as approval, Bhole Baba accepted the post.

In Hindu society the Shankaracharya is comparable to the Pope in Christian society. The first Shankaracharya was born in the eighth century A.D. A great philosopher, yogi, and social reformer, he was one of India's most influential spiritual leaders. During his lifetime he established five monasteries: one in each of the four corners of India, and the fifth in south central India at Karvirpitham. As legend has it, he appointed four of his disciples to head the first four monasteries, while he himself spent the last part of his life in the fifth. Since that time, these five positions have been handed down from generation to generation, with only occasional interruptions. Anyone holding these offices is given the title "Shankaracharya," and is respected as the representative of the first Shankaracharya. Devout Hindus believe (or at least expect) him to be enlightened, all-powerful, and capable of helping people through his blessings. Then, as this belief and the expectations it generated became firm in the Indian mind, those holding the position of Shankaracharya were given one more title: Jagadguru ("teacher of the universe"), an epithet that the heads of other spiritual traditions in India also bear.

The ceremony installing Bhole Baba in the seat of Shankaracharya of Karvirpitham lasted eighteen days, and in due course he was given a new name: Jagadguru Shankaracharya Sadashiva Bharati. But even though this was his official name, most people called him either "Jagadguru" or simply "Bhole Baba."

And so it was that in a matter of a few weeks the sadhu who had so recently been living a solitary life became Jagadguru Shankaracharya, the head of an influential religious institution. Instead of experiencing the presence of the goddess Ganga while the crocodiles sunned themselves beside his meditation seat, he would have to find a way to experience the presence of God in those who now surrounded him. It was not an easy task. Dr. Kurtkoti had been actively involved in the social and religious reformation that was sweeping the land, and at the same time he had participated actively in the social, cultural, religious, and spiritual lives of his followers. Their expectations of his young successor were high. But if Dr. Kurtkoti had been a reformer, Bhole Baba was a revolutionary.

India had just gained her independence from British rule, and society was in turmoil. The spirit of democracy was calling for change, and the spirit of orthodoxy was resisting with all its considerable might. For centuries there had been political, religious, and cultural suppression in India, and the end of British rule unleashed an impulse toward freedom that expressed itself in ways as diverse as the society itself: brahmins were trying to reclaim their antique dignity, the rajas wanted to resume their kingly roles, and those from the lower strata of society were clamoring to share equally in the new democracy. Tension between Hindus and Muslims was at its peak. The age-old Hindu caste system was being revitalized by some, and dismantled by others. Some temples were opened to those of all castes and creeds, while others restricted entry to brahmins and other members of the upper classes.

During this turmoil people naturally looked to their religious and spiritual leaders for guidance. The other four Shankaracharyas supported the view of orthodox Hinduism, but Bhole Baba, as Shankaracharya of Karvirpitham, exercised his power in support of reform. In other words, the majority of Hindu religious leaders supported caste restrictions and women's subservience to men, and

175

attributed the poverty and helplessness of the destitute to their bad karmas. Bhole Baba, on the other hand, took this opportunity to bring the beliefs he had cultivated in the company of men like Mahatma Gandhi and Rabindranath Tagore into practice. He issued directives declaring that every man and woman—rich or poor, educated or illiterate—could enter the temples and worship God. He supported education as the way to uplift human consciousness and achieve long-lasting transformation. Compared to this, Dr. Kurtkoti's reforms had been mild.

At the same time, tradition demanded that Bhole Baba fulfill his role as Shankaracharya. This meant he must maintain the rules and laws, values and dignities for which the monastery at Karvirpitham had been established in the first place. Custom dictated that he make himself accessible to his followers and allow himself to be treated as a holy man. He was expected to sit on a throne-like seat while people worshipped him with incense and garlands. One of his main tasks was to bless the stream of people who visited him day and night. Bhole Baba found this custom hollow and time-consuming.

During his discourses and *satsangas* (spiritual gatherings) he reminded people that although it is good to love your spiritual leader, it is more important that you learn to take care of yourself and discover your own hidden potential—to become a light to yourself and a light to others. He said that blessings work only when you are sincere and honest with yourself. The faithful followers were disappointed when they heard him say this. They wondered if there was something wrong with their Shankaracharya.

Although Bhole Baba was the head of the entire ashram, he was junior—both in age and in tenure—to those who had been with the former Shankaracharya. The senior members of the ashram expected their new leader to give them the same kind of love and attention they had been accustomed to receiving from Dr. Kurtkoti, yet it offended their dignity when he did this—after all, they were the senior disciples of a highly respected spiritual leader and many years senior to this young upstart. While working with the former Shankaracharya they had assumed leadership roles, and now the highest leadership position had been transferred to an outsider and they were expected to work under him. When he accepted the office, Bhole Baba had a vision of creating a community in which love, mutual cooperation, selfless service, and the spirit of self-transformation prevailed. But he did not know what it would take to make this vision a reality. Whenever he tried to convey the message that methodical practice and contemplative techniques for self-reflection are the forces that engender transformation, he was met with sullen resistance by the senior members of the ashram, who felt that he was talking down to them.

He was also heartsick about the ashram environment. Although the people living there had left their homes and worldly connections, they had brought their desire for power and prestige with them. Self-discipline and the practices necessary for self-transformation were at the bottom of their list of priorities. And just as in Indian universities and colleges—wherein teachers are promoted solely on the basis of seniority—in religious organizations the more senior the resident, the more enlightened he is believed to be.

177

Whenever Bhole Baba tried to institute change, he encountered enormous resistance. Before becoming Shankaracharya he had visited many ashrams and other institutions, but always as a guest or short-term student. He had not always been favorably impressed with the teachers, their teachings, or the environment they maintained, but he found no reason to be disturbed about these things—he simply learned what he needed to learn and moved on. Now he was in his own ashram, surrounded by his "followers," who honored him as Shankaracharya while expecting him to teach and behave in a manner that suited their own whims and desires. It was as though the energy of the ashram was trying to tame the guru so he would not act against the wishes of the students. This was an aspect of human behavior that Bhole Baba had not learned about under the tutelage of Bengali Baba, and he began to wonder if he had overestimated his ability to deal with a society so entrenched in traditional and unexamined beliefs.

Yet he wanted to serve and share all that he had gathered from various saints and teachers, so he busied himself traveling, lecturing, and meeting with religious and political leaders. With rare exceptions, the religious leaders did not like his progressive ideas, while the political leaders admired him for his vision and courage. For example, in his dedication to reform Bhole Baba took action to bring the *deva dasi* custom to an end. "Deva dasi" means "servant of God," and deva dasais were women who were forced to live in the temples, serving the priests and giving music and dance performances as part of the daily worship. This custom had reached its fullest expression in the temples of south India, where for all practical purposes these women were slaves. They were not allowed to marry, although they often bore children fathered by the priests and other temple authorities. Such children had no place in society, so they grew up as orphans and beggars. Bhole Baba insisted that this custom be abolished, and to this end he held public meetings and met with government authorities and politicians. After a protracted struggle he succeeded in abolishing the custom, although in the process he incurred the displeasure of many of his own followers.

178

This and other reforms that he led were a threat to orthodox Hinduism, but even though many of those in his own circle disagreed with his ideas, on the surface they continued to worship him as a God-man. Uncomfortable in this atmosphere, Bhole Baba began to reevaluate the merits of his desire to serve humanity through his position as Shankaracharya. And after a long analysis he came to the conclusion that just as people as individuals are attached to their personal belongings, collectively they are attached to their customs, dogmas, superstitions, and prejudices. It is not easy to help them overcome their attachments, especially when they think their attachments are virtues.

Bhole Baba was also missing Babaji. His master had always kept in touch with him in one way or another, and Bhole Baba had expected that Babaji would visit him and be happy to see what a good job his student was doing. But when more than two years had passed without a word, his master's words began to echo in his heart: "No matter how far you have reached in your spiritual evolution you must not stop your practices." Bhole Baba realized he was in an untenable position: teaching others what he himself had no time to practice. He considered this hypocritical and was disappointed in himself.

Bhole Baba was caught in a dilemma: should he continue serving others at the cost of his spiritual freedom, or should he resort to solitude, forsaking the idea of selfless service? He wondered if there was any way to clean up the trash that had entered the sublime tradition of the Vedic sages without involving himself in politics. In the past he had asked his master several times why he did not share his wisdom with humanity at large, and Babaji's only answer had been a gentle smile. Now Bhole Baba was beginning to understand Babaji's solitary life. After a long and deep internal debate he decided that he must leave the post of Shankaracharya lest he lose his own connection with the Lord of Life. Let Babaji decide the best way for him to serve others.

Bhole Baba knew that if he announced his decision to leave his post it would throw the ashram into turmoil, along with the large community of followers throughout the region. If he did not appoint his successor before resigning, he would be thought irresponsible. Yet it would be even more irresponsible to appoint a successor: this would inevitably trigger a fight among the senior monks. So he decided that the best solution was to leave the ashram quietly and let a leader emerge on the basis of his own merit.

179

But how to leave? He was constantly surrounded by people—he was left alone only when he slept and when he went to the bathroom. After some thought, however, he came up with a plan that would allow him to slip away unnoticed. He began to go for long walks. Of course people accompanied him, whether he liked it or not, and he had to wear the garb of the Shankaracharya—saffron robe and wooden sandals—and carry his staff of office. His driver would drop him some distance from the ashram and he would walk for a long time before returning to the car. To reduce the number of people attending him on these walks, he lengthened the walks and changed his route often. Then one day he shocked everyone by asking the driver to give him the keys to the car so he could show the man how to improve his driving. No one had imagined that a spiritual person of his stature would put his hands on a steering wheel. Even today it is unusual for a swami to drive a car; in those days it was unheard of. As the driver sat next to him in shock, Bhole Baba drove to one of the places where he was accustomed to walk; then, after completing his walk, he drove back to the ashram again. He followed this routine for a while, and then one day he asked the driver to stay at the ashram—he would drive himself.

Once alone, Bhole Baba drove to the nearest town and parked the car near a police station, leaving a note asking that it be returned to Karvirpitham. From there he walked to the railway station and boarded the third-class section of the train to Allahabad. He had no ticket, but he looked so imposing that several people offered him their seat—it was evident that he was a respected holy man. When he sat down the passengers felt uncomfortable sitting next to him on seats that were equal to his, so they squeezed themselves into the row of seats facing him. Bhole Baba closed the metal window shade, fearing that someone on the platform might recognize him, and made himself comfortable. When the other passengers asked him who he was, he said only that he was a sadhu on his way to the Himalayas. Despite his repeated requests, no one would sit next to him, and so a whole row of seats remained conspicuously empty. Luckily the train left the station before anybody pressed him hard to reveal his identity.

A half hour later, the conductor came through. Surprised to see such an impressive figure in the third-class compartment, he bowed his head in respect and checked everyone else's ticket. Then he sat down next to Bhole Baba and politely asked who he was and where he was going. Bhole Baba explained that he was a sadhu and requested that the conductor ask no further questions about his identity. He confessed that he had no ticket, for he had no money to buy one, and told the conductor that this was the first time he had committed such a crime. In a mischievous tone the conductor said, "What if I ask you to get down at the next station, or allow you to continue on only if you tell me who you are?"

Bhole Baba replied, "Please don't do such things to me. I need your help. My students are waiting for me at Allahabad station. They will pay for my ticket and any penalty. I promise that when we reach Allahabad I will tell you who I am and why I am traveling without a ticket."

When the conductor replied that his shift would end in Nagpur, long before the train reached Allahabad, Bhole Baba laughed and said, "Then come with me to Allahabad as my guest."

The conductor accepted the invitation and accompanied Bhole Baba all the way to Allahabad, providing him with water, tea, and some biscuits during the overnight journey. At Allahabad junction Bhole

Baba was received by the members of the family of Beni Prasad Tandon, and at that time the conductor came to know who his passenger was. He took a solemn vow not to tell anyone about the incident, and then returned to his home. Bhole Baba stayed for a few days with the Tandon family, and then proceeded to the Himalayas, where he found Babaji.

When he saw his master, Bhole Baba fell at his feet, crying, "Why did you let me accept that post?"

With a smile Babaji said, "I did not order you. You had the desire and you asked my permission. I'm glad you are back. You have seen how worldly temptations follow a swami and how the world wants to absorb a spiritual person. Now nothing will affect you because you have experienced position, institution, and renunciation.

"People expect a lot from their spiritual leaders," he continued. "Do what you can to uplift and enlighten people, but never forget your path."

A few days later Babaji started a conversation with Bhole Baba on a subject he had never before mentioned: marriage. "Most people are married and have children," Babaji said. "Most of the problems in the world center around their relationships—the well-being of family members and relatives, money, jobs, and business. How can you serve them and guide them if you don't have the experience of such things? You should get married. Then you will learn how it feels to live in the world, and that will help you cultivate true compassion for those who are part of families and who are caught in a web of worldly obligations.

"Furthermore, it will knock off the slightest trace of vanity you may have regarding spiritual life. I do not want you to walk on the crutches of Shankaracharya. I want you to be complete in your own right and have respect for yourself—a self-respect not affected by those who condone your actions or by those who condemn them."

Meanwhile the people at Karvirpitham were trying to find out what had happened to their Shankaracharya. Where did he go? Was he still alive? The many followers who did not live at the ashram were completely mystified—some assumed that there must have been a problem at the ashram; others thought the problem must lie with Bhole Baba himself. Some thought he was a coward and had betrayed the tradition; others saw his disappearance as an example of dispassion

181

and fearlessness. Some proposed that they should search for him and bring him back, while others insisted that they should not interfere with the decision of a saint or work against his wishes. In this hodgepodge of conflicting opinions no one was willing to listen to anyone else, and in their own fragmented manner everyone did what they wished. Some searched for him, while others turned their attention to filling the vacancy left by his departure.

A year passed while Bhole Baba remained in the Himalayas. Babaji had made it clear to him that he should return to the world, and Bhole Baba was more than willing to comply, but he did not know where to go. Even though he had cast aside the name Sadashiva Bharati and the title Jagadguru Shankaracharya, he was so well-known he feared that people would recognize him if he went to one of the cities, and that news of his whereabouts would soon reach Karvirpitham. Then instead of gaining experience by living in the world he would get entangled in the religious melodrama he had left behind.

When he expressed this concern to Babaji, his master laughed. "Human memory is shorter than a dog's," he said. "People have many problems to occupy them. Who cares whether you beautify the throne of Shankaracharya or sink into oblivion? Coronation or dismissal of a religious or political leader creates momentary excitement. Ignorant people, not knowing the nature of the world, join in the song and dance for a while but quickly get sucked back into their day-to-day concerns. No one has time for anyone but themselves. The people at Karvirpitham too have their own agenda. Those interested in power and prestige will figure out how to delete you from memory. More than a year has passed since you left that place. Go and do your work."

Babaji instructed Bhole Baba to travel in north Indian cities, such as Lucknow, Allahabad, and Kanpur, and as he did, he kept remembering Babaji urging him to get married. But how? In Indian society, who would think of marrying their daughter to a swami? Still, Babaji had said that he should marry, and so Bhole Baba knew his master must have made arrangements for this in his own mysterious way. He made no attempt to enter a householder's life but left it in the hands of providence.

In *Living with the Himalayan Masters* Swamiji writes about how Babaji's words began to materialize: "When I was in Uttar Pradesh, a northern state of India, people would come to visit me in the evenings and I would give discourses on the Upanishads. One day a girl who had her master's degree in English literature asked me to grant her an interview. She began by asserting that I had been her spouse in a previous life. She talked for two hours and led me to a state where I agreed that it could have been possible. I had never had such a personal audience with anyone for such a long time before. She tried to persuade me that we should get married in this life as well. . . . I started brooding on what it would be like to live with her. I told her that if my master would permit me to get married, it was all right with me. . . . This girl was from a well-known family. Many of her brothers, cousins, and other relatives held high government positions."

That is how Bhole Baba entered the world. The woman he married came from a well-known family, so his renunciation of monastic life was no secret. He started using the name Brij Kishor Kumar, but the general public still referred to him as Bhole Baba. Using a substantial sum of money he had received from Babaji, he started a business in Agra. As a businessman he was Kumar Saheb, but deep down he was still a sadhu who was acutely aware of the hunger of his soul. He did not mind working hard to gather the means and resources to provide for his growing family (by this time he had a son named Mohit), and work hard he did. Before long his business was prospering.

Bhole Baba's devotees in north India were in an uproar and the air was thick with speculation about his marriage; many assumed that he had left Karvirpitham for the sole purpose of marrying this particular woman. My dissertation adviser at the University of Allahabad, Dr. M. P. Lakhera, came from the Garhwal Himalayas where Swamiji was born and told me that after his marriage many of the devotees who had worshipped him became his enemies. They were embarrassed by his "fall" and did not want anyone to know they had been disciples of such a guru. Dr. Lakhera, on the other hand, admired Swamiji, not because of his spiritual achievements but because he was the genius who had been the most beloved disciple of Professor R. D. Ranade at the University of Allahabad. He praised Swamiji because he felt that

Swamiji honored the truth without fear of the criticism that his actions would inevitably bring.

I know about this period in Swamiji's life from many people who in one way or another were associated with him in those days. Among them were Colonel Khaira and his two children, Ravi and Piku, who were close to Bhole Baba then and in the days thereafter. In the 1980s they moved to Canada and since then have been actively involved with the Himalayan Institute in Pennsylvania. As children Ravi and Piku addressed Swamiji as "Uncle," and as adults they still behaved like kids in his presence. Once in Honesdale, when Swamiji was playing with his dogs Raja and Princess, Ravi remarked, "Uncle, no one can train dogs like you."

Swamiji laughed and said with pride, "Do you remember when my dogs captured that robber?"

"Yes, Uncle," Ravi replied. "What a scene that was!"

At the time, Bhole Baba had been living in Agra in a well-furnished bungalow, surrounded by lawns and gardens and encircled by a high wall. The property was protected by two fierce guard dogs that Bhole Baba had trained himself. One night when his wife was away and Bhole Baba was deep in meditation, a thief entered the house. The dogs knocked him to the ground and one of them straddled his chest, put his nose in his face, and began growling softly. The other went to the meditation room and began circling his master, occasionally brushing Bhole Baba's back with his tail. The dog had been trained not to interrupt his meditation, but as soon as Bhole Baba opened his eyes, the dog barked to signal that something was amiss. Bhole Baba followed him and the dogs began to bark and dance around the thief, who was shivering with fear. When the police came they marveled that these dogs were so well-trained they had subdued the intruder without harming him at all.

Bhole Baba's life at home was complicated from the beginning, and Dr. Lakhera told me that the age-old customs and values of the Himalayan brahmin families played a significant role in this. Although brahmins are the highest caste, there are hierarchies within the caste itself, and for a long time the standard practice had been that a brahmin girl could be married only to a brahmin boy from a family of higher status. According to this hierarchy Swamiji's family from Garhwal was inferior to his wife's family. Dr. Lakhera told me, "The members of her family were not willing to forgive Swamiji for the disgrace he had brought on them by marrying their daughter."

Bhole Baba's own relatives added to the complications. They had almost forgotten him and were amazed to see him reemerge in such an unexpected manner. Like his wife's relatives, many of them held influential positions, which drew them into high society, with its rounds of parties and gala social events. Bhole Baba was expected to take part. Relatives on his father's side had not had anything to do with him for a long time, but now they expected him to join their circle. His wife and her relatives considered this to be beneath their dignity—they expected Bhole Baba to uphold their superior position, an attitude that permeated even day-to-day family encounters. This did not bother Bhole Baba much. His long-cultivated habit of loving all and hating none left him at peace with everyone.

185

What did bother him was that his meditation was constantly being interrupted. Although he complied with everyone's demands, working hard at his business and taking care of the family, it did not seem to be enough to satisfy anyone. This did not disturb him, but he was annoyed that his meditation practice was treated like an unwanted stepchild. The family could not understand how he could claim to love them if he sat in meditation for hours instead of spending that time with them. And so the sweetness that concentrates itself at the time of marriage quickly dissipated.

In 1978, when I was working on my doctoral dissertation at the University of Allahabad, I teased Dr. Lakhera by mildly criticizing Swamiji's act of abandoning his family responsibilities to become a swami again. Dr. Lakhera was known for his balanced perspective and it was difficult to make him express his personal opinion about anyone. But I knew that if he disagreed with me strongly, he would hurriedly light a cigarette, inhale, and then speak. And that is exactly what he did.

"There are extremes in every aspect of this great man's life," he said quietly. "He was conceived when his parents were well past childbearing age. As a child he was loved by some and discarded by others. He was essentially raised by homeless sadhus. He received his education from the best of the best schools: Woodstock in Mussoorie, the University of Allahabad, and Oxford; he lived with Mahatma Gandhi and Tagore; and he became Shankaracharya at such a young age—a prestigious position which he tossed away to enter a householder's life, only to be ridiculed and insulted by his new relatives: 'Sitting on the couch cross-legged? How uncivilized of you!' they would say.

"But he is an invincible hurricane that decides its own path and wipes out anything that blocks its way. People now call him Rama, but in him I find the valiant Hanuman, who sees nothing but the goal. If you ever wish to mature in your thoughts, you'd better not speak such words as you just have. They don't fit in your mouth."

Whenever Bhole Baba sought Babaji's advice on domestic matters, the only answer he got was, "Learn to have patience." But finally, he reached his limit. He went to his master, and without any further inquiry or discussion Babaji said, "You have a task and you have not yet completed it. Having examined and compared worldly companionship and spiritual achievements and decided to follow the path of renunciation, you are now letting yourself be tempted back into the world. If you persist and remain within the influence of your current atmosphere, it will take several lifetimes for you to come back to the path."

Swamiji later wrote, "The decision was left to me, but after listening to my master I decided to break this tie and go back to the path of renunciation."

Bhole Baba made arrangements for his wife and two children. He gave them all the worldly possessions he had gathered during the brief time he was living a householder's life, and only after making sure that they were well provided for did he return to his master.

At last Babaji saw his son coming back to him with experiential knowledge of both religious vanity and the pleasure and pain that come with living in the world. He reminded him that it is important to uphold man-made customs only as long as they uplift our consciousness: they are meant to make life easy, not to create complications. "To be afraid of the world is the greatest bondage of all," he continued. "You are complete in yourself. Pleasure and pain, success and failure, death and birth cannot touch even your shadow."

Babaji again initiated Bhole Baba into *sannyasa* (the monastic order), but this time the monastic vows Bhole Baba took freed him even from the rules and laws that enslave monks. With this initiation Bhole Baba was born as Swami Rama. This whole cycle of experience—becoming a monk, renouncing monastic life to enter a householder's life, then renouncing that to become a monk again—confused some people and angered others, who felt he had betrayed the values of the monastic order. Those who were perceptive, however, saw the spirit of the Vedic tradition coming to life in Swami Rama, for in pursuit of experiential knowledge he walked fearlessly on the path of truth.

Swamiji comments on this at length in *Living with the Himalayan Masters:* "There are two well-known paths: the path of renunciation, and the path of action in the world. My path was the path of renunciation. One should not compare paths and think one superior and the other inferior. I certainly do not condemn the path which involves living and working in the world while having a family. That path furnishes the means of living, but is also time-consuming. In the path of renunciation there is ample time for spiritual practices, but limited means like food, shelter, and clothing. The renunciate must depend on the householder for fulfilling such needs. It is not important which path one follows. What is important is the honesty, sincerity, truthfulness, and faithfulness which one has in either path.

"This particular incident brought some humiliation into my life because people put swamis and yogis on high pedestals and look upon them as demigods. In India a swami is expected to live apart from society, without worldly possessions and without any worldly preoccupations. I have met many on the path who live hypocritically because of such expectations. I have heard Western psychologists say that renunciation, and especially celibacy, is ascetic insanity. I leave it to each individual to choose for himself, but it is important to mention here that hypocrisy is a great obstacle. Those who observe celibacy do indeed become abnormal if they do not transform their inner personalities. Those who do not have control over the primitive urges should not follow the path of renunciation.

"The drives for food, sex, sleep, and self-preservation are powerful urges. Each has a very strong impact and influence on human life and behavior. Why should there be such a taboo on sex only? In yoga science all the urges are channeled and directed toward spiritual development. Those who cannot control and sublimate these drives should live in the world and experience their fulfillment in a regulated way. They can follow the path of tantra rather than renunciation. They can transform the fulfillment of these drives into spiritual experiences.

"There is much confusion created by renunciates who impose rigid discipline on their students. This often makes the students dishonest and hypocritical. Is such discipline necessary? Conflict within and without are the signs and symptoms which clearly indicate that one is not on the path of spirituality."

on the TRAIL OF RAMA

SWAMIS IN THE SHANKARACHARYA order usually have one of two terms added to their names—"ananda" in northern India and "indra" in southern India—so the newly ordained Swami Rama found it odd that Babaji had not given him the name "Swami Ramananda" or "Swami Ramendra." He knew that Babaji was not confined to the Shankaracharya order—the sadhus belonging to the Ramanujacharya order also claimed him as part of their tradition. And in that tradition sadhus have the terms "ananda," "dasa," "deshika," or "acharya" appended to their names. It was in their circle that Babaji was known as Baba Dharam Das. Following the standards of this tradition, Babaji could have given Swami Rama the name Swami Ram Das or Baba Ram Das, as he had with some of Swamiji's other guru brothers.

Swamiji also wondered why he had been initiated at Deva Prayag, a town thirty miles north of Rishikesh, where the two branches of the Ganga (the Alakananda and the Bhagirathi) converge. The most famous temple here is dedicated to Lord Rama, but no special sanctity is associated with the place. It is simply where pilgrims stop to perform ancestral rites and pay homage to Lord Rama on their way to famous holy shrines, such as Badrinath and Kedarnath, in the deep Himalayas. But Swamiji knew that Babaji's every action had some meaning, and so he tried to understand what Babaji wanted to teach by giving him the name Swami Rama and initiating him at Deva Prayag.

One day he asked Babaji, "What is my tradition? In the external world, how shall I introduce myself?"

Babaji replied, "I performed your funeral rites at Deva Prayag. Your past is dead—all of it: your worldly identity, and your religious and spiritual identity. You are dead to all traditions, and all traditions are dead to you. Traditions are drunk with religious opium. Have you not seen how much trouble they have created?

"A tradition is not something you possess. Fish do not possess the water they swim in—it supports their life. You receive spiritual nourishment from a tradition. It is an ever-flowing stream of knowledge fed by numberless other streams. There is no such thing as a tradition that is independent of the sources of knowledge flowing from innumerable saints and sages. When a tradition separates itself from other traditions, either it turns into a cult or it dies out. You belong to all traditions and yet you are not the slave of any of them.

"Mount Kailas is your home. You are born to serve Rama, to serve the world of Rama, and to work like Rama. And you are not allowed to return to your home until you have walked in the footsteps of Rama and have completed the journey of self-sacrifice just as Rama did. Rama's mission was to serve not only India and Indians but the whole world. He loved humans and non-humans alike. He built a bridge between big and small, rich and poor, humans and animals, and he healed broken hearts."

In telling me about this, Swamiji broke off his narrative and said, "With that initiation I experienced a sense of indescribable freedom. I was glad to know that Bhole Baba is dead, Sadashiva is dead, Sadashiva Bharati is dead, Jagadguru Shankaracharya is dead, and I was relieved that an identity-free Swami Rama had now been born. Even after birth, this Rama eternally resides in the womb of its creator: my master, the blessed child of the Divine Mother. Whenever the creator pushes this Rama out into the world, he has only one purpose in his mind: Rama, this child of his, must walk in the footsteps of the legendary Rama, who built a bridge between big and small, rich and poor, humans and animals, and healed broken hearts. Since then, I am a citizen of two worlds: the world that exists within my master, and the world outside."

Babaji then told Swamiji to follow the trail of Rama from the city of Ayodhya to Sri Lanka, giving him guidance on how to approach particular shrines and what practices to do there. He completed his instructions with these words: "Before embarking, study the *Ramayana,* for it is the most practical of all the great scriptures. Those who study and practice the spiritual principles outlined therein become free from grief and fear. Hanuman, the wisest among the wise, guides such aspirants to Rama. And on seeing him, the blessed aspirant becomes Rama. Rama is one who remains balanced in all situations and circumstances. Wake up, my Rama! Begin your journey to Ayodhya now. May you search and find Rama."

According to Indian tradition, Rama is an incarnation of Lord Vishnu, the preserver and nourisher of the universe. Whenever righteousness declines and the natural order is disturbed, Lord Vishnu incarnates to restore the higher virtues of life and bring nature back into balance. There have been twenty-three incarnations of Vishnu; Rama is among the most significant. His father, king Dasharatha, ruled a prosperous kingdom in north India. He had three wives and four sons, of which Rama was the oldest. The princes were close—they grew up together, studied together, and got married at the same time. But on the day king Dasharatha announced the coronation of prince Rama to be king in his place, Rama's stepmother—through a complicated series of circumstances—created a situation that forced the king to send Rama into exile for fourteen years and crown her own son, Bharata, instead. And Bharata, who was away when this happened, returned to find his father dead from grief and his brother in exile. Because Rama was the rightful heir, Bharata at first refused to accept the kingdom, but finally, at Rama's insistence that he follow their father's order, he accepted the crown—but only for the period of his brother's exile.

So Rama set out to travel to holy shrines and visit the sages who lived in solitude. His journey took him from his capital city, Ayodhya, in northern India to the Dandaka forest, which at that time stretched from central India far south. And there Rama's wife, Sita, was abducted by Ravana, the king of Sri Lanka. Immediately Rama set out to rescue her, and during the search he met the mighty Hanuman, whose devotion to Rama is legendary, and Sugriva, the king of the

THE TRAIL OF RAMA

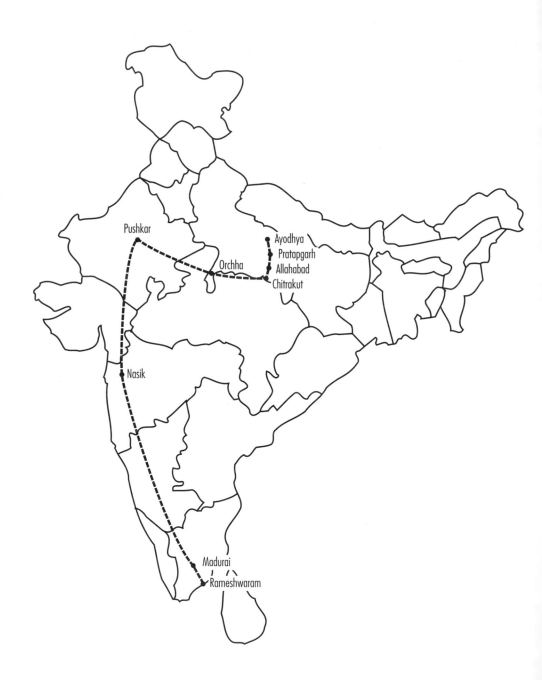

Pushkar

Orchha

Ayodhya
Pratapgarh
Allahabad
Chitrakut

Nasik

Madurai
Rameshwaram

Banara race. With their help he built a bridge across the ocean to transport an army from the mainland to the island of Sri Lanka. After a fierce battle Rama vanquished Ravana and rescued his beloved Sita. The route that Rama followed from the time he left Ayodhya until he reached Sri Lanka is called "the trail of Rama."

Rama's story is the tale of the ideal man who sacrifices his personal happiness for the sake of the higher values of life and the welfare of all living beings. Remaining unperturbed in the face of the grimmest circumstances, he accepts both the announcement of his coronation and the decree of his exile with the same equanimity. He bestows love on people of low birth just as he bestows it on his own brothers. His greatest work is building a bridge that connects two cultures, two races, and two traditions. An invincible warrior, once he conquers his enemies he turns them into friends and works to ensure their peace and prosperity. Although he is the king of kings, he finds time to attend to the concerns of all—down to the stray dogs in the streets of Ayodhya. Even in exile he is able to conquer an enemy as formidable as Ravana—but in his own court he sits defenseless against his citizen's demands that he send his queen into exile. In every situation he upholds dharma, the values that are the foundation of a healthy society.

193

Rama's every act was so impeccable that even in his own lifetime people regarded him as an incarnation of God. The places associated with him came to be regarded as shrines, and following the route he took from Ayodhya to Sri Lanka is considered to be one of the most important spiritual practices that can be undertaken. According to the scriptures, making this pilgrimage ensures the seeker freedom from fear and grief and enables the pilgrim to attain an everlasting state of peace and equanimity.

Modern Ayodhya is situated on the bank of the Sarayu River. Like Banaras, it has hundreds of temples, and with few exceptions all of them are dedicated to Lord Rama, the Divine Mother Sita, and Hanuman. Just as Banaras is guarded by Ganesha and Bhairava, this holy city is guarded by Hanuman. Admission to its inner dimension is possible only through his grace. As per Babaji's instructions, Swamiji's goal in Ayodhya was to offer his homage to Lord Rama and Sita at a special shrine known as Kanak Bhawan. He must go there under the guidance of Hanuman.

Swamiji had visited Ayodhya many times with his master, both as a child and as a young man, and so he was well-known to many of the sadhus in the ashrams. They knew that he was an adept in the practice of hatha yoga and pranayama, and fearing that they would ask him to teach, Swamiji decided to avoid the ashrams and keep as low a profile as possible. To this end he undertook the practice of silence as soon as he reached Ayodhya, lived on the bank of the Sarayu River, and relied on food that was offered to him spontaneously. As instructed by his master, he began an intense meditation on the mantra of Hanuman, which according to Babaji would lead him to Rama, the protector and guide of the eternal city of Ayodhya. It was a thirty-three-day practice, and in addition to doing *japa* (the repetition of mantra), Swamiji visited the main shrine of Hanuman, known as Hanuman Garhi, daily.

By the time Swamiji was completing the thirtieth day of the practice it was August, and according to the Indian calendar it was the month of Shravana. The monsoon was at its height, as it always is in August, and on this particular day it seemed as if the rain was threatening to wash away the entire city.

By nightfall the wind had become fierce. Swamiji's only blanket was soaking wet, and it felt as if the rain and the cold wind would pierce his bones. Seeking protection, he made his way through the black night to a nearby temple. Because he was observing silence he could not announce his arrival, but this hardly mattered, as the temple seemed deserted. It was pitch-black inside. The main hall offered the best protection from the draft, so Swamiji made his way there and sat down. But the temple was not deserted: the guard, who was taking shelter from the storm in a corner of the hall, caught a glimpse of Swamiji in a flash of lightning and approached the seated figure, asking who he was and what he was doing there. Swamiji could not answer without breaking his vow of silence. He tried to communicate in gestures, but they were hidden in the darkness. And when there was no reply to his questions, the guard assumed that he had caught a thief and began to shout and to beat Swamiji with his bamboo staff. With that, the priest and others living nearby rushed to the temple with a lantern. They recognized the man the guard was beating as the swami who had been practicing austerities on the riverbank nearby, and intervened, but by that time Swamiji was badly injured.

When the guard and the priest apologized, Swamiji did not answer, but raised three fingers in a gesture no one understood. They bandaged his wounds, wrapped him in a dry blanket, and tried to make him comfortable. In the morning when the weather cleared, he returned to his spot on the riverbank.

Three days later, on the day that coincided with the annual celebration of Badka Mangal ("Big Tuesday"), Swamiji completed his practice. This is the day when millions of people throng to Hanuman temples throughout India, and Hanuman Garhi, the temple Swamiji had been visiting daily, was completely engulfed by the crowd. Seeing the throng, Swamiji thought: "Those who have come here with so much faith and devotion have done so only because they are transformed by the consciousness of Hanuman. Indeed it is Hanuman himself who is manifesting in the form of those who have come to worship him." He realized that he did not need to go inside the temple to worship that force: it pervades the entire city, guiding and protecting it. And while he was rejoicing in this understanding, someone who looked like a priest approached him and said, "Come with me to Kanak Bhawan. I'll take you to the main temple of Sita and Rama. There you can worship Hanuman as well as Sita and Rama."

Swamiji interpreted the priest's offer as an acknowledgment that his practice was completed. Kanak Bhawan was some distance away, and as they walked, the priest spouted platitudes about the sacredness of Ayodhya, the importance of Kanak Bhawan, and how one attains freedom from all fear and grief just by having the vision of the Lord at that temple. When he mentioned buying ritual articles for worship at Kanak Bhawan, Swamiji pointed out that he was a sadhu and had no money. The priest expressed disappointment and changed the subject.

Unlike the priests in the West, who perform services in a church, Hindu priests working at a temple do not have an established structure or standard of behavior. The big temples usually have officially appointed priests who assist the pilgrims and devotees in performing their worship inside. But there are also dozens of priests (and sometimes hundreds, if the temple is a large one) who work around the perimeter of the temple and sometimes at taxi stands and bus and railway stations. They introduce themselves to pilgrims, take them to the main temple, help them buy the objects they need for ritual worship, and facilitate their entry into the temple. It is understood that the pilgrims will serve them with a love offering. They have no incentive to offer their services either to sadhus or to devotees from the local area, for sadhus have no money and the local people already know their way to the temple.

The man accompanying Swamiji seemed to be one of these priests, and so Swamiji thought it odd that he was being so helpful. But the priest kept up such a stream of chatter that Swamiji had no time to explore the man's intentions. The priest kept abruptly changing the subject in the middle of a sentence, and it occurred to Swamiji that the man might be mentally unbalanced. While talking about Rama, he would ask whether Swamiji had ever been to Ayodhya, and then boast about himself—how well he knew the city, how he would take Swamiji all the way to Rama, how when Swamiji reached there anything he asked would be given to him, how no one he had taken to Mother Sita had ever returned empty-handed, and so on. Swamiji began to wonder if it had been a mistake to accompany this priest, but just as he was considering leaving him, they reached the gate of the Kanak Bhawan temple.

Pointing to a small statue of Hanuman outside, the priest said, "While you do your *puja* here, let me see how things are inside." Swamiji had no ritual objects, nor was he accustomed to performing rituals, so he simply stood in front of the statue of Hanuman. The priest turned to enter the temple gates, but before he had gone more than a few yards he seemed to dissolve among the handful of visitors on their way inside. And seeing this, Swamiji realized that the priest was Hanuman himself. With awe and gratitude, he entered the temple and offered the blossoms of his love and devotion to Sita and Rama, the mother and father of the universe. Then he set out on the trail of Rama.

Swamiji told me about this incident in 1992 while he was talking about some of his experiences with his guru brother Nantin Baba, a young mystic who lived in the Kumayun Himalayas most of the time.

An ardent devotee of Sita and Rama and well-known for his mastery of hatha yoga, Nantin Baba spent the summers in the Himalayas and the winters in Chitrakut and south India. He was fond of pilgrimages, especially to places associated with Lord Rama, and during these journeys he would stop at sites of special significance and recite a Hindi (and sometimes a Sanskrit) version of the *Ramayana*. According to Nantin Baba, the moment you begin to recite the *Ramayana* Hanuman in his subtle form comes to listen.

Nantin Baba's favorite pilgrimage route was the trail Rama followed during his exile, and he had invited Swamiji to make this journey with him several times. But Swamiji never felt inspired to accept. It was only after Babaji instructed him to visit Ayodhya and receive the blessings of Hanuman, Sita, and Rama before he embarked on this pilgrimage that Swamiji began to understand its importance. His encounter with Hanuman in the guise of a priest had opened his heart and filled him with enthusiasm for setting out on the trail of Rama, and he was hoping to travel with Nantin Baba. He knew that during the month of Shravana Nantin Baba was usually to be found in Chitrakut, the region Rama had visited first after setting out from Ayodhya, and he knew that he was not likely to set out on the trail south until the monsoons had passed in the beginning of September. If he combined train, bus, and walking, Swamiji could reach Chitrakut in a matter of days. But he did not want to go by train or bus, because Lord Rama walked this trail barefoot. Furthermore, he wanted to stop at those spots where Rama had stopped for a time. Thus all he could do was pray he would reach Chitrakut before Nantin Baba left.

Swamiji's first stop was Nandigram, about which Swamiji said, "Deception has no power to withstand the air of this place. If someone meditates here even for fourteen days without pretense, freedom from greed and possessiveness is guaranteed. The fortunate aspirant is blessed with insight and the inner strength to discharge his duties selflessly and lovingly."

Before 1992 I had never heard Swamiji make such a strong statement about any sacred place and the importance of visiting and doing practices there. I had been living in the West for more than thirteen years by then, and to some degree I had lost sight of Swamiji's true identity. Many Westerners held him in high esteem as a pioneer in the field of holistic health, and since coming to the United States I had been constantly hearing that he was a great yogi with extraordinary control over his autonomic nervous system and heart, and hearing him lecture again and again on topics related to the health and integration of the body, breath, and mind, his core identity as a Himalayan sage who had spent much of his life in meditation was no longer in the front of my mind. The message he had been giving in the West was "Go within and find within. The Lord of Life resides in the inner chamber of your heart." And even though the Himalayan Institute organized trips to holy sites in the Himalayas under his supervision at least once a year, Swamiji never spoke directly about their sanctity.

198

In 1983 when Swamiji told me about Mount Kailas, I thought that it was special because both Swamiji's master and grandmaster lived there. In 1985 I saw him overcome with emotion when he shared his experience of the vision of the Divine Mother at the Temple of Sixty-four Yoginis in Khajuraho. But at that time my interpretation was that Khajuraho was special because Babaji spent his time there and because it was there that Swamiji had the vision of the Divine Mother. But in 1992, when he began talking about sage Durvasa and his role as the custodian of Ujjain, my understanding of these spiritual sites began to take on a new dimension.

A few days after he told me about his encounter with sage Durvasa in Ujjain, Swamiji told me about his journey on the trail of Rama. Nandigram, the first stop after Ayodhya, is less than fifty miles from the village where I was born. According to scripture, Rama's brother Bharata had lived there for the fourteen years of Rama's exile, and in that region it is customary to go to Nandigram before setting out on any pilgrimage, to worship Bharata and perform the ancestral rites. The town was full of priests who helped pilgrims perform the rites, and then the pilgrims would go on to Banaras, Gaya, and the four standard pilgrimage sites in the four corners of India: Puri in the east, Rameshwaram in the south, Dwarka in the west, and Badrinath-Kedarnath in the north. I never thought of Nandigram itself as having any spiritual significance.

My own visit to Nandigram had been uneventful. I had gone there as a young man at the instruction of a saint, Baba Ram Mangal Das, who lived in Ayodhya. He was said to be a devotee of Rama as well as an adept in the practice of Sri Vidya—the most esoteric practice of tantra. He was also known for his clairvoyance. Language, time, and space posed no barrier to him—he could communicate with anyone, alive or dead. When he was in the mood, he would talk about great souls, like the Vedic sages, Buddha, Abraham Lincoln, George Washington, and Guru Nanakdeva, as well as those whose greatness was overlooked, even by those nearest to them. Baba Ram Mangal Das spoke of such people as if he had lived with them, not as if he were telling a story about them. People believed that he often traveled to holy sites throughout the world in his subtle body and that the great souls also visited him at his ashram in Ayodhya. Once in a while he shared these experiences with his students, who wrote them down and published them.

199

Baba Ram Mangal Das instructed me to go to Nandigram but did not tell me why. When I arrived I was approached by priests, but when they realized I was not a pilgrim they immediately lost interest in me. The barbers were puzzled, for I did not comply with their request to shave my head. (The standard practice is for pilgrims to have their heads shaved and take a bath before performing the ancestral rites.) Not knowing why Baba Ram Mangal Das had sent me there, I wandered aimlessly. But when I returned to the saint he said, "Your soul has been cleansed with the nectar of Bharata Maharaj's love for Rama"—a comment that made no sense to me at the time.

Years later, when Swamiji told me that deception is powerless to withstand the air of Nandigram and that practice done there without pretense bestows freedom from possessiveness, I wondered why. I had noticed nothing special about the place. So I asked him why it was associated with ancestors and why spiritual seekers attach no particular significance to it.

Swamiji explained that when Rama went into the forest, his father, Dasharatha, died from grief. His brother Bharata was next in line to perform his father's funeral and post-funeral rites (shraddha), and because Bharata had lived in Nandigram after his father's death, people believed that he had performed the rites there. Thus they came to associate Nandigram with ancestral rites. But the yogis know that while he was there Bharata undertook an intense practice of austerities and meditation. An ideal son, brother, renunciate, ruler, and yogi, Bharata was one of those rare souls who were completely free from all desires. He sacrificed his life for Rama, ruling the kingdom for fourteen years but never claiming to be king. And all the while he lived in Nandigram he was accompanied by great sages, such as Vasishtha, Jabali, and others. Thus Nandigram and the surrounding area is so charged with the spiritual energy of self-discipline, non-possessiveness, and selfless love that one's practices can be speeded up almost without effort, provided that the aspirant's heart is open to Rama's love, as Bharata's was. What is more, according to the scriptures, that great yogi did not sleep for the fourteen years he did his sadhana there, and so Nandigram is especially conducive to the practice of *yoga nidra* (yogic sleep).

Swamiji told me he resumed his journey to Chitrakut after a short stay at Nandigram, but on the way he stopped at Belha Mai, a beautiful site on the bank of the Sai River. According to legend, Rama and his party arrived there in the evening. The next day Rama bathed in the river and worshipped the Divine Mother, and responding to his prayer, she appeared and blessed him. This took place at dawn, and so she came to be known as Bela Devi ("the goddess who appeared at dawn"). But as time passed the word became slightly distorted, and she is now known as Belha Devi or Belha Mai.

Swamiji's next stop was Shringberapur, a famous pilgrimage site near Allahabad, where the boatman Nishada insisted on washing Rama's feet before letting him sit in his boat. This episode in the *Ramayana* is still celebrated in Indian folklore. As the story goes, this boatman, the chief of his tribe, had been Rama's friend in youth. When they were students living in the ashram of their teacher Vasishtha, he had sensed Rama's divine nature, but custom prevented him from expressing it. When Rama needed to cross the Ganga en route to Chitrakut, however, Nishada claimed the honor of ferrying him across the river. His deepest wish was to worship Rama as a divine being and to honor him as a prince. But Rama insisted on treating him as a friend of equal status. A long dialogue ensued in which Nishada, through his unpretentious love and humility, won Rama's consent to wash his feet and worship him as a devotee worships God. And after Nishada had rowed the party across the river, Rama tried to give him a ring as fare, but the boatman refused to accept it, saying, "O Lord, keep this ring, and when the time comes, row me across the river flowing between life here and hereafter." Thus Shringberapur is identified with Rama's love for all and for the dissolution of the barriers of caste, creed, and social status that divide one person from another. Even today, on auspicious bathing days, groups of women flock to the Ganga singing about this episode in their own melodious dialect.

Continuing along the ancient trail, Swamiji next reached Prayaga Raja, now known as Allahabad. There hundreds of people knew him. He usually stayed with the Tandon family whenever he was in the city, but this time he had come as a pilgrim and so it was not appropriate to accept their hospitality. Trying to follow the trail as faithfully as possible, he went directly to the ashram of the sage Bharadwaja, where according to the *Ramayana,* Rama himself had spent a few days. This place is now occupied by a cluster of temples dedicated to various gods and goddesses, as well as to sage Bharadwaja. Swamiji told me that during the time of Lord Rama, Bharadwaja ashram was situated on the bank of the Ganga, but down through the centuries the river has changed its course and three or four miles of the city now lie between the ashram and the river.

From 1972 through 1979 I lived in Allahabad, just across the road from Bharadwaja ashram. The school of Saint Anthony is on one side of it, and Anand Bhavan, the residence of India's first prime minister, Jawaharlal Nehru, is on the other. Each January I saw crowds of tourists visiting Anand Bhavan and considerably fewer people paying their homage at the one-room temple dedicated to the sage—hardly anyone except residents of Allahabad ever visits Bharadwaja ashram. To me it was only a place to get my groceries and participate in the annual nine-day celebration of Nava Ratri, organized by the local Bengali community.

But as soon as Swamiji mentioned Bharadwaja ashram in the context of his pilgrimage I knew that there must be something unique about this place—something known only to the adepts—and my heart jumped. When I asked him what it was, he explained that Rama had done a special practice there. The standard version of the *Ramayana* glorifies Rama as an incarnation of Lord Vishnu, and the author, Tulsidasa, his ardent devotee, feels no need to describe the spiritual practices that enabled Rama to realize his divine self. But the most ancient version of the *Ramayana,* written by Valmiki, portrays Rama as an ideal man, and in that context it tells us how Rama studied at the feet of the masters, how he undertook intense practices, and how— through self-effort, the blessing of the sages, and the grace of the Divine—he was able to unfold his dormant potentials to their fullest. Tradition has it that in Prayaga Raja, under the guidance of sage Bharadwaja, Rama undertook a practice related to the most valiant aspect of Shakti: Kali, the devourer of time and the conqueror of death. A tiny temple, now known as Kali Mandir, has been built on the spot where Rama meditated on her and received her blessings. Since the beginning of time Prayaga Raja—that is, Allahabad—has been the center of Shakti sadhana. Whenever the Earth has suffered from man-made catastrophes the sages have propitiated the Divine here, and through their efforts they have been able to generate a collective consciousness powerful enough to restore the health and well-being of the planet and the creatures that inhabit it.

I had already read in the scriptures some of what Swamiji told me, but the specific information about Rama meditating on the goddess Kali was completely new. According to the scriptures there are fifty-one Shakti shrines, including Allahabad, scattered throughout India. Lalita (also known as Sri Vidya) is the form of Shakti that presides over this holy city. Yet the impression I got from Swamiji was that Kali is the presiding deity of Allahabad and that the area of Bharadwaja ashram is its spiritual center. I was convinced that if the conversation could be prolonged I would learn something which is found only in the oral tradition.

So I asked Swamiji, "I know from the *Ramayana* that before going into the deeper parts of the forests in central and south India, Rama stopped here and met sage Bharadwaja. It also appears from the *Ramayana* that the sage knew Rama was a divine incarnation and requested that he spend the period of his exile here in his ashram. Rama refused, saying it was too close to Ayodhya, that his presence would attract so many people from Ayodhya that the ashram would be disturbed. Instead he sought the sage's advice about where he should live. The answer he received—'Tell me, O Lord, the place where you do not already exist'—clearly indicates that the sage was an ardent devotee. But as you described it, sage Bharadwaja was also Rama's teacher and an adept of Shakti sadhana, especially the Kali-related practices."

"The sage Bharadwaja was a Sri Vidya adept," Swamiji replied. "There are many names for Sri Vidya. Among the most popular are Lalita and Tripura. Before he moved to Prayaga Raja, Bharadwaja's main abode was the Kashmir Himalayas; the place where he did his Sri Vidya practice is now known as Sri Nagar. He was a great teacher and it was under his leadership that the Kashmir region of the Himalayas became the educational capital of the subcontinent."

203

Swamiji, who always refrained from discussing social issues, now began alluding to them. He said that the Kashmiris have forgotten their roots. People of any caste in India who bear Bharadwaja as their last name, he said, or those whose *gotra* (lineage name) is Bharadwaja, are direct descendants of this sage. One of Bharadwaja's students undertook an intense practice of Sri Vidya under his supervision and as a result received a direct vision of the Divine Mother. So when sage Bharadwaja decided to move to Prayaga Raja he ordained that student to carry on the tradition in Kashmir by putting a *tika* (dot) on the forehead. Therefore that student, and later his descendants, came to be known as Tikavan; and as time passed, these families came to be known as Tiku. Even today the Tikus in Kashmir worship Sri Vidya as their *kula devi* (family goddess) under the name Tripura.

Swamiji said that it was sad that the children of this great sage no longer remember their heritage. Most of them have left Kashmir, and once disconnected from their roots, the sublime knowledge they once possessed becomes dormant in their genes. Looking at me, he said (it was 1992), "One day I want you to remind these children and wake them up. Kashmir is a beautiful place. By knowing their heritage and their connection with the sages, they can create a heaven there or in any other part of the world."

As he answered my questions, Swamiji explained that while Rama was going into exile in the forest, sage Bharadwaja had instructed him to meditate on Kali, the valiant form of the Divine Mother. When he returned from exile, however, Rama stopped in the vicinity of Prayaga Raja and meditated on Lalita, the most beautiful and benign form of the Divine Mother. The place where he did this second practice is a few miles south of Bharadwaja ashram, near the Yamuna River. Swamiji stopped there and paid homage to her before going on.

When he arrived in Chitrakut, Swamiji was relieved to find that Nantin Baba was still there, and for his part Nantin Baba was happy that his friend would be joining him on this auspicious journey. Nantin Baba was a yogi of high caliber, as well as a devotee, fully immersed in the love of Rama. In the kind of *bhakti yoga* (the yoga of love and devotion) he practiced, known as *sakhya bhakti*, God is treated as a friend, and Nantin Baba was indeed Rama's friend. Like Rama, he wore his hair in a topknot and applied sandalwood paste to his forehead. He looked like Rama and behaved like Rama, and he advised Swamiji to do the same during the journey. This would help him maintain a constant awareness of Rama, he said. He often sang a song that can be translated as "Inside Rama, outside Rama, Rama everywhere."

Swamiji translated *The Valmiki Ramayana* in the early nineties, and in the introduction he writes, "During those days, Nantin Baba and I dressed exactly as Rama had dressed, according to the description in Valmiki's *Ramayana*. When we encountered hermits on our journey, they were amazed at the sight of us. Many of them thought we were avatars of Rama and Lakshmana, but this was a case of mistaken identity that we did not relish or enjoy, because we sought to avoid contact with people."

Swamiji had stayed in Chitrakut on several earlier occasions, but Nantin Baba's knowledge of the place far exceeded his. It was like a home to him. While they were there, Swamiji and Nantin Baba stayed at Hanuman Dhara, a holy cave just below the crown of a hill, which contains a statue of Hanuman. Hanuman Dhara—meaning "stream of Hanuman"—takes its name from the stream that flows from the cave. Before meditating on Rama at various sites in the Chitrakut area, an aspirant must meditate on Hanuman in this cave.

Sita Rasoi ("the kitchen of Sita") lies on the crown of the hill above Hanuman Dhara. Legend has it that this is where Rama, Sita, and Rama's brother Lakshmana lived when they first arrived in Chitrakut, and the central pilgrimage spot is where Sita prepared their meals. Faithful devotees believe that the Divine Mother, in the form of Sita, still cooks here for her family, which consists of her beloved Rama and all of Rama's friends and devotees.

Swamiji said, "While we stayed at Hanuman Dhara we went to Sita Rasoi every day."

Seizing the moment, I asked, "Swamiji, did you get your meals from her kitchen?"

I noticed Swamiji dissolving into emptiness for a second before replying softly, "The whole world is her kitchen. That is why creation continues to thrive."

Perhaps the most significant site in Chitrakut is Kamada Giri. When Swamiji spoke of this place he had a hard time getting the words out, and it was clear that his experiences there were too precious to share. When he finally spoke he said, "There are a few places on the Earth which have a non-earthly dimension, and Kamada Giri is one of them. Rama lived here for four years of his exile. Hundreds of sages joined him in meditation and they wanted to accompany him when he left for the south, but Rama asked them to remain at Kamada Giri, promising to stay here in his subtle form for eternity. And because it is the eternal abode of Rama, sages who consider *bhakti* [love for Rama] superior to *mukti* [liberation] have merged in this mountain. These sages are kind and generous. They fulfill the desires of the pilgrims who visit this site, and that is why this mountain is called Kamada Giri ["the fulfiller of all desires"]. How pitiable are those who think of anything other than the Lord of Life while they are here."

Swamiji did not tell me how long he and Nantin Baba remained at Kamada Giri, but he did say that both of them recited the

Ramayana all day long while they were there. And because the standard practice is to complete the entire *Ramayana* in nine days, my guess is they must have stayed there for at least that long.

As winter commences in India, the sun becomes less intense and the mosquitoes disappear. By the end of September the monsoon is over, the rivers become passable again, and the vegetation that chokes the paths during the rainy season dies out. This is the time the pilgrimage along the trail of Rama traditionally begins. In the introduction to his translation of *The Valmiki Ramayana,* Swamiji gives some details about his journey with Nantin Baba:

"On the day of the *purnima* (full moon), resolving not to take with us anything except one blanket, a walking staff, and a water pot, we set out toward the beautiful spot known as Anasuya. (Many sites are known by the names of the renowned sages who once resided there.) This is one of the most picturesque places in the Chitrakut forest. Here we watched the wild animals, saw the huge beehives that hung on the cliffs, and heard the tigers roaring all around us. With the *Ramayana* in our hands, we passed one night on the bank of the Mandakini River. During our journey, we made a fire and spent each night beside it in meditation. We had been instructed by our master not to sleep or nap at night but to take our rest [for] at least three hours after having our noonday meal. . . .

"We did not depend on householders or hermits for our food or sustenance. For food, we would dig up and boil tarura roots, and several other kinds of roots, including gainthi, which is delicious and nourishing. Sometimes the householders who dwelt in the small villages of the area crossed our paths and offered us sattu, a food made of fried gram flour. Life in those days was joyous in a manner that is inexplicable. Words cannot convey the experiences of our journey in a way that does them full justice."

When they left Chitrakut, Swamiji and Nantin Baba went to Sharabhanga, a few miles south. The great sage Sharabhanga had lived at this site. According to the *Ramayana,* when this sage had completed his normal span of life, Indra, the king of the gods, himself descended to accompany Sharabhanga on his ascent to heaven. But knowing that during his exile Rama would visit him, the sage declined Indra's invitation and remained in the ashram instead, resolving to cast off his body only after seeing Rama in the flesh. Many sages in Chitrakut, including Atri and Anasuya, knew about this, and therefore the sage Atri asked Rama to visit Sharabhanga on his way to southern India. When Rama arrived, Sharabhanga offered his homage and then instantly left his body in a manner now known as spontaneous combustion. The place has been considered sacred ever since.

From there, pilgrims generally travel to the nearby town of Satna to catch a train for Nasik, the site of Sita's abduction, several hundred miles to the south. But by doing so they skip many important places where Rama lived and did his practices. According to Swamiji, before setting out on the trail of Rama one must study not only the *Ramayana* but also other scriptures in which Rama's journey is documented, the *Padma Purana* foremost among them.

207

Swamiji and Nantin Baba followed the trail of Rama set forth in the *Padma Purana,* first going from Sharabhanga to Orchha, in Madhya Pradesh. But before reaching Orchha they stopped at a beautiful hilltop Shakti shrine known as Maihar. There, according to local belief, an immortal yogi, Alha, worships the goddess in the early morning before the priests open the temple. According to scriptural sources, in ancient times the Shakti at this shrine was associated with the fine arts, but people nowadays believe she is a goddess who fulfills the worldly desires of her devotees, and so Maihar has become a tantric shrine where the worship is often done with wine and other ingredients pertaining to the left-hand path of tantra.

Their destination, Orchha, is a small town that has been overlooked as a spiritual site in modern times. But masters like Nantin Baba and Swamiji, well-versed in both the scriptures and the wisdom of the tradition, trace the history of Orchha back to the Vedic period. Later, during the time of Rama, it was an important Shiva shrine, and Rama did his sadhana there under the guidance of sage Atri. In the *Padma Purana* this place is known as Rikshavan.

Rikshavan was forgotten until the nineteenth century, when the queen of Orchha dreamed that she visited Lord Rama in Ayodhya. In the dream he told her how much he loved Orchha and how grateful he was to that place, for it was there that he received the blessings of Shiva. He also told her that he missed Orchha and wished she could take him there. The queen woke up eager to visit Ayodhya and bring Rama to Orchha. So she built a temple in the palace, and while it was under construction she went to Ayodhya and found the statues of Rama and his family that she had seen in her dream. She brought them back to Orchha on the back of an elephant, accompanied by chariots, horses, and an entire retinue. (The story of Rama's regal journey from Ayodhya to Orchha is still told in both towns today.) Once in Orchha, the statues were installed at the altar of the temple, which is known as Raghu Nath Mandir.

When he and Nantin Baba reached Orchha, Swamiji had to resort to a bit of trickery. The small kingdoms of Orchha and neighboring Tikam Garh were intimately associated with the family of Bhole Baba's wife. And even though Bhole Baba had renounced the householder's life and had been ordained as Swami Rama, a visit to Orchha would have created a stir. So to avoid being recognized, he hid himself in ragged clothing during his short visit to the temple, and the two sadhus left Orchha immediately afterward.

Continuing to follow the trail described in the *Padma Purana,* Nantin Baba and Swamiji next traveled westward to Pushkar, in Rajasthan, where according to the scriptures the first and grandest *yajña* (group meditation) ever was performed. Sponsored by the creator, Brahma himself, all the gods, sages, humans, demons, snakes, birds, and forces of nature participated in this *yajña,* and there for the first time in history the wisdom of the Vedas was brought into practice.

This was so long ago that the description of Pushkar in the scriptures bears little resemblance to the region today. Then there were three hills and three lakes. The Sarasvati River originated in one of the lakes and flowed from there to the ocean. Now the river and two of the lakes have vanished and the one remaining body of water is so diminished that it can hardly be called a lake. In modern Hinduism, Pushkar is the only place exclusively associated with Brahma, the creator; the adjacent town, Ajmer, is the holiest site in India for Muslims and Sufis.

Before entering Pushkar, Nantin Baba gave discourses to Swamiji about the area—how this place came to be so holy, what the exact pilgrimage sites were, the kind of practices traditionally done there, which great personalities in the past lived and practiced there, the circumstances under which Rama had visited Pushkar, the practice he undertook there, and so on.

Beginning in Chitrakut and continuing to this point, Swamiji and Nantin Baba had been reciting the *Ramayana* every day. Here in Pushkar they decided to do a complete recitation of the *Padma Purana* instead, and undertook a formal scripture recitation called *parayana*. To this end, Swamiji and Nantin Baba found accommodations in a *dharamshala* (guesthouse), where they cleaned the room and prepared three seats: one for the teacher, one for the scripture, and the third for the student. At Swamiji's request Nantin Baba assumed the role of teacher while Swamiji assumed the role of student. Then, following the scriptural injunctions, Swamiji worshipped Nantin Baba as a representative of the sage Vyasa, the author of the *Padma Purana*. As part of the practice they took a bath every morning in the small lake, paid their homage to Lord Brahma, did their meditation, and then had a light meal. In the afternoon they returned to the room, where Nantin Baba took his seat and recited the scripture, expounding on the most relevant portions.

During the sixteen years I was in Swamiji's presence I never saw him reading a book, and could not imagine him sitting in front of someone who read to him. Yet I knew that scriptural recitations are a form of spiritual practice and I was curious about where he and Nantin Baba had gotten a copy of the *Padma Purana*. When I asked him, he replied that they did not have one—Nantin Baba had read the scripture many, many times and knew it by heart. The current version of the *Padma Purana* is actually a compendium of stories, many of which also appear in other scriptures, but to Nantin Baba the *Padma Purana* was a living entity, not a book. He invoked it in his copy of the *Ramayana* and placed it on the seat reserved for the scripture being recited. And every afternoon he told the stories from memory, which is how the scriptures were recited in ancient times.

As soon as Swamiji told me that Nantin Baba had told the stories from memory, I had a mischievous thought: I had read this scripture and found it to be a lengthy manual of typical Hindu sacraments, a textbook of codes of conduct, a guide to holy sites (including Pushkar), and a description of the etiquette associated with the caste system. I knew that Swamiji did not believe in the caste system—but what about Nantin Baba? I asked Swamiji, and he said that in Nantin Baba's version of the *Padma Purana* there was no caste system and no rituals. Yogis like Nantin Baba, he said, do not carry the burden of books: they are the creators and destroyers of the books. Like the scriptures that belong to other religions, Hindu scriptures have been contaminated by the selfishness of priests. Yogis intuitively know which portions of a scripture are genuine and which are interpolations.

210   Then I asked Swamiji how I would know which portions had been interpolated, and he told me to bring him a copy of the *Padma Purana*. At the time, the only copy I had was an abridged Hindi translation published by the Gita Press in Gorakhpur. When I handed it to him, he opened it to the table of contents and crossed out more than half the chapters. Removing his glasses, he commented, "Most of the material in these chapters either describes the values and standards of life in vogue during the Vedic period or propagates the idea of sin and instills fear and guilt. These chapters have nothing to do with the teachings of the sages. They reflect the hypocritical posturing of the priests and pandits who copied the manuscripts down through the centuries."

Then I asked Swamiji if there was a particular episode that Nantin Baba had expounded at length. Glancing at the table of contents, he put his finger on a certain chapter and said, "This is one. Go and read it."

I went to my office down the hall and read the story. It goes like this:

One day King Prabhanjana set out on a pleasure hunt in Pushkar's vast forest. It was teeming with wildlife, and after a short time he spied a doe lying under a bush. Although he knew that creatures living on sacred ground should not be killed, he shot her. The doe was wounded, but to his surprise she made no attempt to escape. And as the king drew closer she spoke to him. "You foolish man," she said, "look what you have done. This was not the appropriate time to hunt me—I was nursing my baby beneath this bush—nor is this the appropriate place to hunt. You well know that this forest is a spiritual site. Because of your actions you will have to be reborn as a beast and live on raw meat."

In terror the king threw himself on the ground before her. "Please forgive me!" he cried. "I acknowledge that I have trespassed on this sacred site, but I did not see your fawn. In that respect I am innocent. Have mercy on me."

"A hundred years from today," the doe replied, "you will encounter a cow named Nanda. When she tells you her name, this punishment will end. But during your life as a lion, you must pause a moment each time before you kill your prey. After you have captured it, explain that anyone falling into your grip is your food and thus you have the right to kill it."

With those words, both doe and king died, and from the king's body there arose a mighty lion. It was unusually large and fierce, and except for a curious habit of pausing for a few moments before killing its prey, it had all the instincts of its kind.

A hundred years passed as the lion hunted in the forest, always following the doe's injunction. Then one day a group of cowherds entered the forest with their cows, and finding a clearing with good pasture and water, they decided to settle down for a while. So they fenced a small area to protect the cows at night and built a few huts for themselves, and soon the place rang with the mooing of cows and the flutes of cowherds.

The biggest and the healthiest cow in the herd was Nanda. She was wise, fearless, and content, but one day she wandered off to graze and was attacked by the lion. As was his habit, he paused before killing her and said, "Today providence has sent you as my food."

"It is impossible for me to protect myself from you," Nanda replied calmly. "Death is inevitable, whether it comes now or comes later. But O king of beasts, I gave birth only a few days ago. My milk is the only source of sustenance for my calf. Even now he is hungry and waiting for me to return. How will he survive if you kill me? Please let me go. I will nurse my calf and give him a few lessons on how to survive. And then, after entrusting him to my friends, I will return to you."

"Your fearlessness indicates that you are wise," replied the lion. "But your attachment to your child belies your wisdom. In this, the last moment of your life, why do you worry about your son?"

Nanda said only, "Please trust me and let me go. If I don't return, may I incur the sin incurred by killing an enlightened sage or a parent. If I violate my promise, may I incur the sins incurred by abusing an animal, failing to help a friend in need, or disrupting another's spiritual practice. Knowing these to be the most heinous of sins, I will certainly return."

"You may go," the lion replied. "See your calf once more. Give him your milk, lick his forehead, and commend him to the care of your friends. Then return promptly."

Nanda set off for the cowherds' enclosure, and when the calf saw his mother approaching he romped for joy. But when she neared him he saw that her manner was grave, and asked her why. Nanda said quietly, "Son, fill yourself with my milk, for I do not know whose milk you will be drinking tomorrow. This is our last meeting. I have promised a hungry lion that I will return and surrender myself to him."

"I will come with you, Mother," the calf cried. "Without you I will die anyway; I would rather die with you!"

"Embracing death in an emotional fit is suicide," Nanda replied sternly. "The best way to love and serve me is to stay here. Now listen to my advice.

"While you are grazing in the forest or drinking from a stream do not be careless, for it is through carelessness that creatures bring about their own destruction. Do not let your greed for fodder lead you to graze in dangerous places, for greed invites failure both here and hereafter.

"Do not be gullible and do not follow anyone blindly. Carelessness, greed, and blind faith are your worst enemies. Do not trust anyone until you have tested them. And do not place your total faith even in someone who seems to be trustworthy, for such trust sooner or later invites fear. For the deliverance of your soul love all, but for your peace of mind, trust only God.

"Make all efforts to protect yourself. Keep yourself healthy but never fear death, for death is the only certainty that life affords. Just as a traveler rests in the shade for a time before continuing his journey, so do we meet for a while before continuing on to our destination. Free yourself from grief."

When Nanda had finished talking to her son, she licked his

forehead and then went to her friends and said, "You are healthy and generous, and you have the means to help others. Please protect my helpless child. For the sake of truth, I must return to the lion."

She then walked in a circle around the entire herd and paid homage to earth, water, fire, air, space, sun, moon, stars, and the protectors of the ten directions, as well as the trees and animals in the forest of Pushkar. "May all the forces of nature and all the divine beings living here in visible or invisible form protect my son and give me the strength to follow the path of truth," she prayed.

Then Nanda returned to the lion. "I have come," she told him. "Please satisfy your hunger with my meat."

But instead of killing her the lion paid her homage. "I have not experienced peace for a long time," he said. "My life has been governed by anger and hunger. But after talking to you, I realize that the practice of truth is the highest of all practices. Blessed is the land where you reside; blessed are those who drink your milk. After seeing you, I have lost interest in life. As a lion I have killed thousands of animals to satisfy my hunger. My instinct forces me to hunt, yet today some inner prompting tells me that life holds more than eating, sleeping, aging, and dying. But I am a lion and have no control over my appetites. Please tell me how I may attain peace of mind and come to know the higher purpose of life."

The cow replied, "My dear brother, in this dark age of ours, charity is the best way to attain peace of mind and come to know the higher goal of life. One who helps others merges in Brahman at the time of death."

"Now I know who you must be!" the lion exclaimed. "You are the embodiment of the blessing I received from the doe I killed a hundred years ago when I was a king! Please deliver me from the bondage of this body and the habits associated with it. I beg you to tell me your name."

"Nanda," she said.

Instantly the lion died and the king rose from its corpse.

As I read this story I tried my best to maintain an attitude of faith in the scriptures, but still a question remained: People hunt animals, and yet the king had to live as a lion for a hundred years because he killed that doe in a sacred place. That seemed harsh. When I next saw Swamiji he asked right away, "Did you read that?" I said I had, and expressed

213

my feelings about the harshness of the king's punishment. "That's the point," Swamiji said. "Actions, good or bad, performed at such sites bear fruit instantly. The king was not an ignorant person: he knew the importance of that place; he also knew creatures living there should not be harmed. Yet he acted against his own knowledge, and an offense committed by one who knows what he is doing is more serious than an offense committed by one who is ignorant. Had the doe been killed by someone driven by hunger who had no knowledge of the sanctity of that place, the act would not have had such drastic consequences."

Then, changing the subject, Swamiji began to talk about the importance of scripture recitation and the value of making a pilgrimage. He explained that to grasp the true intent of a scripture it must be read three times: first you read it before going on the pilgrimage; then you read it at the pilgrimage site; and finally you read it as a means of teaching others and sharing your experiences. He said that if we go on a pilgrimage without knowing the significance of the holy site we visit, we will come back as ignorant as before. Using stories as a tool, the scriptures introduce these places to us and acquaint us with the sages and divine beings living there. Then when we arrive, these places recognize us.

Referring to one of the discourses that Nantin Baba gave in Pushkar, Swamiji said that a seeker must not carry the luggage of logic while visiting sacred sites. He stressed the importance of having faith in the scriptures and being convinced that everything written in them is absolutely true. When you reach the holy site, try to find the places described in the scriptures, he advised. If you don't find them easily, order your intellect to discover them. Ask your heart to convince your intellect that the physical location is simply a doorway to another dimension of reality.

Swamiji explained that the scriptures are an embodiment of revealed knowledge and that the sages to whom those scriptures were revealed are immortal. They are omnipresent—time and space present no barrier to them. The moment you invoke them, they are there. Every holy site has its corresponding scripture, and it is important to read that scripture while you are there. The second reading is totally different from the first—this time it is a spiritual practice. And if you treat the

બેટે !
મેરા આશીષ
मुरल मोड़ जगासे
हो अग्रसर આध्यात्म पथ पर
अवधूत
गंगोत्री हर्दर्द

The future Swami Rama—from his student days to his tenure as Shankaracharya

The view from the trail between Gangotri and Gomukh

The young Bhole Baba

Above: Swamiji's beloved Himalayan peaks

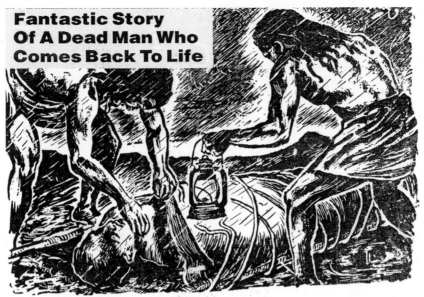

Fantastic Story Of A Dead Man Who Comes Back To Life

DARSAN DAS HELD THE LANTERN WHILE LOK DAS UNCOVERED THE BODY, HE PLACED HIS HAND OVER THE MOUTH. "THIS MAN IS ALIVE," SHOUTED DARSAN DAS.

From *Blitz* magazine

The Bhawal Sanyasi as sketched in *Blitz*

Left: Two views of Mount Kailas from the Lhachu Valley

Banaras as seen from the Ganga

Entrance to the temple at Tungnath

The Tungnath temple

The plaque above the door leading to
Babaji's room at Vindhychal, and the
samadhi shrine nearby

Swami Sadananda

Swami Shivananda of
Gangotri

The Badrinath temple

The hanging bridge at Rishikesh, looking toward the Ganga's west bank

Rabindranath Tagore

The bridge at Rishikesh, looking toward the east bank

Mahatma Gandhi

Temples at Chitrakut

The Goddess Chinnamasta

The Jokhang monastery in Lhasa

The Potala Palace

The Shiva temple at Motia Talab

Swamiji as Shankaracharya

The Jokhang temple

Some of the temples at
Omkareshwar

Below: A few of the
many temples at Ayodhya

A view of Ayodhya from the Sarayu River

Swamiji in Japan, circa 1968

With a Mahikari
member on a later visit

Swamiji with Reverend
Okadasan and
Miss Okada

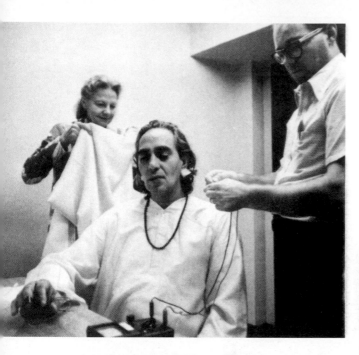

Left: At the Menninger
Foundation with
Dr. Elmer and
Mrs. Alyce Green

Lower left: Receiving an
award from the President
of India

Swamiji at Hansda Ashram in Nepal

The trail to Gomuhk

Hansda Ashram

Swamiji in Nepal, circa 1983

With Pandit Rajmani
and his son, Ishan

"I pray to the Divinity in you."

The temple at Gaya

Swamiji's letter to
Dr. Agnihotri

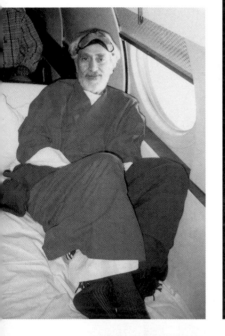

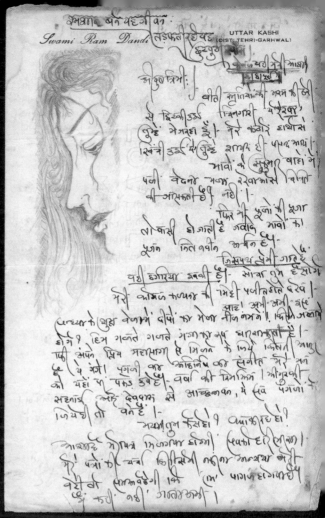

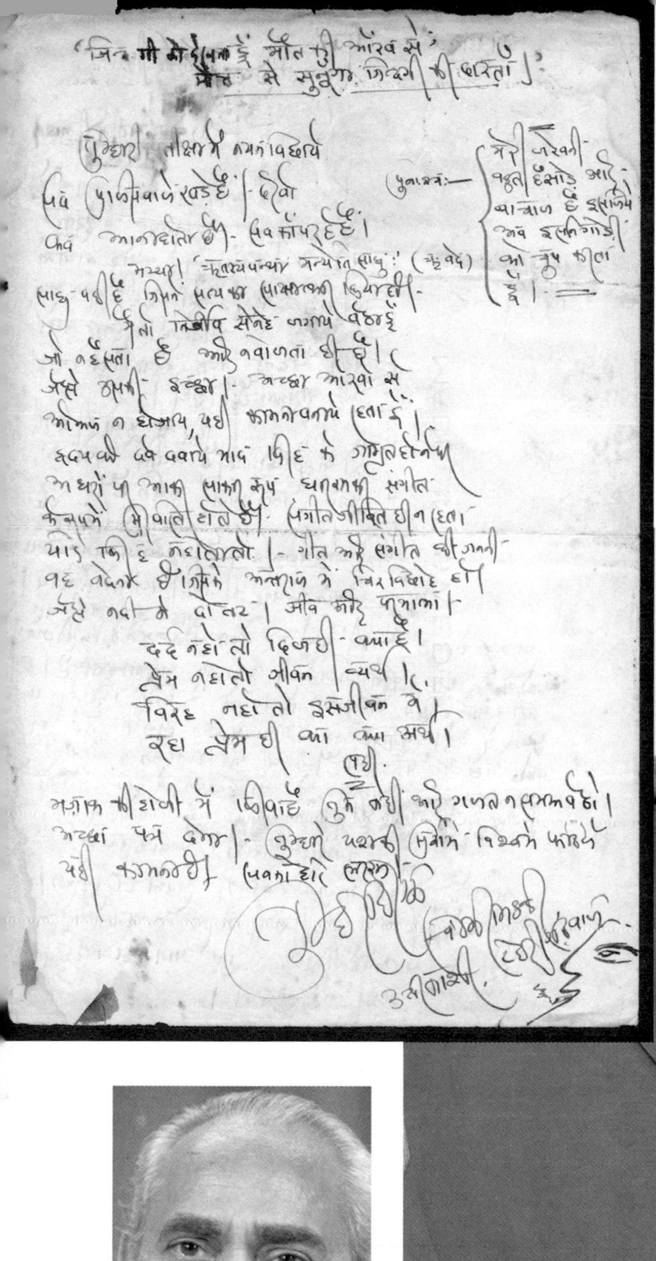

'ज़िन्दगी को देखता हूँ मौत की आँख से;
मौत से सुनता ज़िन्दगी की दास्तां।'

[illegible]

दर्द न हो तो दिल ही क्या है।
प्रेम न हो तो जीवन व्यर्थ है।
विरह न हो तो इस जीवन के,
रहा प्रेम ही का क्या अर्थ।

[illegible]

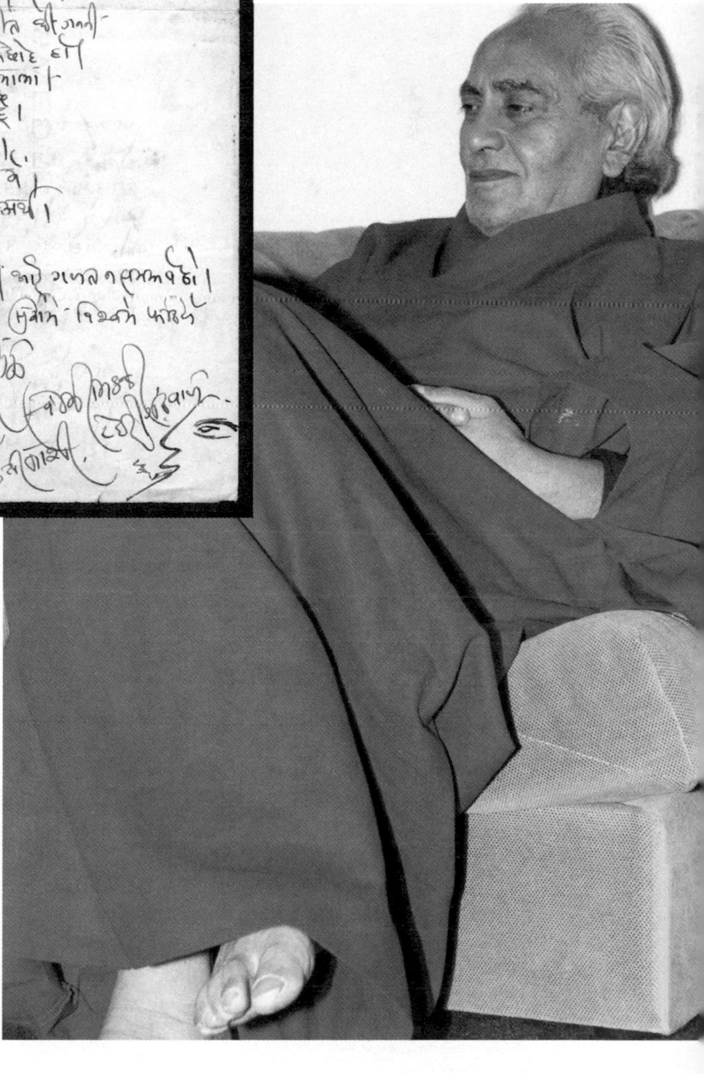

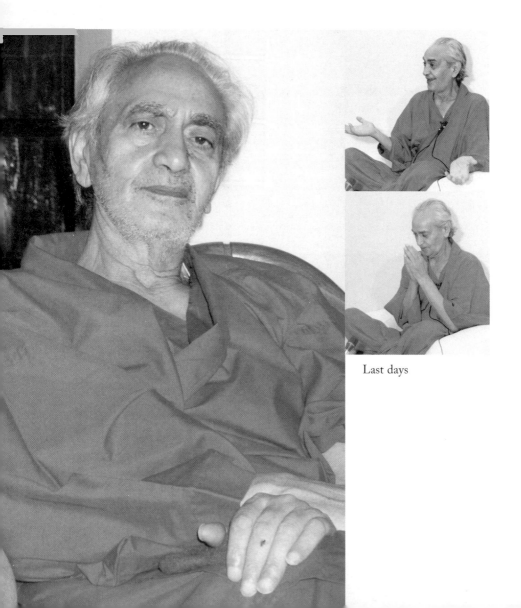

Last days

scripture as an emblem of the spirit of the sages, it will speak to you. The sanctity of the site will enable you to hear it, and your unwavering faith will enable you to understand it. Swamiji also said that it is best if this second reading is done aloud by one who has gained a direct experience of Truth while living at those sites. The role of the pilgrim is simply to listen and reflect on the teachings imparted by that master. This is what is known technically as *parayana* (scripture recitation).

During scripture recitation, Swamiji went on, the practice of austerity—eating, talking, and sleeping less—is of the utmost importance. Avoid all company that distracts you from your primary goal. Don't mix with the local residents and do not associate with those who have come as tourists. Incorporate the teachings into your daily routine, something which is possible only when your consciousness and the consciousness of your teacher operate on the same wavelength. Allow yourself to merge with the teacher.

215

In this environment, Swamiji continued, spiritual virtues such as simplicity, innocence, purity, and sharpness of intellect begin to manifest spontaneously and you no longer hear these stories as stories; rather, they become a living truth. Let intellectuals dismiss them as myth and let others search for a symbolic meaning in them. But if you wish to be a spiritual seeker, you must open your heart and connect it with the hearts of the sages whose consciousness is not confined to this material world. Through the eyes of the soul they see that which cannot be perceived through the senses. Once you become one with them, however, this suprasensible reality is as visible to you as the material world is to ordinary people. Whatever you understand, begin to practice. Whatever you cannot understand, leave to the knowers of the Truth.

Once the recitation of the *Padma Purana* was completed, Nantin Baba and Swamiji left Pushkar for Panchavati, stopping on the way at Vidisha, Ujjain, and Omkareshwar. Panchavati is where Ravana abducted Sita, and its best-known site is the Shiva temple, Tryambakeshwara. The nearest town, Nasik, is approximately a hundred miles northwest of Bombay. To Nantin Baba the whole forest of

Panchavati (the Dandaka forest, which covered most of central and south India in Rama's time), especially the area through which the river flows, was the dwelling place of Rama, and singing the hymns of the *Ramayana,* he and Swamiji roamed the forest. Sharing these experiences, Swamiji wrote:

"Panchavati was infested with deadly, poisonous snakes, but to our surprise we discovered that snakes are the most ancient and intelligent creatures on the Earth; they will not hurt or harm others if they are not disturbed. One day there in the forest, we came across a king cobra standing on its tail, fully extended to a height of ten to twelve feet! It was a thick, black cobra and it created a memorable sight. Without a word, we changed our route.

"Encountering tigers, boars, and other wild animals was part of the daily routine, and on days that we did not happen to see any of these wild forest dwellers, we missed them. After finishing our morning ablutions, we would go to work digging roots, which we later roasted for our day's food. At first we decided not to carry any food for the next day, but after a while we changed our minds and carried a few roots with us. Occasionally we encountered other travelers on the trails that cut across the wild area, and they would offer us jwar, bajara, and other grains or foodstuffs. Sometimes we accepted these gifts. Because the area was so rugged, the entire journey was arduous, but the experiences were thrilling. Whenever we stopped we would first collect wood to make a fire, and we always sat next to it for our daily meditations. We often made our humble dwelling places on the banks of rivers, where we could get water without difficulty."

After traveling more than a month, Nantin Baba and Swamiji arrived at Uti, a large lake in the state of Karnataka near Mysore. It is now a resort, but in ancient times it was an exalted spiritual site. In Rama's time Uti was known as Udakmandalam, which means "circle or body of water." And in this holy lake, according to the *Ramayana,* a sage lived in a celestial palace he had created through his yogic powers. Nearby is the ancient kingdom of the Banaras, whose citizens became Rama's allies in freeing Sita from Ravana. Swamiji briefly describes his experiences there in his introduction to the *Ramayana:*

"There is a famous lake there called Udakmandalam or Uti. Palaces and beautiful mansions have been erected around the lake.

216

Upon arrival we asked the caretaker of the Mysore palace to give us shelter for a few days. Summer was approaching and because Uti was a favorite spot, this 'Queen of the Hills' became crowded with visitors. The caretaker kindly gave us the use of a small room behind the palace, where we lived and from which we roamed around in the mountains for many days.

"After arriving at Udakmandalam our food habits had to be changed, and we started taking ordinary meals, such as bread, vegetables, and dals. During this time we visited Goodlur, Coimbatore, and other places of interest. We surveyed the whole area. There is a community called Torah in the vicinity of Udakmandalam. Even to this day, historians and anthropologists differ in their opinions about the origins of this community. The inhabitants are an unusually tall, handsome, and healthy people who like to live close to nature and whose menfolk wear long hair and beards. They are agriculturists who grow potatoes as their main livelihood. Nantin Baba and I wanted to observe their way of life. We imagined that perhaps they were the descendants of the great king Sugriva of the Banara race mentioned in the *Ramayana*."

217

Next, the two sadhus stopped at Madurai, one of India's most famous holy sites, although it is often overlooked by Rama's devotees. According to Nantin Baba it was there that Lord Rama and his entire army stopped for the last time to gather their resources—spiritual as well as material—for their assault on Lanka. Madurai is a stronghold of Shakti sadhana (worship of the Divine Mother), and according to the tradition of the Himalayan sages the Divine Mother resides there in her most exalted form: Sri Vidya. Madurai had been one of Babaji's favorite places in south India and Swamiji had come there as a young man to study the right-hand path of tantra, especially the discipline pertaining to the practice of Sri Vidya. With its majestic and well-kept temples, learned brahmins who embody the knowledge of the Vedas, and adepts of right-hand tantra, Madurai outshines the rest of the country in preserving India's heritage.

Although generally Swamiji went out of his way throughout the journey to avoid meeting anyone he knew, he told me that in Madurai he made a point of visiting the learned brahmins at whose feet he had sat while learning about Sri Vidya. Referring to those brahmins,

Swamiji commented, "They are the *devas* [the divine beings] in the flesh. They are the ones who, through their study, practice, and selfless love for all creation, invigorate the soul of the Earth. It is because they exist that the planet does not sink into an ocean of utter confusion. Their whole life is sadhana. They eat, drink, sleep, walk, and talk as a service to God. They procreate so that they may continue doing the work of the sages in the form of their children. Not only their meditation and ritual worship, but even their most ordinary actions are an integral part of their spiritual awareness; for them, nothing else exists. It is in respect to brahmins of this caliber that the scriptures proclaim, 'May the people of the world learn the standards of an ideal life by watching how the first-borns [brahmins] of this land conduct themselves.' Without meeting these great souls our pilgrimage to Madurai would have been incomplete, for they are the blessed children of the Divine Mother."

218

With their blessings and the blessings of the Divine Mother, Swamiji and Nantin Baba next set out for Rameshwaram. Sri Lanka is the final destination on the trail of Rama, but Rameshwaram, a small island connected to the mainland by a bridge, is the last stop on the trail of Rama in India. Clusters of shrines dot the island, but the main shrine is a famous Shiva temple (also known as Rameshwaram), where according to tradition the Shiva lingam was installed and worshipped by Lord Rama himself before he began building a bridge to Sri Lanka.

As soon as they reached the island, Nantin Baba and Swamiji bathed in the ocean and then entered the Rameshwaram temple complex, where they observed the custom of bathing in water drawn from twenty-one different wells. These are barely a hundred yards from the shore and the water table is high, yet the water is not salty, but sweet. Then, after paying homage to Shiva at the temple, Swamiji and Nantin Baba visited other shrines on the island, finally arriving at Dhanush-Koti, which means "the tip of the bow," the second most significant shrine on the island. As the story goes, in order to transport his army to Sri Lanka, Rama built a bridge connecting the Indian mainland with the island. When the war was over and Rama had emerged victorious, the new king of Sri Lanka asked that Rama demolish the bridge for the safety of Lanka. Honoring his request, Rama destroyed the bridge by pushing it with the tip of his bow. The place where he stood when he performed this action came to be known as Dhanush-Koti.

Just as he had in Pushkar, Nantin Baba took the lead in scripture recitation here, this time reciting the chapter of the *Ramayana* known as "Sundar Kanda." It is a short chapter, and he completed the recitation in less than an hour. Then, with Swamiji again assuming the role of the student, he elaborated on the inner significance of the bridge.

As Nantin Baba expounded on the text, he explained that the sages had blessed Rama with infinite insight and strength. He could have vanquished Ravana single-handedly, Nantin Baba said, but killing Ravana was not his goal—his goal was to bring an end to Ravana's oppressive rule. Killing an enemy does not destroy that enemy's animosity; that lives on in one form or another, waiting for the opportunity to express itself in violence. It can be destroyed only through communication and proper understanding. The bridge built by Rama is a symbol of this, linking as it does two races and two ways of life. If after making a pilgrimage to this holy site we are not inspired to transcend our ethnocentric awareness and thus create bridges among human hearts, our journey has been in vain. Everywhere there is conflict between old and new, North and South, East and West, materialism and spirituality, and there can be no peace unless these issues are resolved. Those whose life is not touched by the light of Rama remain victims of their own inner conflicts. They are bound to be torn between the call of the soul and the demands of the senses. To a genuine seeker the holy site of Dhanush-Koti grants freedom from all such conflicts.

Nantin Baba also said that while creating a bridge, it is important to avoid imposing your customs and cultural values on those whom you are helping. Customs, rituals, and dogma are like baskets containing the seeds of life's higher values, seeds that address the needs of the soul; the baskets are only containers. Once you have planted those seeds in new soil, let them grow on their own terms. Then, by destroying the bridge, Rama teaches us to walk away once the seed has been planted—a subtle message not to impose one's customs, rituals, and dogmas on others. His action also exemplifies non-attachment. Perform your actions selflessly and lovingly, and when the work is completed, simply walk away.

219

Swamiji and Nantin Baba spent a few days at Rameshwaram and then took the ferry to the island of Sri Lanka. Nantin Baba had never gone beyond Rameshwaram during his previous pilgrimages and was not familiar with the sites associated with Rama in Sri Lanka, but by employing various means of transportation, Swamiji and Nantin Baba traversed the central and northern portions of the island for a month. They found that the people of Sri Lanka remember the story of Rama but do not think of Ravana as an evil king. In their eyes he was an unmatched warrior, a learned scholar, a staunch defender of his country and race, and an ardent devotee of Shiva. And during their travels, Swamiji and Nantin Baba met many Shaivite scholars and adepts.

Swamiji and Nantin Baba also visited Buddhist monasteries, which have preserved what they consider to be the purest form of Buddhism, known as Theravada. When the monks in one of the monasteries realized that Swamiji and Nantin Baba were yogis from the Himalayas, they greeted the two with a tremendous outpouring of love and respect. And when they learned that Swamiji was fluent in the Pali language, they asked him to give some discourses on the canonical Buddhist texts (which were originally written in Pali). According to tradition a pilgrimage is not complete without an act of charity, and the highest act of charity is sharing one's knowledge with others, so Swamiji took this as an opportunity to complete his pilgrimage by teaching these monks the scripture *Vishuddhi Magga* ("The Path of Purification"). Pleased, the monks presented him with a Sanskrit manuscript called *Kumbha Karna Ramayana*, one of the rare yoga texts that describes the techniques of *yoga nidra* (yogic sleep). When discussing this text with me, Swamiji said that both Ravana and his brother, Kumbha Karna, were great yogis, but in those days many considered them demons because they used their power and wisdom for their own sense gratification rather than for the welfare of humanity.

This proved to be Nantin Baba's last pilgrimage on the trail of Rama. From Sri Lanka the two sadhus returned to the Himalayas, and Nantin Baba traveled deeper into the mountains. As Swamiji wrote, "Eventually my friend Nantin Baba dropped his body in the Himalayas. I am still strong and alive to narrate a few more stories."

$\mathscr{the}$ MISSION BEGINS

AFTER HE RETURNED from the trail of Rama, Swamiji settled down in Uttar Kashi for a while. It is my good fortune to have met many of those who knew him during that period. The first were Maya Tandon and her husband, Shivnath, whom I met in Minneapolis in 1979. Maya's father had been Swamiji's friend since their days together at the University of Allahabad, and the couple had known Swamiji from early childhood. I spent many evenings with them and soon came to realize that these two were a repository of information about Swamiji's life after he renounced the position of Shankaracharya.

Then in 1980 my own destiny took an interesting turn. I was at the headquarters of the Himalayan Institute in Pennsylvania when Swamiji arranged my marriage to the daughter of Dr. S. N. Agnihotri, another of Swamiji's friends from the university. I had never seen the young lady in question, but I was in seventh heaven over the prospect of becoming part of a family that had long been near and dear to Swamiji. What is more, Dr. Agnihotri and Maya's father, Dr. Tandon, were so close they were like two peas in a pod. By the time I got married Dr. Tandon was no longer alive, but I had access to the letters that Swamiji had written to both Dr. Tandon and Dr. Agnihotri. It was my father-in-law who told me about Swamiji's life after he returned from the trail of Rama.

Swamiji lived in Uttar Kashi from 1958 to 1961 in a secluded cottage in Tekhla, a village three kilometers from the town. In 1996, accompanied by several of my American friends, I went there in search of the exact location of that cottage. We stayed in the guesthouse. From there we visited the famous Shakti and Shiva shrine, and as soon as the priest, Pandit Murari Lal Bhatt, discovered we were Swamiji's students he made elaborate arrangements for us to perform the ritual ceremonies in the temple there.

I asked the priest if he had known Swamiji personally, and he exclaimed with tears of joy, "I have known him since I was a child! In those days Swamiji lived in Tekhla. He was the most unusual swami I had ever seen. He was tall and straight like bamboo and radiant like fire. His eyes were so bright and piercing that no one could look straight into them. Even on cloudy days he wore dark glasses. His walk was as fluid as the wind moving through the grass. He had a transistor radio. None of us had ever seen one, and since he carried it inside his robe, we thought he was singing without moving his lips. When we asked him about this, he said, 'It's a miracle.' After we discovered the source of his music we called him 'Transistor Wale Baba.' As he walked around the temple, I used to hold his fingers and walk with him."

The pandit told me the exact location of Swamiji's cottage and said that the cottage had a name: Shanti Kuti. So early the next morning we set out to find it. We found ourselves instead at Shital Kuti, the ashram of Baba Shital Das. We thought we had come to the wrong door, but it turned out to be the perfect place to visit first. The resident sadhu, Vasant Dev, had known Swamiji well and was overjoyed to learn that we were his students. Although thirty-six years had passed since he had last seen Swamiji, to him it seemed like yesterday.

He invited us inside and asked one of the other sadhus to make tea for us, and while it was being prepared he told us that his gurudeva, Baba Shital Das, and Swamiji had been great friends. When I asked where Baba Shital Das was now, he replied that he left his body in Nepal, where he had lived with his own master. As most of Babaji's students had "Das" appended to their names, this aroused my curiosity. I began to wonder whether Baba Shital Das had been one of Babaji's

222

students, and I became even more curious when Vasant Dev said he did not know the name of his grandmaster.

So I asked where his gurudeva had lived before coming to Uttar Kashi and he replied, "As far as I know my gurudeva and Swamiji met in Rishikesh, and from there the two came to Uttar Kashi. My gurudeva lived in this cottage, and Swamiji lived in the cottage near the crown of the hill. I remember often in the afternoons Swamiji either came to visit my gurudeva or my gurudeva went to visit him. Both were accomplished yogis, and many aspiring sadhus from Uttar Kashi wanted to learn from them. But since Swamiji lived up the hill, it was hard to reach him there. Furthermore, he was quite strict with his schedule, so often it was my gurudeva who taught yoga to the sadhus."

By this time tea had been served, and the conversation became more casual. I began reading the Hindi verses written on a wall of the room, and I saw that most of them came from the sayings of "Saint Kabir Das," so I asked him if Baba Shital Das had belonged to the order of Saint Kabir Das, and he told me that he had. As he said this he opened his medicine box, took out some pills, and swallowed them with his tea, saying that he had become old and the mountain weather was no longer suitable for him. He had gone to the Himalayan Institute Hospital that Swamiji had built near Dehra Dun, where he had gotten the medicine, and he had made several attempts to see Swamiji while he was there, but with no success. That night I wrote a note to my friend Dr. Anil Singhal, who worked at the hospital, telling him who Vasant Dev was and asking that he be given special care.

When we had finished our tea I asked Vasant Dev to take us to Swamiji's cottage, and while we were driving he told me that at the end of his stay here, Swamiji had started a dispensary in Uttar Kashi and gave his cottage to the doctor who worked there. The doctor was no longer alive, he said, but his children still lived in the place. As soon as our car stopped in front of the house a gentleman came out, but when we asked if Swamiji had ever lived there, he said nervously, "No, no. No swami ever lived here." He went back to the house and shut the door.

Vasant Dev laughed and said, "That fellow is afraid you people might claim the house." We took some pictures and drove away.

223

Dr. Agnihotri, my father-in-law, told me that during the first part of his stay in Uttar Kashi, Swamiji was withdrawn, but as time passed he became more accessible. He began traveling to north Indian cities during the winter, mainly Lucknow, Kanpur, and Allahabad. Finally in 1963 he moved to Allahabad, where he lived at a place now known as Shiva Kuti, and once again reconnected with his old university friends, Dr. M. P. Lakhera and Dr. G. R. Sharma. During this phase of his life Swamiji began interacting with others and expressing his opinions on religion, spirituality, health, and yoga science and philosophy in a way that indicated he was preparing himself to embark on a mission.

Dr. Lakhera told me that Swamiji had the unique ability to be away from the crowd and still attract those with whom he wanted to interact. His favorite topic was the dynamics of death, and he would bewilder doctors and scientists by draining the blood from half of his body (which turned white) into the other half (which turned deep red). At other times he would make the pulse in one wrist vanish while the pulse in the other remained perfectly normal. Then he would explain how, by practicing yoga, one can attain complete mastery over oneself. He said that the mystery of life lies in the knowledge of death, and through the practice of yoga one can discover the dynamics of death. A human being who dies a normal death is reborn and starts the journey of life all over again. "To start with A, B, C and at the time of death lose everything you have learned, and in the next life to start again with A, B, C!" Swamiji would exclaim. "What a waste of time! The yogis retain their memory by casting off their bodies without dying. When they enter a new body they can pick up where they left off."

Dr. Lakhera said that before this period Swamiji had never exposed his yogic accomplishments to anyone. But now he began openly challenging doctors and other scientists, telling them they needed to broaden their understanding of the subtle mysteries of life. Then he would demonstrate how limited their knowledge was by performing one yogic feat or another. Once in the presence of Professor G. R. Sharma, Dr. Lakhera, and Mr. Anand Pratap Singh, among others, Swamiji demonstrated how a yogi can die for a few hours, preserve his body, and enter it again. When he himself "died," the witnesses were shocked and worried. But he had told them beforehand that they should not disturb the body, that he would "come back to life" exactly two hours later. Which he did.

After each such demonstration Swamiji would talk about the Upanishads and the *Yoga Sutra,* saying with authority that the practices his onlookers had witnessed are described in the scriptures, and adding that if humanity's true potential is to be known, spirituality and science have to be brought together. Then he would switch the conversation to religion and explain that although all religions have their origin in revelation and direct experience, with the passage of time they come to embrace a set of superstitions and dogmas, and consequently the truth is obscured. Within two years a large number of professors, physicians, attorneys, and judges in Allahabad, inspired by Swamiji, organized a series of public lectures, and soon Swamiji was in high demand in other cities as well.

225

The kumbha mela is a grand spiritual festival held in Allahabad every twelve years, which always attracts millions of people from all corners of India. The 1964 kumbha mela was no exception. At the invitation of the Vishwa Hindu Parishad, one of the nation's largest Hindu organizations, Swamiji delivered a series of lectures on religion and spirituality which awakened thousands of hearts from religious and intellectual slumber. Many of those who attended felt as if their heads were on fire when Swamiji blasted hypocrisy, sectarianism, blind faith, the caste system, and the oppression of women. Those who believed firmly in temples and priestly ritualistic ceremonies were amazed to hear him say that spirituality cannot be confined within the walls of temples, mosques, or churches. And as they continued listening, they heard that spirituality can be practiced without dependence on others—that they could experience God in their daily lives. Those who held the preconceived notion that a swami is a Hindu religious leader who must therefore advocate Hinduism were distressed to hear that Swamiji did not have a preference for any religion. He drew a clear distinction between Hinduism and *sanatana dharma* (the eternal teachings as outlined in the Vedas). He reminded his listeners that the Vedas do not belong exclusively to Hindus or even to Indians, but are a treasure house of information about the truth that belongs to all humanity.

Many Hindu leaders and their followers were outraged by Swamiji's claim that other religions are as good as Hinduism, and it made them uncomfortable to hear him say that identifying with a religion is one thing, and practicing the spiritual principles and higher values of life set forth in that religion is something else entirely. Those who follow a religious leader, he said—whether Hindu or Christian— are sheep, while those who embrace the teachings of the *Bhagavad Gita* or the Bible and practice those teachings in their daily lives are transformed from sheep to human beings; they alone are true Hindus and true Christians. Such sincere practitioners will be blessed with the knowledge of eternal truth, he said, and thereafter their consciousness will expand beyond the boundaries of any religion.

226   Swamiji soon became a center of controversy, and this attracted even larger crowds. And as the crowds grew, he began to add more fuel to the fire. He started every lecture in a gentle, loving manner, but at the climax he turned into a raging storm, blowing away misconceptions about God, heaven, hell, and dependence on priests and pandits. Then his stormy aspect would subside and he would again become a gentle saint. In this masterful way Swamiji channeled the sentiments of his listeners toward the eternal teachings of the sages and convinced them that truth can be experienced not by listening to lofty discourses but by doing sadhana.

Everyone listening to his words was deeply affected, although in radically different ways. Those who were broadminded and receptive to the truth were thrilled, but those who were narrowminded were offended and angered, and for months after the kumbha mela Swamiji and his ideas were a topic of hot debate in the city. Two years later his lectures were compiled, edited, and published in Hindi under the title *Yuga Dharma Kya* ("What Is Eternal Dharma?"). This was Swamiji's first book.

After the 1964 kumbha mela Swamiji began to appear in public more often. By now twelve years had passed since he had renounced the position of Shankaracharya, and during that time he had taken care to keep himself out of the public eye. But even though he was now becoming more visible, he still did not let a crowd collect around him. He spoke only on subjects that were not appealing to the public at large, and he did not speak at temples—they attract people from all walks of life, the majority of whom believe that glancing at God in a temple will make all their problems vanish. Swamiji's teachings did not appeal to them, as this passage from *Yuga Dharma Kya* makes clear:

"In our present circumstances narrow man-made 'isms' can no longer help us. The practices of the existing religions have been confined to monasteries, temples, churches, and mosques. In your own heart haven't you questioned the usefulness of a religion that can be practiced only in designated places? Does it make sense for religious practices to be separated from everyday life?

"India is such an unfortunate country that every year a few gods incarnate but the problems of our society always remain the same. When are you people going to overcome your illusion that by sitting around a guru you will overcome your problems? A guru is very important, but even more important is to practice what he teaches you. A guru can show you the path but it is you that has to walk on that path. If a guru tells you to have faith in him—that he will do everything for you and you don't have to do anything for yourself— better you get rid of such a guru. Many rich people have built big temples for God. Do they or their children have less miserable lives than those who have not built such magnificent temples? Wake up! Realize your own potentials and awaken them. Make yourselves healthy and strong. Organize your life in a way that enables you to take care of your duties and obligations and at the same time attend to the needs of your body, mind, and soul. How can you worship God when you are physically unhealthy and mentally confused?"

Many people still remembered Swamiji as the Shankaracharya and did not expect his talks to undermine the value of rituals and temples. But he emphasized the importance of yoga, including practicing yoga postures and breathing exercises, following a healthy diet, and meditating. These teachings were indigenous to India but they had been forgotten by most Indians—only a handful of sadhus and learned people who were well-grounded in both the Western and Eastern systems of education were familiar with them. For this reason Swamiji usually spoke at places frequented by intellectuals and educated seekers. In Allahabad, for example, he gave lectures at the University

227

of Allahabad and the Public Service Commission; in Kanpur he spoke at the Indian Institute of Technology. These places allowed Swamiji to convey the message of the Vedas and the Upanishads to those who understood its value, and the audiences appreciated his emphasis on the importance of creating a bridge between ancient wisdom and the modern sciences, between spirituality and materialism.

At one such lecture Swamiji said, "The power of science and technology must be guided by the highest principles of ethics, morality, and spirituality. Science and religion, technological discoveries and spiritual wisdom, must come together. Today there is no balance between science and spirituality, and as a result science seems to be moving toward self-destruction. Instead of bringing peace, science has been creating fear. With the help of science, humanity has reached the nuclear age. Scientific discoveries have brought a great increase in our standard of living, and as far as physical comforts based on material objects are concerned, we are far better off than our ancestors. But peace of mind has declined many times more than comforts and luxuries in the external world have increased. No matter how many things we invent with the help of intellectual knowledge, we cannot free ourselves from inequality, fear, and doubt. In order to find that freedom we have to withdraw our attention from the external world and make our minds inward. The solution to human problems can be found in the inner chamber of one's own heart. Mind and intellect are the finest tools both for knowing the objects of the world and for exploring the truth within. However, they need to be trained so that they can discriminate right from wrong and the good from the pleasant."

In addition to giving occasional discourses at institutions of higher learning, Swamiji taught the Upanishads to a select group of people, such as Dr. Agnihotri, Dr. Tandon, Dr. Kulkarni, Narendra Mohan, and Roshan Lal. Many of those sessions took place at the home of Dr. Sunanda Bai, a surgeon at Kanpur Medical College. Swamiji often stayed at her home when he was in Kanpur, and it was there that the idea of establishing the Himalayan International Institute of Yoga Science and Philosophy was conceived. I visited Dr. Sunanda Bai many times between 1980 and 1997. She was a great lady, one of those rare students of Swamiji's who had thoroughly imbibed his teachings.

228

Like Swamiji, she was a strict disciplinarian who tolerated no nonsense and who dealt with day-to-day situations in the light of spiritual knowledge. But in her personal life she was a bhakti yogi, an aspirant whose life was filled with love for Swamiji. Among all of his known students, she was perhaps the only one who had met his master in person and had his photograph in her possession.

I gathered from my conversations with Dr. Sunanda Bai that Swamiji's life was filled with his experiences of the sages—both ancient and modern. He loved his master deeply, and it was obvious from the way he spoke that to him Babaji was one of the ancient sages—the seers of the mantras, the custodians of revealed knowledge. Swamiji spoke as if he had learned the scriptures directly from the ancient sages. His deep love and respect for the sages was, as Dr. Sunanda Bai told me, "often misconstrued by ignorant people. Some thought Swamiji considered the sages to be God or that he did not believe in God."

Swamiji taught the scriptures with authority—not as a teacher but rather as an instrument of the sages. He presented even the most complex subjects in the simplest language, always emphasizing the practicality of the teachings. To him only the knowledge that brings freedom and everlasting peace is valid knowledge; the rest is merely an intellectual exercise. As Swamiji put it in *Yuga Dharma Kya:*

"People have long been experimenting with the objects of the world, seeking a way to find lasting happiness. This experiment seems to be unending—so far humanity has not discovered a lifestyle that creates happiness. Many people in the past have experienced higher reality and concluded that happiness lies not in the material world, but within. Yet their experiences have not become the experience of all. Out of many, only a few follow the footsteps of these enlightened ones, and they are the ones who attain happiness. They live in the world and yet remain above it.

"Without inner illumination, external life cannot be made pure and ideal. External life must be illuminated by the divine light within. Freedom from pain and misery can be achieved by unveiling the secret of the inner life. The moment the veil is lifted and the ego attuned to the higher self, our thought, speech, and action accord with the will of the Divine. Once there is attunement between the divine will and our worldly activities, we enjoy freedom here and now. One who has free access to the world within and without becomes a citizen of both worlds. He attains freedom, and eternal peace is his."

As Swamiji became more and more active, he felt the need to have a place where he could serve people in an organized way, so he bought a piece of land on the bank of the Ganga in Rishikesh and built a two-room ashram there. Swamiji was quite familiar with the site, for ever since he was a boy he had spent many nights there with his master. It was known as Prashant Tati ("the peaceful bank"). In the late 1960s, when Swamiji built the ashram, the whole area was forested. Wild elephants swam across the river and roamed this part of the forest, and the only human settlement was the ashram of Kali Kamli Wala, which held a Sanskrit school and a few teachers, students, and resident sadhus. An adept named Nirvanji lived on the premises and was like one of Swamiji's godfathers. Babaji had often sent young Bhole there to stay with Nirvanji while he himself traveled higher into the mountains, and even when Swamiji was an adult Nirvanji treated him like his child. This great sage lived in a small, box-like wooden hut, but he refused Swamiji's repeated invitations to move into a more comfortable room when Prashant Tati was built next door. (The hut was preserved until the 1990s and many of us who had heard about Nirvanji would visit it in his honor whenever we were in Rishikesh.) Another sadhu living on the premises of Kali Kamli Wala ashram was famous for his ability to attract elephants. Some thought his ability was due to his being a great adept and a devotee of Lord Ganesha; others thought that because he was fully established in the principle of non-violence, the elephants could not retain their beastly instincts in his presence. But the truth was that the sadhu had been a mahout, an elephant handler, in south India before becoming a sadhu, and he kept chunks of gur (raw sugar) in his hut to feed to the wild elephants when they came to eat the tall grass growing in the vicinity. Swamiji told him repeatedly that he should not feed the elephants—they would come to expect it, and if their expectations were not met they would become angry and might very well hurt him.

And sure enough: one night a bull elephant came looking for a handout. The sadhu gave it a chunk of gur, but the elephant wanted more. So the sadhu gave him another. When the elephant became even more demanding, he fed it all the sugar he had. But as he was giving it the last chunks, the dominant male of the herd arrived. To avoid a confrontation, the first elephant left—but the sadhu had no more sugar. And when no sugar was forthcoming, the dominant male grabbed the sadhu with his trunk, lifted him overhead, and smashed him to the ground. Swamiji told this story during a lecture in Honesdale to illustrate how expectation breeds disappointment, which can in turn breed violence.

Soon after the two-room ashram building was finished, Swamiji saw a leper sitting on the riverbank adjoining the ashram. His hands and feet had been almost completely eaten away by the disease and his face was disfigured. Lepers and other beggars lived five miles upstream around Lakshman Jhula, a popular pilgrimage site, and Swamiji wondered how the man had made it this far downstream without help. As soon as the leper saw Swamiji he demanded food and water, but no matter how much Swamiji served him it was not enough, and the more Swamiji tried to please him the ruder he became.

He remained in front of the ashram day and night shouting foul and abusive words. When Swamiji offered to take him wherever he wanted to go, the leper replied that this was his place and he would not move. When Swamiji offered to bathe him and clean his wounds, the leper told him that it was none of his business. He seemed to be afraid of water. After several days of continuous disturbance Swamiji thought of leaving the ashram for a while—but if he left, he thought, what would happen to the leper? And leaving the ashram because of this man's annoying behavior did not seem appropriate.

Almost a week passed, and the leper was getting louder and more abusive every day. Then, early one morning when he was hurling his abuse at Swamiji, Babaji arrived. He immediately walked up to the leper, shouted at him, and kicked him so hard he rolled off the bank and fell into the Ganga! Swamiji could not believe his eyes. What he saw next was even more bewildering: as soon as the leper touched the water, his body healed, and he was handsome and radiant as he stepped

231

out of the river. He and Babaji then bowed to each other, and without a word the radiant man turned and walked across the Ganga. Within a few minutes he entered the forest on the other side and vanished.

When Swamiji asked who this man was, Babaji replied that he was one of the seven sages who had taken on the leprosy of thousands of people all over the world. Many times Mother Ganga had begged him to give the disease to her, but he refused to burden her with the problems of so many people. Many other sages had also wanted to share the pain with him, but driven by his inherent compassion, he kept it all for himself. As he told me about this incident Swamiji stopped in mid-sentence and said, "Since that day, my master had a white spot on his right foot."

It was during this visit to Rishikesh that Babaji told Swamiji the time had come for him to deliver the message of the sages to the whole world. "There is so much pain in every aspect of life," Babaji said. "Disease, starvation, fear, and grief are everywhere. But no matter how much experience you have gained in the world and in your inner life, you are still inert. To serve others you need inexhaustible wealth—the wealth of inner strength and insight. So before embarking on this journey, receive the blessings of the sages. Go to our cave in Manali and commit yourself to an intense practice for eleven months. There in the cave, close your eyes so you can perceive without seeing. Observe silence, so that later you can speak effectively. Do not use your hands for any worldly purpose, and later success will fall into them of its own accord."

The cave in Manali lies in the Himachal Pradesh region of the Himalayas. In the tradition of the Himalayas the sage Parashurama is the protector and guardian of this region, and the cave is associated with Vasishtha, one of the seven sages. For a long time I assumed that Swamiji had gone there only to do an eleven-month practice. And in *Living with the Himalayan Masters* Swamiji mentions the Manali cave only in this context. Throughout the book Swamiji talks about other holy sites in the Himalayas, and later he took groups of students to visit them. But he never took a group to the cave at Manali. It was to be several years before I learned why.

When Swamiji talked about this cave and the practice he did there, he explained that just as scientific discoveries have to be tested and verified under strict laboratory conditions, so do spiritual principles. Scientific theories relate to the forces of the external world, and therefore scientific labs are equipped with material tools and devices. Spirituality is concerned with inner reality, and to verify this inner truth one has to work in the laboratory of the inner realm. The mind itself is the lab; meditative practices are the tools. As he wrote in *Living with the Himalayan Masters*, "The sages systematically teach you the method of going deep into meditation. They say, 'This is the first step, the next, the third,' and so on. They will describe certain symptoms that arise out of meditation. When a particular symptom appears then you know you are going to that step. In this way you attain the highest degree of concentration. They keep a strict watch on you so that you remain undisturbed and do not go through suffering of any sort."

In the same book Swamiji also describes at length how he lived in the cave, what he practiced, and what his experiences were: "My food was mostly barley and mountain vegetables, some juices, a glass of milk in the morning and one in the evening. In the limited space of the cave . . . I would do a few postures regularly and would sleep for two to three hours only. The rest of the time I remembered my guru mantra and meditated or gazed. Three times a day I did pranayama vigorously but very cautiously.

"The entrance to the cave is closed, but there is an outlet for the waste to wash away and a tiny needlepoint hole in the ceiling of the cave where a single shaft of light can enter. This tiny hole is to aid in concentrating the mind on a single point. This happens spontaneously, even if you don't want it to happen. You don't have to make any effort to concentrate in that situation, because there is only one ray of light and nothing else. In such isolation what will you do the whole day if you don't learn meditation? If you don't do meditation you quickly become imbalanced. You have no choice. . . .

"Dwelling in the cave for the first two months was very difficult for me, but later I started enjoying it immensely. The science of raja yoga teaches *samyama*—inner transformation through concentration, meditation, and samadhi. During this training I discovered that without living in silence for a considerable time, maintaining a deeper state of meditation is not possible.

"After eleven months I came out of the cave. It was five o'clock in

233

the evening on July 27. I was asked not to stay outside in the sun for the first week. I had difficulty in adjusting to the external world. Everything looked different, as though I had come to a strange new world. The first time I went to the city it took me forty minutes to cross a street corner because I was not accustomed to so much external activity. But gradually I became able to deal with the world. Coming back to the external world I realized that the world is a theater where I could test my inner strength, speech, emotions, thoughts, and behavior.

"After the completion of this training I was prepared to come to the West. I did not want to leave my master, but he insisted. He said, 'You have a mission to complete and a message to deliver. That message is ours, and you are my instrument.' My master then instructed me to go to Japan. He told me that I would meet someone in Japan who would help me come to the United States."

234

Before embarking on his journey to Japan, Swamiji asked Babaji about the exact nature of this mission. He knew he was to deliver the message of the sages as outlined in the scriptures—but there are hundreds of sages and thousands of scriptures; it was not easy to choose some and disregard the others. Furthermore he was quite aware of the cultural barrier dividing the Eastern way of thinking from the Western. So Swamiji asked his master, "What shall I teach the students who wish to learn from me? Shall I teach the religions of India and convert them? Shall I ask them to follow the Indian culture?"

Swamiji knew the answer, of course, but since he did not know how long it would be before he would have another chance to tease his master, he posed the questions anyway. The answer he got was, "You foolish boy."

So Swamiji pressed him further. "Then what shall I teach them? The culture in the West is entirely different. Our culture does not allow anyone to get married without the consent of other family members, while the culture in the West sanctions a free social life. Christians can marry anyone they choose, and the Jewish people do likewise. Their ways of worshipping God are set, while we worship the way we like and follow the path of enlightenment we choose. They are in the bondage of fixed ideas in their way of worshipping and in certain ways of thinking, while we are free-thinkers in the bondage of social laws. These two ways of life seem to be quite apart. How can I deliver your message to the West?"

"Though these cultures live in the same world with the same purpose of life, they are each extreme," Babaji replied. "Both East and West are still doing experiments on the right ways of living. The message of the Himalayan masters is timeless and has nothing to do with the primitive concepts of East or West. Extremes will not help humanity to attain the higher steps of civilization for which we all are striving. Inner strength, cheerfulness, and selfless service are the basic principles of life. It is immaterial whether one lives in the East or West. A human being should be a human being first. A real human being is a member of the cosmos. Geographical boundaries have no powers to divide humanity.

235

"'Free yourself from all fears' is the first message of the Himalayan sages," Babaji continued. "The second message is to be aware of the reality within. Be spontaneous and let yourself become the instrument to teach spirituality without any connection to religion and culture. All spiritual practices should be verified scientifically if science has the capacity to do so."

After receiving these instructions Swamiji went to Kanpur, where Dr. Sunanda Bai bought him a ticket for Tokyo. He then traveled to Calcutta, where he boarded Cathay Airlines for the flight west. It was 1968. As Swamiji was fond of telling us, he began his journey to Japan with eight dollars, which in those days was the maximum amount of currency one could take out of India. While changing planes in Hong Kong he ordered a cup of tea and some biscuits, for which he paid four dollars, plus a dollar tip. Thus he landed in Tokyo with three dollars in his pocket and no idea of where to go or how to start Babaji's mission. Yet he was confident that the plan would unfold with time. His master had said that he would meet someone in Japan who would help him come to the United States.

His presence at the airport created quite a stir. "I was wearing my white dhoti and kurta with a shawl over my shoulder," he told us later. "When I walked, my wooden sandals made a loud noise on the bare floor. It attracted everyone's attention. When I walked to customs after claiming my luggage, one of the officers checked my carry-on bag while the other officers and the crowd watched curiously. I did not speak Japanese and the officer did not speak English, so we did not understand each other. He said something when he found an apple in my bag, and I assumed he was saying that I couldn't bring it into the country. So I told him that I had gotten the apple in the airplane and I would be happy if he took it.

"One of the other customs officers knew a bit of English, and when he heard me offering the apple he laughed and said, 'Perhaps he is from another planet.' Then the officer asked me which country I came from, and I replied that I had come from India—the Himalayas. Without further inquiry he let me go."

As he cleared customs, a distinguished-looking gentleman approached Swamiji and asked him where he had come from and where he would be staying in Japan. Swamiji replied that he was coming from India and would be staying with a friend. And when the man asked who that friend was, Swamiji, not knowing what else to say, replied, "Perhaps you are that friend."

The gentleman did not seem particularly surprised at this answer. As he drove Swamiji to his home in Tokyo he told him that an old sage had come to him in a dream the night before and said that the sage's son would be visiting Japan and instructed him to make all the arrangements for him there. The man went on to explain that his only son was suffering from hepatitis. The doctors held out no hope for him. He asked Swamiji to heal him.

At first Swamiji was concerned about starting his mission by healing someone and thus creating expectations in those who heard about it. He knew that such miracles become the ground for a cult, and people begin to worship the miracle worker instead of practicing what he teaches. However, if that was how his master wanted things to unfold, then it would be so. Within a matter of days the boy began to recover, and as the days turned into weeks he regained his strength.

His host was convinced that this holy man had come to Japan only to save his son. But because Swamiji was from the Himalayas, his host introduced him to Okadasan, the spiritual head of the Mahikari organization. Swamiji described Okadasan as a kind and generous man who emphasized living a virtuous life and serving humanity. The members of the Mahikari organization believed that he had been a Himalayan sage in his previous life and regarded him as a prophet. Before Swamiji arrived in Japan, Okadasan had had many visions of a sage in the Himalayas, and when Swamiji spoke about his master and described his appearance, Okadasan realized that the sage appearing in his dream was Bengali Baba. His joy in meeting the spiritual son of this sage was boundless, and with reverence he asked Swamiji to impart the secret teachings of this sage to him. Babaji had given Swamiji a sacred rock, and Swamiji gave it to Okadasan. Thereafter the two men began spending their days together.

Hundreds of thousands of members of Mahikari came to know about Swamiji and his relationship with their beloved founder, and in the evenings they came by the thousands to receive his blessings. Their faith in him was so deep that they believed his *darshana* (glance) was enough to bestow healing energy. Occasionally Swamiji would give public discourses at Mahikari and other institutions, but he quickly discovered that the majority of those who came were interested in receiving his blessings and a selected few were interested in learning about the teachings of the sages.

At that time Japan was in the throes of a great cultural change. For centuries the Japanese people had regarded the emperor as a divine incarnation and had found solace in following their time-honored customs. Now the younger generation was searching for a faith and spiritual structure that could help them experience inner freedom. Buddhism had long been the dominant religion, and the Japanese version had its own unique flavor. It retained the element of love and compassion while embracing the indigenous customs, beliefs, and ritual practices of Japan. The different forms of the martial arts, for example, had become an integral part of this religion.

In the realm of science and technology Japan was as advanced as the Western world, but in the realm of religion and spirituality it was still searching for direction. Swamiji found this amazing. "People were progressive and ready to break all barriers to succeed in the world," Swamiji told me. "But in terms of exploring the inner dimensions of life, they had yet to rediscover the great spiritual wealth that was buried in their own heritage. I wished Buddhist masters and the masters of the Shinto tradition would bring forward the great wisdom of ancient Japan and enrich the lives of modern Japanese. Japan is blessed with a rich cultural heritage. I wished the Japanese would divert their focus from worshipping their religious leaders and start searching for the truth independently. Since the end of World War II the whole nation had been striving for material success and had undoubtedly achieved it, but their lives had become extremely hectic. To cope with stress, sickness, and problems at work and at home people put their faith in miracles in spite of their education and sophistication in other matters. But I was very happy to see that the Japanese are hardworking, honest, and sincere. Certainly one day they will play a pivotal role in bringing the various cultures and traditions of the world together."

Swamiji lived with Okadasan for six months. In these months, both leaders discussed the proper way of creating a bridge between East and West, ancient and modern, science and spirituality. Swamiji eventually decided that he had been sent to Japan to renew the link between Okadasan and the lineage of the Himalayan sages, and since that had been accomplished, he explained to Okadasan that his master had wanted him to go to the United States and deliver the message of the sages there. Okadasan immediately made arrangements for Swamiji to travel to America and provided him with a generous sum of money. Before leaving, Swamiji promised that he would visit Japan at least once a year—a promise he honored as long as he remained active in the West.

Swamiji's first stop in the United States was Hawaii, where he met with several members of the Mahikari group he had known in Japan. From there he found his way to Seattle and then to Detroit, where he made his first public appearance. There a group of doctors was galvanized by Swamiji's approach to filling the gap between science and spirituality and arranged for him to travel throughout the Midwest, giving lectures in homes, in churches, at colleges, and even in motels.

He visited many cities in those early days, but in time Chicago and

Minneapolis emerged as his main centers of activity. Marion Peterson, one of Swamiji's oldest and most beloved students, told me that the first lecture Swamiji gave in Chicago was downtown at the Pick Congress Hotel. The minister of the Unity Northwest Church invited her to attend, but she declined because she had no interest in hearing a swami speak—in fact, like most people back then, she did not know what a swami was. A little later that same minister invited Swamiji to lecture at his church in suburban Arlington Heights, and it was there that several people who were to become Swamiji's students first met him, Marion included. Another woman who was there that night, Shirley Walter, had been teaching hatha yoga for the local park district, and Swamiji inspired her to begin offering classes in her home. Before long he was giving classes there too, and with his guidance Shirley and her sister, Linda, organized their first yoga center in the basement of Shirley's home. This was the first formal yoga group Swamiji was affiliated with, and he attracted so many people that the group soon outgrew that space.

239

In those early days Swamiji was traveling constantly, teaching yoga classes and giving lectures on a broad range of topics; he even taught cooking classes. In the universities and hospitals he spoke on the scientific dimension of spirituality, holistic health, and the effect of concentration, relaxation, and meditation on the endocrine glands and the nervous system. In those settings he explained how meditation can be used to reduce stress and help one discover one's own inner healing force.

At the invitation of Unity, Unitarian churches, and interfaith organizations, he lectured on aspects of spirituality common to all traditions. He reminded the audience that "unless you discover the sacred link among the great traditions of the world you cannot live peacefully with anyone. If you cannot see the sacred bond that holds different members of the family together, you cannot live peacefully within your own family. This sacred link, this sacred bond, is the Divine within you—that which is eternal, that which is not subject to death, decay, and destruction."

When he lectured at Hindu temples Swamiji made startling and often provocative statements: "While living in America you cannot raise your children as Hindus or even as Indians," he would say. "Why are you filling their minds with confusion? You tell them they are Indian and insist that they behave like Indians and hold on to their Indian heritage and values. But when they ask you, 'What is this Indian heritage?' you fail to answer them. You have neither the time nor the interest to practice the disciplines of your tradition, yet you expect your children to be the upholders of that tradition even though they do not know what it is. Children are intelligent. If you don't pollute their minds with your long-cherished prejudices and conflicts, they will grow as healthy members of humanity."

In YMCAs, YWCAs, and yoga studios he adopted a different approach. There he taught most of the basic aspects of yoga, mainly the physical postures. However, even when leading hatha workshops, he introduced philosophy and spirituality, making sure that people did not mistake yoga for a mere set of physical exercises. He always made it a point to explain that hatha yoga is part of a larger program for physical and mental well-being and spiritual enlightenment. Every hatha yoga class he led ended with a period of meditation. Presenting a holistic model of the teachings of the Vedic sages was always his main goal.

Almost everyone who attended these lectures and workshops had the distinct impression that Swamiji was speaking directly to them. At the end of a session he would often say, "Now I will answer your questions. Do you have any questions?" At such times his answers were straightforward—sometimes too straightforward for comfort.

For example, a woman once asked him, "Swamiji, when the mind is in a great deal of distress and emotional turmoil, how do I know whether I should listen to my heart or struggle with the situation I'm in even though staying in it is painful?"

In a forceful tone, Swamiji boomed, "Better you shape up yourself! Your husband is a good man. Why are you hurting him and hurting yourself? Better you don't chase other men. Take care of your husband, yourself, and your children." The next moment he looked at the audience, and pointing to the woman with a smile, said softly, "I know her very well. She is my daughter and I love her." This allayed the woman's embarrassment somewhat, but left her bewildered: she had never met Swamiji, yet apparently he was acquainted with even the most private circumstances of her life. At the end of the lecture, as he walked through the audience to the door, Swamiji put his hand on the woman's head and said lovingly, "Come and see me. I will help you."

Such encounters were common—that is just one example among hundreds. Even when people had not asked him a question or drawn attention to themselves in any way, Swamiji might look at them and say something like, "Don't worry about your son. I will pray for him. He will be fine." Or, "No need of running here and there. Start practicing. You will find your answer." Or, "It has nothing to do with arthritis. Check with a dentist. You may have a problem with your gums."

The hundreds of people who had such experiences called them miracles, but when I tried to talk with Swamiji about them he would simply say, "I am just an extension of my master." On one occasion he gave a more elaborate answer: "I am just an instrument. What do I do? Nothing. My master is the one who sent me to the West. He told me that I would meet my students and colleagues in the States. He's the one who arranged everything for me. People came to me out of the blue. At first I did not know anyone. People heard me speak, and those who hardly knew me arranged more lectures for me; the media too took an interest in my work. Had I not known my master, I too could have considered all this a miracle."

241

As Swamiji's biographer, I think of this phase of his mission as a period of miracles. People came to know him in extraordinary ways, and once they met him they found him transforming them in extraordinary ways. He knew the inner potential of those he met, and without waiting for them to ask he gave them what they needed. This was true for those who met him just once, for those who studied and practiced under his guidance, and for those who became teachers and served him by helping him carry out his mission.

Swamiji worked day and night, and to many people it was evident that he was always accompanied by his master. He had no choice but to teach and guide those who came to him. Even when he wanted to rest more than just a few hours a day, his master would not let him. Years later, during one of his lectures in Honesdale, Swamiji lovingly called his master a slave driver and told the following story:

Swamiji was staying in a Minneapolis hotel, where he was scheduled to give a lecture. His schedule had been particularly hectic of late and he was running a low fever. Half an hour before the lecture was to begin there was a discussion among his students to the effect that Swamiji should rest and send someone to speak in his place, and in the end Swamiji sent one of his students to give the lecture, and lay down to rest.

He had been reclining on his side for a few minutes when he felt something crawling in his ear. A student who had stayed behind with him checked the bedding, but found nothing. Swamiji lay down again, but the sensation returned. Again the bedding—pillow, pillowcase, and spread—were given a good going over, and again nothing was found. After this had happened a few more times, Swamiji's assistant called housekeeping and asked for a new set of bedding—pillows and all. But even with the new bedding Swamiji felt something crawling in his ear the minute he lay down. By this time almost thirty minutes had passed.

His assistant suggested that he had been traveling so much that perhaps the sound of the airplane was stuck in his head. The assistant happened to have a set of earphones with him and suggested that wearing them might help, but when Swamiji put them on, the crawling sensation was even stronger. He jerked off the headset and threw it on the floor, shouting, "It must be there! Now it must be there in the earphones!"

"No, Swamiji, it's not possible. There must be something wrong with you," said his assistant. Swamiji insisted that the young man check the earphones—and when he examined them under a lamp he exclaimed, "You're right! There is a bug in here—but how is that possible?"

Swamiji got up and, like an angry teenager, shouted, "I know that I'm your slave! I'll go and lecture!" He washed his face, combed his hair, threw his shawl over his shoulder, went to the hall, and gave the lecture.

When he saw his master later in India, Babaji said, "I'll become a bug if necessary, but I'll make sure you do your work and don't become lazy."

SPIRITUALITY *and* SCIENCE

SWAMIJI ALWAYS CALLED his teachings the message of
the sages. The philosophical aspects of what he taught were derived
from the Vedas and the Upanishads; the principles of holistic health
and the body-mind connection, which were some of his central
themes, were derived from Ayurveda, the *Yoga Sutra,* and tantric texts.

His lectures invariably began with a salutation to the Divine: "I
pray to the Divinity in you." Then if the topic was related to health or
psychology he would repeat his standard phrase: "A human being
is not body alone, not mind alone. Between body and mind there is
something called breath. A human being is a breathing being too. If
you want to be healthy and happy and if you wish to experience everlasting peace and tranquility, better pay attention to your breathing."
Only after explaining the importance of breathing, the sitting posture,
diet, and exercise, would Swamiji address himself to the announced
topic.

If the lecture was related to religion, philosophy, or spirituality,
he would begin by saying: "All religious traditions of the world have
their source in one single truth. This truth is the goal of all religions.
Methods may differ from each other, but methods have no power
to divide humanity. The sages do not belong to a particular caste,
creed, or nation. The message of the sages is universal. According to
them the first and foremost priority of a man is not to see God but to
know himself.

"Self-realization is the main theme of the sages' message. And self-realization means you know yourself at every level: at the level of your body, breath, mind, and soul, and at the interpersonal level. The more you know yourself, the better you will understand the world around you. And the more you understand the world around you, the more realistic your expectations of the world will be. The more realistic your expectations, the fewer disappointments you will experience. Lacking self-knowledge, you will remain in the grip of false expectations of yourself and the world around you, and that will make you miserable. A miserable person has no time or energy to contemplate on the higher truth. Therefore, if you want to experience a higher level of reality, better you renounce your self-created misery. And you can do that."

244

Here in the United States, Swamiji lectured and taught in much the same way he had in India between 1963 and 1968, taking a scientific approach toward health and spirituality. In India people listened to him because he was their "Swamiji," a holy man, a Himalayan sage, and a former Shankaracharya. The occasional demonstrations of yogic practices he performed lent extra weight to his teachings. But those demonstrations did not motivate the members of his Indian audience to practice what he taught. Their preconceived notion of Swamiji as a holy man impelled them to follow him, and they were happy simply identifying themselves as his disciples. Few saw Swamiji as anything more than a "God-man." Only Professor R. S. Tandon and a few others drank coffee with him, played cards, and made jokes. When the hour grew late, they would ask him to leave so they could get a few hours of sleep before teaching their classes.

In the West it was his straightforward, clear-cut approach to spiritual unfoldment in a holistic context that people found impressive, and their way of looking at a swami and his teachings was radically different from that of the people in India. Many Westerners were experiencing the limitations of material success and were looking for a new way of life that would be more fulfilling. They were interested in Eastern concepts only to the extent that such concepts contributed to their inner growth and happiness.

The culture in the United States made it possible for people to see

Swamiji as both a person and an adept. Unfettered by excessive devotion, Americans were able to see Swamiji as he was in the moment, and they were able to see nuances that were lost to the majority of Swamiji's students and followers in India. For example, the stories told by the students in Chicago in the early 1970s show that even though Swamiji was highly evolved spiritually he was also very practical and down-to-earth—he taught only what people needed to learn. People were impressed with Swamiji because in him they found both profound wisdom and spiritual power, and yet he laughed, joked, and took an interest in their daily lives and ordinary concerns.

Swamiji had been traveling constantly from the time he first arrived in the States, staying in any one place for only a few days. That changed when he went to live at the Menninger Foundation in Topeka, Kansas, in the fall and winter of 1969. This came about because a Minneapolis physician, Dr. Daniel Ferguson, was so fascinated by Swamiji's ability to demonstrate control over his autonomic nervous system, heart, and circulatory system that he got in touch with a colleague, Dr. Elmer Green, head of the Voluntary Controls Program in the research department at the Menninger Foundation. Dr. Green was researching the mind-body relationship and the mind's capacity to regulate physiological processes, including those thought to be involuntary. And when Dr. Ferguson told him about this Himalayan adept, Dr. Green invited Swamiji to come to the Menninger Foundation and perform some yogic feats under laboratory conditions to demonstrate the relationship between mind and body. Swamiji readily accepted.

245

Accompanied by Dr. Ferguson, Swamiji first visited Topeka on March 28, 1969, for a weekend. Once there, he explained to Dr. Green, his wife, Alyce, and their associates that, according to the sages, all of the body is in the mind, but not all of the mind is in the body. The body is meant to serve the purposes of the mind, just as the mind is meant to serve the purposes of the soul, he told them. All bodily functions are under the command of the mind, he said, but because people have lost touch with their minds they have no control over many of the functions of their bodies. Instead of trying to understand the dynamics of the mind and delving into its various faculties, most people are unaware that the mind is the finest tool for exploring the reality within and without.

Swamiji made this statement knowing that he was talking to a group of hard-core scientists who would not listen to such lofty spiritual doctrines unless they could be proven scientifically. Swamiji said unequivocally that he had come to the West to create a bridge between science and spirituality, and, further, that he had the ability to broaden the understanding of scientists by demonstrating some of the ways in which the knowledge of modern science is limited. He told the scientists that if humanity ever wishes to attain the next level of civilization, it must overcome these limitations. Then Swamiji announced that he could stop his heart without suffering any harm. When the Menninger scientists asked him whether he would be willing to demonstrate this, he said, "Of course. That's why I have come."

Preparations were made, and Swamiji was hooked up to an EKG machine. Doug Boyd, who was later to become Swamiji's secretary and personal assistant during his stay at the Menninger Foundation, gives a detailed account of these initial demonstrations in the introduction to his book *Swami*. Although Boyd was not present during these first laboratory sessions, Dr. Green gave him an account of them when he offered Boyd the opportunity to work with Swamiji.

Boyd asked, "'Swami Rama wasn't getting feedback when he stopped his heart in the lab, was he?'

"'No, there was no feedback. He sat in the experimental room where all the subjects are run, and he was wired up to the polygraphs in the control room, but that was a demonstration rather than a practice or a training session, and there were no visual or audio feedback signals. By the way, Swami didn't actually stop his heart, you know. In fact, what really happened was that his heart rate jumped from seventy to about three hundred beats per minute. This is called atrial flutter. In effect, he stopped his heart from pumping blood for about seventeen seconds. Dr. Marvin Dunne, a cardiologist at the University of Kansas Medical Center, identified the type of record and said that it is associated with a drop in blood pressure and fainting, and sometimes death. . . .

"'You know, the swami said he was willing to stop his heart that

246

way for three or four minutes. I told him I'd be sufficiently impressed if he did it for ten seconds. As a matter of fact, I was surprised that he was willing to try it at all because he had told us when he first came that in order to safely stop his heart he had to fast for three days. Now I think that he may have two techniques. In the demonstration that he was referring to when he talked about fasting he may actually stop his heartbeat and produce a flat EKG record. But when he offered to do this heart-control demonstration I was surprised, because for one thing, I thought we had completed all the experiments we were going to do at that time, and for another, we were at the dinner table with him and Dan Ferguson, the doctor who first told us about him. The swami was going to give a talk in the conference room the following morning, and then he and Dr. Ferguson were to get on the plane for Minneapolis. Alyce and I had taken them out to a restaurant and we were just finishing a big dinner. We were telling him how we appreciated his contribution to our research, and all of a sudden he exclaimed, "I'm sorry I didn't stop my heart for you. I know you wanted to see that." I said, "That's all right, you can do it next time." And he said, "I'll do it tomorrow!" Alyce reminded him that we were eating, not fasting, and said that I was not willing to help him endanger his life. Do you know what he said? He said, "My heart is my toy and I can play with it if I want to!" He finally convinced us.

247

" 'So the next day we did the heart-control experiment. Swami had insisted, and after he assured us he would only do it for a few seconds and would be perfectly all right, we agreed to go ahead. We had to start a little earlier in the morning than usual so that we could get him wired up to do the experiment, and get finished before he had to give his talk. I sat with Swami in the experimental room and Alyce and Dale were in the control room with Dr. Ferguson and Dr. Sargent, a Menninger doctor. Swami had asked Alyce to call over the intercom when his heart stopped. The verbal command, "That's all," was supposed to be Swami's signal to do whatever he had to do to return his heart to normal. They hadn't expected to see what they saw on the EKG polygraph. We had thought perhaps there would be a flat line for about ten seconds. So there was a delay in giving the signal, "That's all," because they were in there watching the polygraph and wondering what the rate of three hundred beats per minute meant in someone like Swami Rama.

"'Of course I had no idea what was going on. The swami was just calmly sitting there. At the signal, "That's all," he established a solar plexus lock by pulling in his stomach and tightening his diaphragm. I asked him how he went about stopping his heart. Then Alyce called me over the intercom, saying, "Would you come in for a minute and look at this record?" When I went back to the swami I said, "Your heart didn't stop the way we thought it was going to. Instead, it started beating at about five times its normal rate!" And he said, "Well, you know, when you stop your heart this way it's still fluttering in there." It was interesting that he used that word because when Dr. Marvin Dunne, professor of cardiology at the University of Kansas, saw the electrocardiogram he called it atrial flutter. After Dr. Dunne had talked about the record awhile, he said, "By the way, where is this man? What happened to him?" I said, "Nothing. We took off his wires, and he went up and gave a lecture!"'"

After the lecture Swamiji returned to Minneapolis, and a couple of weeks later, on April 16, he wrote a letter to the Greens promising to return to the laboratory in the fall for further demonstrations. He then continued traveling and teaching and was in great demand. People from all walks of life, especially college students, educators, physicians, and psychologists, came to learn from him.

In the late summer Dr. Green held a formal meeting to discuss the prospect of Swamiji's working at Menninger as a consultant to the Voluntary Controls Program, and it was at that time that Dr. Green asked Doug Boyd to be part of the ongoing "Swami Rama Project," as Swamiji's personal assistant. Boyd writes: "The prospect of being involved in the Swami Rama Project fascinated me. Over the past several months I had been watching Eastern influence growing in the West, and I had come to see that the 'New Age' that was now so often spoken of would be the concurrent result of Western growth in the East and Eastern growth in the West. For over ten years I had been working with Asians who were developing the pragmatic systems and practical skills that had always been thought of as the Western way. My involvement in the Swami

Rama Project would be a chance to participate in another aspect of this same global process. . . . As his secretarial assistant at the lab, I would have the opportunity to observe his techniques."

Boyd's job description stated that he would schedule Swamiji's research activities, appointments, and lectures, answer the telephone, take dictation, transcribe recordings, handle all correspondence, and edit Swamiji's written materials. He was also responsible for recording the research data and summarizing the key points. He and Swamiji were to stay in the Greens' home. Boyd was to be available to Swamiji around the clock. His job description included handling Swamiji's financial transactions and arranging for any special dietary needs. "It was a fascinating prospect," he writes. "Inevitably I was to become acquainted not only with the teachings and talents of this Himalayan yogi, but also with the man himself."

On September 9, 1970, Swamiji returned to Topeka, this time for a long stay. He was not yet settled in his room when Mother Nature came to the flatlands of Kansas in her full glory to greet her Himalayan son. When the siren sounded to warn of an approaching tornado, everyone in the house prepared to take refuge in the storm cellar. Over the din of the radio, the siren, the wind, and the rain Alyce Green called for Swamiji to come downstairs. He replied that he would be along in a few minutes, so she sent Boyd up to get him, thinking he did not understand the urgency. But even after Boyd explained the danger, Swamiji was not alarmed. Boyd tells us what happened next: Swamiji said, "'We have not yet begun our work, and the wind comes to blow away the swami, the doctor, and everybody else? This is impossible!' He walked majestically into the living room, his shawl cascading over his outstretched arms, and seated himself on the love seat in the corner.

"Alyce and I went to the hall closet, where Elmer had cleared the trap door and was peering through the opening to see whether the dirt below was wet. I had hoped that Swami would follow, but since he did not, I went back to the living room. He was still talking. 'Troubles may come and go, troubles may take us by surprise, but why is it that we should have to fear? What are these announcements of disaster? What are these whistles and these speakers to drive intelligent people under their houses?' I stood in the doorway and looked at him. I was not sure how to persuade him or whether I should try. 'Go do as you like,' he said, 'jump through the floor.' He gracefully lifted his legs, and without using his hands, he folded himself into a lotus posture. Then he folded his arms across his chest. 'I shall remain here in full view of the reality.'" This is how Kansas greeted the Himalayan sage, and how the Himalayan sage introduced himself to Kansas.

Swamiji dominated any space in which he moved by the sheer force of personality. He was six feet one inch tall, and when he walked with his head held high he was quite imposing. Yet he was friendly and emitted an energy that drew people to him. I lived with him for twenty years, both in India and the United States, watching how he walked, slept, ate, shopped, worked, played, interacted with others, and dealt with administrative matters. I observed his hobbies—how he sometimes appeared to be driven by them, and how at other times he drove them away. I found him masterful in everything he did. He executed projects of all sizes with precision and efficiency. He knew how to cook, clean, do his laundry, and make his bed, and he carefully instructed his students in these matters. For example, he gave cooking classes and demonstrated how to clean dishes without wasting water. But when it came to taking care of his own needs, he sometimes seemed comically incompetent.

Boyd observed many of these same traits, and his account gives us a sense of what Swamiji was like: "Living in the Greens' home with Swami Rama was to mean a considerable change in my lifestyle. I realized this the day the swami arrived, and I knew it around five-thirty the following morning when he knocked on my bedroom door and shouted, 'Hey, Douglas! How about a cup of tea?' The tea-making became an important part of the daily routine, and wherever the swami was, I was to be nearby, ready to come forth with the hot tea and milk in a moment's notice. Swami often called it 'tilk,' and he preferred it in a tall glass with equal parts of strong tea and hot milk and a few healthy spoonfuls of honey. . . . I could easily disregard my alarm clock, but not the booming voice of the swami and not his need for his morning tilk. Once he told me that if I could teach him the tea-making procedure, including the technique of operating the knobs on the kitchen stove, he could avoid disturbing me in the early mornings.

I taught him the procedure, for the sake of his ever-expanding enlightenment, but I wanted to go on preparing his tea and to be awakened when he stirred in the mornings.

"At first it amazed me to find this yogi adept, this master of 'involuntary' processes, so inept at such everyday procedures as preparing tea; but I learned that Swami had been accustomed to being waited on hand and foot in India. It was not that he had insisted on it—this was the manner in which devout followers treated their teachers. Swami Rama was a particularly important swami, as he had once been a Shankaracharya in southern India. Shankaracharyas are influential religious and spiritual leaders in the Hindu hierarchy in India.

"Swami Rama is perhaps the only man ever to have 'escaped' from this position, having felt, as he described it to me, like a bird in a gilded cage. No one but a true scholar could ever be selected for the high and holy post of Shankaracharya; but Swami's had been a life of vigorous study, and he had spent many long days voluntarily chained to a chair so that he could not get away from his books. Sometimes he appeared to me to be an expert in all things knowable—from metaphysics to history to horticulture. Yet having his daily needs and wants anticipated and provided for without his even having to identify and verbalize them left him inexperienced in the practical procedures of daily living. Swami was an interesting combination of self-mastery and incompetence. I knew the complications and confusions of technological America would be even more overwhelming for this Himalayan yogi than for the usual foreigner, and I wanted to spare him the additional culture shock of having to make his own tea. . . .

"In the first days, Swami Rama and I spent the mornings at home, and several times he called me upstairs to sit in his room with him and listen to his tape recordings of classical Indian music and devotional singing. . . . But most of the time he was wordless. Sometimes we sat in silence for hours. He would sit absolutely motionless in his lotus posture with his eyes half closed and his back and neck so straight he looked taller than usual. At those times he seemed old and venerable. . . . He was always obviously pleased with all that I prepared for him, and that made me feel good. . . .

"The Greens' home was directly across the street from a large landscaped park that was bordered with weeping willow trees. It had a zoo, a rose garden and greenhouse, a swimming pool, tennis courts, and lots of green lawn, and a little open train with a bell and a high-pitched whistle gave people rides around the perimeter for thirty-five cents. Every lunchtime while we sat at the table the train went around and around with its ludicrous whistle, and every day Swami noticed it and remarked about it. Two or three times he ran to the window so that he could see the people as they rode past behind the weeping willow trees.

"One day I told him that the Greens had ridden the train with their grandchildren, but that I had never experienced it. I had been meaning to, I explained, but had never gotten around to it. 'I realize I'm going to have to see to it that I get to ride on that train,' I said jokingly, 'since I know that every aspirant must either satisfy or repel all desires in order to achieve non-attachment.'

"He listened to me with obvious amusement, but then for a moment his face grew serious and he become thoughtful. Suddenly he smiled again, and his eyes lit up. 'We'll do it!' he said. 'Definitely we'll do it! You make all the necessary arrangements!'

"'Yogis and exotic people often have several distinct natures, several aspects of their beings,' Elmer had once said to me. 'The swami is a man of three aspects as I see him: a wise old man, a middle-aged man, and a young boy,' and within these first days I had been able to see his three beings. At times of quiet contemplation and in our evening meditations he was a dignified and sagelike old man. Most of the time he was his bold and jaunty middle self, and at rare and unexpected moments he was simply a child. Though his highest yogic nature was probably in the aspect of the old man, I believed it was his middle self that did the demonstrations in our laboratory and performed extraordinary yogic feats. And I believed that the child in him would one day have us riding the train."

Every afternoon Swamiji spent two hours in a soundproof laboratory cooperating in psychophysiological experiments. It was Boyd's job to bring him to the lab, get him seated at the table, and provide a cup of hot tilk whenever he needed it. The normal procedure was to hook Swamiji up to three machines: an EKG (electrocardiograph), an EEG (electroencephalograph), and an EMG (electromyograph).

His assignment was to go into different states of meditation so that researchers could assess the effects of these varying states of mental activity on the body. Afterwards a team of researchers would interpret the data recorded on the heaps of polygraph paper that piled up during that day's session.

During these sessions the researchers were interested in seeing whether it is possible for a human being to relax the brain and nervous system, thereby giving complete rest to the mind, without falling asleep, and whether it is possible to produce different kinds of brain waves at will while remaining awake and aware of the external world. Scientists have arbitrarily divided brain-wave patterns into four bands—beta, alpha, theta, and delta—and they have correlated these four patterns with various states of mind, from the most tranquil to the most agitated. But before demonstrating his ability to produce a particular brain wave at will, Swamiji first had to acquaint himself with the equipment and with the significance of the lines on the graphs. For example, he would focus his mind on his mantra; later he would think of catching a train at a crowded station—shouting, yelling, and pushing other passengers; then he would think of sitting quietly on the bank of the Ganga and gazing at the forest across the river. After the session was over the scientists would show him the graph and explain how wiggly, jerky, or relatively flat lines were associated with beta, alpha, or theta brain waves. When the line on the graph was quite smooth, almost flat, they told him that particular pattern was a delta wave.

After two weeks of daily sessions Swamiji announced that he was ready for the formal experiments to begin, but before long he came up against the limits of technology. Here is Doug Boyd's account: "Soon Swami could announce he would produce so many minutes of theta, so many minutes of delta, go back up to beta, produce alpha for so many minutes—and then do exactly what he said he would do. Finally he ceased to be impressed with that achievement. One day he enthusiastically suggested that he would like to help develop the means to demonstrate the existence of additional waves or patterns that our electroencephalographs seemed unable to measure and record. He thought that by working with Elmer and with the people in the Biomedical Electronics Laboratory he could help them develop more

253

sensitive instruments and thereby prove the existence of more significant states that they seemed not yet to have discovered.

"'You don't understand,' Elmer explained. 'This is all there is. You can go from a flat record—that is, from zero cycles per second—all the way up to twenty-four, twenty-six, twenty-eight, as many cycles per second as you can produce, and it will be accurately indicated on the polygraph. And the whole spectrum—the entire range of electrophysiological activity of the brain—is divided somewhat arbitrarily into these four bands. That's simply a matter of definition. So zero to four hertz is delta, four to eight is theta—and this you know because we've defined these before—eight to thirteen hertz is called alpha because that happens to be what the guy got first from his subject when he was naming these patterns, and any frequency from thirteen on up is defined as beta. So there isn't anything else.'

"Swami was now able to produce patterns within any of the four frequency bands. But apparently he had come to the realization that he was able to do more than showed. 'All this is nothing,' he said, 'only simple exercises. Something is missing here, there must be some more patterns—something more than this beta, alpha, theta, delta.'

"'Aha! there is something else,' Elmer responded. He and I both just got the swami's point. 'You have to remember these machines are measuring the physical activity in your physical body. What these patterns are showing is not necessarily states of mind, but only states of brain.'

"'Not necessarily states of mind, and certainly not states beyond mind,' I added, remembering Swami's saying that meditation is a state beyond mind.

"For a few moments Swami sat silently in thought. I imagined him feeling that he had reached the limits of what he could demonstrate in the areas of concentration and meditation. He suddenly realized that all the magnificent variations he could achieve in his internal states of consciousness could not be paralleled with equally magnificent changes in the patterns on the polygraph.

"'Then what's the use of all these machines?' he asked.

"'Ah, but for what they're doing, they're extremely useful. They're useful for demonstrating the psychophysiological principle, the mind-body relationship. What we're saying is that changes in physiological states affect mental-emotional states, and conversely, changes in mental-emotional states produce physiological changes. The extent to which this is true can be studied with physical measurements made by physical machines because we can see how changes in the body are related to changes in subjective mental and emotional states. This is a tremendous step, and what you are doing is useful in making this step. You'd be surprised how many people, even doctors and scientists, think we're only bodies—nothing more than bundles of largely involuntary chemical-electrical responses. And they've not only hypothesized this, they've already concluded it. We are going to have to first break those conclusions; we're going to have to smash all the premature theories in a scientific way so that science can move on. Eventually we may find higher principles: we may find how higher states of consciousness relate to the mind-body relationship. And maybe someday science can make nonphysical measurements with nonphysical instruments.'"

255

Swamiji subjected himself to these scientific experiments, but he was not a guinea pig; he was a teacher. He had come with a mission to teach, train, transform, and introduce the reality that transcends our known territories. In mid-September a group of nine people met with Swamiji in a conference room. The original purpose of the meeting was twofold: to help Swamiji become better acquainted with the culture of Western science, and to learn the system of concentration and meditation from him so they could better understand what he was demonstrating in the lab. Those attending sat on chairs, but when Swamiji observed that they looked stiff and awkward, they decided to hold the next sessions in the Greens' living room, where people could sit comfortably on cushions on the floor. When Swamiji gave his first lesson on the sitting posture, he began by emphasizing that in order to gain a deeper level of meditation it is absolutely necessary for a meditator to sit in a comfortable, stable posture. He demonstrated how to sit with the head, neck, and trunk erect, explaining that before attempting to meditate one should relax all the body's limbs and organs and learn the basic principles of proper breathing. As time passed, these sessions became more and more inspirational. Finally

Swamiji began teaching the philosophical aspects of yoga. His teacher-missionary spirit became more and more evident, as is obvious from Boyd's record of his teachings: "'Man is in search of peace, bliss, wisdom, and happiness,'" Swami Rama told the group. "'We are all trying to achieve that everlasting happiness which is gained through knowledge which is gained through peace which is gained through method. For happiness we need peace of mind. For peace of mind we need mind control. For mind control we need method. We need a definite process with which to completely cut off the mind from the contact of the senses—from the sensations and objects of the outside world. . . .

"'The mind should be free from all turmoils. Buddhist scriptures, Hindu scriptures, Tibetan, Tao, and Confucian scriptures all speak of ways to make mind free. In the beginning there are different methods, but they all meet in the same place. All paths lead to meditation, for there is only one goal and that goal is meditation. Meditation is the only path to freedom—freedom from anxiety; freedom from pain, anger, distress, and depression; freedom from all sorrows, all fears, and all bondages. And meditation is the only path to knowledge.'"

Swamiji always concluded these inspirational, philosophical, and spiritual discourses with practical lessons. Here is one example: "'Your work starts with your lungs. Why with the lungs? Why not with your arms? By controlling the motion of the lungs, mind's movements come under control. By controlling the motion of the lungs, by increasing the capacity of the lungs, by making the lungs strong, you make the respiratory system very regular. Now, by making the respiratory system regular, you bring the vagus nerve under control. By bringing the vagus nerve under control, you gain control of the sympathetic and para-sympathetic systems.'"

As part of these practical lessons, Swamiji taught a particular breathing exercise known as *bhastrika* (bellows breathing), a technique that involves a loud and forceful exhalation, which empties the lungs completely; then an equal volume of air is inhaled gently and smoothly. The key lies in keeping the spine straight and avoiding any jerks in the chest, during either exhalation or inhalation. This breathing is done repeatedly and rapidly. He ended this lesson by saying, "'You should practice this method for one or two weeks, and then we will go on

256

from there. And next time we will talk about your stable posture, because you should do this in your stable posture. So practice as I told you, and do not use your mouth. Mouth is the emergency gate only—not for breathing exercises and not for ordinary breathing. Why? Because mouth has no filter.'"

Despite all these demonstrations, teachings, and practical lessons on yoga and meditation, life around Swamiji was full of fun. Laughing, joking, and making plans for someone's life (whether or not that person agreed) were normal elements in his behavior. For example, he decided it was time for Doug Boyd to get married and insisted he would make all the arrangements—he would select the furniture, the house, and the bride. When Mrs. Green suggested that Boyd himself might have other plans, Swamiji brushed it off. "He can't do that," he said. "He must get married. And if he doesn't listen to me I will exert pressures—subtle pressures from behind. We have ways of doing such things." Swamiji looked serious and was quite persuasive—this was a trait that Boyd thought of as "the insistent arranger."

257

The longer Swamiji stayed in Topeka the more he aroused the curiosity of the Menninger staff. Some began to perceive him as a threat. As Boyd recounts, "There were a few researchers who reacted to him with mixed emotions. He stimulated their interest because they knew he could do some unusual and remarkable things, yet at times he seemed a threat to some of their preestablished conclusions about the laws of the universe and the nature of the electrochemical organism called man and to their conclusions about the supremacy and finality of contemporary Western science."

One day Swamiji got into a heated debate with a psychiatrist in Dr. Green's office. Swamiji knew that this man doubted what he had been seeing in the lab, and so Swamiji deliberately made strong claims about the power of a one-pointed mind. By using psychokenetic energy, he said, he could move an object from a distance. When the psychiatrist expressed his skepticism, Swamiji asked Dr. Green to arrange an experiment so he could demonstrate this ability.

"The knitting needle experiment," as it came to be known, was carefully controlled. In a room sealed from drafts, Swamiji sat cross-legged on a couch wearing a mask over his mouth and nose. Four feet away there were two knitting needles—one fourteen inches long and the other ten inches—mounted on a small metal spindle so that a gentle push would make them rotate horizontally. Swamiji asked Doug Boyd to burn a stick of incense and place a metal container of cold water on his right. He also asked Boyd to sit on his left, warning the young man that if he touched Swamiji he would get a powerful shock. If Swamiji began tipping to his left, he said, Boyd should gently push him back toward center with a four-inch plywood board, two and a half feet long, provided for that purpose. All observers, including Dr. Green and Boyd (twelve in all), examined Swamiji's mask, the needles, the light, and checked for any possible source of airflow in the room. When the experiment began, Swamiji started to murmur a mantra so quietly that it was almost inaudible. (During one of our conversations Swamiji told me that this was the seed mantra *krim*, preceded by what is known as a *sabar* mantra.)

258

What happened at the culmination of the mantra recitation is best described by Boyd: "He [Swamiji] used a strange-sounding mantra I had never heard before; he increased the tempo and the pitch of his chanting as he went on repeating it until finally he reached a piercing, high-pitched crescendo that ended in a sound like 'r-eee-eee-eeem.' Two things happened simultaneously: I felt a sensation of electricity in my body, especially in my chest and on the right side of my face, and the object moved. My first instantaneous impression was that the electric shock sensation was some sort of hypnotic phenomenon that made the object appear to move. The second impression that flashed through my mind was a vivid recall of the only other such shock experience in my memory, an incident at a mountain cabin in which some teenage friends fooled me into holding a wire attached to a portable generator and when they turned the crank, I could not let go. But now the shock faded instantly. Swami asked Elmer if he wanted him to do it again. Elmer said yes and the swami resumed his chanting, beginning softly and slowly again. I decided that what I had felt was merely an emotional response to his eerie 'ee-eee' sound. Then it happened again. The same 'r-eee-eee-eeem!' sound, the same intense tremor of electricity, and the needles turned on the spindle. No, it was not just an emotional response, it was a real physical sensation.

"The needles had indeed moved, and everyone must have seen it, for though they had turned only a few degrees, they now rested in a different position. The needle point in front of the swami's face had moved toward him as the long hand on a horizontal clock face would move—counterclockwise—from about the nine to the seven. When the swami turned to face Elmer, I noticed his eyes: they looked wet and strained.

"Swami maintained his calm manner as the mask was removed and the observers got up and left. 'It was not of much use,' he said to Elmer and me when there were only the three of us in the room. 'The one who was doubting before is doubting even now.' . . .

"I went up to the second floor for a cup of hot water and a tea bag, and I thought about the demonstration and Swami's feelings. I did not know enough to explain what Swami had done, but I did feel that he had succeeded. Twice the needles had moved on the spindle, and it seemed evident to me that it had not been caused by the force of air from Swami's lungs. If the needles had moved as a result of his breathing, they would have moved at a different point in time, they would have moved in the opposite direction, and the lamp suspended on its cord would have been affected also, causing the spot of light to move from the object. In addition, there was the electric current phenomenon that I felt both times when the needles turned. In any case, something had to cause the needles to move, and that something had to be explicable in natural, not supernatural, terms. It had to be real energy to act as it did upon a physical object. I could not think of any facts or theories I had learned in my high school or college science that would preclude the possibility that energy sufficient to move an object could be generated in a human body and directed through the eyes or even through thoughts. Those who choose to deny the possibility would have to rely on their personal feelings and traditional beliefs.

" 'I don't think anything could have been done to make that demonstration any more convincing,' I told the swami, handing him his cup of tea. 'People cling to their doubts and beliefs as a matter of choice. No demonstration can ever influence anyone's beliefs, Swami. . . . If we were to prepare the control systems more elaborately, they would simply think you have a more elaborate cheating system worked out.' "

259

When I heard about this experiment I was curious about how Swamiji had made the needles move. Had he not used the mantra, I would have assumed that he did it by using the power of his sight, which he had cultivated through the practice of *trataka* (gazing)—for I had seen him incinerate a piece of paper and crack glass from a distance by gazing at them. I also wondered why Swamiji had two needles mounted on the spindle instead of just one.

When I asked him, he said, "I was thinking of making several experiments, but it is so disappointing—even scientists are closed-minded. During this experiment I had channeled the energy through my eyes, but it was not necessary. I did it so that at least by looking at my strained eyes the scientists could put together some explicable theories of the movement of energy through visual means. I was moving the object not away from me but toward me. I was pulling it rather than pushing it. In the scriptures this is known as *akarshana* [attraction]. There are six tantric *kriyas*, known as *shat karma*. Attraction is one of them. I had two needles, and my plan was to focus the energy in each needle in a manner that they first attract each other and then repel each other. This process of repelling is *vidveshana*, another of the six *kriyas*. Then I had planned to demonstrate *stambhana* [immobilization]. During that time I had planned to stop a moving needle suddenly, then combine the two different *kriyas* and let one move while the other remained stationary.

"But I saw no point in doing such things—these people had already made up their minds. Now you can see why the scriptures define these practices as forbidden. And ultimately such experiments have no positive effect on one's physical, mental, or spiritual growth. The purpose of doing these things is to inspire people and let them know that the practices described in the scriptures are authentic and that a human being is equipped with boundless potentials and that there are ways to unfold them."

Although Swamiji continued to participate in the experiments at the Menninger Foundation, he knew that they would not bear much fruit, and so he shifted part of his attention to making public appearances. His first series of lectures, held in an auditorium at the

Menninger Foundation, was mainly attended by professionals from the veterans' hospital, teachers and students from Topeka's Washburn University, members of the nearby Ananda Marga ashram, and some Menninger employees. In these lectures Swamiji maintained his scientific approach to health and well-being, but he spoke more as a philosopher and spiritual teacher than as a researcher. He usually began by reminding people that yoga is not a religion but a path of self-discovery. "Meditation is an inward journey," he would say, "and on this inward journey you come to know who you are, where you have come from, what your intrinsic traits and characteristics are. By knowing the inner dimensions of your life you can form a realistic image of yourself, and thereafter you will not be affected by the false image created by others and imposed on you. In short, meditation introduces you to yourself. Once you know your true self it will be easy for you to figure out your relationship with the world, as well as your relationship with the Lord of Life. Then you will come to understand that no religion in the world is better than another. You will not be caught in religious conflicts."

261

Boyd paints a vivid picture of these lectures: "Swami made an impressive appearance in public. He walked majestically back and forth across the stage in his sandals, gracefully cast his long shawl over his shoulders, and used his hands and voice in an aesthetic manner. Every Friday evening he spoke for two hours or more, but he had no difficulty holding the attention of everyone, young or old. He talked about mind, Eastern and Western views of mind, and the yogic disciplines of controlling the mind and its functions. He spoke about the meaning and process of meditation, and in what he called the practical part of these lessons, he taught some postures, breathing exercises, and even Sanskrit chants. 'I know many people think that these yogis and swamis from India have just come to force their ways and methods of meditation on other peoples and their ways of life. . . . If you will throw out of your minds this idea that this is a swami from the East and that you are from the West—that will be better. The real truth is the same truth for all, and the truth has nothing to do with religion, and the methods are for each individual to choose and develop for himself.'"

"'East is East and West is West' is a primitive idea," Swamiji's master had told him. Now he was delivering that same message, telling his audiences in Topeka that people all over the world are searching for peace and happiness regardless of which tools they use to reach the goal.

The Ananda Marga ashram also held its meetings on Friday night, and some of the members who attended Swamiji's lectures invited him to come and speak to members of their organization. So after his lecture at the Menninger Foundation, Swamiji would go to another place and speak to that group. As a result of these and other interactions with people outside the Menninger laboratory, Swamiji's popularity grew and people began to telephone him.

Boyd writes: "One day he agreed to give a private consultation in his office to someone from 'outside,' and from that day on it became a regular occurrence. He had already been using some hours of his mornings talking privately with interested Menninger people, and one of the doctors at the clinic who was interested in comparing yogic medicine with Western methods talked with him occasionally about a couple of his patients. In addition to this, he had frequent private meetings with some of the members of the training group. It was my job to keep his appointment book, and now that his door was more or less open to the public, his calendar became full to overflowing. With his ashram lectures, his instruction sessions for our training group, and now a waiting list of appointments to fill up all the hours and quarter-hours that remained when he was not either in the lab or preparing for it, there was almost no time to stare at the phone or watch for the arrival of the mail. It seemed to me that the busier he got, the more he enjoyed himself. . . .

"One afternoon while he was at home he spoke with Pat Norris on the telephone, and after they had talked for many minutes, he suddenly said, 'Come here. I want you to come here. Can you come now? I want to see you right away.' Pat was a professional clinical psychologist who worked at the Kansas Reception and Diagnostic Center in Topeka. Because she was a member of the training group, and because Swami had requested it, she left home immediately for the Greens' residence to meet the swami, wondering what he wanted with her that could not be handled on the telephone. While Pat was on her way, the swami sat in the living room hurriedly writing something on a piece of paper. With a look of satisfaction he glanced over what he had written, folded the paper, put it in his pocket, and waited for Pat to arrive.

"'Ask me something!' he said abruptly the moment Pat had sat down beside him.

"'Like what?' Pat wondered. 'Ask you something about what?'

"'Something about anything. Just ask. Put to me whatever question you want.'

"She was thoughtful for a moment, supposing that the swami must at least have some topic in mind and wondering what it was. Nothing in their telephone conversation had suggested that she should have something to ask about, and now only seemingly silly questions came to mind.

"'Why do you hesitate? Ask! Ask!'

"So she asked some brief, simple question about her future. Swami did not offer an answer. He only looked at her blankly for a moment and told her to ask something else. Perhaps that had not been a suitable question. Trying to come up with a more thoughtful question, she asked something more specific, something about whether she should plan or could expect to continue her postgraduate studies.

"'All right,' the swami said. 'Ask me another.'

"Pat felt puzzled. He had told her to ask about anything, but he apparently had no intention of making any response. He had not even seemed to pay much attention to the questions. She considered carefully for a minute and thought of a more personal question.

"'Ask me another.'

"Pat decided that the swami was no doubt trying to learn what sort of things she felt she needed to be advised about. But she had more or less pulled those questions out of thin air. For her fourth question she tried to think of something the swami might feel more like answering, another personal question that sounded even more meaningful.

"When she had worded her fourth question as sincerely as she could, the swami smiled at her, pulled from his pocket the piece of paper on which he had written, and handed it to her.

"She unfolded the paper. There, in the order she had asked them, were her four questions. And there were the swami's replies.

263

"One cold morning in early December a member of the Ashram Association came to keep her appointment with Swami. Swami was in one of the conference rooms with our training group, who now met with him each morning for a series of talks on the yoga sutras of Patanjali, and on this day he was late in concluding the session. As I returned to my office after the talk carrying the large stereo tape recorder through the hallway, I saw the lady sitting in the lobby holding her three-and-a-half-year-old son in her lap.

"On that Friday night after the Tower Building lecture when Swami had spoken at the regular meeting of the Ashram Association, this lady had approached him as we were on our way out and attempted to talk with him about her little boy. The boy apparently had chronic asthma and was susceptible to pneumonia and several times recently had nearly died from nighttime attacks. He was under the care of a doctor, but she was worried because he was not improving. The lady had wanted to tell Swami about the agony and fear of being awakened in the night by her child's wheezing and gasping for breath. She had seemed to have a hard time getting through to the swami. He had allowed himself to be distracted by the many people who came up to thank him for coming, to make some comments or to say goodbye to him. But for some reason he had not even seemed to notice the one person who had something really urgent to say. Then, just as she had given up trying to talk to him and he had taken his leave and was already out the door, he had suddenly turned around, gone back inside, and sat down by her. So she told him about her child. The swami had slowly closed and opened his eyes a few times as though he were either tired of all the people or else feeling sleepy. Finally he had spoken softly, as though to himself: 'The problem is the child's *heart*.' Then he had looked at her and told her that her doctor ought to do an electrocardiogram, suggesting it might be helpful to have an EKG to examine. The next day she had an EKG taken without consulting her regular doctor.

"Now she had come and brought her son with her, and when I went to tell the swami that his appointment was waiting, he and Elmer were having a conversation. They went into his office. Swami took from his desk a number of pictures of holy men and told the boy he wanted to give him one. He got the boy to choose the one he wanted. The boy picked from the group a modern-looking image of Christ, and Swami told his mother to take it home and hang it in his room. She reported that she was having a difficult time over that EKG. When she had spoken to her doctor the doctor had reacted to her as though there were something wrong with her for having consulted with a swami. She had to mention the swami, she explained, because the doctor wondered why she had an EKG taken without consulting him. When she told him about the swami, he told her she might consult another doctor.

"Eventually, examination of the EKG by a cardiologist did reveal that there was an abnormality or a malfunctioning of the child's heart.

"'How did you happen to think of the EKG?' Elmer later asked the swami.

"Swami recalled the night when he had sat beside the lady after his talk at the Ashram Association meeting. 'I called the boy, and he came to me in his astral body. I said, "What's the matter with you?" And he said, "In this life I have a defective heart."'

"At this writing the boy's condition is greatly improved, and his mother attributes his well-being to the fact that the EKG incident forced her to change doctors and led her to the 'ideal' doctor for her boy, the fact that the swami 'blessed' the boy and continued to meditate for him, and the fact that the picture of Christ still hangs in his room."

In many Indian cities, such as Kanpur, Allahabad, Bombay, and Delhi, there are hundreds of people who have had similar extraordinary experiences with Swamiji. In Kanpur alone there are easily a hundred people who were either healed by him or had their questions answered simply by coming into his presence. In Allahabad Swamiji shattered bulletproof glass with his intense gaze, and in Rishikesh he brought a bucket of water to a boil with the energy in his finger. At the residence of Mr. Anand Pratap Singh, the personal assistant of one of the cabinet ministers, Raja Dinesh Singh, he materialized a Sri Chakra from thin air. Each of these events was witnessed by a number of people. Indians are accustomed to seeing and hearing about such "supernatural" occurrences, for there have been a number of yogis who, like Swamiji, have extraordinary mastery over themselves and the subtle forces of nature. In the West, however, such things are so rare that even if people see them with their own eyes, they still have a hard time believing they actually happened. As Swamiji discovered, this is true even when such demonstrations are conducted under strict laboratory conditions.

But Swamiji was not discouraged. His mind was focused on his mission: Create a bridge between East and West, spirituality and science, regardless of the obstacles. He was not a licensed health practitioner and he did not prescribe medicines, but he offered to teach yogic techniques to those who visited him when he knew those techniques would be helpful. One of the staff psychologists, for example, was suffering from a crippling disease. His doctors had exhausted all their resources and so he came to Swamiji, who wanted to help him by working with his prana through the means of some simple breathing techniques. To this end, he had asked Boyd to type up some of his notes on the idea of prana and the means of working with it, and he had given them to the psychologist, who showed them to some of his colleagues.

266

The yogic concept of prana is widely known and accepted today, but thirty years ago it was virtually unheard of. At the Menninger Foundation, Swamiji explained prana by saying that it is the subtle energy—the life-force—that holds the body and mind together, adding that if we want to lead a healthy life it is important to keep this energy in a balanced state. Breathing is the most obvious manifestation of this subtle energy. Normally when we breathe, Swamiji would explain, one nostril is more open than the other, and so we supply more air to our lungs through that nostril.

The few pages on prana that Swamiji gave to the psychologist he was trying to help read in part: "When the balance between the flow of the right and the left nostril is upset, the 'pranic' energy is affected by it, and the result is some sort of physical ailment, sometimes trivial and sometimes serious. If we want to cure ourselves of disease and restore the balance of life, we should try to restore the balance between the flow of the breath. The breath flow should therefore be carefully studied for the purpose of getting rid of diseases. Not only does breathing oxygenize the blood but it also stores up 'pranic' energy. The breathing not only coordinates the positive and negative currents of the body but also attracts desirable and undesirable conditions. This is done by the operation of the magnetic law of attraction and repulsion. . . . This 'pranic' energy, if it is wasted, causes diseases."

Green and Boyd recognized that Swamiji was expressing what to him was a familiar truth in a typical Indian manner. But one of the research psychologists who had been antagonistic toward Swamiji for some time read the material and insisted that Swamiji be prevented from seeing the psychologist who had come to him for help and also be prevented from making any further pretense in the area of health and healing. It made no difference to this antagonist that his colleague was seeking Swamiji's help voluntarily. He believed that the pages about prana that Swamiji had given to this man proved that Swamiji was insisting that all diseases could be cured by breathing more or less through the left or right nostril. He accused Swamiji of cruelly creating false hopes. Dr. Green knew that what Swamiji had "meant by his words was something quite different from how they were interpreted by the man they had angered," but because of the potential legal complications, he asked Swamiji not to see the psychologist again. As Boyd observed, Swamiji "was more saddened than angered. He had really liked that psychologist, and he had said so many times. He talked so much about that man, both at home and at work, that I knew he felt more enthusiastically hopeful about what he might accomplish with him than about anything else he had done at the Menninger Foundation."

Doug Boyd's book *Swami* leaves the reader with the impression that Swamiji was disappointed by his experiences at the Menninger Foundation. But in my personal experience with him he never seemed disappointed, no matter what the situation. When events took a sudden and unpleasant turn, he was not at all affected. In fact, he always reminded his students that expectation is the source of all misery. So after I read *Swami* I asked him if he had been disappointed at what happened there.

"Not really disappointed," Swamiji replied. "But yes, I expected more than I should have. I knew there are all kinds of people in the world. Driven by their *samskaras* [the subtle impressions of their past] they see things in different ways, and that is why the same phenomenon, the same truth, is interpreted in different ways. That is what happened there.

"But it really did not matter. My work at the Menninger Foundation served a purpose. The point wasn't how many doctors and researchers participated in the project, or how many of them appreciated what I did and how many disagreed with me. The point was that it created a stirring. Yogic practices were brought to the attention of educated and scientifically minded people.

"My collaboration with those scientists helped me find my students, friends, and colleagues, who would carry on the mission later. In the four months I was there a great number of educated people from the States, as well as other parts of the world, came to know about me, and a great part of the credit goes to the Menninger Foundation. I'm even more grateful to those who resented me or my work, for it is they who gave me the incentive to make myself available to a wider range of people—and that's what my master intended.

"I am a fakir [a carefree person who depends totally on God] and as such I had no reason to do any of those demonstrations. At the behest of my master I subjected myself to those experiments, and when I noticed that a good number of people had gathered around me, I decided it was the perfect time for me to establish an independent organization [the Himalayan Institute]. And from that platform we could broadcast the message of the sages."

For me, this conversation raised another question. Many other masters, such as Swami Vivekananda and Swami Rama Tirtha, had also brought the message of the sages to this country and had broadcast it without leaning on science. The gap between spirituality and science had existed for ages, and neither spiritual leaders nor scientists felt the need to fill it. So why was this scientific experimentation on a spiritual subject so important now? Why had Babaji given Swamiji the task of creating a bridge between spirituality and science, East and West? Why is that so important? And why did this process of bridging the gap between spirituality and science have to begin at the Menninger Foundation?

When I expressed this to Swamiji, he said, "Today science is growing at an extremely fast rate. Scientific discoveries are contributing to the production of endless worldly objects. If the spiritual understanding of life and the world in which we live doesn't grow at the same speed, then human civilization will become so lopsided it will collapse."

Then, out of the blue, he said, "Elmer and Alyce Green are very special people. During our first meeting I felt that Mrs. Green was my own mother. When I finally went to stay with them I could not control my emotions. I was compelled to tell them everything about my master, to the point that later I felt it had not been appropriate. I have not spoken to anyone about my master at such length as I did to the Greens. I always kept my master in the deepest chamber of my heart, but here, to my surprise, I talked so much about him. Later I learned from my master that the Greens are special souls and were yogis in their previous lives. They had been blessed with the gift of serving humanity and providing direction. And they will continue doing good work, relieving others' pain until the last breath of their lives.

269

"The Greens gave me their love. While living in a scientific atmosphere they did what they were supposed to do. Had they not done that—had they followed me blindly and admired yoga too much—they could have become instrumental in killing the true spirit of yoga. Yoga science would not have found its rightful place in the field of holistic health and might have become a cult instead. And just because a few people were critical of me, it aroused more curiosity among others. My master works in so many strange and mysterious ways.

"A spiritual and charitable organization established by him would never be accepted by the scientists as an authentic source of empirical knowledge. Unless a researcher with a big degree spends millions of dollars in 'research' at a prestigious university and proves that eating a heavy meal loaded with fat and sugar late at night is injurious to health, people will not hear it. When saints and yogis teach these simple truths from their personal experience, people ignore them and continue to suffer. Had I taught mind's mastery over the body without doing those demonstrations at the Menninger Foundation, people would have said, 'He's a Hindu swami trying to impose his culture on us.'

"After those demonstrations I established the Himalayan Institute, which is respected by all—Christians, Jews, Hindus, Buddhists, and Muslims. Men and women from all walks of life—scientists, doctors, teachers, students, and businesspeople alike—come and learn the universal principles of spirituality without any hesitation. As long as the Institute maintains its credibility it will continue its work of bridging the gap between ancient and modern wisdom, East and West, spirituality and science. People will participate in the Institute's work, for they know that the work entails healing human hearts and rediscovering the sacred link which connects all spiritual traditions of the world."

ROOTS *in the* WEST

AFTER WORLD WAR II ENDED in 1945, the United States was blessed with a booming economy, and Americans began to experience all the comforts and luxuries that prosperity brings. New economic opportunities drew people away from their hometowns and extended families, and this new mobility gave them greater freedom at a personal level. But it also deprived them of the emotional support and guidance that flows from an extended family. People made more money in less time and had more leisure. Television and other forms of mass media flowed in to fill it. The growing prosperity in the external world, coupled with a growing sense of emptiness in the inner world, gave rise to the culture of the sixties and experiments with alternative lifestyles, religious beliefs, and spiritual practices.

Swamiji knew that to create a bridge between East and West, between spirituality and science, he must thoroughly understand the elements unique to each, as well as the elements they have in common. At the Menninger Foundation and during his lecture tours, he made a careful study of the cultural psychology of the West, especially the United States, and saw clearly what was missing in American society. Family ties had been loosened, old values were falling away, new values had not yet been formed, the link between spirituality and science was broken, and even though the economy had engendered an insatiable desire for an endless number of objects, deep down people were questioning the purpose and meaning of life.

Even before he left India, Swamiji had been aware of the direction Western society was taking. And in an attempt to get some clear instructions from his master, Swamiji had explained the cultural differences between East and West to him and then asked, "These two diverse ways of life seem to be quite apart. How can I deliver your message to the West?"

His master had replied, "Though these cultures inhabit the same world with the same purpose of life, they are each extreme. Both East and West are still doing experiments on the right ways of living. The message of the Himalayan masters is timeless and has nothing to do with the primitive concepts of East or West. Extremes will not help humanity to attain the higher step of civilization for which we all are striving." These words from Babaji were like a beacon, guiding Swamiji as he formulated his mission in the West.

Swamiji left the Menninger Foundation in mid-December of 1970 and went to India for a few months. When he returned to the United States in the spring, he made Chicago his main base. He had no ashram or center of his own, so he stayed in various hotels and motels in the metropolitan area. The students who were closest to him kept track of his itinerary, ran an informal office for him from their homes, and helped people from other cities locate him when he was in Chicago. Many invited Swamiji to stay with them, but his long-cherished habit of living in solitude kept him in hotels. This caused some consternation among Indian families, for whom hosting a swami is a great honor. Even today, some Indians in Chicago refer to Swamiji as "the hotel swami."

In the spring of 1980, when I was new to this country and still living in Minneapolis, a gentleman of Indian origin said to me, "Swamiji is a great sage and the leader of our Hindu dharma, but it is odd that he associates with Americans and has no time for us. Even when he did not have a place of his own, he stayed away from his own countrymen. Now he has a big center in Pennsylvania and smaller ones all over the country, but it is impossible to have *satsanga* with him." It was obvious to me that this man was annoyed with Swamiji—because he was Indian he felt this gave him a special claim on Swamiji.

Shortly afterward, when I joined Swamiji at the Institute's head-quarters in Pennsylvania, I noticed that we two were the only Indians there. I wondered why, so one day I repeated that gentleman's remark to Swamiji, adding, "There are over sixty residents here, but except for you and me, there are no Indians."

"My mission is not confined to Indians alone," Swamiji replied. "My master has sent me to create a bridge between East and West, science and spirituality. I have been given a job: to create a platform where people from all faiths and all walks of life interact with each other, learn from each other, share the best they have, identify the weaknesses they have inherited from their backgrounds, and make plans to overcome such weaknesses. Read *Living with the Himalayan Masters* and see what my master has said: 'To get freedom from all fears is the first message of the Himalayan sages. The second message is to be aware of the reality within.' Like other ethnic groups, Indians are afraid of losing their cultural identity while living in this melting pot called 'America.' India is an old country with an ancient and multi-dimensional culture. Indians are accustomed to harboring lofty ideals, but these ideals are rarely reflected in their actions. That is why, despite its great wealth of wisdom, India has been suffering for the last fifteen hundred years.

273

"During the first few years of my stay in this country I visited many Indian families and organizations, but only on rare occasions did they want to learn something from me. Most of the time they made sure that I knew how much they knew about everything. They told me what I should teach and how I should teach. They criticized Americans: Americans are of loose character; they are materialistic; they have no respect for their parents; they don't know how to discipline their children; they have no loyalty to their spouses; they eat beef; they have no idea that Hinduism is the mother of all religions, and so on. There were so many factions among them that if I associated with a particular Indian family or organization, I was automatically dragged into party politics. The saying 'two heads, three opinions' is as true among Indians in America as it is in India. Extending my love to a particular group meant inviting animosity in general.

"I introduced the knowledge of the sages without associating it with Hinduism, and the result was that broadminded Indians, whether they were Hindus, Sikhs, or Jains, came to study with me alongside the Americans. I love Indians, but I love their children more, for they are more openminded and have a wider perspective on life than their parents.

"Through these children there will come a time when people of Indian origin living in the West will realize that the wisdom of the sages documented in the Vedas is the soul of Hinduism. Rituals, religious ceremonies, and various forms of sectarianism are but Hinduism's outer garments. Indian families in America will understand the value of my master's mission in the West when their children start asking, 'Who are we? Where are our roots? What is our heritage? Are we superior to others? If yes, then in what respect?'

274

"My master said, '"East is East and West is West" is a primitive idea. That the West has much to share with the East is beyond doubt, but the East has much to contribute to the West. The flower of the West without the fragrance of the East is a flower in vain.' I have always remembered this. Working in the Indian community exclusively, confining myself to Hinduism, and delivering the message of the sages from a Hindu platform would have ruined my master's mission. That is why I kept myself apart and why I preferred to live in hotels."

Still, living in hotels was not an ideal arrangement. Vegetarian food was hard to come by in those days, and Swamiji found himself eating a lot of pancakes. Tilk—a special preparation of tea boiled in milk with cardamom, ginger, saffron, and sugar—was his favorite drink, and to make it for him his students had to smuggle a hot plate into his room. Then there was the mess. Swamiji had many visitors, and while the student prepared tilk for them, the milk often boiled over, and even when it did not, it often got sloshed onto the carpet. And it was hard to wash up in the bathroom sink. To make things worse, Indian families often brought food for Swamiji, and the strong aroma of Indian spices drew the attention of the hotel management— who were also understandably annoyed by the candle wax stuck to the carpet and the small holes burned into the rug by candles and incense.

Furthermore, in the midst of a hectic schedule of traveling, giving lectures, and teaching workshops, Swamiji was contributing articles to the magazine *Voice of the Himalayas,* published in Kanpur, India, and it was difficult for him to do his writing while staying in temporary quarters. When he returned from a weekend in another city he would settle into a new hotel room, and his students would have to bring paper and a typewriter. Swamiji would sit in one corner giving dictation to someone, who wrote it out in longhand while another person typed in the opposite corner. The work would normally continue until one or two in the morning; as soon as the students left, Swamiji would take a bath and meditate.

Eventually the group in Chicago realized that this gypsy life was ridiculous—Swamiji should have a permanent place to live and do his work, and those working with him needed an office. So they went to him and proposed forming a non-profit organization as a means for furthering his mission. Swamiji agreed, and the incorporation papers of the Himalayan International Institute of Yoga Science and Philosophy of the USA were filed on June 23, 1971.

275

The new Institute rented a house in the Chicago suburb of Barrington, where Swamiji began lecturing and holding teachers' training classes. In the mornings he taught hatha yoga, pranayama, and relaxation techniques, and in the evenings he gave discourses on spiritual subjects. Now that he had an office, people could call and make appointments, and his travel arrangements became more organized. The teachers he trained began to offer classes throughout greater Chicago and in other cities. As soon as the Institute was incorporated, branches and affiliated centers began to spring up all over the country and in other countries.

Swamiji maintained a rigorous schedule, lecturing in different U.S. cities four days a week and returning to teach in Chicago on the weekends. He would travel to India in the fall and return to Chicago in the spring, and on his way to and from the East he would stop and hold seminars and conferences in Great Britain, Holland, Switzerland, Belgium, Germany, Italy, France, and Spain. During his first appearance in a new city he would demonstrate his mastery over his mind and his voluntary control over the supposedly involuntary systems of the human body. In his next presentation, however, he always spoke about how to be healthy at the physical level and happy at the mental level. He taught simple techniques of hatha yoga, pranayama, concentration, and relaxation as a means to explore the inner dimensions of life. His non-religious, non-sectarian approach to health and spirituality drew people from all faiths and from all walks of life, and everywhere he went, the media carried stories about this scientist, yogi, mystic, and philosopher. Within a matter of two years Swamiji had been written about in scores of newspapers and magazines and had appeared on dozens of radio and television shows.

This was also the time that a host of scientists, professors, and health professionals joined Swamiji in different capacities. One of them, Dr. Rudolph Ballentine, came to play a pivotal role in the growth of the Himalayan Institute. A young psychiatrist, Dr. Ballentine was familiar with yoga and Eastern philosophy and was deeply interested in the methods of self-transformation found in the Eastern traditions. He had been on the faculty of psychiatry at Louisiana State University School of Medicine in New Orleans, and in that city's French Quarter, in the late sixties, he had also co-founded a free clinic dedicated to helping street kids, most of whom had problems with drugs. But after becoming involved with the practice of yoga he realized that in order to be really effective, he needed more knowledge and insight. And so, adventurous and carefree, he decided that the best way to get it was to travel to the East, where traditional knowledge was still honored.

Early in 1972 he set out. From Europe he went overland to Beirut, but after being there a short time he felt a sudden inner command to go to India immediately. An hour later he was in a taxi to Damascus, from where he caught a plane to Karachi, Pakistan. Traveling by a variety of conveyances, he crossed into the Punjab to Amritsar and made his way to Delhi in the early spring of 1973. In Delhi he realized that he must learn Hindi before venturing further into yoga, so he visited the Department of Hindi at Delhi University, where he found a professor who agreed to tutor him in his home.

When Dr. Ballentine arrived for his first lesson, the professor asked if he was part of the group of physicians and psychologists who had been brought from America by someone named Swami Rama. Dr. Ballentine knew nothing about that, so the professor showed him an article about the group that had appeared in that day's newspaper. Dr. Ballentine took down the information in the article and learned that the group was at Swamiji's ashram in Rishikesh. So Dr. Ballentine wrote a letter asking about their work and mission. A week later, an American voice on the telephone replied on Swamiji's behalf, explaining that the group would soon be back in New Delhi and suggesting that he meet them there. Although he was ill, Dr. Ballentine kept the appointment, and when he arrived at the hotel he was greeted by a psychologist, Dr. Alan Weinstock.

The hotel was abuzz with activity since a famous sitarist was about to begin a performance in Swamiji's honor, and when Dr. Weinstock brought Dr. Ballentine to the door of the concert room and presented him to Swamiji, Swamiji barely looked up, muttering offhandedly, "Yes, I know, I know. Seat him up front beside me." This did not make a very good impression on Dr. Ballentine.

After the performance Swamiji invited him to his room and asked abruptly, "Why are you in India?" Before he could answer, Swamiji said, "If you came to find a teacher, you won't succeed: they live in the mountains. Besides, I can teach you anything you need to learn."

Dr. Ballentine was shocked by what seemed to him the man's insufferable arrogance. Trying not to sound as irritated as he felt, he replied, "I really don't think you can teach me anything, Swami Rama. However, if you can help me, I would appreciate it."

"What kind of help do you need?" Swamiji asked, totally unaffected by the implied insult.

"Well, you see, my visa is about to expire, and I want to stay in this country longer so that I can learn more about yoga," Dr. Ballentine replied.

"Come back tomorrow," Swamiji said.

When he arrived the next day, he was taken to a room full of devotees—Indian ladies with their daughters, men of importance—all sitting on the floor before Swamiji, posing their questions. Swamiji looked at them, offered a few sentences of response, and then turned to Dr. Ballentine and proceeded to answer his questions—the questions he had in his mind but had not spoken. The answers were crystal-clear, and they rang true. Dr. Ballentine began to suspect that this man might, after all, be able to teach him something—perhaps a great deal.

After some time Swamiji sent everyone away and turned to Dr. Ballentine. He signaled to one of his assistants. "Bring in Mr. Pandey," he said. When a well-dressed Indian man entered and took a seat, Swamiji explained to him, "Dr. Ballentine is a psychiatrist from America. His visa is expiring. Can you help him?"

"Of course, Swamiji," the gentleman replied. "All he needs to do is let me know for how long he needs the visa, and I will get it for him." Then Swamiji looked at Dr. Ballentine and said, "Mr. Pandey is the head of CBI [Central Bureau of Intelligence], the equivalent to your FBI director. He will take care of your visa problem. Is there anything else I can do for you?"

278

Dr. Ballentine was stunned. His plans, organized around writing a research proposal and visiting a sponsor for it in Bombay (so that he could get a visa extension), were suddenly unnecessary. What to do now? "Well," he heard himself say, "I had a few thousand dollars with me, and half of it is gone. I do have some concern about being financially able to stay in India." Before he could say more, Swamiji turned to one of his assistants and said, "Bring in Mr. Sharma." Mr. Sharma, he explained, was the largest exporter of brass artifacts in India. "Dr. Ballentine is a sincere seeker," Swamiji said to Mr. Sharma. "He may need some assistance financially."

"Of course, Swamiji," the gentleman replied, bowing. "He should let me know where he is and how much money he needs. I'll wire it immediately."

With no more work to do to get a visa, with his financial worries allayed, and with this man before him who seemed to have the answers he wanted, Dr. Ballentine began to see a new possibility opening.

"Where are you going from here?" he asked Swamiji. "Maybe I could come along?" It seemed like an appropriate question. After all, Swamiji had suggested that he could teach him what he wanted to know.

"I'm afraid that's not possible," Swamiji replied. "But perhaps we can meet again later."

From Dr. Weinstock, Dr. Ballentine learned that Swamiji would soon be going to Chandigarh to attend an international conference on yoga. Dr. Ballentine had read about the conference and had considered going, for many of the best-known authorities—those Indians who wrote on yoga in English—were to be there. He had seen their books in the Delhi University library, and was eager to hear them speak.

So Dr. Ballentine said goodbye to his Hindi teacher, put his belongings in storage, and caught a train to Chandigarh. When he arrived there, after dark, he hired a *tonga* (a horse-drawn buggy) and asked the driver to take him to an inexpensive hotel. They visited several places, but all were closed or full. To make matters worse, no one seemed to have heard of an international conference on yoga. He was discouraged.

"I know of one more hotel," the driver said. "It's the Oberoi." That was an expensive place. Dr. Ballentine didn't want to waste money, but he was tired, not well, and needed a place to sleep. So he agreed.

279

An hour later he had had a bite to eat from room service and felt better. But he was not pleased: here he was on a wild-goose chase, looking for a yoga conference that didn't seem to exist, and wasting his money on an expensive hotel.

At that point the phone rang, and when he picked it up the voice of Dr. Weinstock said, "Swamiji wants you to come to his room right away." Dr. Ballentine looked at the receiver in disbelief.

"What?" he asked, baffled.

"Room 115," Dr. Weinstock replied.

When he arrived, Swamiji asked, "What took you so long?"

Dr. Ballentine was instructed to return to Swamiji's room at nine the next morning so they could go to the conference. He was elated. He would, after all, get to hear the learned men he had read about.

The conference was being held in a great hall. The room was crowded and the panel of eminent experts was already seated on the stage. But the moment Swamiji entered the room the speaker stopped, and both those in the audience and those on the stage rushed from their places toward him, pushing and elbowing in an effort to get near enough to touch his feet. Dr. Ballentine was puzzled: Why were these authorities on yoga trying to touch the feet of Swami Rama?

It took more than ten minutes for the commotion to subside and for Swamiji to make his way toward the stage. The speaker was about to resume, when Swamiji interrupted. "I am sorry to disrupt your program, but there is an important person from America who is here to address you," he announced. The speaker quickly joined the audience, and Swamiji said to Dr. Ballentine, "Go up on the stage."

"For what?" he asked, taken aback.

"To speak," Swamiji answered.

"About what?" he asked, his eyes growing wide.

"Whatever you want," Swamiji answered.

Dumbfounded, Dr. Ballentine stepped up onto the stage and faced the hall. Slowly he began to talk about his interest in yoga and the parallels he saw between yoga and psychotherapy. He talked about his questions, his vision of how the two could come together. When he ended, he heard applause. The authors he had come to hear approached the stage to express their interest and admiration.

His brief talk had lasted only about half an hour, but it had mesmerized experts and audience alike. They had not expected a Western physician to launch such a profound inquiry into the interface of Eastern and Western ideas. Dr. Ballentine himself was surprised at his spontaneous presentation.

After this experience, the dormant fire in Dr. Ballentine burst into flame and he could no longer return to the practice of conventional medicine or psychiatry. So he joined Swamiji and dedicated himself wholeheartedly to the work of the Himalayan Institute. Under Swamiji's guidance he studied Indian philosophy and immersed himself in the wisdom of Vedanta, yoga, Ayurveda, and homeopathy. And in addition to learning about different approaches to physical, mental, and spiritual well-being, he committed himself to intense meditation practices as taught in the tradition of the Himalayan sages. Like Swamiji, he too began lecturing on ancient wisdom and giving workshops on the principles of holistic health. In addition, he established a network of holistic health clinics in different cities around the United States.

Although Swamiji remained the main force, the combined efforts of Dr. Ballentine and the other teachers trained in the tradition generated so much activity that the Institute outgrew its rented space, and early in 1975 it acquired a three-acre plot in the Chicago suburb of Glenview. The property included a house, a cottage, and a big building—all run-down—and throughout that early spring, students and volunteers worked day and night to fix up the buildings and clean up the grounds. The grand opening was scheduled for May 5.

When I asked my friend Gus Gatto about this period, he said, "It was awe-inspiring to see how hard Swamiji worked and how little he slept. He busied himself traveling, lecturing, and writing, but he still managed to keep us hopping. A bunch of boys with no experience did the renovation work, and the girls did the cleaning and fixed our meals. In those days the residents had no rooms of their own—they worked all day long and late into the evening, and then pushed the furniture and construction tools into a corner, spread their sleeping bags wherever they found space, rolled them up again in the morning, and went back to work. Sometimes the girls fixed lunch; at other times Swamiji ordered food from an Indian restaurant. Even though we were all working day and night, the grand opening was only a few days away and there was still a mountain of work to do. Swamiji had invited VIPs, such as the Indian Ambassador to the United States, the Indian Consul General, the mayor of Chicago, and a number of other prominent people from both the Indian and American communities.

"On May 4, the day before the opening, the place finally began to take shape. Swamiji was walking around in the late afternoon giving last-minute instructions, and Anne Aylward, the first chairman of the Institute—whom Swamiji affectionately called Mama—walked into the main hall, where some of the students were hanging the curtains. Looking at the large magnolia tree just outside the big window in the back, Anne remarked, 'Wouldn't it be wonderful if that magnolia were in bloom?' Spring was late in Chicago that year, the trees had not leafed out yet, and the buds on the magnolia were still tightly closed.

"Swamiji walked into the room just then and asked, 'Hey, what are you people talking about?'

"Mama said, 'This tree won't blossom for weeks, but we were wishing it would be in bloom for the opening.'

"Swamiji looked at the tree for a moment, then put his arm around Mama and said, 'That will be my gift to you. It will bloom tomorrow.'

And sure enough: the next morning the large magnolia tree just outside the picture window in the main hall was covered with blossoms."

Swamiji rarely did such things in public, but in private his magic touch was much in evidence. The culture of the sixties had reached its climax. Recreational drug use and casual sex had become the norm among many groups of young people. Swamiji's teachings attracted those who were interested in self-help and self-transformation, but most of them came to him only after they realized how much harm they had already done themselves by living a careless life. Swamiji did not promise these young people instantaneous bliss or a quick transformation. Instead, he subtly imparted something so potent that they wanted to stay with him.

Many young men and women, however, had joined the Himalayan Institute hoping that Swamiji would ordain them as renunciates, thinking this would solve all their problems. Swamiji told these students repeatedly, "You attain freedom not by running away from the world but by renouncing the unwanted part of yourself. To attain freedom from inner slavery, you must study yourself. Study the dynamics of your mind and discover how skillfully it tricks you. Once you are clear in your mind and pure in your heart, you will see that this world is a beautiful place and you are a beautiful being. There is no need to renounce the world. While living in the world you can be happy, peaceful, and creative. There is no need for renunciation."

Swamiji always approached health and spirituality scientifically. He made sure that his teachings, which had their source in the Vedic tradition, were not mistaken for Hindu religious ideas. But because he was a swami and came from India, it was hard for people to realize that he was unfettered by religious and national affinities. Swamiji reminded his students again and again that simply changing religions and adopting a new lifestyle will not lead anyone anywhere. It is self-transformation—an everlasting inner transformation—that will bring true fulfillment in life.

Despite this repeated reminder, many young people hung around Swamiji wearing ochre clothes, which they had heard was the color of purity, renunciation, and holiness. Swamiji often playfully greeted such a person by saying, "How are you, Your Holiness?" Then turning to a bystander he might say, "Do you know why I consider her holy? Because she has holes in her head." And still, some people refused to hear what Swamiji was trying to tell them.

For example, one young woman in Chicago, who had become one of the Institute's best hatha yoga teachers through her sincere practices, wanted to become a renunciate. Although she was married, she begged Swamiji to initiate her into the monastic order of the Himalayan sages. Swamiji told her that she should stay with her husband and learn to perform her actions skillfully and selflessly. There was no need, he said, to renounce her family, culture, and religion.

At the time, an Indian pandit who was well-versed in the scriptures and an expert in Hindu rituals was spending a great deal of time at the Institute with Swamiji. The young lady told the pandit of her spiritual fervor and often discussed her goals with him, so the pandit approached Swamiji and pleaded with him to fulfill the desire of such a sincere seeker. Swamiji refused outright, saying that renunciation was not her path. Soon afterward Swamiji left for India. After he had gone, the woman divorced her husband, and the pandit, using his authority as a Hindu priest, performed the rituals to make her a swami. The other students were confused and disturbed: they knew that Swamiji had told her not to become a swami and wondered why the pandit had performed this ritual for her. They wondered how a pandit, who was not a swami himself, could ordain someone as a swami by performing a ritual ceremony. They were curious to know what she really got from this ceremony other than changing her normal clothes for ochre robes.

Then, while Swamiji was still in India, this newly ordained swami started behaving as if everyone should treat her like they treated him. This was even more distressing to the Institute community, and some people left as a result. Others waited for Swamiji's return. Some of them tried to contact him in India, but to no avail. The organization was in turmoil. Swamiji pretended he did not know what was going on and simply allowed the drama to unfold, letting his students learn from the events themselves. Eventually the young swami renounced her renunciation and returned to her husband. I have no idea how the pandit faced Swamiji, but the students who had harbored fantasies of leading a spiritual life simply by becoming a swami got the lesson and turned their attention to self-discipline and self-reflection.

In addition to confusion about the meaning of renunciation, there was considerable confusion within the community about spirituality itself. The hippie movement had attracted all kinds of people to the United States. They came from all over the world, but especially from India, Tibet, China, and Japan, and the general impression Americans got from this influx was that anything out of the ordinary is spiritual. Kung fu, karate, tai chi, Reiki, dream therapy, mind reading, clairvoyance, astrology, tarot cards, hatha yoga, different forms of meditation—all were lumped together in the broad category of spirituality. The most alluring spiritual teachers were those who promised miraculous experiences, such as *shakti pata* (the direct transmission of spiritual energy), out-of-body experiences, astral travel, the vision of gods and goddesses, and other forms of psychic experiences.

By contrast, Swamiji's approach to spirituality was scientific. He taught people to be practical and not to be influenced by false promises. "Only the experience that leads to a long-lasting transformation within is a valid experience," he would say. "Seeing red or blue lights in your head or hearing voices does not make you spiritual. You still remain the same even after experiencing such things. Learn the techniques to make your body healthy and your mind balanced so that you can use your healthy body and sound mind as tools to explore the deeper dimensions of life." At a practical level, he taught hatha yoga, pranayama, proper diet, relaxation techniques, and meditation. But he knew that his students must be exposed to the teachers of different traditions and cultures and that they must figure out for themselves whether or not the path they were following was the right path for them.

So Swamiji decided to host an annual congress, to which he invited teachers, scholars, and religious leaders from a wide variety of traditions. The first, held in June of 1976, lasted three and a half days, and it was a real eye-opener. As speakers, Swamiji invited Sufis, Sikhs, and Buddhists; Jewish, Christian, and Islamic clergy; Native American shamans; Zen masters; swamis from various orders; yogis from various schools; health professionals (conventional and unconventional); and scientific researchers. All of them had their own brand of charisma and expertise, and all of them had a following. Swamiji knew that some were not what they seemed, yet he invited them anyway.

Some of the speakers shared experiential knowledge, which people could practice to improve their quality of life; other presentations were intellectually sound, but boring and of no practical value. Yogi Ramananda from India demonstrated the amazing yogic feat of breaking an elephant's chain with the power of his breath. In one session a young man demonstrated his extraordinary retentive power by asking twenty volunteers from the audience to tell him a long series of numbers. When he finished listening to the numbers provided by all twenty, he pointed at each person, in no particular order, and recited their numbers precisely. In another session, a yogi claimed his kundalini was awakened and demonstrated this by attaching wires to his head that were connected to a doll several yards away. At the moment when he told the audience that he was now activating his *sushumna* (the central channel in the subtle body), he pressed a button on a remote control hidden in his voluminous robes, and the doll's eyes lit up. And then there was the teacher who, shortly before his scheduled lecture, took a tablet of LSD. When it took effect, he declared he was in samadhi and sent word that anyone who wished could come to his room and bask in his presence.

285

Chicago is a cosmopolitan city, but people passing by the hotel were astonished at the sight of speakers in their orange robes, pointed hats, or shaven heads walking with their entourages. Some who attended found the conference thrilling, others were disappointed. Many complained that in spite of his own scientific and holistic approach to health and spirituality, Swamiji had invited speakers who were charlatans, cult leaders, and in some cases, simply deluded. Others were grateful to Swamiji and the Himalayan Institute because this congress put them in the company of so many great masters. Some felt they had learned a great deal; a few were convinced that their kundalini had been awakened. The consensus was that the congress provided a rich, if somewhat confusing, environment.

Swamiji himself spoke only three times during the congress. On

June 17 he greeted the speakers and the audience with some brief opening remarks on the importance of the gathering. Then he gave two lectures: the first on the evening of the 19th, and the second on the afternoon of the 20th. By the time he walked to the podium to give his last lecture, he was fully aware of the mixed reactions.

Addressing the audience, he began in his typical fashion: "I pray to the Divinity in you. I am grateful to all the speakers who have been so kindly sharing their knowledge with you. I'm glad you are listening to them attentively. You Americans are great people. I love you and I have great respect for you. But you people have a serious problem: you are trying to find the solution to your problems in the external world. Let me tell you—the objects of the world are disappointing. You have made all kinds of experiments in the external world. Today you can fly in the air, and you have already landed on the moon. But you are not able to understand the importance of turning your mind inward and finding the truth within. Unless you know yourself, unless you know your body, your mind, and the center of consciousness—which yogis call Atman— you will remain alien to this world. You will not be able to adjust yourself to the world around you. Happiness comes from within.

"In the pursuit of happiness you have tried all sorts of things—sex, drugs, and hundreds of other things—and you know that such things cannot make you happy for long. But still you continue to run into the external world, trying to learn the art of health and happiness from this teacher, from that priest, from this guru, from that swami. But let me tell you that unless you find the teacher within, these teachers and preachers in the external world cannot make you happy. You must learn to light your own lamp. An external object can simply show you the way, but ultimately you have to walk on the path by yourself.

"If you are not clear about the goal and purpose of life, then no matter how clear the instructions you get from external gurus, you will be haunted by fear and doubt. The fear and doubt will not allow you to walk on the path wholeheartedly. Therefore, first you sit down and contemplate on the urgent issues of life: What am I doing? Why am I doing it? What is the purpose of my life? What do I want to achieve in life? What did I do in the past? What were the consequences of my previous deeds? What lessons did I learn from my past actions? Which of my actions were healthy and conducive to my growth, and which were not? Where did I make a mistake, and how can I not commit the same mistake again?

"This is called contemplation. During the practice of contemplation, be honest to yourself. Listen to your inner voice. Make sure your inner voice is not contaminated by the noises of your mind. Your own sincerity and honesty will help you hear and heed the voice of your soul. Once you come in touch with that inner voice, the theories and practices taught by the teachers in the outside world will begin to make sense. You will instantly know which particular practice is really sensible and meaningful, which particular practice is truly helpful to your growth, and which other practices are just a waste of time.

"There are three kinds of aspirants: some are like elephants, others are like ants, and a few rare ones are like honeybees. An elephant is a strong, powerful animal, but is not able to separate the grains of sugar from sand. An ant can separate sand and sugar. But a bee gathers the sweetness from all different sources and mixes it skillfully to form honey. Similarly, there are three kinds of students. Some students are not able to distinguish the great wisdom from dogma, superstition, cultish practices, and ceremonies; they remain confused about spirituality. Another kind of student has enough insight to see the difference between the genuine and the fake, between useful and useless practices, but is not strong from within. The best students are those who are blessed with both insight and inner strength. They gain knowledge from all possible sources, and modify the knowledge to suit their needs, for they know exactly what they are trying to achieve in life.

"The Upanishads, the great scriptures of the East, say that this world is full of light and darkness, good and bad. You as a human being have the capacity to distinguish light from darkness and good from bad and embrace only that which is full of light. Don't waste your time running around from this teacher to that teacher. Don't expect Swami Rama or anyone else to give you enlightenment. How can you expect that if I eat for you, you will attain freedom from hunger? Expecting that you will overcome your hunger by having someone else eat for you is a false expectation. Do not listen to those who give you such expectations.

"Be practical. You have a body, but you are not body alone. You are

287

a thinking being too, for you have a mind. In order to be healthy and happy, you must learn the dynamics of your body and mind—their relationship and how they are connected to each other. Between body and mind there is something called breath. You are a breathing being too. Breath holds the key to your physical and mental health. Proper diet and exercise ensures your physical health. Proper thinking and one-pointedness of mind ensures your mental health. But without proper breathing you cannot have a good grip on either your body or your mind.

"When you learn to eat properly and exercise properly, breathe and think properly, you don't become a Hindu or a Buddhist; you simply become a good healthy person. With a healthy body and clear mind, you can practice your religion more efficiently and creatively. Once you are healthy in body and clear in mind, you can easily contemplate on the higher purpose and meaning of life. Once you have clarity of mind, you will not need an Eastern swami or Western preacher to tell you what is good for you and what is not good for you. Therefore what I tell you is to learn those techniques of holistic health and spirituality that can help you become healthy and strong, clear and energetic.

"This is a scientific path. All yogic practices can be verified scientifically. Yoga is a spiritual science. To practice this spiritual science, you do not need to change your religion. There are no commandments in yoga. Yoga requires self-commitment. Self-commitment is the basis of self-discipline, and self-discipline is the key to self-transformation. It is self-transformation that will bring you everlasting joy—not changing your clothes or your lifestyle or becoming part of a particular group or organization."

This presentation brought the congress into perspective for most of the audience. Those who had been confused felt that their questions had been answered, and afterwards activities at the Institute took on new life. In the fall, Swamiji returned to India.

At the time this was going on, I was going through a crucial phase in my own life. I had just completed my master's degree and had entered the doctoral program in the department of Sanskrit at the University of Allahabad. Family pressure was forcing me to find a job, but my personal ambition demanded that I find something more fulfilling than simply trading time for money. After twelve years of intense study of Sanskrit and the scriptures, I knew that the purpose of life was more than being born, growing into adulthood, struggling for worldly success, becoming old, and dying. I was convinced that it is better and more satisfying to shine for a flash than to smolder for years. When my parents and sisters were not uppermost in my mind, I thought of leaving everything behind and finding a master who could introduce me to the Lord of Life. But as soon as I remembered my family I would think of finding a job so I could fulfill my responsibilities to them. In fact, I had applied for jobs in several places, including the University of Allahabad and the Indian Institute of Indology, located on Ring Road in New Delhi.

I visited New Delhi for the first time when the Indian Institute of Indology called me for an interview in September of 1976, but it quickly became clear that they had already selected a candidate and were simply going through the motions of interviewing others. So with a mixture of relief and disappointment I returned to the home of my host, Mr. Anand Pratap Singh. Mr. Singh was a member of the royal family that had ruled the state of Amargarh, where my family had been *raja purohit* (royal priests) for many generations.

The next morning was the first day of Nava Ratri, the nine days dedicated to the Divine Mother Durga, so I got up early, took my bath, and did my practice of *japa* and scripture recitation. After breakfast I was sitting on the lawn when Mr. Singh came out and said, "Hey, Rajmani! Do you want to see Delhi?"

Naturally I did. We drove by the residences of prominent politicians on South Avenue, and he pointed out the house of Jawaharlal Nehru, India's first prime minister, on the Tinmurti Road. Eventually we pulled up in front of the Ashoka Hotel. Handing me a ten-rupee note, he said, "I have an important meeting in this hotel. It might take some time. You see Nehru Park across the street? You can walk around for a while and go back home whenever you wish. If you get lost, get a three-wheeler; you know the address."

This was my first visit to Delhi and everything looked wonderful—I had never seen such beautiful buildings or wide streets, and

289

I was impressed by the huge, well-maintained park, where I wandered aimlessly. After a while I found myself on the other side. There was a tall building across the road, with a sign on the top reading "Akbar Hotel." In Allahabad, Banaras, and other cities that I was familiar with, restaurants were called hotels, and I was amazed at the size of the building and was curious to see how many people would be eating in such a place. As I drew near the entrance a car pulled up, and when the doorman opened the door I walked in along with the guest. I was overwhelmed by the huge lobby and completely bewildered by the absence of food. My first thought was that this was an important place and I should not wander around, but I dismissed it when I remembered that I was the guest of Anand Pratap Singh, who held a high governmental position, and once people knew that, no one would bother me. So I wandered around until I reached a place where I saw a door slide open, people come out, and others go in. Then the door closed. A little later it happened again, so out of curiosity I went in myself. The door closed and there was a strange sense of motion, and when the door opened again, I saw that the carpet outside was different. I was no longer on the same floor. Suddenly it dawned on me that the "room" I was standing in was a lift, an elevator. I had heard about lifts, but this was the first one I had seen. I noticed a lighted number "9" above the door. A bit scared, I got off.

To cover my fear and feeling of foolishness, I started walking around in the small lobby on that floor, pretending I was waiting for someone. I was standing at the window, amazed at how small the trees in Nehru Park appeared to be, when I heard a sweet voice behind me saying, "Bete [sonny]." No one there knew me, so there was no reason to pay attention to that voice, but the lobby was so small that I could not ignore the tall, handsome man walking toward me. He was dressed in silk kurta and pajamas (traditional Indian garb), and wore a rudraksha mala around his neck. Without hesitation he put his hand on my shoulder and said, "When did you come?"

"Yesterday," I replied. I felt I knew this man, and certainly he seemed to know me. It seemed awkward to ask who he was, so when he took my hand I walked with him. His suite was just a few steps away and we were inside in no time. He sat on his bed, and gesturing for me to sit on the bed in front of him, said, "I can't believe how you have grown. So what are you doing these days?"

"I'm working on my Ph.D." I replied.

"What's the topic?"

When I replied, "The philosophy of Sri Vidya," he chuckled.

"Philosophy of Sri Vidya!" he exclaimed. "You can get your Ph.D. and D.Litt. at the snap of your fingers. But tell me, when are you going to do the sadhana?"

He asked with such authority that it shook my whole being. It was both an invitation and a challenge. Who was this man? For the past five years I had been searching for a master who could teach me Sri Vidya, the heart of the esoteric sciences described in the scriptures. In that time I had met more than twenty teachers, scholars, and saints who were renowned for their knowledge of Sri Vidya, but I found that most of them had only book knowledge—knowledge that was not satisfying to me. Yet they were the ones who invited me to study with them. The few who were adepts told me flatly that I must learn this science from one who has been my master in previous lives. And when I asked them how to find him, they told me lovingly that he would find me, just as he had found me before. Among such great adepts was Swami Sadananda from Allahabad, who told me, "He gathers his sheep before it's dark. Do not worry, he will find you; he will introduce himself to you."

291

As soon as I remembered those words, the identity of the man before me hit like a bolt of lightning. I knew this was the master that Swami Sadananda and the other adepts of Sri Vidya had been re- ferring to. But this man was so pleasant, casual, and engaging that I had no time to absorb this. After a brief silence he said playfully, "I have heard about Sri Vidya. There are some scriptures that talk about this science. Do you know any of them?" I told him the name of a few Sri Vidya scriptures and he started asking questions, as though he knew very little about this science and was intrigued by my knowledge. My childish self was flattered and I answered his questions, although my explanation was somewhat choppy because part of my mind was still trying to grapple with the puzzle of this man and our relationship. A tall, handsome man cannot be a sage, I was thinking. Sages do not live in crowded cities, and especially not in luxurious buildings. The sweetness of his voice and the peaceful aura of his countenance proclaim that he is a great soul, but his eager questions and his silk garments suggest he may well be a prince with scholarly tastes. The question "When are you going to do the sadhana?" kept echoing in my mind, and my heart told me that this was my master.

All the while, I was expounding on Sri Vidya, encouraged by his enthusiastic attention, but in twenty or thirty minutes my meager store of knowledge was exhausted. Then, so skillfully that at first I did not notice what he was doing, he began to expound on the subject himself. I was embarrassed at my presumption and immaturity, but what he was saying was so inspiring that it never occurred to me to interrupt and apologize for my ignorance. I was totally absorbed in his words—my dreams were coming true.

After a while, the telephone rang. He picked it up, listened for a moment, and said, "Send him up." The gentleman who came to the door a few minutes later was as surprised to see me as I was surprised to see him: it was none other than my host, Anand Pratap Singh. Mr. Singh immediately put his head at the feet of this mysterious man, who said, "Anand, why did you hesitate to bring him here?"

"Sarkar [Your majesty], before bringing him here I wanted to have your permission," Mr. Singh replied.

The man said, "I have been waiting for him for a long time."

As soon as Mr. Singh sat down, the mysterious man resumed our conversation about Sri Vidya. In five minutes or so the telephone rang again. Mr. Singh picked it up, listened for a moment, and said, "Sarkar, Peelu Modi is on the phone."

"Tell him I am busy. I will call him later," the man replied.

Peelu Modi was a member of parliament, one of India's top politicians and businessmen, and hearing his name I wondered again, "What is going on here? Anand Pratap Singh—himself a prince and secretary to His Highness Raja Dinesh Singh, India's Minister of External Affairs—is sitting here humbly attending to this man's telephone calls. And a person of the stature of Peelu Modi calls him—and he has no time to speak to him because he is busy talking to me?" While part of my mind was pondering this and another part was absorbed in listening to his profound words on Sri Vidya, Mr. Singh picked up a thin book of black and white photos, and when he opened it the cover caught my eye. It said "Swami Rama of the Himalayas" and carried a photo of the man sitting in front of me. When I saw the name and photo, everything coalesced: this is Bhole Baba, the sage who is the master of Sri Vidya.

At this—I don't know how—my body swung around and I fell into his lap. I lost my awareness. I don't remember how long I stayed in that state. All I remember clearly is that Swamiji was wiping away my tears. When I regained my normal awareness, I had a clear memory of an indescribable state of wonder and joy in which I had been absorbed. I tried to hold on to it. Then I heard Bhole Baba/Swami Rama saying, "I have been waiting for you. When are you coming to the States? You have to help me." He told me to get a pen and paper and he would make a synopsis of my thesis. I got up to get the items from the desk, and I felt drunk. My mind was drawn to reexperience the joy it had tasted a few moments before, but by the time I brought the paper and pen Swamiji had thrown a thick veil over my memory. Today the only thing I remember is that it superseded all the joys known in this world. Just the longing alone to reexperience that joy overshadows all the joys and sorrows of this world.

Swamiji dictated the table of contents for my thesis, and then he talked to Mr. Singh about Indian politics for a while before turning to me again and talking about my parents and sisters. Out of the blue he said, "Don't worry about them. I will take care of them. They are my responsibility. Your responsibility is to do your practice and get ready to come to the United States." Then he picked up the telephone and called one of his students in the United States and told him to make arrangements to fill out the immigration papers and sponsor my visa.

The three days that followed were intense. I had a hard time knowing whether Swamiji wanted me to come with him to the States or accept a teaching position at Delhi University—or if he was simply testing my patience, mental clarity, and stability. But once that phase was over I found him to be kind and straightforward. In spiritual matters he was serious and precise, but in the normal course of events he was casual, spontaneous, and jolly. No matter what the situation, he was imposing,

293

and in his presence I felt as though I were drowning in humility—in part because I knew he was a great sage and in part because his personality was so dominant that I felt timid. The realization that he was my master inspired me to ask questions and learn from him, yet the part of me that was overwhelmed by his very presence wanted to hide in a corner. To help me out, Swamiji lightened the environment by joking and telling stories about his experiences in the West.

One day he told me a story, which he later repeated several times during his lectures in the United States, about a woman who had come to see him in Chicago. A doctoral student at the University of Minnesota, she was writing her thesis on yoga, and as part of her field work she made an appointment to meet him. During the interview she asked about *siddhis,* the supernatural powers that yogis acquire in the course of their practices. She had heard several accounts of Swamiji's voluntary control over his autonomic nervous system and believed he was able to perform these yogic feats because he was a siddha master. She had also heard from a few of Swamiji's admirers that he was such an accomplished master that he was not affected by physical and bio-logical needs: he was beyond hunger, thirst, the sensations of heat and cold, pleasure and pain, and so on. She had also heard that Swamiji did not sleep. When he coughed a few times during the course of the interview, she thought, How is it possible for an accomplished yogi to suffer from a cough? When one of the residents interrupted the interview to tell Swamiji his lunch was ready, this woman could not believe it. When she asked him if he ate, he replied, "Of course I eat."

She said in amazement, "But yogis are beyond hunger and thirst!"

"What do you mean?" Swamiji said sternly, and got up and went into the bathroom. When she got over her shock, she decided that Swamiji was a hypocrite—he taught yoga and claimed to practice it, and yet he ate food and went to the bathroom. She was so upset, in fact, that when she returned to Minneapolis she organized a group and led a crusade against Indian yogis and swamis.

I asked Swamiji how she could have such a shallow understanding if she was a Ph.D. candidate. I said that anyone with the slightest common sense understands that all living beings—humans and non-

294

humans, yogis and non-yogis—must eat and eliminate as long as they are alive.

"That's the problem," Swamiji chuckled. "Intellectuals often lack common sense. That is why their work is not practical. In this woman's case, there were many other forces leading her to conclude that swamis and yogis are fakes. She had read hardly any authentic texts on yoga, and lacking knowledge of Sanskrit, she had no access to yogic literature. She had heard a few lectures on the *Yoga Sutra*, especially on chapter three [the section that describes supernatural powers]. She had heard amazing stories about me, and when I did not measure up to her expectations, she was disappointed.

"It's not her fault. Often devotees make up extraordinary stories about their gurus to impress others and lend themselves credibility—if their teacher is great, then they must be great too, or at least destined for greatness. Such devotees create a guru cult, contaminate the sublime tradition of the guru-disciple lineage, and in the process they misguide the novice seekers."

295

I found Swamiji totally unpredictable. Some days it seemed as if he were waiting for my visit, and he would spend hours alone with me. And during such sessions he spoke on every subject imaginable. One of his favorite topics was the dynamics of death. He talked about *parakaya pravesha* and explained that the knowledge of, and mastery over, the dynamics of death is one of the central themes of our tradition. He described how his master and a few other adepts demonstrated their mastery over the process of dying for him when he was young. Although I did not completely understand what he was telling me, the subject was so fascinating that each time we met I found myself hoping he would introduce that topic again. There were other times when I would go to visit him that I would wait in the lobby for hours, perhaps all day, and if I was lucky I got to see him for a few minutes.

I noticed that Swamiji did not want people to know where he was living, what he was doing, or indeed anything about his comings and goings, and I quickly realized that I must not let anyone know I was spending time with him or even that I knew him. The same was true of the practices he taught. He would teach me the next level of discipline only if I could keep my lips sealed in regard to what he had already taught me.

I had an opportunity to attend Swamiji for an unbroken sequence of twelve days and nights during the first four months that I knew him. And looking back on it, I realize that this was one of the most precious periods of my life. It happened like this:

At the end of September, for no apparent reason, Swamiji told me to visit my parents and return as soon as possible. So I traveled to the remote village in northern India where they were living, stayed one night, and returned to Delhi. Since he had said "Come back as soon as possible," I decided that I should see him before letting anyone else know I was in Delhi. The only luggage I had was a small bag containing an extra set of kurta and pajamas, a towel, a set of underwear, and a few toiletries. I had brushed my teeth and combed my hair on the train, and I was all fresh. When I arrived at the hotel around seven a.m. the receptionist told me that Swamiji had moved to another suite and was waiting for me there. And when I got to his room, even before I had touched his feet as a gesture of respect, he said "Khush raho, khush raho. [Be happy, be happy]. I'm tired of seeing and talking to people. You stay here and make sure no one disturbs me. Tell the reception people not to forward any telephone calls; in fact, tell them that I'm not available." With these instructions, he went into the bedroom and closed the door. I sat in the living room. After several hours Swamiji came out and told me to go and eat something and come back quickly. He gave me the room key and told me to open the door without knocking and sit quietly in the living room. And that's what I did.

At two a.m. he came out again and told me to leave and return at sunrise. But where could I go? Showing up at Anand Pratap Singh's home in the middle of the night did not seem right, especially since I had not told him I was in Delhi and spending time with Swamiji. Yet I could not afford even the cheapest hotel. Then a thought flashed in my mind: Why waste time going anywhere? Dawn was only a few hours away and I could pass the time across the road, under the trees in Nehru Park. It was closed, so I climbed the six-foot iron fence, avoiding the spikes on the top, and dropped down into the grass. I walked around and exercised to keep warm, and just before dawn I found a spigot and brushed my teeth and bathed. I returned to the hotel at sunrise.

My routine for the next eleven days did not vary: sit on the couch and either do *japa* or sleep. I trained myself to wake up at the slightest sound from the bedroom that indicated Swamiji would be coming out. Whenever he entered the living room and I sensed I was not needed, I ran to the nearby Sarojini Nagar Market to get a few chapatis and a little dal.

On the twelfth night, around two a.m., Swamiji said, "Now you go," as he always did, but as I was picking up my bag, he asked, "Where do you stay?"

"In Delhi," I replied.

"Where in Delhi?"

"Over there, across the road."

"Where? With someone?" he asked.

I said, "It's a wonderful place—very peaceful."

Then he asked firmly, "But where?"

"In Nehru Park, under the trees."

He was quiet for a moment; then he raised his hand in a gesture of blessing, so I bowed my head. Putting his hand on my head, he said, "There will always be a shelter for you. But where do you eat?"

"In one of the *dhabas* [roadside restaurants] in the Sarojini Nagar Market."

At that he said, "There will always be food for you; you will not go hungry." Then he ordered tea, milk, and some biscuits. This was the first time in these twelve days that he had either talked to me or offered food.

The conversation that followed helped me understand that even when Swamiji was active in the world, he was hardly in the world. The snowy peaks and glacial streams of the Himalayas were his real abode. The ancestral cave on Mount Kailas was his playground. People may perceive Swamiji as a scientist, a yogi, a philosopher, a poet, and a philanthropist, but that night I realized he was the blessed child of the Divine Mother. His inner and outer world was saturated with her presence. "No one is anyone's guru," he told me, "no one is anyone's disciple. The Divine Mother alone is the teacher, and through her unconditional love she appears before a sincere seeker in the form of a guru. Seeing a difference between her and a guru is maya—and unless we tear this veil of maya, we will never have inner peace."

Then Swamiji assumed a commanding tone and said to me, "Complete your thesis. Go to Assam. There are several manuscripts in the library of Gauhati University. Kamakhya is also nearby. This is where the Divine Mother will appear in the form of a guru and open the door to eternity."

I said, "But I have already found her in the form of you."

"You don't understand," he replied. "The ritualistic practices are not part of our tradition, but you are being prepared as a teacher. You should know the path of rituals too. It is in Kamakhya that the Divine Mother will make arrangements for you to practice that aspect of Sri Vidya. It involves rituals and the worship of Sri Chakra, and once you have learned that aspect of the practice I will teach you the next one." With these instructions Swamiji dismissed me. I did not see him again for ten months, but I was able to keep track of his activities through Anand Pratap Singh.

In the spring of 1977, Swamiji returned to the United States. This time he traveled much less, focusing most of his energy on writing, and in the summer he wrote *Living with the Himalayan Masters*. People still remember how powerful and elevating the atmosphere was around Swamiji during the two months he was dictating that book. The students worked in shifts, taking dictation by hand, typing the material, editing it, and setting the book in type as each chapter was completed. Dr. Agnihotri, Swamiji's friend from their days together at Allahabad University and later his student, was present at these sessions, and calls *Living with the Himalayan Masters* "a revealed scripture." He remembers clearly that during the dictation Swamiji appeared to be slipping out of this world when he talked about his experiences with the adepts. Everyone working on this project found the work spiritually charged, and all have their own stories to tell. One in particular is worth mentioning. It was witnessed by many people.

It was late evening. Swamiji had just finished dictating a chapter and was in the mood to talk about his master. As he talked he mentioned some intimate details of Babaji's life and even elaborated on some of the practices he had taught him. The assembled students were enthralled, and urged him to include the material in the book. Swamiji declined, saying, "It exposes my master and me to the public. My master does not like to come in the limelight." When the group refused to take no for an answer, Swamiji reluctantly agreed and dictated the story. It was quickly typed and the pages were put in front of Swamiji. The door was closed and there were about a dozen people sitting in the room, when suddenly the door popped open, a breeze blew in, swirled around, picked up the newly typed pages, and swooped them out of the room. They were never seen again.

When *Living with the Himalayan Masters* went into production, Swamiji resumed a hectic traveling and lecturing schedule for a few months. In the winter he went to India for a short time, returning to the States again in early spring. By then the book had been published and was performing its own miracles. The Glenview center already had more residents than it could comfortably hold, and the waiting list was growing. Many people in Chicago and the other cities Swamiji visited wanted to do more than attend a lecture now and then—they wanted to study with this Himalayan master for an extended period. So the staff began to look for another place, one that not only could hold dozens of residents but that also would give the Institute room to grow.

Within a matter of a few months they found the Kilroe Seminary of the Sacred Heart, just outside the small town of Honesdale in northeastern Pennsylvania. Swamiji found it ideal for his mission. Located on more than four hundred acres, it included a main building with over a hundred rooms, an auditorium, a conference room, a library, an industrial kitchen, and several classrooms. A smaller building in back, which had housed a group of nuns, contained several more rooms, a kitchen, and a chapel. Both buildings were brick and well-built. The seminary occupied the grounds of an old dairy farm, and the large barn was still in good condition, as were most of the outbuildings. There were also two small farmhouses and a picturesque pond on the property. Set in the rolling hills of the Poconos, this beautiful wooded campus was only two and a half hours from downtown Manhattan and three and a half hours from Philadelphia;

the Wilkes-Barre/Scranton International Airport was only forty-five minutes away. It was a perfect location: far enough away from major cities to be peaceful, yet close enough to be easily accessible.

Swamiji immediately set about raising funds, and the Institute purchased the Honesdale property before the end of the year. By the summer of 1978 the Institute's new headquarters was firmly established, and now Swamiji's mission really took off. Students began to pour in from all over the world to participate in a monthlong Self-Transformation Program, in which they learned not only the fundamentals for maintaining physical health and well-being but also the practical techniques of self-reflection and introspection. It was through this program that Swamiji created an atmosphere in which seekers could discover the meaning and purpose of life. As Swamiji explained it, "The Self-Transformation Program offers the tools and means for spiritual unfoldment and total well-being while residents enjoy the comforts granted by modern science and technology. This allows the students to discover the best of themselves; it has been the core of the Institute's residential program since the beginning."

That summer several Ph.D.s and M.D.s who had been studying with Swamiji joined the Institute's faculty, and the small holistic health clinic that had been operating in Glenview expanded and became the Combined Therapy Department. Under the direction of Dr. Ballentine, it assumed a leading role in the newly emerging holistic health field. Another physician, cardiologist John Clarke, also joined the team, giving added energy to the merging of spirituality and medicine.

Once they were settled in Honesdale, Swamiji inspired the faculty to serve humanity themselves, not only through lectures and workshops but also by writing articles and books. He had his own style of getting people to work. Out of the blue, for example, he would remark in a lecture, "Did you know, Dr. Ballentine is writing a book on meditation? He has already started it." Then he would look over to where an amazed Dr. Ballentine was sitting and ask, "Dr. B., when are you going to finish that book?" Addressing the audience again, he would say, "If you don't get this book in your hands by spring, let me know. I will spank Dr. B." He would frequently tell someone to write a book, and then within days begin asking if it was finished.

Swamiji's own style of writing was also unusual. Just as with any project, once he began writing he would stop only when the book was done. Students worked in shifts: one took dictation by hand while another typed the material from the previous session. The editor did not wait for the whole book to be finished, but edited one chapter while the next was being dictated. Then once the manuscript was completed Swamiji invariably expected it to be published before the next seminar—a matter of weeks or sometimes even days. This made it necessary for the Institute to have its own press, and a small one was purchased and installed in a rented space in town. It quickly became apparent, however, that the speed at which Swamiji was writing, and insisting that others write, required more equipment and space. So a team of residents began renovating the dairy barn, and by the spring of 1980 part of it had become a fully equipped press—complete with a two-color Heidelberg printing press and collating, cutting, and binding machines—while another part housed the art department, offices, and the shipping, packing, and warehouse of the Himalayan Institute Press.

301

With the monthlong Self-Transformation Program, the long-term Residential Program, the Combined Therapy Department, and a well-established publishing program all in place, Swamiji's mission was now firmly rooted in the West. From now on all he had to do was provide it with continuous nourishment, which he did by teaching at the Institute's main campus in Honesdale and various branch centers, and lecturing in major cities throughout the United States and Europe.

GRACE *in* ACTION

AS SWAMIJI'S ACTIVITIES picked up speed in the States, my immigration papers were completed in India, and in October 1979 I went to Delhi to catch my flight to New York. I had not seen Swamiji since the previous spring, but just as I was about to depart for the airport Mr. Anand Pratap Singh told me that Swamiji had arrived in Delhi and wanted to see me. I went to the Akbar Hotel immediately. After a brief greeting, he looked at my ticket and said, "It is from Delhi to New York. How are you going further?"

"I don't know," I replied. "In fact, where am I going? The ticket has come from someone in Minneapolis. Am I going to Minneapolis? And Swamiji, I do not know English. What is going to happen to me?"

Swamiji was quiet for a moment, and then said, "Somebody will meet you at the airport in New York. He will make all the arrangements for you. You will go to the Institute. There you will know where you need to go and what you will be doing. Now you go."

My lack of English made the journey an ordeal. I had never been on an airplane before, and every announcement was a source of anxiety, for I had no idea what was being said. At Frankfurt we had to deplane, go into the terminal, and then return to the gate and board the plane again. I had an Oxford pocket dictionary and tried to use it to decipher the signs in the airport, but after a series of guesses and failures I realized the signs were in German. Immigration at Kennedy Airport was a nightmare. When I finally made it through customs, my anxiety overwhelmed me. There was a huge crowd outside. Where should I go? How would I recognize the person who had come to pick me up? I was trying to look into everyone's eyes. Then I saw a man carrying a sign that read "Pandit Rajmani Tigunait." Thank God I could read at least that much English.

My memory of this meeting is vivid—it was like the joy that desperate devotees experience when they see God. The man holding the sign was the manager of the Institute's East West Bookstore in Manhattan. He took me there and handed me over to Dr. John Clarke, who drove me to the Himalayan Institute in Pennsylvania. Here arrangements were made for me to go to one of the yoga centers in the Midwest affiliated with the Himalayan Institute, where in his own mysterious way Swamiji began training me.

During the first few weeks others passed on to me some of Swamiji's encouraging comments: "Panditji is a brilliant man." "He will do a remarkable job." "Once he begins speaking, he will shock people." But when Swamiji called me around Christmas, probably from India, he said, "What's wrong with you? All day long you hide yourself in your room. You have become a bookworm. That is not the way to learn. Spend time with others. The more you talk and the more you hear others speak, the faster you will learn. You have a big English vocabulary now, but you do not know how to form sentences. Your other problem is that you still think in Hindi. Stop thinking in Hindi! I want you to learn American culture and the psychology of the people there. I want you to teach." Swamiji ended the conversation with this powerful command: "Don't behave like an arrogant brahmin!"

Hearing this, I tried to interact more with others and improve my English. But I knew my limitations. My grammar was poor, my accent terrible. I did a good job vacuuming, washing dishes, cooking, shoveling snow, running the mimeograph machine, and sealing envelopes. But how could I teach? I spent more time with the residents, particularly Rolf and Mary Gail Sovik and Barbara Hicks (now Kamala Gerhardt), and they kindly coached me not only on my English but also on the American way of life.

Then one day I received a message from Swamiji: "I'm so disappointed that it is almost three months he has been in the States and still he has not started teaching." A thought flashed: I should begin with the *Bhakti Sutra*. With the help of the commentary I could easily expound on the theory of the yoga of love and devotion, and to add a practical dimension, everyone could do some chanting. This would give me a chance to speak to a small group who would also participate. Words began to flow and I recognized that my English was better than I had thought.

In early spring Swamiji returned to the Honesdale campus. I was missing him and often thought of calling or writing, but my sense of worthlessness stopped me. From some sources I heard that Swamiji was happy with my progress, and from others I heard that he was disappointed in me. I knew that in either case he would guide me and do whatever was best for me. Then one day Maya Tandon, who lived just a few blocks from where I was staying, advised me to call Swamiji. She had known him since childhood and knew how to interpret his words, especially those he did not speak. But she and her husband, Shivnath, were experts in keeping their lips sealed and speaking only that which was absolutely necessary, so it took me almost a week to get Swamiji's comments about me out of them. They went something like this: "After coming to the States this boy has forgotten me. What can I do? He doesn't speak to me."

It was the month of May. I began calling Swamiji in Honesdale but could not reach him. Each time I called, his secretary told me that Swamiji was resting, or lecturing, or that he was simply not available. I persisted until finally one day his secretary told me that Swamiji wanted to know why I was calling and what I needed from him. I told her that I hadn't spoken to him for a long time and just wanted to talk to him. She said she would give him the message. The next day I called again. But this time, instead of using the hold button, the secretary put the phone down and I heard her tell Swamiji that I was on the phone again. "What should I tell him?" she asked.

I heard Swamiji say, "Tell him I am busy."

Then I heard her say, "I've got to go, Swamiji. There won't be anyone here for a while to answer the phone for you." Then she picked up the receiver and told me Swamiji was busy and hung up.

I knew that if I waited a few minutes and then called, Swamiji would answer the telephone himself. So that's what I did. He picked up the phone and even before I could say anything he said, "Why are you bothering me? What do you want from me?"

"I want to see you, Swamiji."

"Why?"

"Because," I replied, "it's been a long time and I have not seen you."

"So what?"

"No, Swamiji, please give me your permission to see you."

At that he shouted, "If you have already decided to see me, why do you need my permission?"

"Because it is not appropriate for me to come without asking."

His tone changed. "I've been dying to see you for all these months, and here you are sitting there in Minnesota. Today I am coming to Chicago. Come and see me there."

I told Rolf and Mary Gail Sovik of my plans and they generously made the arrangements for me to take a night train to Chicago. I arrived on a Tuesday morning and made my way to the Glenview center. When I went to Swamiji's room Anne Aylward, who was the Institute chairman at that time, was with him. She said in a puzzled tone, "Swamiji, is he the one you were talking about? He's just a boy."

Swamiji smiled and said, "So what? I'm still a young boy of my master." Later I learned that Swamiji had spoken highly of me to all the residents and they were expecting a wise, mature man.

The atmosphere at the Glenview center was delightfully relaxing. A young lady, Sujata (now Suzanne Grady), had the privilege of attending Swamiji, and we became friends in no time. She told me Swamiji's favorite drink was tilk, and taught me how to make it. Within a matter of hours I felt totally at home.

That evening Swamiji asked me to accompany him to a lecture he was giving in downtown Chicago. Gus Gatto drove us into the city, and on the way Swamiji asked about my experiences in America. He asked about my activities in Minnesota in detail, and explained that it is natural to go through culture shock when plunging into a society markedly different from your own. We were passing through a street with a lot of neon lights, and he pointed to one building with a large flashing sign and asked me if I knew what it was. I said, "No."

So he looked at Gus and said, "Gus, you have to bring Panditji here."

"Are you kidding, Swamiji?" Gus replied. Then he whispered to me, "You don't want to go to that place unless Swamiji has hidden the missing piece of your enlightenment there. It's a strip joint."

Swamiji chuckled. "You just wait, Gus. I'll make sure Panditji becomes familiar with every aspect of your culture."

We arrived a bit early at the church where the lecture was being held, but as soon as we got out of the car Swamiji was surrounded by a crowd. Some touched his feet and others shook his hand. Swamiji singled out a few people and disappeared with them into a private room while I mingled with the crowd. When it was time for the lecture to begin, Gus stepped up to the microphone to introduce the Himalayan Institute and Swamiji, and the topic. I sat down in a back row of the big hall. There was pin-drop silence as Swamiji walked up to the stage, folded his hands, bowed his head, and began to speak:

"I pray to the Divinity in you. The topic given to me this evening is 'Wave of Beauty and Wave of Bliss.' According to the sages of the Himalayas, beauty and bliss are inherent attributes of the Absolute. The Absolute Transcendental Reality is like an ocean of beauty, an ocean of bliss. The life-force is like waves that continuously emerge from this ocean and subside in it. The entire world comes out of this beautiful, blissful Divine Being. And after completing the cycle of its outward expansion, it dissolves again into the Divine Being. The purpose of life is to know that you are a wave of beauty and bliss. Just as waves in the ocean are not separate from the ocean, you are not separate from the beautiful and blissful Divine Being.

"You suffer from a sense of worthlessness because you do not know that you are a beautiful person. But you have an inherent urge to experience your inner beauty and joy. Not knowing how to turn your mind inward, you are trying to find beauty and joy in the external world. You have become dependent on others. When someone tells you that you are beautiful, your face lights up and you say, 'Thank you. You made my day.' You put on makeup, and when your sweetheart does not admire you, you feel terrible. Since you do not have the direct experience of that part of yourself which is beautiful, you look for confirmation from outside. And when you don't find it, you become disappointed.

"Once I was in London. A young man came to see me with his girlfriend. He asked for my blessings. I asked him why he was marrying her. He said, 'Because she is beautiful and I love her.' I told him that he needed a better reason than that to have a successful marriage. He told me, 'Swamiji, you don't understand. She is beautiful.'

"I told him to come back with her after the marriage and I would give my blessings. The first thing every morning, they used to call each other. One day he thought of surprising her with a visit instead. So he drove to her apartment and knocked at her door. She came out in her nightgown and he was shocked to see her face. He told her he had come to give her a surprise, and then he left quickly. He came to see me, and the first thing he said was, 'Swamiji, she is ugly.' I told him that if you are going after the beauty of the body, you will be disappointed. Childhood, adolescence, adulthood, and old age are natural conditions of the body. The body is subject to change. There is a beautiful self within you, within her, within everyone. If you learn to love that beautiful self within, you will come in touch with the blissful aspect of the self. It is the inner beauty that manifests in the form of a smile on your face."

Swamiji went on speaking for almost thirty minutes. Then he said, "Now I'm open for questions and answers. Do you have any questions?"

Somebody from the audience got up and asked, "What do you mean by inner beauty?"

In a booming voice, Swamiji replied, "Here is a great scholar who has done his Ph.D. on this very subject." He gestured at me and said, "Please get up." Hesitantly, I stood up. He asked me to come to the stage. My legs began to tremble. Hundreds of people were looking at me and I felt as if I would collapse back into my seat. Then Swamiji spoke in Hindi, "*Chal, chal, chal* [come, come, come]." I don't remember how I managed to reach the stage or how the microphone came to be in my hand, but I spoke for ten or fifteen minutes. I have no idea what I said. Whatever it was, people seemed to understand it and like it. I have been lecturing ever since. We have seen that Swamiji employed a similar tactic with Dr. Ballentine. In fact, that is how he trained a score of students and transformed them into teachers.

A few days later, when Swamiji was flying back to Pennsylvania, I asked him how long he wanted me to be in Minnesota. "Why do you want to be in Minnesota?" he inquired to my surprise. "Come with me to Honesdale." I said that I had to pick up my clothes and books, and he said, "They will pack everything up and send it to you." And so it was that in mid-June of 1980 I came to live with Swamiji at the Institute's headquarters.

At the Institute I saw a new aspect of Swamiji's personality. In India he had seemed to be a kind and wise sage whose thoughts, speech, and actions were permeated by love for his master and the Divine Mother. There he spoke to me on esoteric subjects, such as how to cast off one's body voluntarily, the importance of piercing the innermost energy channel (known as the Brahma nadi), meditating on the presence of the immortal sages, and healing others from a distance without letting the person know how the healing had come about.

In India I had also seen in him a mysterious and sometimes mischievous man, for it was hard to decipher the intent of his actions. There he was a man of paradox. He lived in luxurious hotels, and at night when everyone was gone he spread his blanket and slept on the floor. When he traveled or appeared in public he wore custom-tailored suits, but among the sadhus he assumed his old role, sitting in front of the dhuni dressed in a simple kurta and pajamas.

In Minnesota I found many people who described Swamiji as a scientist-yogi. To them he was great because he could stop his heart and was able to channel his blood so that it flowed only in particular arteries. I also met others who believed that even when Swamiji was involved in the world, he was totally absorbed in samadhi, that he knew everything about all the students initiated in the tradition, and that he could be approached only through his leading disciples. So those people followed and even worshipped the leading disciples, hoping that through their blessings they would one day receive the grace of the master. Through personal interactions with the followers, however, I learned that some leading disciples made promises on

309

Swamiji's behalf which I felt, from my own experience with him in India, that Swamiji would never have given. But the followers believed everything the leading disciples said, and when their expectations were not met, many of them felt betrayed by Swamiji himself.

For example, one of the leading disciples told his followers, "I have not yet reached that level of realization, but in the nighttime, through the grace of the lineage, I am fully connected with Swamiji. Every night, between twelve and three, in my meditation I attend to my students no matter where they are. Tomorrow during my meditation I will give you a gentle push. I will lead you to the next level of your spiritual height. Thereafter if you meditate every day at precisely three in the morning, I will accompany you in your spiritual journey. It is my master's promise that in three months' time you will reach the summit of realization." Most students who had been promised such a "push" could not get up at that hour and felt guilty about it; the few who did force themselves awake every morning at three o'clock did not see the promised result and were tired and groggy most of the time. To my amazement, they continued to love their teacher but gradually became angry at Swamiji. They were convinced that it was he who was refusing to give them what had been promised.

Things were quite different in Honesdale. Here Swamiji was like the head of a big family, easily accessible and full of good humor. He played with the children, joked with the adults, often cooked his own meals, and enjoyed parties as much as he enjoyed working with the residents to beautify the grounds. The atmosphere was so relaxed and the residents were so much a part of him that, unlike the people in India, they did not feel the need to run after him and ask for his blessings.

In administrative matters, however, Swamiji was a stern taskmaster. Within a day of my first meeting with him in Delhi I learned that he did not like slowpokes. But until I moved to Honesdale I had no idea that he had equally exacting standards where work and self-discipline were concerned. By 8:45 a.m. he expected everyone to be working—and working hard. He was likely to show up anywhere at this hour—the kitchen, the print shop, the business office, the art department, or anywhere else on the grounds. The first few times he discovered that someone was not where they were supposed to be, doing what they were supposed to be doing, he would gently explain the importance of regularity and the value of being responsible. If the pattern didn't change, he would scold, and if that had no effect, he would dismiss that person from the program.

Early in my stay at Honesdale he asked me to accompany him on his morning walks, which normally began by making the rounds of the main building. One day at six a.m. he stopped at the door of the meditation room, where everyone was supposed to be at prayers, and quietly surveyed the room. Then he went to the men's wing and shouted, "Where is David? Is he still sleeping? Wake him up!" When the person he was calling for emerged, Swamiji reproached him: "Don't be lazy! If you want to be a healthy and happy person, wake up on time. Never miss morning prayers. Go and knock on all the doors. See who else is not awake. In fact, from tomorrow, you should ring a bell in this hall at 5:30." Then he stalked out.

In the course of our walks he would make remarks like, "This is a beautiful boulder; we should use it somewhere." "This dead branch doesn't look nice." "We should plant some flowers here." "This trail needs to be marked properly." And as soon as he returned from his walk he would call the person in charge of maintenance and give him instructions, even though it was before breakfast. And the maintenance coordinator knew that the instructions should be carried out that day.

During these walks Swamiji tossed out remarks like, "Americans are great people. They are generous and hard-working, but they are spoiled." Or, "Modern people want to have fun, but don't know how to distinguish fun from self-indulgence and self-destruction." Standing at the top of a big hill on the northeastern side of the property, he would gaze across the valley and say, "There is so much beauty and abundance in nature. How unfortunate are those who don't see it." While I lived with him in India I had learned that none of Swamiji's words or actions were meaningless or random, and I knew that there must be some reason why he took me for these walks, and there must be a reason why he made such remarks.

One morning when I was with him he called Bala (now Janet Lindgren), the coordinator of the residential program, and said, "Pan-

311

ditji is the spiritual director of the Institute and he is in charge of maintaining the discipline on campus." I remained quiet but wondered what he meant by "discipline." When Bala left, I asked him, and he said, "Make sure everybody is present at morning and evening prayers. Make sure they eat on time and sleep and wake up on time and go to hatha yoga and breathing classes regularly."

I realized that this would not be an easy task. Before I could teach discipline to anyone else, I would have to discipline myself. Swamiji emphasized the importance of self-discipline and self-motivation in every lecture he gave, and had often explained to me that motivation from inside is the key to self-transformation. And by ordering me to maintain discipline he forced me to figure out how to help the residents motivate themselves. I tried my best and made some head-way, but I could not measure up to his expectations. For example, one morning around lunchtime Swamiji was walking through the central corridor in the main building when he stopped at the back door and shouted to someone: "Get Panditji!" When I arrived he pointed to an apple that had been left on the coatrack and roared, "Is this how you are maintaining discipline? People are leaving apples and cups and plates all over the building!" I quietly acknowledged my carelessness and told myself that discipline meant more than making sure that people got up on time, attended prayers regularly, and ate on time.

I found myself wondering what discipline really was, but unless Swamiji himself was in the right mood, it was hard to ask him a question in private. Normally questions vanished in his presence, and if they didn't, there was a realization that the question was trivial and that it would be a waste of Swamiji's time to pose it. Yet when I was alone my mind kept returning to this question of discipline.

That weekend there was a seminar on superconscious meditation, and the title of Swamiji's lecture was "Preparation for Meditation." Swamiji started his lecture in his typical style: "I pray to the Divinity in you. How are you today? Are you comfortable? Do you like the food? . . . The topic given to me this morning is 'Preparation for Meditation.'" But within a few minutes he dropped the topic and started talking about discipline.

He said, "Discipline means cultivating qualities and qualifications that enable you to become a disciple. Let me tell you the difference between a student and a disciple. A student comes, takes some classes, and goes away. He may practice a part of what he has learned and ignore the rest. He still has doubts and fears regarding the teacher, the teachings, and his own ability to practice the teachings. A disciple is he who has an organized mind and knows the value of his time as well as the value of his teacher's time. He is determined to undertake a practice, for he knows it is the practice that makes one perfect. There is a silent understanding between teacher and disciple: 'I will teach provided you practice.'—'I will practice no matter what.'

"In this circumstance both teacher and disciple follow certain disciplines. At a spiritual level the teacher makes himself available whenever the disciple needs his help. The only thing the teacher asks from the disciple is: 'Be disciplined.' The first step in disciplining yourself is to overcome your carelessness. To start and complete your practice, first you have to organize your external and internal life. And you can do so only when you are not careless. A vigilant person alone can make the best use of his time and learn the art of how to be creative and productive. According to the sages, carelessness is the mother of all sins. So many times you do not want to make a mistake but due to carelessness, you commit mistakes. Carelessness is a negative trait that resides in the dark and dull corners of the mind. Unless you throw away this trait you cannot discipline yourself, and unless you discipline yourself, you cannot deserve to be a disciple. True wisdom is imparted only to the disciples, whereas information is disseminated to all students and followers."

Swamiji continued to amplify on this theme, and it seemed as if this whole lecture was for me. It finally dawned on me that the apple left on the coatrack had been an excuse to make me ponder the meaning of discipline. It was a reflection of someone's carelessness, a symptom of a disorganized and scattered mind. This is what causes us to miss our practice, wake up late, or waste our time gossiping, I realized. This is what causes us to be sloppy in our thought, speech, and action.

At the same time that Swamiji was answering my question in the lecture, others in the audience found him answering theirs. This was typical. Swamiji never remained focused on the announced topic for

313

long. He would often begin by remarking, "In today's lecture I am going to teach you something very profound and provocative, provided you pay attention." Then he would wander off the topic. But surprisingly, every member of the audience emerged awestruck: "That lecture seemed to be just for me," they would say. "He answered all my questions."

Swamiji's real day started at ten in the evening, when the work that required his one-pointed attention began. That was when he either dictated his books or listened to the edited version of something he had dictated earlier. The work continued until one or two a.m. From time to time Kamal, his secretary, or other students who often attended him (such as Kevin and Wendy Hoffman) or I prepared a midnight snack for him, which normally consisted of kheer (rice pudding), or vermicilli pudding, and tilk. Then came the toothbrushing ritual. One of us would bring water, toothpaste, a brush, a Water Pik, and an empty bowl to his living room (which was also the work room), and he would brush his teeth while making jokes ("This is Swami Rama's tooth *puja* [worship]"). He would take out his dentures, point to the gold in them, and say, "You know, I have the most expensive mouth. In the olden days women used their jewelry as a savings bank. These days swamis like me use their mouth as a safe-deposit box." Then he would get up, stretch his body, and say, "Now starts the peak hours of Swami Rama. You people go and rest. I have to start my work. Good night, everyone."

Every night, just as I was about to leave with the others, he would ask in a commanding tone, "How far have you completed your thesis?" or "How many more chapters are left?" Because I knew that he would call me again around six or seven in the morning and ask the same question, I realized from his question that he was expecting me to work through the night. Often strongly, sometimes gently, he would say, "Sonny, you have to complete your thesis this year." Furthermore, he insisted that I write my thesis in English. That made the task doubly hard, for there were few books in English on the philosophy of Sri Vidya. Most of the texts were in Sanskrit and some were in Hindi; so I had to read and think in Sanskrit and Hindi, organize the material in English, and consult the dictionary to find the appropriate terms. And the only time I had for serious thinking and contemplation was after I left Swamiji's room in the early morning hours. This is how he forced me to learn how to survive with little or no sleep. I developed a special way of sleeping: I would fall asleep at odd moments (after lunch, perhaps), reclining on one side with my head propped up on my forearm. Within thirty minutes my wrist would begin to hurt and I would wake up. Since I could rarely afford to sleep more than thirty minutes, the body figured out how to derive complete rest in that short time.

In July Swamiji led a silence retreat exclusively for the faculty and directors of Himalayan Institute branches and affiliated centers. Because I had to finish my thesis I was not participating, even though Swamiji was giving instructions on *yoga nidra* (yogic sleep) to this special group every afternoon. However, one day toward the end of the retreat he told me to join the others while he gave instructions on this practice. I arrived late to find him in the midst of explaining that when you are awake your mind resides at the center between the eyebrows; during the dreaming state it is at the throat center; and during deep sleep it is at the heart center. He said that the important thing in yoga nidra is to pass quickly through the intermediate state of dreaming, which requires training your mind to spend as little time as possible at the throat center while it travels from the eyebrow center to the heart center.

Practically speaking, yoga nidra is a practice that allows you to fall asleep at will, remain aware of yourself, and return to the waking state at will. It is a conscious sleep, unlike the normal sleeping state, in which you are not aware of your internal state. Entering a state of sleep consciously and returning to the waking state at will is possible only when you allow your mind to rest at the eyebrow center. The first step is to program your mind to fall asleep in odd situations while keeping part of your mind alert so that you remain aware of your plan to wake up at a certain time. When Swamiji said that, I said to him in Hindi, "Swamiji, I have been doing that every day without using any of these techniques."

Swamiji replied, "Yes. You thought you were not using any techniques, but the circumstances I created led you to invent the techniques unconsciously."

Then Swamiji went on to explain the prerequisites for practicing yogic sleep. Regulating the four primitive urges (food, sex, sleep, and the desire for self-preservation) is the ground for self-discipline, which is itself a prerequisite for any advanced practices, including yoga nidra. "On this path," Swamiji said, "you must first awaken your *sankalpa shakti,* the power of will and self-determination. Do not undermine your capacity. Never say that you cannot do it. Instead, overcome your resistance. Expand your capacity. Laziness is the greatest obstacle. It resides in the domain of the mind, and from there it influences the body. A person lacking vigilance interprets his laziness as tiredness of the body and attributes it to weakness and chemical imbalance. Laziness is the most subtle obstacle in sadhana. You can overcome this obstacle by preventing your mind from becoming a slave to your body and senses. You must order your body and senses to function under the leadership of your mind, and also let your mind know that it is simply an instrument of the soul. Infuse your mind with the power of determination. The power of will and determination is an attribute of the soul. The technique of yoga nidra helps you organize your body, senses, and mind, but it is the power of will and determination that gives your body, senses, and mind the energy to carry out your plans—to fall asleep while still remaining awake, and to get up exactly when you decided to get up. Willpower is the key."

Hearing this, I realized that Swamiji had trained me to overcome my tendency to laziness without my knowing what he was doing. He had a genius for teaching his students what they needed to learn without their knowing they were being taught.

Every year in July the Institute celebrates Guru Purnima, the day of the full moon dedicated to honoring the tradition. The summer of 1980 was my first opportunity to be around Swamiji on this auspicious day, and I wanted to follow the time-honored custom by offering him a garland. I did not know where to find good-quality, fragrant flowers, so my friend Bala came to my rescue and prepared a garland of roses for me. The night before Guru Purnima, I asked Swamiji if I could come and see him early the next morning. He readily agreed.

I arrived at his door carrying the garland on a silver tray and found it unlocked, so I knocked gently and walked in. Swamiji's room was empty, but the blanket and the pillow on the floor where he sat were molded as if he had somehow slipped out of the blanket without disturbing it. I checked the kitchen, the conference room, and the bathroom, but there was no sign of him.

To me this was a most auspicious day and I did not want my mind to dwell on worldly matters, especially while I was in Swamiji's room, so I sat down next to his blanket and began to meditate. But my meditation was disturbed by the anticipation of his return, and I was continually opening my eyes to make sure he was not standing next to me. Finally, frustrated by my anxiety, I got up and locked the door and once again checked the suite of rooms. They were empty, so with no further anxiety I closed my eyes in meditation. About half an hour later I caught a familiar scent, and when I opened my eyes I found Swamiji sitting in front of me as if he had just slipped back into his blanket. Instantly the thought flashed through my mind that he had gone to see his master, and I was so overwhelmed that I forgot to bow my head and greet him properly. Instead, I blurted out, "You were with Babaji!"

He simply smiled and, looking at the garland resting on the tray, asked, "What is there?"

Overcome, I picked it up and without really knowing what I was doing, I put it around his neck. Earlier, I had planned that I would walk into his room, touch his feet, offer the garland, stand a few moments reciting a prayer, touch his feet once again, and receive his blessing. But now I forgot it all. I stood in front of him totally blank, as though there were no head on my shoulders. All I remember is that after a few minutes of silence he took the garland off and, holding it in his hand, said, "This is for you." Spontaneously, I lowered my head in response, and as he was putting it around my neck I heard him say, "*Tapasvi manasvi varchasvi bhava* [May you be committed to *tapas* (self-discipline), may you be filled with the power of determination, may you be enlightened with divine radiance]."

All day long I was drunk with this experience. It was too much to contain, yet I had to keep my lips sealed. These initiations must always be private. So I busied myself with interior monologue: "How fortunate I am to have a master like Swamiji as my guru. How fortunate are all the residents to get to spend so much time with Swamiji. Being in his company is like being in the company of God. Time and space present no barrier to him, and therefore he knows everything about his students. Thinking of him is like meditating on God."

In the evening, hundreds of guests and residents gathered in the auditorium to celebrate this auspicious day. A group of people were chanting "*Jai gurudeva; jai, jai gurudeva* [Hail to gurudeva]." But when Swamiji entered the auditorium the chanting stopped, and as he walked to the front he said loudly, "Hey! Why did you stop? Do you know I have a gurudeva too? Today I'm going to tell you what is 'guru.' People have lots of erroneous notions about it." By this time he had reached the stage.

He sat down, closed his eyes, and was quiet for a few moments. Then he spoke: "The word *guru* is a very pious word. In fact we don't use this word by itself. It is always accompanied by the word *deva,* 'bright being.' We always say 'gurudeva.' The word *guru* means 'one who dispels the darkness of ignorance'; *gurudeva* means 'divine being, the bright being that dispels the darkness of ignorance.' Gurudeva is the one who dwells in the innermost chamber of our heart and guides us in all situations and circumstances of life. It is the inner light.

"People think that a particular human is the guru. That is a big mistake. Just like you, me, and everyone else, that human guru is born and dies one day. Whereas, gurudeva is immortal. It is unborn and not subject to death, decay, or destruction. Since the beginning of history, people have been trying to find guidance from this guru, that teacher, this priest, that swami. But so far they have not been successful.

"No matter how many books you read and how many teachers and preachers you study with, you can never be completely free from your doubts and fears. Unless you are free from doubts and fears, you cannot commit yourself to your practice wholeheartedly. Unless you practice wholeheartedly, you cannot gain direct experience. Without direct experience, you cannot have true solace.

"When you receive guidance from the Divine Being within you, your doubts and fears vanish. You no longer feel a need to validate your path, your way of life. Inner light infuses your heart with an unshakeable conviction. Your conviction becomes the source of your strength. When the lamp of conviction is lit by the Divine, you become immeasurably strong.

"To avoid frustration and disappointment, search and find the teacher within, the gurudeva within. In the light of the inner guru you will be able to distinguish what is right for you and what is not, what is good for you and what is not. If you cannot distinguish right from wrong, good from bad, you will always remain a victim of abuse and exploitation by the external world.

"No matter how enlightened your guru is, he cannot guarantee your enlightenment. He can guide you; he can show you the light. But it is you who have to go within, find and embrace the light within.

"There are not very many perfect masters. And even if you are fortunate enough to meet one, he will not interfere in the law of providence. He will help you in identifying your strengths and weaknesses. He will help you learn how to overcome your weaknesses and cultivate inner strength. If it is appropriate, if it is the right time, and if it is in conformity with the divine will, he will light the inner flame on the altar of your heart. Before doing so he will make sure that you understand the value of self-responsibility, that you understand how to keep the flame alive and how to bask in its light. This is called preparation for receiving divine grace.

319

"Let me explain further. It is your job to gather the lamp, the wick, and the oil. When this preparation is done, the dormant light within you inspires the awakened light within the teacher to light the lamp. In other words, it is at the request of the teacher within you that an enlightened master is spontaneously motivated to serve the eternal flame that resides in you.

"A true teacher never gives false expectations to his students. He never says, 'You serve me and I will do the practices for you.' Let me tell you strongly and clearly: Just by being around a great person, you do not become a great person. Just by being around an adept, you don't become an adept. By doing what an adept did, you become an adept. Look at the great masters: Krishna, Rama, Buddha, Christ. Millions of people knew them, and thousands of people lived with them—but how many were enlightened? Hardly one or two. These great masters were powerful and compassionate, and yet people around them remained ignorant and miserable. In fact, very few made an effort to take advantage of the wisdom of these masters, and as a result almost without exception all of the followers of these great teachers suffer from hatred, jealousy, greed, anger, desire, attachment, and ego, just like those who did not have a chance to be in the company of these great souls.

"This Guru Purnima, the full-moon day, is a reminder that your gurudeva is within you. That bright being manifests in you in the form of enthusiasm, courage, self-confidence, self-trust, self-motivation, and faith in God. On this occasion, you make a resolution to commit yourself to your practice with renewed energy. Don't be dependent on anyone, including the physical form of the guru. It is important that you love and respect your guru. Have faith in him—but don't make the mistake of identifying your guru with the body. Rather, conceive of the guru as the sacred light, the sacred fire. That sacred fire is not different from you. It is you."

This lecture gave structure and direction to the monologue I had been having with myself all day. It helped me look at Swamiji, Babaji, his master, the prince of Bhawal, and other sages in an entirely new light. And that day my own journey took on a new form. I began to contemplate on how the guru is the sacred fire, and in what sense the sacred fire is not different from me or any of us. How is it us? What does it feel like to have a direct experience of that fire?

In the United States, Swamiji's multifaceted personality came into full view. In India I had seen him only as a kind but mysterious sage. He no longer gave discourses there, although he taught the esoteric aspects of spiritual disciplines in private. He was hard to locate in India. Except when he was in Delhi, no one knew where he was or what he did. In the United States he made himself available to the public. He had an itinerary and people knew where to find him and when. Here the teacher, orator, writer, administrator, and humanitarian aspects of his personality dominated his mystical side.

The most colorful of Swamiji's many aspects was the teacher. Today as I look back over my notes I find that he made a deliberate effort to demonstrate the distinction between a spiritual teacher and a preacher. During the course of his lectures he would say, "Many of you seek a teacher or guru in another person and then attempt to find a father figure or a mother figure in that teacher. You build high expectations, and when things do not work out as you imagined, you blame the spiritual path for your disappointment. But the scriptures tell us that the teacher is the omniscient Divine Being. A physical guide may be anyone in whom the divine light manifests, but it is the omniscient Divine Being, the inner light, who actually shows us the way.

"There is a vast difference between a preacher and a spiritual teacher. Preachers train us to become part of a group, which often sets us apart from the rest of humanity and constricts our consciousness. Preachers tell us to have faith in them and in their words. Spiritual teachers, on the other hand, expand our consciousness. They are not rigid or dogmatic. True teachers do not take credit for their work, for they know that they are simply working on behalf of the sages of their tradition. Such teachers and their teachings can never engender a cult, because they are inclusive and openminded."

321

No matter what the subject, Swamiji would begin every lecture by paying homage to the Lord Within. Then he would look at the blackboard to see what the topic was supposed to be, and usually start with some variation of the following: "A human being is not body alone, not mind alone. Between body and mind there is something called breath. If you want to be healthy and happy at both the physical and mental levels, you need to understand the secret of breath. Breath is like a customs officer: anything that is exported and imported between body and mind passes through the breath. The secret of longevity and inner purification lies in working with the breath."

Then, depending on his mood, Swamiji would either elaborate on this topic or go on to explain the mystery of the mind. "Mind is the cause of both bondage and liberation," he would say. "Our modern system of education teaches us how to cultivate only the conscious part of the mind. The vast unconscious remains unexplored. Unless you learn to penetrate your unconscious and gain a direct experience of the contents stored there, you can never free yourself from the subtle impressions of your past. Failure to know your unconscious mind causes you to remain caught in the snares of fear and anxiety. Meditation is the tool for gaining access to your own unconscious."

Swamiji would then elaborate on the dimension of life that transcends the range of mind: the Atman, which he always translated as "the center of consciousness." He would say, "If you want to enjoy life to its fullest, know yourself at every level: body, breath, mind, and consciousness. You are a citizen of two worlds: the world outside you, and the world inside you. Creating a bridge between these two worlds is called 'sadhana.'"

Often someone would ask a question, such as, "I have been trying my best to do my practice, but it is a struggle. What should I do?"

Swamiji would reply, "No matter how methodical and authentic the practice, it becomes mechanical if it is not greased with love. Cultivate love for your practice. Only then will you be able to continue doing your practice for a long period of time without frustration. While involved in spiritual practice, be nice to yourself and be nice to others. Do not hurt yourself and do not hurt others. Stay within your capacity, and try to expand your capacity as you keep getting stronger and more established in your practice."

Then he would get sidetracked. "Grease your duties with love," he would say. "You can live happily in this world only when you learn to perform your actions lovingly and skillfully. Yoga means the art of performing your actions lovingly and skillfully. It teaches you how to live in the world while remaining above it. Learn to enjoy the objects of the world without getting attached to them. To find purpose and meaning in life, you don't need to renounce the world or run away from your duties. The call of duty is very powerful. Learn to discharge your duties lovingly, selflessly, and skillfully. By doing so you become free here and now."

From an analytical viewpoint, Swamiji's lectures did not seem to be organized. He would jump from one subject to the next with little or no regard for the announced topic. But his presence was so compelling that people would lose themselves in him. And as the words flowed from his mouth, his listeners would hear exactly what they needed to hear. Each member of the audience heard Swamiji addressing their specific concerns and issues.

In almost every lecture Swamiji's thundering conviction about God and the way to experience God in daily life came through. He consistently said that he was not teaching religion, nor was he representing Hinduism or any other "ism." In fact, he would use the word "God" in the beginning of the lecture, but would soon drop it in favor of "the Divine" or "the Divine Being." He would say, "God is not hungry for your worship. God is ever-present, complete, requiring nothing. If you want to serve God, serve him by being a good and productive resident of creation. If you cannot add more beauty and joy to this world, then at least leave it as clean as you found it. Do not create pain for anyone. The Divine within you, whom you call God, feels delighted to see you working hard for the welfare of the world. The Divine resides in the cave of every heart and witnesses all our deeds; and seeing that we are involved in kind and selfless deeds, he feels happy. What difference does it make to the Divine whether or not we beat our drums and blow our conches as a means of worshipping him?

"The goal of sadhana is not to see God or to become divine. You are already divine. To experience your divine nature, first you have to become human. Due to our animal tendencies, the divinity remains hidden within us. Anger, hatred, jealousy, greed, attachment, desire, and egoism are the expressions of our animal tendencies. These tendencies arise from four primitive urges: food, sex, sleep, and the desire for self-preservation. To climb the ladder of divine experience, first you must subdue the animal tendencies. Then you will become fully human. The human within you will pull the divine toward you. Then you will not need to run after divinity. Unfoldment of the divinity within will lead to contentment."

When he was not lecturing or teaching, Swamiji was simply a man—a complete man. This was apparent in his every action. When he played tennis, he looked and acted like a teenager: he shouted and laughed, making comments with each stroke, teasing his partners and opponents, and joking with those gathered around the court. The children knew that when Swamiji finished playing, he would take them on his lap and pass out candies. When he was surrounded by children he became a dignified grandfather, talking lovingly to them and asking whether their parents were behaving well with them. At other times, when the children saw Swamiji outside—walking, working in the garden, or making a fire—they would run to him immediately. Swamiji often asked them, "Who loves you the most?" The children would shout, "Baba!" Sometimes he asked, "How much do you love me?" Throwing their arms wide open, they would chorus, "This much!"

At times the children visited Swamiji's room with their parents, and there they enjoyed complete freedom. They would race to him and jump into his lap while Swamiji tickled and teased them. They crawled all over him, pulling his hair and sometimes even biting his nose. Once a little boy crawled into a pillowcase (with the pillow still in it) and hopped around the room like a frog to get Swamiji's attention. The child's father caught him and whispered, "Don't do such things in Swamiji's room." Swamiji heard that and intervened: "Let him enjoy. Don't ruin his childhood." Then he began to play with the boy himself.

In his lectures, as well as in private meetings with parents, Swamiji voiced his concern about the disintegration of families and its effect on children's well-being. On several occasions he said, "If you are concerned about the future, care for your children lovingly and selflessly, for they are the caretakers of the future. Whatever you give them today will come back to you tomorrow. There is a difference between planning for the future and worrying about it. They alone can plan who have a good grip on the present. People waste their time holding on to the past and worrying about the future. Unfortunately parents pass this tendency on to their children. From such an empty present, an empty future emerges."

In the fall of 1980 Swamiji gave a series of lectures on family life and child-rearing, which later took the form of a book, *Love and Family Life*. That same year Swamiji founded a children's school at the Institute and took an active role in designing a curriculum that could be incorporated into the Montessori system. He held classes during which he taught parents and teachers how to let the best in the child manifest, stressing the importance of disciplined love. He taught them how to allow the children to express their creativity and to be fearless and communicative.

Swamiji, who except for a brief interval lived a monastic life, was amazingly wise about children and family life. Once a little boy started biting the other children in the school. This went on for months. His parents and teachers did everything they could think of to stop it, but nothing worked. Finally one day the boy's mother told Swamiji what was going on. He said, "There are worms in his stomach. They are biting him, and so he is biting others. Talk to Dr. Clarke and see if Cina 1M [a homeopathic remedy] in split doses is appropriate for him." A few days after he was given one dose, the boy stopped biting.

On another occasion, while he was walking on campus Swamiji met a young woman who had gotten married a few months earlier. When he asked where her husband was, she said he had gone on vacation. Swamiji let it pass, but when the man returned, Swamiji took him aside and asked him why he had gone on vacation alone. "I needed some space, a vacation for myself," the young man said.

"Sonny, be sensitive," Swamiji replied. "If you learn to communicate with your wife and develop a loving relationship, you will have lots of space and your whole life will become a vacation."

325

Swamiji was not only mysterious, he was mischievously mysterious. He clearly had a kind heart, yet his actions often appeared unkind. This was confusing to me as well as to others. For example, he would often promise to teach a student an advanced practice and then fail to appear at the appointed time and place. Or he would tell a student, "Relax and take it easy. You should take better care of yourself," but within days he would give the student a mountain of work and demand that it be done right away. Or he might praise a woman one day and call her a bitch in public the next.

Once Swamiji invited a student to see him, showered the young man with love and blessings, and before dismissing him, said with feeling, "You have no idea how much I love you." But a few days later he called the coordinator of the Institute's residential program and criticized that same student. "What's wrong with him?" he said. "He's not following the program properly. He's undisciplined and should be asked to leave." The coordinator asked the student to go, but he refused, saying he had come here to study with Swamiji and would not leave until Swamiji told him to go. Swamiji refused to see the young man, but he gave no further instructions to the residential coordinator. Other residents got involved in the situation, and when it was thoroughly complicated, Swamiji summoned both coordinator and student and said, "You people should learn to communicate with each other."

It took months for both parties to realize what Swamiji was trying to teach them. This scene repeated itself, with endless variations, again and again. Sometimes it resolved itself easily, but often those involved left in frustration and confusion.

I too got a taste of this way of teaching. It began a few days after Guru Purnima in 1980. When he was talking about sadhana one day Swamiji said, "Don't pretend to be something which you are not, for hypocrisy is one of the greatest obstacles on the path of self-realization." Then early one morning he called me to his room and asked me to read the portion of my dissertation which I had written in the past few days. Around 8:30 Swamiji's secretary came in and told him that seven people had been waiting for mantra initiation since 7:30. Swamiji told her to make all the arrangements for the initiation and tell them that he would call them soon. She left, and Swamiji resumed listening to my reading. After a while he began expounding on the material and giving me specific instructions about which books to read and how to find other material. Around ten o'clock his secretary returned and told Swamiji that people were still waiting. He replied, "Yes, yes. I know. Tell them to wait. I will soon be with them." And he went on instructing me.

At eleven, she came again and said, "So, Swamiji, should I tell them to come back tomorrow?"

At this, he got up abruptly and said, "No, no. Panditji will initiate them right now." He stretched and looked at me and said, "Panditji, you initiate them." And he walked away.

I did not know how to give mantra initiation or even which mantra to give. So I followed Swamiji a few steps, hoping for instructions. But he stopped suddenly and said in a stern voice, "Go and take care of them. I have lots of work to do. And do it quickly, because you have to cook lunch." Then he walked away.

I went to my room totally bewildered. Swamiji had yet to give me a formal mantra initiation, so I did not have that as a guide. I remembered the process of initiation as described in the scriptures, but it is long and ritualistic, and I had learned from observing Swamiji for the past four years that he never performed rituals. Furthermore, it took just a few minutes for him to initiate someone. I wondered what to do. From several other teachers I had learned many, many mantras but I did not have complete faith in any of them. I knew hundreds of mantras from the scriptures, but most of them are long and hard for Americans to pronounce. Furthermore, both Swamiji and the scriptures enjoined: "Teach only what you have practiced." According to the scriptures, however, the mantras I had practiced so far were highly secret—I was not supposed to even talk about them. So I could not give the mantras I had practiced, and I could not give those I had not practiced. What should I do? I began to cry, but I could not waste the time—Swamiji had told me to "do it quickly."

I went to the initiation room, having no idea what I would do. Then, as each student came and sat down in front of me in a meditation posture, my heart was flooded with spontaneous prayer: "O Lord, Master of all previous Masters, I don't know what I am doing, and yet I am doing it because Swamiji said to. I am not sure whether I have fulfilled the job of being a good student, yet I am sitting at the seat of the teacher, initiating others. Time is so short that I cannot even pray. Therefore, I beg you to transform me into a good conduit so that only the mantra which is appropriate for this student of yours flows through me. Please rescue me today and prevent me from practicing hypocrisy. Once this is over I will ask Swamiji how to initiate properly." At this, my mind became blank, and suddenly a simple word flashed. I said the word aloud several times so that the student would get the proper pronunciation. I repeated this process with each student—seven times in all. Then I rushed off to cook lunch.

While cooking, I planned how to tell Swamiji which mantras I had given and ask if they were appropriate. But when he came to lunch he was occupied with so many other matters that I did not feel it was appropriate to ask him about the initiations. Then when lunch was over, just as I was about to ask, he said, "Bete, can you make a cup of tea for me?" The subject did not come up again.

For the next eleven months Swamiji rarely initiated people at the Institute. And each time I gave someone a mantra, I would pray and confess to God that I was ignorant and did not know what I was doing. I was angry at Swamiji because he was not giving me a chance to ask him about mantra initiation. I knew he was a great master, yet I wondered why he had created a situation in which I had to pretend to be something I was not. I remembered his saying that hypocrisy is one of the greatest obstacles on the path of self-realization. I knew that if I disobeyed him I would fall from the path—but practicing hypocrisy would cause me to fall from the path too. At times I thought of running away from the Institute, thinking it would be easier to maintain my love and respect for Swamiji from a distance. Then another thought would flash: "No. He knows what he is doing. I have no ill intention. I do not wish to misguide others. Therefore I am not practicing hypocrisy." But still my anger persisted.

In June of 1981 the Institute held its annual congress in New York. At the end, as the guests were leaving, Swamiji walked into the hotel lobby and went straight to Brunette Eason, a student from Chicago who had been studying with him since his early days in the United States. He asked her to come to Honesdale, where he would ordain her as a teacher and initiator in the tradition. Brunette canceled her flight back to Chicago and came to the Institute, and when she arrived Swamiji told her that he would see her the next morning at seven o'clock. Brunette waited in the lobby for Swamiji for five hours. At noon he appeared, put his hand on her shoulder, and said lovingly, "Brunette, I told Panditji to teach you fifty, sixty mantras. He is going to write down those mantras and then I will discuss with you further." So when Brunette next saw me, she said, "Swamiji told me you are going to teach me fifty or sixty mantras. When are you going to do that?"

Trying to hide my surprise and dismay, I said, "After lunch." This triggered my anger again—I thought, "Now I'm being forced to involve others in this. Good! This way Swamiji will come to know what I have been doing."

When lunch was over I took Brunette to Swamiji's conference room and started writing down the mantras I had been giving to students for the past eleven months. Then, in the middle of the session, I thought of writing down a variation of a very special three-syllable mantra, called Bala Tripura, which according to the scriptures is supposed to remain secret. I had never taught it, but I argued to myself, "Why keep it secret? Then again, I must not violate the rules laid down in the scriptures." Finally I decided to do both—violate and not violate. So I broke the mantra into three parts and wrote each syllable as a complete mantra. Then I wrote a combination of the first and the third syllables, the third and the first, the second and the first, and so on. And finally I wrote down all three syllables in the proper sequence as a complete and independent mantra. Then I continued writing and explaining the other mantras I had given.

At the end of our session Swamiji walked into the room, and I got up and handed the paper to him. Swamiji looked neither at me nor at the paper. He spoke to Brunette, sat down quietly, and then started reading the mantras. Regarding the first few, he commented, "Good. Very good." Then he crossed out the combinations of syllables I had created from the Bala Tripura mantra. When he came to the main mantra, he crossed it out several times. Giving me a sidelong glance, he said in Hindi, "Do not play with the mantras." I was relieved—the mantras I had been giving for the past eleven months were the proper ones. But still I wondered about the origin of all the mantras I had written down. Did they have a scriptural source?

That evening around 10:30, as I walked into Swamiji's room, he asked, "Panditji, did I ever show you those scriptures?"

I said, "Which scriptures?"

"The ones I brought from my grandmaster in Tibet," he replied.

When I said he hadn't, he asked his secretary to get them, and she returned with what looked like a bundle of rice paper and handed it to Swamiji. He gave the bundle to me and asked me to open it. It was wrapped in a red cloth. I unwrapped it and found a pile of unbound, oblong sheets stacked between two boards. The thick coating of sandalwood paste on the top board told me that someone had been worshipping the scripture.

Not knowing where to begin, I picked up a stack of sheets from the top and carefully laid them aside. I could not believe my eyes: there before me were all the mantras I had written down for Brunette a few hours earlier. They were in exactly the same order. Even the syllables of the Bala Tripura mantra were there, and they were crossed out in exactly the same manner that Swamiji had crossed them out on my paper. I was flooded with awe and elation. Swamiji looked at me and said, "So you think I have not been teaching you?"

Spontaneous words slipped from my mouth: "Forgive me, Swamiji, for my childish behavior and my shallow understanding of you. I have practiced many of these mantras, but still I wonder: Which one is my guru mantra?" But as soon as I said it, an incident from the past flashed before me that brought a mantra into my mind. I knew it was my guru mantra. I was just about to say as much to Swamiji when he said, "Yes, that's your mantra." Then he asked me to make tilk for him.

While he sipped, I found him in the perfect mood to entertain my questions about mantra initiation. In fact it seemed as if he was waiting for me to give him the opportunity to expound on the mysteries of sadhana and the role of God's grace and self-effort. All I said was, "Swamiji, it is beyond my comprehension how such things happen."

"The grace of God is always pouring in, but generally people have a hole in their minds," Swamiji said. "How can you retain God's grace? Sealing the hole caused by fear, doubt, hatred, anger, jealousy, greed, desire, and attachment is an integral part of spiritual practice. Once you make all sincere efforts and are truly exhausted, then you cry out in despair, and that spontaneous cry is the highest form of prayer. It opens the channel of devotion, leading to a state of ecstasy. This state of ecstasy is God's grace. Grace is the fruit you receive from your faithful and sincere efforts.

"Self-realization is a matter of revelation. That comes through God's grace. However, relying on God's grace and abandoning self-effort, especially in the early states of sadhana, is a big mistake. God's grace is like rain that falls over a vast area without any regard for the particular spots that it will benefit. It rains on the unjust and the just alike. And even after it rains, the land that does not have good soil, or soil that can hold the water, will remain barren. But when it rains on land that is fertile and has been properly prepared, seeds sprout and plants thrive. Only when we are fully prepared can we receive, assimilate, and benefit from divine grace.

"Divine grace often dawns in the heart in a mysterious way. When it happens, we are awestruck; we are pulled into a state of wonder. Freedom from fear and doubt is the surest sign that we have received the grace of the Divine. Thereafter, worry and grief disappear forever. This is what the scriptures call 'immortality.'"

Activities at the Institute accelerated with each passing year. By 1981 the Combined Therapy Department was in full swing and a graduate-level program in Eastern studies had been established. The number of faculty members and residents was growing. Many of the original residents were married and had children, so the Institute had established its own Montessori school on campus. In the midst of all this, in the summer of 1981, a strange drama unfolded.

One of the board members was wealthy and had donated a large sum of money to the Institute. He and his family did not live on campus, but had a house nearby. They were close to Swamiji and had been associated with the Institute since the mid-seventies. This man claimed to have spiritual aspirations, but he was arrogant. People tolerated him because of his position, his wealth, what appeared to be his closeness to Swamiji, and his generosity to the Institute. Swamiji tried his best to help him transform himself, but met with little success. His arrogance remained legendary.

That summer the man's daughter got sick, and he and his wife made an appointment for her at the Institute's clinic. When the girl did not appear for her appointment, the doctor called the man's home to check on her. The man answered and gave the doctor a tongue-lashing, shouting that he should have come right over to see the girl rather than waiting for her to keep her appointment, and implying that he was worthless both as a person and a physician. The doctor was deeply offended but managed to avoid expressing his feelings. His path crossed Swamiji's a few minutes later, however, and Swamiji asked, "How are you, sonny?"

"Fine," the doctor replied, but his face said otherwise. Swamiji took his hand and led him to his room, and when he heard the story Swamiji called Dr. Ballentine and told him to make sure the man did not return to the campus. In the ensuing commotion several residents left, and Swamiji and the Institute became the target of a barrage of accusations and a lawsuit or two.

Watching it all, I wondered if such an abrupt and harsh action on Swamiji's part was really necessary. Couldn't it have been done more diplomatically and skillfully? By this time I had learned that it was more fruitful to pay attention to the lessons rather than to events themselves, but even after long contemplation, this lesson eluded me. Months later the episode was still draining away time, energy, and money, and many people were still gossiping about it. So one day I expressed my puzzlement to Swamiji, who said, "He is my student. If I don't discipline him, who else will do it? A teacher must not operate under the influence of fear or temptation. Furthermore this is the Himalayan Institute, an ashram where people should be living in peace and harmony. Love and discipline are the foundation of an ashram. A superiority complex and sense of self-importance destroy the peace. There is a time for everything. People come and people go. If you understand the divine plan and if you see your part in a situation that is unfolding, then play your role joyfully. If you do not understand, simply watch that situation from a distance without involving yourself.

"If you pay attention, you can learn something from this kind of drama. See? People don't necessarily come to a spiritual teacher or a spiritual organization for spiritual reasons. Even if they have a spiritual motive at the beginning, some people soon lose sight of it. And such people pollute the ashram environment.

"'Ashram' means 'place for complete rest,'" he went on. "The ashram environment and the practices undertaken there provide a complete rest for your body, mind, and soul. An ashram is not a place for socializing, nor is it a place for debating philosophical and religious issues. And certainly it is not a place for politics. Self-discipline and self-analysis are the grounds for ashram life. You come to an ashram to learn, to practice, and then you return to the larger world to test how far you have progressed on the spiritual path. If you wish to become a permanent ashramite, it is the duty of the teacher to lead you through the fire. Blessed are those who endure the heat, for one day they shine and give light to the world. An ashram without a *sat guru* [true teacher] and inspired students is just like any other community."

$\mathcal{the}$ PATH OF FIRE AND LIGHT

IN 1981 SWAMIJI'S HEALTH seemed to be deteriorating, and medical tests showed that he was bleeding internally. Doctors could not pinpoint the source, but Swamiji had told a few people that his time in this world was nearly over and he must return to his eternal abode in the Himalayas. He then made some changes in the Institute's constitution and appointed Dr. Ballentine the head, handing over to him all responsibility for guiding the Institute, both spiritually and administratively. In the early fall Swamiji returned to India and went directly to the Manali cave where he had done his eleven-month practice before coming to the West. Within a week his health was restored and he had been inspired to establish an institution in India similar to the one headquartered in Pennsylvania.

From Manali, Swamiji traveled to Chail to formulate his plans. He stayed for the next five months at the Maharaja Palace Hotel, formerly the summer palace of the king of Patiyala, and spent his days writing a commentary on the *Bhagavad Gita*, playing table tennis, taking long walks, and meditating in the company of his longtime friend and student, Dr. S. N. Agnihotri. The two had taken up residence in the hotel's largest suite, the Honeymoon Cottage, and the presence of these aging "spiritual honeymooners" was a source of constant surprise to the young lovebirds who flocked to the luxurious hotel.

From here Swamiji sent a message to the Honesdale headquarters saying that he wanted to build an institute for the study of Vedic culture and civilization in India, explaining that for centuries India has suffered from an inability to draw on its own inherent wealth. The Indian system of education was two hundred years old, he said, yet few institutions prepare their graduates for more than routine clerical and teaching jobs. If the land of the sages is ever to wake up and recognize its potential, he explained, there must be a revolution in the field of education. And there was another problem: in the race for modernization, urban India was embracing unhealthy elements from the West— the very elements Westerners themselves were now trying to eradicate at home. India is not able to separate the valuable attributes in Western culture and civilization from those that are harmful. So, he said, before the Indian intelligentsia became polluted by excessive materialism, before spiritual, social, and family values disintegrated, and before stress reached epidemic proportions, it was important to ready the means and tools to reverse this trend and reestablish peace and prosperity within and without. He explained further that the bridge connecting East and West had to have a firm footing in both hemispheres; so he appointed Dr. Ballentine, Dr. Clarke, and me as the coordinators and told us to outline a project that would draw on all aspects of the Vedic tradition and disseminate that knowledge in its land of origin.

This message brought a wave of joy and excitement to Honesdale—joy because Swamiji had regained his health and once again become active, excitement because he was relying on the Institute to help carry out his mission. Government officials in the states of Punjab and Hariyana expressed interest in the project, and it appeared as if the Institute would be granted a two-hundred-acre plot of land in Hariyana, near Delhi. Within a matter of months, however, another political party came into power, and government support for the project evaporated. Meanwhile members of the royal family of Nepal, who had long been Swamiji's students, asked him to implement this project in their country. It had been one of Babaji's favorite places, and as a young man Swamiji had lived with his master in Nepal's Namcha Bazaar and at the shrine of Mukti Nath, so he had a special affinity with this mountainous country.

So it was that before returning to the Institute in the spring of 1982, Swamiji visited Nepal. The panoramic view of the snow-clad

Himalayan peaks captivated him, and as he climbed a small hill he remembered that when he had been there with his master, long ago, Babaji had looked at the Gauri Shankar peaks and said, "When I'm not in this body, these will be your mother and father." Local villagers happily agreed to sell Swamiji the land he needed, and so he founded the Hansda Ashram in the village of Banepa, on the outskirts of Kathmandu. Everyone was excited at the prospect of having an institution in their country where people from all over the world would be coming to study various aspects of Eastern culture and civilization. And before leaving for the United States, Swamiji put together a team under the leadership of Bharat Gurung to oversee the construction and landscaping in his absence. Bharat Gurung did a superb job, and by the time Swamiji returned to Nepal at the end of the summer there were already a few buildings, complete with electricity, and a well-groomed trail leading to the ashram.

335

That summer in Honesdale Swamiji occupied himself and the rest of the Institute with construction projects and landscaping. He gave only a few lectures. From sunrise to sunset he was outdoors working with the residents as they cut trees, burned brush, and cleared away rocks, underbrush, and fallen timber to make room for trails, lawns, and gardens. They planted trees, established flower beds, and sowed grass. That year the only way to be around Swamiji was to put on gloves and take part in the "rocks and roots" brigade. Guests and residents alike joined him every day when he made a fire and cooked his mountain bread on the open flame. Sometimes he roasted potatoes and prepared a special dish called "bharta."

While all this was going on, the children hung around Swamiji, trying to charm him by gathering twigs and throwing them in the fire or showing him the newts, frogs, and toads they had captured in their sand pails. There was poison ivy and poison oak everywhere; Swamiji warned people to wear gloves, but over the course of the summer almost everyone had a rash from it at one time or another. But the work went on. At night Swamiji either worked on his book *Choosing a Path*, counseled students, or had long telephone conversations with people in Nepal.

The period from the summer of '82 to the summer of '84 was the era of construction both in the United States and Nepal. Swamiji spent most of his time in Nepal and India, and a number of community projects began to emerge around Hansda Ashram. With Swamiji's generous support the little school down in the valley hired teachers, and the children began receiving a proper education. Swamiji started a dispensary, and Dr. A. P. Singh from Kanpur and Larry Xavier from the States took charge of it. They served more than two hundred patients in each twelve-hour day. Hansda became Swamiji's semi-permanent home for a while, and students from all over the world made their way to Nepal to see him. The Institute began taking groups to Hansda in the spring and fall. Swamiji scheduled an international conference on yoga and holistic health in Kathmandu's Yak and Yeti Hotel in March of 1984. But shortly before the conference, an event took place that broke Swamiji's heart.

It was early March, and Hansda Ashram by now had three buildings and could easily accommodate twenty guests. Early one morning Swamiji came out of his room for his usual walk, made his way to the highest point in the ashram, and gazed intently in the direction of the village. All morning he made repeated trips to this little knoll, an expression of deep sadness on his face. No one knew why, but just before noon, the news arrived: a number of people had been murdered in the village early that morning. The survivors, the messenger said, were terrified and were huddled together sobbing. Swamiji gave a long sigh and said, "This is not a place for people like us. My Lord, such brutality! We will leave this place on May 15."

Swamiji announced his decision to leave Nepal during the conference. Everyone was dismayed, but when they asked why, all he would say was, "I cannot tolerate brutality." Yet the construction and landscaping continued and even picked up momentum. And because Swamiji was working so hard and with so much love, they all assumed that he had no intention of actually abandoning the ashram. He asked people from the Institute's headquarters to send grass seed, and in due course seventy pounds arrived and was planted. A week later Swamiji said, "It will take a long time for this lawn to grow. We don't have enough time. Can we get some sod?" The practice of establishing a lawn with sod did not exist in Nepal, but Swamiji was not deterred. People thought it was a lunatic plan, but he told students who were coming from Honesdale to fill their suitcases with sod, and when the customs officers opened these gigantic suitcases at Kathmandu airport, they found carpets of earth and grass. They had never seen such a thing, but most of them knew about Swamiji and his Hansda Ashram so they allowed this strange cargo to pass into the country.

The work continued. May 14 arrived and there was still no sign that the ashram was about to be closed. Swamiji was tending the gardens and giving directives to the people running the nearby dispensary and school. In the afternoon he asked several times, "So what is the date today?" "So when are we supposed to leave this place?" He also said, "We can't leave unless the work is completed. The lawn has to be watered and there is some weeding to be done over there." Then he looked at a flower bed—the plants were just coming out of the ground—and said, "Don't you want to give me a smile before I leave?"

337

The next morning Kiran, my sister-in-law, who was attending Swamiji at that time, went to his room to ask if he was ready for his morning tea. "Yes," he said. "But wait. What's the day today? It's the fifteenth, isn't it? I'm supposed to leave. How can I have tea here?"

"Swamiji, please have your tea," Kiran said. "Then think of leaving." He agreed, but the moment he emptied the cup he picked up his bag, walked out of his room, and told the students staying in the ashram to pack at leisure and join him at the Yak and Yeti. As he passed the flower bed, he saw that all the plants were in full bloom, and touched the flowers lovingly, speaking to them as though they were little children. "Thank you for giving me such a sweet smile," he said. "Always be happy, even when you are about to return to dust."

Dr. Agnihotri, describing Swamiji's departure in a letter to me, said, "Swamiji walked out from Hansda Ashram just as Lord Rama left his father's palace. He did not look back once." Swamiji rarely mentioned that ashram again, but the idea of establishing an institute for Vedic culture and civilization continued to grow in his mind.

Shortly after leaving Hansda, Swamiji returned to the States. The residents were overjoyed that he would be spending more time with them in Honesdale, but their happiness was tempered by the fact that he had abandoned such a beautiful place. Everyone wondered why he had devoted so much time and energy to building the ashram. Didn't he know what would happen? No one had the courage to ask him, but one day in a lecture, without providing a context, Swamiji said, "Only ignorant persons associate success with the fruits of their actions. Krishna was a great warrior—wise, and the knower of past, present, and future. Sixteen times he fought off the enemy who attacked his capital city. When the seventeenth attack came, Krishna abandoned his capital, and people called him a coward. But only after leaving his original capital was he able to establish a new capital, on the island of Dvarika, that was protected by the ocean from all four directions. While residing there he completed his mission peacefully and happily." Hearing this, I knew that Swamiji would start his project elsewhere and on an even grander scale.

338

In the fall of 1985 Swamiji called from India and asked me to join him there with my wife and our three-year-old son, Ishan, as soon as possible. He was in Tikam Garh, a small town in central India. I had no idea why he was there or what he wanted us to do, but we flew to Delhi and from there flew to Khajuraho. Then we drove to Tikam Garh, arriving at suppertime. Swamiji had booked the entire guesthouse, and thirty or forty people were staying there, all in a festive mood. Swamiji, dressed in a silk shirt and slacks instead of the traditional garb of a swami, greeted us and told us to have our meal as soon as we were ready. But when we went to the dining room we discovered that he had not yet eaten. Feeling uncomfortable about dining before he did, we went to him and asked if we could bring his meal to him. "No, you people should go ahead and have your supper," he said cheerfully.

The next morning the guests gathered in the dining room, but again there was no sign that Swamiji had eaten. So we went to him, and again my wife asked if she could bring him his meal, but again he said no and told her to eat. When she insisted that she couldn't eat until he did, Swamiji looked at me and said with a smile, "Can you talk to this silly girl?" When I said that I didn't understand myself, and so I couldn't explain it to her, he replied, "Meera, you go. I'll send Panditji later." After she left he said, "I cannot have meals here because this place and the people here are associated with this body," he said, pointing to himself.

I was surprised. "Swamiji, what do you have to do with this place?" I asked. "You were born in the Garhwal Himalayas, not here in central India."

"Mohit is getting engaged," he replied. "My master made me promise that I would take a full part in all things associated with his marriage, just as any father would do. But neither he nor the people around him understand that after taking the vows of renunciation a swami does not associate with his family and relatives. I can't tell Mohit this, because my master ordered me not to, so in me Mohit sees only his father. Still, I must adhere to *sannyasa dharma* [the traditional values of renunciation], and here everything revolves around family affairs from my past. But I cannot use anything, including food, belonging to this place unless it comes to me as alms."

A solution flashed in my mind. Because we were traveling with a three-year-old, we had brought lots of granola, dried milk, raisins, and cashews from Honesdale, and I asked if it would be appropriate for him to eat that food. He said, "You have saved my life! I knew that if Meera was around, some food would appear." For the next three days, as the engagement festivities continued, Swamiji lived on granola, raisins, nuts, and tilk made from dried milk.

As it turned out, the couple did not marry, but during our stay in Tikam Garh I saw an aspect of Swamiji I probably would never have seen otherwise: how masterfully he balanced two worlds—the mundane and the spiritual. Dressed in a two-piece suit and a shirt of raw silk, he appeared to be actively interested in worldly matters—making jokes, exchanging gifts, and discussing family concerns. On the other hand, when he was alone with Anand Pratap Singh (who had accompanied him from Delhi), and me, he was a sage whose heart overflowed with memories of his master.

After the engagement festivities were over we accompanied Swamiji to Khajuraho, a small town about one hundred kilometers from Tikam Garh, known for its cluster of ancient temples covered with erotic figures. We arrived at noon. Swamiji had not eaten a proper meal in several days, so we went directly to the Oberai Hotel for lunch, and while we were eating he explained that Khajuraho had been the scene of many delightful experiences with his master. He must have seen that we were not able to comprehend his feelings, so he said, "The Temple of Sixty-four Yoginis is like my mother's courtyard. That is where I had my first vision of her at the age of seven. After lunch I will take you to her."

After lunch he sat with us in the hotel lobby talking about some of his childhood experiences with his master. "As a young boy, I was very mischievous," he said. "I had no sense. Sometimes I would put pebbles in the soup just to see how the old sadhus would react when they bit down on one. I used to pull my master's hair and even open his eyelids with my fingers when he was in meditation. One day my master was very much annoyed by my misbehavior. I'm telling you, he was really fed up. He complained to the Divine Mother while he stood in the Temple of Sixty-four Yoginis here in Khajuraho. Like a madman he shouted at her, 'What have I done that I must tolerate his misbehavior and apologize to the sadhus for the disturbances he causes?'

"He grabbed me, swung me into the air, and again shouted at the Divine Mother, 'Make him learn how to behave, or take him back!' Then, just as he was about to hurl me at the statue of the goddess, the Divine Mother appeared and held me lovingly in her lap. After a while she handed me to Babaji, saying with a smile, 'From now on, he'll be a good boy.'" Swamiji paused for a moment, and then said, "I'll take you to her. She is my mother." Then he went outside and stood in front of the hotel and looked toward the temple. From the expression on his face it seemed as if his soul were already transported there and only his body remained.

We got into the car and set off, but the road was closed for construction. It was already 2:30. Our flight to Delhi was leaving at four o'clock, and it was impossible to walk to the temple and back and still catch our plane, so Swamiji said, "Don't worry. One day I will take you to her."

Three days later I was staying with Swamiji at the India International Centre in New Delhi. When the opportunity presented itself, I asked him, "Please, Swamiji, when are you going to take me to her?"

Swamiji said softly, "I will take you there."

"Swamiji," I added, "the scriptures say that after you see her you become her, that there is no difference between you and her. You have seen her. Can't you show her to us even without taking us there?"

At this, Swamiji's countenance changed. "I'm always with her," he said, "Even when I am outward-oriented and thus not aware of her, she is with me. Tomorrow I will show her to you." Then he called Anand Pratap Singh, informed him that he would visit the next morning, and instructed him to empty one of the rooms in his house and have it cleaned thoroughly.

The next morning Swamiji summoned two more of his students, Roshan Lal Kanodia and Usharbudh Arya, and told all three of us to bathe, put on clean clothes, and meet him at Mr. Singh's home. When we arrived, our host took us to the empty room where Swamiji was sitting. In a manner at once imposing and kind, he asked each of us what we wanted from him. All of us said, "Your grace and blessings." Swamiji replied, "Don't be emotional. What will you do with my grace and blessings? Ask for something that you can use in your life." Then Swamiji began listing *siddhis*—clairvoyance, mind reading, knowledge of the future, astral travel, Shiva Bali (a special meditation during which the goddess appears and accepts the offerings in person), and so on. He instructed us to write them down, and then he looked at each of us and demanded, "Ask for any of these *siddhis*. One or two of them will be enough for you to become great. You can earn lots of money, have a big following, become popular, and then you can do many, many good things in life. I too will become free, for then you will be able to carry on my master's work."

All of us were speechless—none of us accepted his offer. This went on for several minutes: Swamiji offering us extraordinary gifts and scolding us for refusing to accept them. Finally he asked each of us to stand in one of the four corners of the room while he himself stood at the threshold. Speaking in Hindi he said, "I am the gatekeeper of thy treasury. Whatever gift you have in store for these children, may it be given to them." At this we heard a sharp rap and instantly saw a red cloth with an object on it spread in the center of the room. "See what

341

has come," Swamiji said—but none of us had the courage to step forward and look at it closely. So Swamiji walked into the room and demanded that I pick up the object and look at it from every direction. I did, and told him it was some kind of yantra. At this, Swamiji addressed his master in a joking tone: "It's not fair. When I asked for something, you gave me some sweets—candies, jalebi—and when they ask, you bring with you the Divine Mother. Why not? There is greater love and affection for grandchildren than for children."

Taking the yantra in his hand and addressing us, Swamiji continued. "You know what is happening in the cave? This is missing, and the sadhus living there are upset with me. They know that no one other than me can transport this yantra from that place. It is a special Sri Yantra. Who wants to have it?"

All of us were silent. Then Swamiji said, "Anand, you are so caught up in politics that you have no time to take care of it. Usharbudh, you travel constantly." Looking at me, he said, "You have no interest in rituals, and these external emblems require ritual worship. Roshan, you keep it." With that, Swamiji handed the yantra to Roshan Lal.

I remained in India with Swamiji for four months. On different occasions I asked him where that yantra had come from and what I was supposed to have done after seeing it. He usually remained quiet, but once he said, "It came from our ancestral cave." Another time he said, "My master used to carry it in his hairlock." On still another occasion he said, "What difference does it make where it came from? You tell me, what difference does it make in your understanding of reality?"

I told him, "At the first instant, it was overwhelming. Then it was thrilling. Later, as time passed, it seemed like a dream. As I remember it today, the experience fills my heart, for it confirms that you are the custodian of the sages' wealth, and I feel grateful that you have accepted me as your student. But it brings a sense of sadness too, that I waste your time. Nine years have already passed. I don't see much difference in me now than when I first saw you in 1976."

At this, Swamiji's indifference evaporated, and once again he was talking to me the way he did during our first meeting in the Akbar Hotel. "The value of such experiences lies in confirming your conviction that such yogic feats are possible," he said lovingly. "It helps you understand that the tradition of the sages is eternal. It is an ever-flowing stream of knowledge. In the bed of this stream lies the infinite wealth of *shakti* [power], *bhakti* [love for the Divine], *vairagya* [dispassion], and all the *siddhis* [yogic accomplishments]. Masters in the tradition are immortal, ever-present, omniscient, kind, and compassionate. They are ever-engaged in finding their students. They guide those who are stranded along the path. These masters are not confined to their physical body. They can guide their students while residing on the other side of the globe. They can guide their students even if they left their bodies centuries ago. And this realization can fill your heart with love for them. But if you do not do any sadhana, this love remains lame; it cannot lead you anywhere. Just because you have a great master or belong to a great tradition, you do not become great.

"This type of experience gives you momentary inspiration," he continued. "If you are vigilant you will take advantage of it. If you are not vigilant, slowly this experience will fade away, and you will be left with nothing."

343

Hearing this, I asked him, "What should I do that will cause this experience to become a ground for my spiritual unfoldment?"

"First try to understand the difference between the experience you gain directly from within and the knowledge you gain from outside," Swamiji said. "You think the vision of the Sri Yantra is your direct experience, but in reality it is not. Just because it appeared in an extraordinary fashion, you think it is very special. I made a big show of asking you people to take a bath, to put on clean clothes, and I made you stand in the four corners of an empty room—in essence, I created an impressive atmosphere. All this together makes you feel that this Sri Yantra is very special. Had I done it in a less formal way, you would have thought it was magic and it would not have seemed as sacred.

"This experience has not added anything to your inner fulfillment, self-confidence, or self-trust, and it certainly has not contributed to your understanding of yourself. It proved that I could do such things, but so what? If I kick you out or commit some fraud with you, the value of this whole experience will be wiped out.

"There are two ways of gaining knowledge: direct experience, and external sources," he went on. "The knowledge you gain from your direct experience is complete, self-evident, and fulfilling. The knowledge you gain from external sources, including your physical guru and the scriptures, is incomplete. It requires evidence of validity and it is not satisfying. No matter how impressive it may appear, the knowledge gained from the external world cannot help you loosen the knot of worldly snares. Such knowledge is simply a burden. By gaining it you may become more informed, and you may tell impressive stories to others, but you cannot be enlightened. People have gone through a great deal of pain to know the truth directly, for they have understood that such knowledge alone could give them freedom. For direct knowledge, you have to do sadhana."

"There must be special practices," I said, "to achieve these kinds of experiences. And don't we have to commit ourselves to such practices one-pointedly?"

"Yes, there are special practices," Swamiji replied. "But before you commit yourself to any advanced sadhana you should be clear why you are undertaking such a practice. What are you expecting from it? Are you realistic in prioritizing the different goals of your life? Have you organized your external life? Sadhana is a matter of interior research. It is totally different from the research conducted in the external world. In the external world the researcher finds subjects for his experiments, but in interior research you must become the subject yourself. This is a difficult task. You must assume the attitude that 'I am the researcher, I am the laboratory, and I am the subject.'

"To have the conviction that you can successfully pursue your research, you must first gather sufficient information by studying the scriptures and learning from those teachers who have already practiced that discipline. Intense practice does not mean that you renounce the world and become a monk. Organize your life in the external world; preserve your physical and mental energy for your higher pursuit. Stay focused and don't be distracted by the charms and temptations of the world."

From September to December Swamiji traveled throughout northern India, Bihar, and central India, and I was lucky enough to accompany him. It was during this time that Swamiji took me to

Banaras and showed me where he had done his practice of the *gayatri* mantra in early adulthood. He also took me to places in Banaras that are not known to casual pilgrims or other visitors—places where accomplished yogis and informed seekers convene to do their sadhana. He took me to the famous holy site Gaya in the state of Bihar, and there he showed me the place where, as the young Bhole, he had met the Pebble Baba.

Thirteen kilometers from Gaya is Bodhi Gaya, where the Buddha attained enlightenment. There Swamiji made me sit in front of him under the bodhi tree while he explained the core of the Buddha's teaching: the four noble truths. He told me that the Buddha was one of the most practical of teachers, and explained that in his teaching he did not concern himself with whether or not the soul existed, or with whether there is or is not a God. The Buddha was a kind soul. He wanted people to know the reality that life is full of pain: to recognize this fact and make an effort to eradicate it. Only when you know the exact cause of pain—whether it lies in the body, mind, consciousness, or somewhere in the external world—will you be able to remove it, he taught. And once the cause of pain is removed, you attain a state of freedom. You are fully established in compassion and wisdom. "That is enlightenment," Swamiji said.

345

Swamiji took me to a dozen other places in the vicinity of Gaya and Bodhi Gaya, explaining the spiritual significance of each. He told me stories about Vedic sages as well as Jain and Buddhist masters who had done their practices there. Then we returned to Banaras and took a taxi to a shrine in the foothills of the Vindhya Mountains. There, at Gerua Talab, Swamiji showed me the place where his master had lived and the two-room structure that was built in his honor in 1917. In front of this building there was a *samadhi:* the burial ground of a saint named Bhole Baba. When I asked about this Bhole Baba, Swamiji said only, "He was a yogi who here took *bhumi samadhi* [burying oneself up to the neck before casting off the body]." I visited that place again in 1995 with a group of forty people from the States, and there we met two sadhus, neither of whom knew of Swami Rama but both of whom knew that Bhole Baba was a disciple of Bengali Baba. In fact one of the sadhus had been Bhole Baba's direct disciple and had been among the students who finished filling the pit after Bhole Baba left his body. According to him, Bhole Baba took *bhumi samadhi* in 1958. When I told Swamiji about this shortly afterward, he said, "After spiritual people die, their followers make up such stories," and changed the subject. This answer did not satisfy me—I still wonder who that Bhole Baba was.

During those four months Swamiji moved from one place to another like a storm. His travels had a spiritual flavor, except in Delhi, Rishikesh, and Dehra Dun. In those three places he was swamped by people. The telephone rang constantly, and he issued a constant stream of directives. All this activity centered around finding a piece of land where he could build the institute for Vedic culture and civilization.

Then one day his mood shifted abruptly and he began talking about building a hospital instead. His students and followers came up with all kinds of ideas and innumerable proposals. Each wanted Swamiji to build the hospital in their hometown, and they all had good reasons: Haridwar is the best place, because the hundreds of homeless sadhus and beggars there need medical services; Dehra Dun is a commercial center in the Himalayan foothills with excellent schools, where the children of the professionals who would staff the hospital could get a good education; Mussoorie would be ideal, because of the altitude and the purity of the mountain air; Kanpur would be perfect, because its millions of people would provide limitless scope for growth. Others argued that the hospital should be somewhere deeper in the Himalayas to benefit the people living in the mountains, and besides, the hospital was being established by Swamiji and must be located in a spiritual place.

After weighing all the pros and cons Swamiji agreed to build a hospital, which he named Sanjivani Aushadhalaya, in the city of Dehra Dun. A group of local doctors enthusiastically joined the project, and Swamiji asked them to form a society and get it legally approved by the government of India. He assured them that it would be fully funded by the Himalayan Institute in the United States—in fact, there was no shortage of money. They should envision a magnificent hospital. Then, having given these instructions in the spring of 1986, Swamiji left for the States.

Back in Honesdale he busied himself teaching, writing, and raising funds. That summer he was engrossed in music. He told everyone about how he had become obsessed with music as a teenager and how his master had become so fed up that he asked the other sadhus to destroy his vina. He told about how his master had ordered, "No more of this noisy music for forty years." Then he would laugh like a mischievous teenager and say, "Those years are up. Now I can practice music again." And practice he did. Day and night it was music, music, and more music. He taught the residents to sing Indian music, and he sang with them. He brought musicians from India and elsewhere. He played the vina, the tabla, the harmonium, sitar, tanpura—any instrument he could get his hands on. Once he telephoned me at three in the morning and said, "Do you want to hear my tabla? You stay on the telephone. I'll put the receiver next to the tabla." Then he started playing. It was my meditation time, but I listened for two hours. Then at five, he picked up the telephone and said, "How do you like it?"

347

I said, "It's marvelous, Swamiji. May I come and join you?"

"Yes, come," and he hung up. When I got to his room he gave me a lesson in voice training. This went on for a few hours. He let me go only when I was so hungry that I had no voice left. It was like that all summer. Anyone with even the slightest interest in Indian music could become his friend and spend hours and hours with him. Watching him so absorbed, one would think that music was the surest—or let us say, the only—way to attain samadhi.

Meanwhile back in India members of the group to which Swamiji had entrusted the work on the hospital became active—not in planning what to do, but in scheming how to do it in a manner that would be of greatest benefit to themselves. I was often with Swamiji late into the night and heard him talking to people in Dehra Dun and Delhi. He would say, "I don't have much experience in setting up an organization in India. God has given you all these skills. I know you can do everything. There is so much suffering, especially in this part of the country. You people are healers and the leaders of society. You know what to do and how to do it. I will ask my students to contribute to this project. You people should not have any worry about money."

One evening, after just such a conversation, I asked Swamiji how things were going. He said, "They are doctors with established practices. They are prosperous. I thought that they would do a good job helping and serving their own people, but they are more interested in serving themselves. What a disappointment!"

I asked him why he was playing the innocent—didn't he know that a person without spiritual aspirations has no boundary around his desires? And didn't he know that, usually, local people are the worst enemies of their locality?

Swamiji's answer was simply, "Everyone deserves at least one chance." Eventually Swamiji withdrew himself, and the society of doctors fell apart. Thereafter he instructed people he knew well to search for a piece of land between Rishikesh and Dehra Dun, and asked some of his students to do the paperwork necessary to form the Himalayan Institute Hospital Trust.

348

This particular summer Swamiji gave very few lectures outside the Institute. Instead, he offered a special seven-day intensive at the Honesdale campus, which he called The Path of Fire and Light. Before this retreat began, he praised it repeatedly. "I'm going to give the essence of sadhana," he said. "I'm going to teach how to meditate properly, how to apply your *sushumna*. If you are really interested in *bindu bhedana* [piercing the most subtle knot at the eyebrow center], don't miss this opportunity. So many of you think you have been practicing yoga, but you are not progressing because you do not know how to practice it properly. This will be the most advanced seminar ever held at the Institute." All over North America Swamiji's students were excited. He was finally going to teach "the real stuff."

I was as excited as everyone else. In 1983 when I had read Swamiji the part of my Hindi translation of *Living with the Himalayan Masters* that dealt with the mystical fire, he had promised to teach this mystery to me. At the time he had said, "We should offer an intensive course on this subject. It will help people. The course will be called The Path of Fire and Light." In my imagination I had gone all the way to learning the esoteric techniques of awakening kundalini, igniting the fire at the navel center, cultivating healing power, and even mastering the technique of casting off my body through spontaneous combustion.

Finally the opening day arrived. Swamiji was scheduled to lecture every morning, and he had assigned the afternoon and evening sessions to other faculty members. Gathered in the auditorium for the first lecture, everyone was ready to absorb every single word of wisdom that would flow from Swamiji's mouth. The room was packed. The cameramen who filmed his lectures made sure they wouldn't miss a single thing. There was pin-drop silence as Swamiji entered slowly from the back of the room and ascended the stage. Then in his typical fashion he stepped to the podium, folded his hands, and said, "I pray to the Divinity in you. This is a very special seminar. You will benefit from it immensely, provided you pay attention. It is called 'The Path of Fire and Light' because it will lead you from darkness to light. But in order to reach the source of light you have to endure the heat of sadhana. That is why it is called the path of fire. It is a very demanding path. It requires that you have full commitment.

349

"Before I teach you the actual techniques, let me tell you that on this path of fire and light, the teacher can only give you guidance. He can tell you what this path is made of, how to prepare to walk on this path, how to walk on this path, how to overcome the obstacles, and how to make certain you're walking forward and not backward. But do not expect anyone else to walk for you; it is you who have to walk on that path. If anybody tells you that he will give you enlightenment, that he will show you God and will take care of all your problems, don't listen to that person. He is a fake.

"Now let me tell you what is this fire. This breath is fire. As long as you are breathing, you are alive. From the center of consciousness arises the wave of the life-force. This life-force turns into breath. You can call breath a ripple of life. Breath is that which animates you. The length of your life is measured in the number of your breaths. Before you are born, providence puts a boundary around your life span by allotting you a certain number of breaths. When you run out of your allotted number of breaths, you die. Therefore breath is the key to health and longevity.

"Breath is living fire. What is oxygen? What do you do with oxygen? Oxygen is fuel. When fuel burns, it releases energy—heat. Where does that energy reside? It resides in the fuel itself. Therefore fuel is the container for the dormant energy. So is the case with oxygen. It is the container of living energy—the life-force. There is a fire within you. That fire ignites the oxygen, and thus the energy contained in the oxygen is released into your body. That energy is a source of nourishment. When the fire within you is extinct, when there is no spark of life left in you, then no matter how much oxygen is pumped into your body it doesn't work. So don't confuse breath with the air you breathe. It is more than that. It is very subtle.

"This science has been described in the tradition as Shiva Svarodaya. Shiva means 'consciousness'; 'svara' means 'melody, music, ripple, wave'; 'udaya' means 'rise, manifestation.' This science describes how the wave of life arises from the primordial pool of consciousness. According to this science, life is a beautiful poem. There is rhythm in it; there is melody in it. To enjoy life in its fullness, you must learn the music of the life-force, with all its currents and cross-currents: rhythm, beat, and melody. Once you learn the music of the life-force, there will be no sorrow left for you in life, for then you will know that the composer of this music is within you. That composer is no one other than you. You are the center of consciousness. You are eternal.

"Propelled by the forces of providence, the ripple of the life-force emerges from the center of consciousness, and propelled by the same force, it again subsides in consciousness. Once you understand that, you will no longer be affected by doubt and fear, grief and anxiety. You will be transformed. Your divine nature will shine forth. But my telling you this is just intellectual knowledge. These flowery words don't help you understand the essence. You will get the essence only when you practice.

"For a genuine and everlasting transformation, you must practice a systematic method of self-discipline and self-training. For the sake of curiosity you may study and entertain yourself with a variety of philosophical doctrines, but those theories work only when you learn to apply them to yourself. Applying theoretical knowledge and living with it in daily life is called 'practice.'

"People have formed a habit of leaning on others. They want others to help them and tell them what to do and what not to do. This is a bad habit. You are a human being: take charge of yourself. By becoming dependent on others you suppress your self-motivation. Without it, you cannot accomplish anything. Summon your willpower and throw aside the fear of failure. Soon you will notice success kissing your feet."

Then, as usual, Swamiji's focus shifted off the main topic. He explained that students in the tradition are taught how to recognize a teacher. Then he told a story about Nirvanji, a great sage who lived in a tiny wooden hut in Rishikesh for more than seventy years. Once as a young man, Swamiji said, he had accompanied Nirvanji to a spiritual conference in Haridwar, where a famous swami from Banaras was lecturing on the spiritual dimension of alchemy and how yogis use mercury to perfect their body, purify their energy channels, and conquer the mind. This is a well-known practice of yoga called *vajroli kriya*. According to the scriptures the practitioner of this discipline takes mercury into his body through his generative organ. But the scriptures do not describe what happens to the mercury, how it affects the body, how its poisonous effect is removed, or how the mercury is removed from the body. The general belief is that the yogi sucks the mercury through his generative organ and channels it to his brain, where it not only induces a state of samadhi but enables the yogi to attain mastery over his body and mind and even to attain immortality.

351

After listening for a while to the famous swami, Nirvanji got up and said, "*Sadhu ka chhora* [Boy of a sadhu], can you demonstrate any of these things?" The swami from Banaras did not know who was asking this insulting question, but he had seen a dozen or more respected sadhus from Haridwar and Rishikesh stand up to honor him. Realizing it would be a mistake to show off, he admitted that he was speaking from books. He went on to say humbly that he had been searching for someone to teach him, but so far he had not been successful. Then he invited Nirvanji to come to the stage and teach this science—the mastery over mercury that leads in turn to the mastery of body, breath, and mind.

When Nirvanji took the stage, he explained that to do any practice, first you have to learn how to sit properly and how to breathe properly. Practice has to be systematic.

With that, Swamiji brought the lecture to a close, saying, "Tomorrow I will teach you the complete system of sadhana."

After his lectures Swamiji would normally ask in private, "So how did you like the lecture?" This particular day he asked the question as usual, and of course he expected a positive answer. But my answer contained its own kind of question. I told him the lecture was very good, and then added, "But Swamiji, you tricked people again. Did Nirvanji give a demonstration? Did he elaborate on *vajroli kriya?*"

"Yes, Nirvanji did demonstrate," Swamiji replied. "You see, just as in religion, in yoga and spirituality there are lots of superstitions. People do not try to verify their beliefs. When you take mercury through the generative organ, where will it go? It will go to the bladder or to the testes. There is no tube or pipe from there to the brain. So how can it go to the brain from there? Mercury is liquid at room temperature. When you do certain pranayama practices and raise the temperature in the pelvic area, mercury turns into vapor and is absorbed into your bloodstream and circulates through your body. The toxicity of mercury is well-known. And if you have not trained your body to tolerate that, you will get mercury poisoning, which may result in renal failure, nervous disorder, memory loss, and a number of other problems. Only after you have unveiled the mystery of fire within your own body can you practice this *kriya*. It is a very advanced practice. Only the accomplished hatha yogis venture to do this *kriya*."

Then Swamiji asked me to bring a thermometer. When I did, he broke it and the mercury scattered on the floor. He asked me to pick up the tiny, shiny droplets. I couldn't—they were sliding here and there. Then Swamiji passed his hand over the droplets in a sweeping motion and they all coalesced, forming one huge drop. He picked it up as though it were solid metal, put it on my palm, and asked me to knead it. I couldn't because it slid all over. Next he put a paper towel in a bowl and had me place the ball of mercury in it. Then he asked me to get a bowl of water and a towel. When I did, he washed his hands in the bowl and wiped them.

Then he picked up the mercury, put it in his left palm, and stirred it with the index finger of his right hand. His eyes were focused on the mercury and it seemed as if he was either meditating or repeating a mantra. Within a minute I noticed that the mercury was losing its sheen, and soon it turned into a black paste. As Swamiji continued stirring, the paste got drier and more condensed, until only a tiny bit of black powder remained in his palm. Then he wiped his hand with the towel and told me he had absorbed the mercury into his body through his palm and could pass it out again through his urine anytime he wished.

Then he talked about how alchemists in Europe used mercury during the medieval period, and explained its medicinal uses as described in Ayurveda and Chinese medicine. He warned, however, that most of this science is now extinct. What remains is not complete enough to guide people in using this science either for healing or for spiritual awakening. Furthermore, he told me, using mercury is risky—even one little mistake can be fatal. There are some rare yogis who have preserved this knowledge, he said, but they keep it secret because they know that human beings are good at misusing, abusing, and distorting the esoteric wisdom.

By now some time had passed, and he asked me to clean the bowl and dry it with the towel. When that was done he urinated in it, and those shiny droplets of mercury could be seen resting on the bottom.

353

After this demonstration, Swamiji went on elaborating. "Mind, breath, and sexual energy can be compared with mercury. Like mercury, they are unstable and it is hard to capture them. Mind, breath, and sexual energy are interconnected—when one is unstable, the other two become unstable; stability in one brings stability in the others. Mercury is an amazing substance. Its behavior is unpredictable. Its behavior changes in response to mind, breath, and sexual energy. The yogis discovered that by stabilizing mercury it is possible to bring the mind, breath, and sexual energy under control. Once you gain mastery over this triangle, you become master of all the visible and invisible forces of nature. Yogis have used the science of mercury for healing themselves and healing others. They have used this science as a doorway to *surya vijñana* [the esoteric solar science]. Through the science of mercury they unveiled the subtle mystery of fire."

The next morning everyone joined Swamiji in the auditorium, hoping he would teach them something new—an advanced practice which would transform them miraculously. But after praying to the Divinity in all, Swamiji began: "The problem with you people is that you don't practice systematically. You are spoiled by this Coca Cola culture—open the bottle, drink, throw the bottle away, and move on.

That's what you do with your practice too: you learn something, practice for a few days, then move on to the next guru, the next mantra, the next practice. You are hopping. This is a reflection of your hopping mind.

"You can't help yourself, because you have bad breathing habits. You don't know how to breathe properly. When you examine yourself, you will find that you have a shallow breath, noisy breath, jerky breath, and there is a pause between your inhalation and exhalation. As long as there is shallowness, jerkiness, noise, and pauses in your breath, you can have neither a quiet mind nor a healthy body. For any practice, you need a strong and healthy body. When you practice regularly, in one sitting posture, for a long time, your body will become still, your breath serene, and your mind tranquil. Then you will realize that although you have a body, you are not the body. You will also understand that the body is a wonderful instrument and that you should take care of it properly. An unhealthy body dissipates the mind—you then have no time to work with other aspects of yourself. That is why maintaining physical health is an integral part of spiritual practice."

354

Swamiji continued lecturing in the same vein. Then looking at Dr. Ballentine, he asked, "Who is teaching this evening? Dr. B, are you? I will ask Dr. Ballentine to teach you the principles of good health tonight. I will also ask Kevin Hoffman to check your posture, because without the proper sitting posture you cannot practice anything."

Many people in the audience were disappointed: Swamiji was back on the same old theme; he hadn't taught them anything new. Others finally realized that they must practice and master the basics, because it is only on the ground of the basics that advanced practices can be introduced.

The next morning Swamiji started again. "Today I am going to teach you the real practice. You will understand the value of it, provided you pay attention." He went on: "As part of systematic meditation, first you learn to sit with your head, neck, and trunk straight. It is the healthiest and most comfortable way of sitting. When you sit this way, the pressure at the base of the spine creates heat, and as the heat increases, the pranic force expands and rises upward. Because the spine is straight and the nervous system relaxed, the pranic energy flows freely upward along the spinal column toward the head. In this pose you are free from sloth and inertia. Without the proper posture you will face numberless obstacles in your meditation. And meditation is the core of all practices."

At the end of each lecture during the course of the seminar, Swamiji said that the next day he was going to teach a unique and methodical practice. But he kept coming back to the basics. He called people up to the stage to look at his posture, to check his breath. He even demonstrated a special technique of hatha yoga and pranayama known as *agni sara*. On the sixth day of the retreat he began to talk about the fire of kundalini that resides at the base of the spine, and said that the path of fire and light is the path of inner awakening: on this path you learn to make the best use of your present level of physical and mental energy to awaken the infinite potential lying dormant within you. This dormant force is called kundalini shakti. And he again reminded the audience that in this inner awakening, breath is the key. Once again he promised that the next day he would reveal the secret.

355

On the seventh morning he said, "I'm going to take you through a shortcut. The shortcut is to cut your ego. Offer it to the higher self. Throw your trash in the fire that resides in you. That fire is the inner guru. This fire is all-pervading, but for practical purposes it resides in two main locations in your body: the navel center, and the guru chakra, the center above the eyebrow center. Meditation on the fire at the navel center helps you overcome the obstacles caused by the two lower chakras. These first two chakras are the centers of self-preservation, hunger, sleep, and sex. These are the four fountains from where the numberless streams of emotion emerge.

"The mind of a weak person is like a fish swimming in the turbulent streams of emotion. But when you gain access to your navel center and learn how to throw your animal tendencies arising from your primitive urges into the fire of the navel center, you become strong. You become the master of yourself. Meditation at the navel center will help you become strong physically and emotionally. The fire at the guru chakra has an entirely different quality. The light emanating from the fire at the guru chakra carries a spiritual quality. Meditation at the guru chakra will help you gain clarity of mind, overcome your doubts, gain the right understanding of yourself, and receive the grace of the Divine.

"Tell me, what do you want me to teach you? Meditation at the guru chakra or at the navel center?"

The audience couldn't make up its mind. Some asked him to teach about the fire at the navel center; others insisted on hearing about the fire at the guru chakra. Still others wanted both.

Swamiji then told his students to be practical and systematic. "When you work with your navel center you will have fewer obstacles to face. The fewer the obstacles, the easier the journey will be. Therefore, in my opinion, this year you should learn how to meditate at the navel center. Next year I will teach you meditation on the guru chakra. Meditation at the guru chakra will enable you to open the door to self-realization."

Then Swamiji went on to describe the method of *agni sara*, a hatha yoga technique for fanning the fire at the navel center. He asked members of the audience to come up to the stage and observe how his buttocks contracted inward when he exhaled, and how at the culmination of the exhalation he pulled his entire pelvic and abdominal muscles toward the navel center. Then he asked the Institute teachers whom he had personally trained to make sure everyone in the audience learned the proper technique of *agni sara* before they went home.

A few weeks after this seminar Swamiji left for India, where the hospital project awaited. When he arrived, some of his students showed him a tract of land between Dehra Dun and Rishikesh that seemed to be ideal. There was a road, access to electricity, and miles of farmland around it for future expansion. The small airport on an adjoining tract ensured easy access to Delhi and other major cities in north India. It was just what Swamiji had been looking for. The project took off. It started as a small dispensary with an outpatient facility, expanding from there, and in a little more than six years there was a well-equipped, thoroughly modern hospital on the site. Swamiji began to spend seven or eight months in India each year, returning to the United States for four or five months in the spring and summer.

356

During this phase of his life I saw a radical shift in both Swamiji's pattern of working and his lifestyle. Before the hospital project began, India was a place of retreat for him and Swamiji led a quiet life there. Except when he stayed in Delhi or visited Kanpur, hardly anyone knew where he was or what he was doing. In those days, he visited his real home—the Himalayan peaks—in the fall. In the winter he spent his time in remote spots tucked away in central India's Vindhya range. But once the hospital project began he was always surrounded by people whenever he was in India. Twenty hours a day he was either holding meetings, negotiating with villagers for land, entertaining politicians, going over plans with architects, builders, and landscapers, recruiting doctors and other staff, or monitoring construction work.

At one time more than a thousand workers were employed on the site, creating a hive of activity previously unknown in the area. And in a society where nothing gets done unless you grease the palms of everyone, from top to bottom, Swamiji was trying to accomplish this enormous task while adhering to the practices of truth, love, and self-less service. This infuriated the local politicians, who wanted to make sure they would get a piece of this gigantic pie in one way or another. But Swamiji would not bribe them or comply with their demands in any way, and so they worked hard to discredit him. For example, they misguided the innocent villagers, convincing them that Swami Rama and his Himalayan Institute Hospital Trust would become a source of misery for them. By establishing this hospital, they said, Swamiji was bringing a Western influence to the area that would damage their noble culture and spiritual heritage. Swami Rama may have been born in the Himalayas, the politicians told the villagers, but he is an American swami. Why should he do anything here? He is loaded with money because he is a CIA agent.

The villagers did not know any better. For centuries they had been living in fear—manipulated, misguided, and exploited by their leaders. Politics, here and in the other underdeveloped parts of India, motivated by money and power, had long revolved around religion, racism, and caste. So now, in addition to everything else, Swamiji had to waste time dealing with corrupt local leaders—sometimes politely, and at

357

other times through various legal means. This was indeed a trial for a sage who had spent his entire life meditating on the Lord of Life and quietly dispensing his love to all living beings.

When he returned to the States each spring, Swamiji looked tired. He attributed this to jet lag, but my heart said that it was a seven-month-long tiredness. Neither I nor anyone else, however, had the courage to advise him to rest, for we all knew his conviction: "In the tree of life there are two immortal fruits: hard work, and remembering God." Swamiji's return always brought a joyful awakening at the Institute. The residents knew when he was back, but they respected his privacy. They saw him only when he wanted to see them. But they had figured out a system of knowing when Swamiji was out playing tennis or walking around the grounds, and would gather around the tennis court or go walking themselves, happy just to get a glimpse of him.

Beginning in 1987 Swamiji became increasingly less visible and less active in his traveling and teaching. He began to spend most of his time meditating, with his music, and writing books. He lectured only occasionally. He did, however, maintain the tradition of offering a seven-day intensive each summer on The Path of Fire and Light, and this is when students from all over the country, Canada, Europe, and elsewhere, came to see him. The flavor of his lectures also changed. On one hand, he continued emphasizing the importance of mastering the basics of sadhana—that is, sitting and breathing properly, eating light and nutritious food at the right time and with the right mental attitude, exercising, and maintaining a regular schedule. On the other hand, he began adding more and more esoteric elements to his teaching. It was during this phase that Swamiji began talking about the "shortcut," the advanced technique of *bindu bhedana* (piercing the most subtle knot at the eyebrow center), and *shakti pata*, the divine grace.

Now every summer he would say, "Life is short, and the journey is long. I want you people to wake up. Waste neither your time nor mine. I have told you many times that anything I have is for you. I love you and I appreciate your generosity and selflessness. But what have you done so far for yourself? Have you thought what will go with you when you leave this place? The fear of death still haunts your mind, because you do not know where you have come from and where you will go once you leave this place. Dying without knowing the meaning and purpose of life is the greatest loss.

"Many times I promised that if you want, I will teach you the higher disciplines of yoga, which are taught in our tradition. I can teach you *yoga nidra* [yogic sleep]. That will give complete rest to your body. In a short period of time you will become more energetic and productive. It will also help you cultivate the ability of intuitive diagnosis. I can also teach you the technique of *bindu bhedana*. That will help you disentangle the knot created by the most subtle obstacles. Then you will be free from all doubt. Fear will vanish once and for all. In the absence of doubt and fear, your relationship with yourself and others will improve tremendously. You will be totally transformed. Your understanding of yourself and the world outside you will be changed. Even the shadow of sorrow will not be able to touch you. But I feel sad that so far no one has come forward.

"You people give me money. What will I do with that money? I have to find a way of freeing myself from worldly things. That is why I am establishing this hospital. Soon I will be gone. The memories of our life together will linger in your mind. You will miss me, and I will miss you."

This message awakened a number of students, and during The Path of Fire and Light seminars they asked him to teach both *yoga nidra* and *bindu bhedana,* but Swamiji always resorted to the same old pattern of teaching the basics, although in a somewhat modified manner. When he taught The Path of Fire and Light for the first time, he emphasized proper sitting and breathing, and included the advanced techniques of pranayama, *bandhas, mudras,* and visualization in the accompanying practicums. That year, the central practice was *agni sara.* Later, *shavasana,* relaxation incorporating sixty-one points in the body, and the technique of yogic sleep gained prominence.

As the years passed, Swamiji became more and more focused on explaining the mystery of the mind and the importance of constantly maintaining a state of cheerfulness. "Happiness is your own creation," he would say. "If you expect something or someone to make you happy, then forget it. Achieving the objects of your desire will not make you happy. It may give you a momentary thrill or feelings of security, but you will soon be engulfed by fear of loss. Happiness is a condition of the mind and is created by your conviction that nothing in this world is worth worrying about. The more you maintain this conviction, the stronger the habit of happiness you form. Only a happy mind can receive and contain spiritual wealth."

One Sunday morning, just as I was leaving for Swamiji's ten o'clock lecture, the Institute's general manager phoned to say that Swamiji wanted to see me right away. I ran from my home to Swamiji's room in the main building and rang the bell. With a voice like thunder, he shouted, "Come in!" As I entered, I noticed that his hair was disheveled, and he looked angry and disappointed. But before I was close enough to bow my head, he blasted at me, "What's wrong with you? You are ruining the Institute! Everywhere things are falling apart because of you. I did not expect you to be so egotistical and uncommunicative."

Besides the general manager, two other faculty members were present. I looked at them, hoping for some clue as to what was the matter, but everyone remained quiet. So I said humbly, "Swamiji, I don't know the context." This response enraged him even further. "You have been insulting people!" he bellowed. "Your ego is so swollen that you don't think anybody else knows anything!" Then he looked at the other three and shouted, "I don't want this Institute to be destroyed because of him!"

One of the faculty members reminded him gently that it was after ten and he was late for his lecture. "Am I in such a good frame of mind that I can lecture?" he shouted. Then, without looking at any of us, he snapped, "Go and take care of this crummy lecture!" We all looked at each other, trying to figure out who he meant; then the other three all looked at me. The message was clear: I was the one who should go. But I had just been told that I was egotistical and I didn't think anyone else knew anything, so I didn't want to lecture unless Swamiji ordered me to. I gave Swamiji a pitiful look and asked, "So, Swamiji, should I go?"

"If not, do you want to chew my brain?" he snapped. "Get out from here!" As I was leaving the room, he shouted, "After the lecture, come back—we have to resolve this once and for all!"

I washed my face, drank some water, and then walked down to the auditorium. Later I came to know that shortly after I left Swamiji's room, he asked the others to leave also and told them he would meet with them later to discuss this matter further. He then combed his hair and came out of his room and walked through the corridor where normally people waited for him when they knew he would be on his way to the auditorium. Seeing a few people standing there, he said, "What are you people doing here? Isn't Panditji lecturing? Go to his lecture!" Everyone left. Suddenly he called out to one of them, Rita Gara, and told her to sit in the back of the auditorium and he would send someone to get her later. By the time Rita arrived I had begun my talk and was making jokes about Swamiji in an attempt to soften the audience's disappointment at seeing me instead of him. About half an hour later Swamiji sent for Rita, and they chatted awhile. Then he asked, "So how was Panditji's lecture? What was he talking about?"

361

She told him, "Panditji is a lot of fun. He was joking about you, making people laugh. And they began to enjoy listening to him talk about the topic."

Swamiji replied, "He's a good boy. I love him very much."

When the lecture was over I went to see Swamiji, expecting even more thunder, and possibly lightning, but to my surprise he pressed the button to open the door without saying anything. And as I entered, I found the energy in the room totally different. An aura of tranquility surrounded him. While I was approaching him, he raised his hand and said, "*Aa ja, aa ja* [come, come]," and as I bowed my head he put his hands on my shoulders and said, "I'm proud of you. Happiness is the most precious virtue. A happy mind alone can retain the gift of knowledge."

I said, "Swamiji, how can I be happy when you are not happy with me?"

"You tell me," Swamiji replied. "Despite all the scolding and accusations, why did you not become upset and sad? You were making jokes!"

"Because I know that you love me," I replied. "If I make a mistake, you will correct it."

Then Swamiji put his hand on my head lovingly and said, "That's called *bhakti*—love and trust together. A person joined in bhakti remains ever-cheerful. He also attains *shakti* [inner strength] and *siddhi* [all yogic accomplishments]. There is nothing higher than bhakti.

Freedom from doubt, fear, and the bondage of karma are the fruits of bhakti. People lacking bhakti don't receive the full result of their sadhana despite their knowledge and sincere practice. And they often lose even what they do achieve.

"Remember," he went on, "this world is not worthy of your trust, but it does deserve your selfless and unconditional love. You must love all. But have complete trust only in the Divine and in those in whom divine virtues are awakened. This advice of mine will help you carry on my mission and protect you from falling into the traps created by the world."

Swamiji's annual Path of Fire and Light lectures enabled people to understand that yoga is more than postures and breathing exercises; it is more than meditation on breath, mantra, or visualizing a sacred image; and it is more than sitting around a teacher chanting or discussing philosophical texts. They came to realize that yoga is more than a therapeutic paradigm addressing the health of body and mind. It is a complete science and addresses the issues of a human being as a whole, as well as the place of the individual and all of humanity in the grand scheme of creation.

People sensed that what Swamiji had not taught was vaster by far than what he had taught. They realized that the tradition of the sages is not confined to teaching a particular aspect of yoga, nor is it concerned with a particular culture or group, and they wanted to know more about the tradition—the sages, the scriptures, their teachings, and the knowledge that has been transmitted orally from generation to generation. In response, Swamiji instructed me to offer a year-long complete course on the tradition and techniques of the Himalayan masters, which I did in 1991–92.

At the end of this course he agreed to teach one of the most important scriptures of the tradition: *Saundaryalahari*, The Wave of Beauty and Bliss. During this seminar students saw an aspect of Swamiji which they had only glimpsed in his books *Love Whispers* and *Living with the Himalayan Masters*. This was the first time he spoke in any detail on tantra and Shakti sadhana; now he talked about the Divine as Mother and allowed the students to know that his personal path was the path of Sri Vidya. He explained that Sri Vidya is the most esoteric and sublime of all yogic paths. "The masters of Sri Vidya view the Divine Mother as the highest reality," he said. "Bliss and beauty is her intrinsic nature, and the universe is her manifestation. It is she who manifests in the form of the universe; therefore the universe is beautiful and blissful. Everyone and everything in the universe is the child of Divine Beauty and Bliss. The Divine Mother is an infinite ocean of bliss, and all the manifestations of the universe are waves in that ocean. Like drops, we are an inseparable part of those waves. Quantitatively we may be smaller than the ocean, but qualitatively we are the same.

"Further," he told us, "everything in this manifest universe is connected to everything else, and experiencing the fullness of our own beauty and bliss depends on having a direct experience of this connection. This law applies at every level of our existence. Nature is the manifest form of the Divine Mother, the transcendental ocean of beauty and bliss. To enjoy her protection, love, and care, we must live in her lap. The more we distance ourselves from her, the further we distance ourselves from divine love and protection. Exploiting nature is like abusing our own mother. Out of ignorance we fail to see that we are constantly receiving nurturance from the sun, moon, stars, air, fire, and water. We are made of these forces; they are integral to us. Even the force of gravity is a form of sentient love emitting from the heart of the planet. It holds us fast to the bosom of the Earth. Punching holes in the ozone layer is like drilling holes in our skulls. Destroying the forests is like hacking away our own limbs. Allowing the soil to erode is like ripping off our own skin.

"According to the adepts of Sri Vidya, worshipping nature is the core of spirituality. 'Worship' means living in harmony with nature, actively contributing to her well-being, and refraining from harming her. Once we are in harmony with nature we begin to experience divine love and grace manifesting everywhere, and our hearts open spontaneously. As this happens, the curtain of duality is lifted and we no longer experience ourselves as entities separate from her. This experience erases our fear of death, because we now realize that we have been with her all along: there is nothing like being born or dying. We are drops of bliss emerging from the wave of bliss and subsiding into

363

it again. We are no longer bound by the cycle of birth and death, for we know birth is like coming into the lap of our mother, and death is like returning to her womb."

In 1976, during my first few days with him, Swamiji had re-marked, "No one understands me. There will come a time when no one will be able to understand my actions and speech. That is when I will disappear in the Himalayas and no one will find me." Beginning in the early nineties, I noticed that his actions were becoming increasingly incongruent. Here at the Institute, he began to gradually withdraw from contact with people—he cut down on lecturing, on giving private audiences, and on his involvement in administrative matters. When he did teach, he usually focused on the virtues of non-attachment, desire-lessness, and turning the mind away from the world and making it inward. Most of the time he stayed in his room, and when he came out it was only to play tennis or take a short walk. Once he remarked to me privately, "You know, I'm intensifying my practice. Can you believe how low Swami Rama has fallen? There was a time when I could cast off my body in less than three seconds; now it takes more than three minutes. Shame on me! But now I'm going to get back to my original state."

I knew Swamiji never said anything without a purpose. And there-fore I tried to see if there was any marked change in his speech or action. I couldn't see much, for he still played tennis, worked on books, watched Hindi movies, and talked to people on the telephone. He made jokes, played with the children, raised funds, supervised the hospital project by phone, and entertained guests and visitors. The only change I could see was that, overall, he was more withdrawn and seemed to be meditating long hours—that was obvious from his eyes. But this change was not significant enough for me to draw a con-clusion about his saying that a time would come when no one would understand him.

My anxiety gave me no rest. I continued pondering: Swamiji had said, "I am intensifying my practice." It is not Swamiji's nature to praise himself or expose his sadhana to anyone. He had also said, "There was a time when I could cast off my body in three seconds." Is he thinking of casting off his body? Then suddenly I was struck by something: the change in his name. His letterhead now read "Dr. S. Rama" instead of "Swami Rama." When I saw it for the first time it shook me; then I was thrown into a state of deep contemplation. I thought about how in 1952 he had cast aside his name, Sadashiva, along with Bharati, a term attached to some of the swamis of the Shankaracharya order. Then he was ordained as Swami Rama. And I remembered how, after this initiation, when Swamiji asked his master what his tradition was and how he should introduce himself in the external world, Babaji had replied, "Your past is dead, and that includes not only the death of your worldly identity but also your religious and spiritual identity. You are dead to all traditions, and all traditions are dead to you. . . . You belong to all traditions and yet you are not the slave of any of them. Mount Kailas is your home. You are born to serve Rama, to serve the world of Rama, and to work like Rama. You are not allowed to go back to your home until you have walked in the footsteps of Rama and have completed the journey of self-sacrifice, just as Rama did. Rama's mission was not only to serve India and Indians, but to serve the whole world. He loved humans and non-humans alike. He built a bridge between big and small, rich and poor, humans and animals."

365

But I could not stop pondering: What happened to "Swami Rama"? Who is this "Dr. S. Rama"? In that past year I had heard Swamiji remark several times, "I am fed up with this swami business." Had he decided to drop his identity as a swami? My heart began to pound when another thought flashed through my mind: Has he decided to drop his body completely? Then I thought, No, no, he is not permitted to go to Mount Kailas until he has completed the journey of self-sacrifice. I knew my mind was too small to comprehend the vastness of Swamiji's being, but I could not stop myself from trying. I began to notice that more and more miraculous experiences were associated with him—experiences that had nothing to do with the medical or scientific realm. Rather, they were esoteric, and many of them centered around death.

For example, once when his secretary, Kamal, was rubbing his feet she noticed small, hard lumps in his soles, and when she pressed them firmly, small pebbles came out. She asked Swamiji how they got there and he said, "From walking barefoot in the mountains."

Another time, Swamiji was dozing on the couch with his body completely covered by a quilt. Julie Hobing, one of the students who often attended him, came in and asked if he would like to have his feet rubbed. When Swamiji said, "If you like," she put her hands under the quilt and began to massage them. He fell asleep, but after a few minutes she felt his feet become smaller and softer. Curious, she lifted the quilt and looked. She couldn't believe her eyes: his feet were those of a woman, the most beautiful she had ever seen. Instantly her curiosity gave way to the realization: "Neither the sight nor the touch belong to this world. They are divine." She did not say anything about this to Swamiji, but in her private time she tried to capture those extraordinary feet in sketches—but none came close to what she had seen. Then one day when she was sitting at the kitchen table in Swamiji's apartment, he walked in and looked at what she was drawing. When he asked her what she was drawing, she replied, "Something I saw a few days ago." He paused and then said, "You are very fortunate: you got a glimpse of the Divine Mother."

Another time, my wife and I arrived at the court at Swamiji's usual tennis time to find there was no indication yet that Swamiji was coming out. We started to play, and as we hit the ball back and forth we noticed that a big monarch butterfly seemed to be chasing the ball. Then after a few minutes the butterfly started to fly around me. It was so close I had difficulty hitting the ball without hitting the butterfly. Whenever I went to pick up stray balls, the butterfly was there before me, sitting on the ball. Then it came and sat on my hand. From there it flew to my right cheek and then to my left cheek. It felt as if someone was kissing me and saying goodbye. Then the butterfly flew away. I followed it as it flew toward Swamiji's apartment and disappeared.

After a while Swamiji came out, and as soon as he saw me, he asked, "Did you see Rita Gara?" Whenever Swamiji was in residence in Honesdale she spent as much time as possible at the Institute, and whenever Swamiji played tennis she would run after the stray balls and bring them back to him. I knew she had been hospitalized with end-stage pancreatic cancer, and so when Swamiji asked if I had seen her that afternoon I replied in surprise, "She's in the hospital."

"No, no," he said. "She left her body today and came to say goodbye to us." I asked him how soon a person can get a body after death. "There is no set rule," he replied. "She loved us very much and she needed a locus [a body] to say goodbye before her unconscious dissolved into the collective consciousness of nature. Creatures like butterflies do not have a very crystallized consciousness, and so that butterfly's body could be used for a short time to express her feelings."

On another occasion Swamiji abruptly asked Kamal to locate a bird's egg, which he said would be somewhere outside near his apartment. She found it and brought it to him. Then he waited for the egg to hatch. When the tiny bird emerged, no one knew what kind it was, so it was hard to tend it. Swamiji cared for the baby bird himself. He would put drops of water in its mouth and would sometimes place it on his couch while he sat on the floor. Kamal gave me regular reports on the bird's condition: Now it's lifting its head; Now it can walk; The bird isn't eating anything and Swamiji is worried; and so on. Then one morning, while Kamal was preparing breakfast for a small group of Swamiji's students visiting the Institute from the Caribbean islands, a frying pan suddenly fell on Kamal's toe. At the same moment Swamiji's booming voice came from upstairs: "Kamal!" She went upstairs immediately and found that the moment the skillet had hit her toe, the little bird had run head-on into a radiator and died. Swamiji gave the body to Kamal and asked her to bury it.

Later Kamal asked me, "Panditji, do you know who that bird was?" When I said I didn't, she said it was the great sage Nirvanji, who used to look after Swamiji. She told me that Swamiji had been concerned because she had been destined to be in a fatal accident, but Nirvanji prevented it by dying for her in the form of a bird.

And then there was the time, in the summer of 1992, when my sister called me early one morning from Delhi and told me that my father was being rushed to the hospital in Allahabad and I should come immediately. She gave me the telephone number at the hospital, and for two hours I tried to call but couldn't get through. Around six o'clock, I told my wife that I was going to stand outside Swamiji's door, and whenever it opened I would ask him what I should do. But just as I was about to leave for his apartment, Swamiji called, and before I could say anything he asked, "What's the matter?" I told him about my sister's call and he said, "No, no, you go immediately. You start driving. When you reach New York, give me a call: by then we'll have a ticket for you. Don't worry." An hour after my plane left, Swamiji called my wife and asked with great concern, "Did you hear anything from Panditji? How is his father?" When Meera said she hadn't heard, he hung up, but he called almost every hour with the same questions. Around noon Swamiji saw her in the hall of the Institute's main building and asked again. She said, "Swamiji, he is still in the plane and I have not heard anything from Allahabad."

At this Swamiji replied, "He was already dead, but he loved Panditji so much that he could not leave without seeing him. And due to his attachment to Panditji, he was in great pain. So I put him back in his body. Now he will stay in his body until Panditji reaches there, and leave only after he has seen him."

When I arrived in Allahabad thirty-six hours later, I found my mother and sisters happy because my father's condition had improved. They told me it had been very scary: he had stopped breathing on the way to the hospital and his stomach was swollen. But by the time they reached the hospital gate, he began to breathe again. They said he was suffering from hepatitis B but was now on an IV, resting comfortably, and talking. When my father saw me, he was thrilled. He couldn't believe I was really there and kept asking, "Is it really true that you are here? How are the children? How is Meera?" But six hours later his condition deteriorated. His eyes had become totally yellow and his tongue was so swollen he was having a hard time speaking. Then his breath became shallow and he began to hiccup. I saw all the signs of death and asked him to bring his attention to the center between the eyebrows and to remember his mantra. He smiled and with great difficulty said, "Oh Bete, now I know." When I asked what, he said, "A few days ago I was dead. But I was sad because I could not see you. Then Swamiji came and brought me back. Now you are here, and my desire is fulfilled. Now it is my time to go."

I asked him, "Do you have any fear?"

He replied, "When we have a master like him, what is there to fear?"

I asked, "Do you know where you are going?"

He said, "Wherever he is. It is totally up to him where he wants me to be." With that, he closed his eyes and departed.

Back in the States three weeks later, I found a marked change in Swamiji's attitude toward me. It seemed as if he did not like me. In fact, it seemed as if he did not even know me. Yet he was very nice to my wife and children. I noticed that he was treating Dr. Ballentine the same way. Dr. Ballentine, who once could spend hours and hours with him, now had to make an appointment to see him, and even then he got only cold treatment. Similarly, now when I came to Swamiji's room he would usually look at me coldly and say, "What's the matter? What do you want to ask?" If I was feeling bold and sat down anyway, he would say, "Go and do your work. Don't waste my time." He was not hard on the residents, but he was not very friendly either. However, he was nice to the guests and to the students who came from elsewhere to visit him. This pattern continued all the way through the summer of 1993.

One day he stopped me in the hall and said, "You never told me you have translated the *Tripura Rahasya*. When did you translate it?" The *Tripura Rahasya* is a tantric text consisting of a dialogue between the sages Parashurama and Dattatreya. Some of my professors from the University of Pennsylvania, who were on the editorial board of the State University of New York (SUNY) Press, had proposed that SUNY publish this manuscript, and Dr. William Eastman, director of SUNY Press, had sent the formal publication agreement for my signature. When I explained to Swamiji that I had translated it in 1984 as part of my coursework for a second Ph.D., he said, "You should have shown me the manuscript. It is a very important scripture of our tradition. It should be published by the Institute. Bring the manuscript." I did, and he said, "We'll start working tonight." He took the manuscript and told me to come back in the evening.

That night when I went to his room Swamiji was working on the manuscript with Deborah Willoughby, then the editor of *Yoga International* magazine. I sat for a few minutes; then he said, "What are you doing here? You go and do your work." And every afternoon after that, he told me at the tennis court, "It is a very important scripture of our tradition. There are lots of mistakes in it. Thank God it reached my hands. Otherwise it could have been a blunder. Tonight I will call you and we'll go through it." Every night I sat downstairs in his kitchen area so I would be available when he called. But he never did, although he always made the same remark at the tennis court.

Meanwhile, Swamiji was playing an interesting drama with Deborah. He was making every attempt to prove to her that my translation was sloppy. He told her the most misguided part of the translation was the mirror analogy running through the scripture that describes the relationship between our consciousness and the empirical world. For some reason Swamiji did not like this, and made fun of me. "What's wrong with Panditji?" he would say. "Instead of knowing the truth directly, he always prefers to see its reflection in a mirror." Finally, he threw up his hands and told Deborah, "We will never attain freedom from these mirrors!" To others he said that I was blinded by my arrogance and was unable to see that I was misrepresenting the tradition. He would say, "Thank God I got the manuscript. Otherwise, this man could have ruined it." He virtually retranslated the entire text.

Then one evening at the tennis court he said, "Bete, we did lots of work. There were many, many mistakes. We fixed it. But we should go through it once again. Tonight you should come and we will finalize it." That night he called me upstairs just as I sat down in the kitchen, and when Deborah read the first verse, he said, "No, no. Read the corrected version." When she said she was reading the corrected version, he said, "Okay then, correct it." With the second verse he said, "What happened to my translation?" Then he looked at me and said in Hindi, "What's wrong with her? I told her not to change anything, but these editors have big egos." Switching back to English, he said, "Fix it." And he dictated the translation. Deborah and I looked at each other. This final "correction" was exactly the same as my original translation. The same scene was repeated for the next few verses— Swamiji kept criticizing Deborah to me in Hindi, saying she had changed the content without his approval. Finally I asked, "Swamiji, should we go back to the original translation?"

He said, "Which original translation?"

"The one you did in 1984 at the University of Pennsylvania," I replied.

Swamiji smiled and said, "Tell her, tell her." So I told Deborah that the original translation had been done by Swamiji under my name, and that I would explain to her later how and why. Then Swamiji told her to go back to the original translation, polish it then and there, and that would be the final manuscript. Deborah still wonders what the whole exercise—which seemed to waste a month of Swamiji's time—was all about.

For the next ten days Swamiji was very kind to me. He called me to his room every night and talked about great sages—Bhagwan Parashurama, Dattatreya, Durvasa, and Guru Gorakha Natha. He then spoke of the places where, he said, these masters still live, and described the sadhana that enables an aspirant to see them with the naked eye. It was during this time that Swamiji unveiled the mystery related to the eleven-month practice he had undertaken years ago at the Manali cave. We were talking about Parashurama, and I said, "Swamiji, Parashurama was an enlightened sage, an incarnation of Lord Vishnu himself. But the questions he posed to the sage Dattatreya in the *Tripura Rahasya* seem childish. For example, he told Dattatreya that he was tired of his own uncontrolled behavior and did not know how to deal with his guilt and self-condemnation. How could he be a Brahma rishi [the highest-caliber sage] if he was suffering from such tendencies?"

371

Swamiji's response was that both Parashurama and Dattatreya are immortal Brahma rishis. They are omniscient divine beings, ever-engaged in guiding and helping humanity. To teach others, these masters bring themselves down to the level of ordinary human beings, go through all kinds of ups and downs, and then work hard to restore their own inner equilibrium. During such self-designed and self-directed dramas one of the sages assumes the role of seeker and the other the role of master. Parashurama is asking practical questions, and by answering them, Dattatreya is offering his guidance to seekers throughout the ages.

"No one is more generous and kind than Bhagwan Parashurama," Swamiji added. "That is why before sending me to the West my master sent me to the Manali cave to receive his blessings. The roots of the Himalayan Institute are deep in the soil of the blessings of these sages."

As soon as Swamiji told me about Parashurama's connection with the Manali cave, a thought flashed: That is where Swamiji had gone in the fall of 1981 during that mysterious week he was ill. I also remembered that his master had left his body soon afterward. And when Swamiji returned to the States in 1982, he told several people that his master had given him ten more years in which to complete his work.

Furthermore, for the next ten years Swamiji often told people that his time in the West was drawing to a close. Then early in the summer of 1991 he told Deborah Willoughby that he had returned to the West against the wishes of his master.

Now sitting with him in the summer of 1993, it all came together: it was in the Manali cave that Swamiji had been granted a few additional years to complete the work he had begun. But this realization stirred another question: Who was it that gave him the few extra years of life: Babaji, or Bhagwan Parashurama? I knew the question came from the child in me and that Swamiji would not entertain it. But I asked anyway. And even as the question came from my lips, I was thinking, "Why am I doing this?"

He answered like a mother patting her baby. "What difference does it make? They are all immortal."

372

The rest of the summer was intense—delightful to some, painful to others. Those who were drawn to the Institute from all over the world received the gifts, both worldly and spiritual, they were seeking from him. But some of the residents found his actions unkind. I did not find them so, but I did notice a marked difference in his dealings with certain people who had once been close to him. Some families had been living at the Institute for more than fifteen years and Swamiji had always treated them as his own children. They had visited him often, and he in turn went to their homes, had meals there, played with their children, and sometimes even cooked for them. But now he spoke to them only when they crossed his path, and then he said only a sentence or two. He gave love and attention to some for no apparent reason, and asked others to leave immediately, again for no apparent reason. Some of the students who felt neglected left in frustration while Swamiji was still at the Institute; many others left soon after he returned to India.

Shortly after his departure, the whispering began. Rumors about Swamiji's misuse of money and his inappropriate behavior with female students began to make the rounds. More than a dozen students who had been close to Swamiji at one time or another (but had left the Institute—in some cases a decade or more earlier) now joined the drama and took an active part in making accusations about him and the Institute's officers, including myself. And these accusations began to appear in newspapers, both in the United States and India. Swamiji remained silent and continued focusing his energy on building the medical complex in Dehra Dun. This silence fueled the negativity of those who were already suspicious, confused those who did not know him well, and frightened those Institute officials who were concerned about their professional reputations. Legal protocol demanded that Swamiji defend himself or take some action to prove his innocence, but he showed no inclination to do so.

A year later I visited Swamiji in Rishikesh, and when the opportunity presented itself I expressed my desire to know from him the reason for his silence on this matter, which was apparently hurting his mission. Swamiji replied, "As a swami, I have taken a vow not to defend myself. Those saying negative things about me are my students, my spiritual children. Onc day I took them into my heart. I prayed to the lord of my life, my master, to bless them with unconditional love. I promised the sages of our tradition that I would serve these students until they reach their final goal. And now, for such a trivial reason, I should abandon them? If I do so, my prayers and blessings will become meaningless. My master's mission will be crippled, and I will be responsible for that. Divine will supersedes all human plans and endeavors. Remember, divine will always contains the seeds of the highest good."

So as this drama played out, I watched it in my dual role as Swamiji's disciple and as an officer of the Institute, waiting for the forces of the cosmos to unveil, in their own time, the meaning of his statement, "There will come a time when no one will be able to understand my actions and speech."

In my heart I prayed to Swamiji, Babaji, and all the sages, especially those he had talked about in the summer of 1993, to give me the strength and insight to embrace the reality of the rest of his statement: "That is when I will disappear in the Himalayas and no one will find me."

ᴀᴛ ᴛʜᴇ ELEVENTH HOUR

IN 1986, WHEN SWAMIJI DECIDED to build a hospital in the foothills of the Himalayas, he dropped his original idea of building a center for Vedic culture and civilization. He never mentioned that project again. Instead he focused his energy on the problems of poverty, illiteracy, and substandard healthcare in India. And in addition to establishing a hospital, medical college, and nursing school, he undertook a rural development project that included programs for adult education (including ways to generate income) in remote Himalayan villages. Then out of the blue, he again began to show an interest in Vedic culture.

It happened in the late summer of 1993. A group of Indians living in New Jersey had been coming to the Institute for some time. They knew Swamiji well and were familiar with his broadminded approach to spirituality, holistic health, and the well-being of humankind and had invited him to lecture in their community one Sunday afternoon. Swamiji asked me to accompany him.

Before the lecture there was a program of music and singing, so when Swamiji walked onto the stage the audience was in a devotional mood.

He began in his typical style: "I pray to the Divinity in you. The core of spirituality is to know yourself at every level. You have a body, but you are not the body. You have a mind, but you are not the mind. Both body and mind are given to you as instruments to express the Divinity that shines in you. You are entitled to have all the objects of the world at your disposal. The purpose of worldly prosperity is to make you comfortable. Worldly objects help you free your body and mind from inconveniences. If you learn to use the objects of the world skillfully, body and mind become a source of joy and do not present a barrier to your spiritual growth. But if you do not know how to put your worldly resources in the service of your body and mind, you live a miserable life. When you are deprived of worldly objects, you suffer, and when you are bombarded by worldly objects, you suffer. When you live a balanced life and learn the art of becoming successful in the world without losing sight of the higher purpose and meaning of life, you become a source of happiness to yourself and to others."

Then suddenly Swamiji's tone changed. "I feel sad that you people are not paying attention to yourselves. Here in this country, where everything is in abundance, I see people suffering from poor health. Among mainstream Americans, awareness is growing—cigarette smoking and alcohol consumption have gone down. Americans now go to health clubs; they are practicing yoga postures; they jog and run; they are learning the principles of a healthy diet. The life span of the average American has gone up tremendously. But Indians living in America are generally the most unhealthy of people. In an attempt to become part of American society, Indians living here embrace those unhealthy habits of consuming meat and liquor that Americans themselves are trying to get rid of.

"Many of those Indians who are vegetarian think that just because they are not eating meat, their diet is healthy. You people also associate a vegetarian diet with religious purity. As a part of your religious activity you do lots of fasting—but when you fast, all kinds of sweets loaded with starch, fat, and dairy products are part of your 'fasting.' Even in the normal course of life a healthy person would have a hard time digesting the food you consume during the fasting.

"No one ever tries to understand: What kind of religious practice is this? By doing such practices you also expect that all your problems will be solved: your children will become obedient to you; you will become successful in business; you will become a holier person; and God will be happy with you. I do not see how all these things are possible. In fact, the result is in front of you. By the age of forty, Indian men have all kinds of problems: back pain, arthritis, coronary disease, high blood pressure, diabetes. The same is true with Indian women. Your children don't listen to you. They don't care for Indian culture or rituals. God is always with you, but fear and doubt, anxiety and worry still haunt your mind.

"So far I have not heard of anywhere in the United States where Indians have a community center where they can go, do some exercise, have some formal classes on diet, nutrition, meditation, and relaxation, and discuss the issues related to the cultural crisis they are experiencing and the problems with their children. You are expecting too much from your temples, swamis, and other religious leaders. You think that by visiting your temples occasionally and by arranging a *katha* [scripture recitation] you will preserve your heritage, and your children will uphold the legacy of your forefathers. This is not going to happen.

"Be practical. Be realistic. If you want to maintain your identity, you need to know who you are. What is your source? Where are your roots? What is so great about your culture? What are its strengths and weaknesses? In which particular areas has Indian society accumulated unnecessary trash? Have the desire to embrace the healthy elements of your culture, and have the courage to get rid of those elements which are damaging and disgraceful. When you pay attention, you will find that all cultures in the world have such elements; Indian culture is no exception.

"You are too much involved in rituals. Your children do not understand the meaning of those rituals and they do not find ritual worship interesting. They are living in a cross-cultural atmosphere. They need to know the unique characteristics of their Indian culture before they can develop any respect for it. The only exposure they have to Indian culture is Indian movies, which they do not really like. They don't understand the language, the film quality is poor, and the plots are repetitious—corruption, crime, and unrealistic love stories. If you want to expose your children to Indian culture and its sublime heritage, you need to be more skillful about it. Bring forward authentic wisdom and present it in a tasteful manner."

A great number of people in the audience took Swamiji's message to heart, and after the lecture was over they asked him to guide them in setting up a center where they could do more than just talk about

377

their culture—where they could practice the core of it. On the other hand, many did not appreciate Swamiji's straightforward message. They had been expecting him to talk about Hindu dharma, quote the scriptures, lead them in singing devotional songs, or give an inspirational speech about the greatness of Hinduism. Their disappointment was apparent. Some left before the lecture was over; others stayed for refreshments after the lecture and shared their negative feelings.

As we drove back to Honesdale, Swamiji expressed his concern for Indians living abroad. "The situation is not great in India either," he said. "There are lots of religious people trying their best to do something for their country, but often their effort lacks vision. The leaders of India are primarily concerned about their sectarian ideology and their institutional mission. If they rise above this, they identify their mission with Hinduism. I don't see a leader in modern India actually promoting the aspect of Indian heritage that stresses the spirit of India: the teachings of the Vedic sages, which is the source of all traditions that originated in the East."

For the next few days, whenever I saw Swamiji in the evenings, he returned to this topic. "Something terrible has happened to the Indian psyche. There was a time when India had the capacity to absorb and assimilate Shakas, Huns, Kushanas, and all others who entered the land as invaders. Indian kings fought with them—sometimes they were defeated, sometimes they triumphed. But never in the history of ancient India could any outside force alter the philosophy and spirituality of India. On the contrary, often invaders settled down and became part of India, leaving no trace of religious or ethnocentric differences.

"But for some reason, fifteen hundred years ago, the teachings of the Vedic sages shrank into Hinduism, and Hindus became concerned with preserving their identity by separating themselves from Buddhists and Jains. Instead of practicing what the great masters of the Vedas and Upanishads had taught, they denounced the teachings of Buddha and Mahavira, who were an integral part of the same ancient tradition. The country became weak and the culture full of vanity as religion and politics commingled. This is when people became wedded to sectarianism: 'My way is better than yours; my spiritual leader is more enlightened than yours; I am more dedicated to my group, guru, and god than you are to yours.'

"Now this tendency has gotten worse. In India, politics is contaminated by religion and caste identity. Religion is suffering from personality cults, superstitions, and dogma. Just like people in India, Indians living abroad are not able to overcome these tendencies. In fact, they are doing their best to pass them on to their children, and when their children resist, they feel disappointed. They believe in miracles. They want priests to perform rituals and thereby change the mentality of their children. During the summer hundreds of swamis visit Indian communities, give their discourses, perform ceremonies, and build a few more ashrams and temples. But the problems remain the same."

One evening I said, "Swamiji, this is the first time in seven years I am seeing you so much concerned with the preservation of Indian culture, and I—"

379

Before I could finish he said, "I am not concerned with Indian culture, Indians, Hindus, or any other group living inside India or outside India. I am interested in the teachings of the sages—the seers of the Vedas. Their teachings are as fresh today as they were thousands of years ago. They were interested in seeing humanity grow and prosper. They taught the gospel of love. I am interested in reintroducing the Vedic legacy to humanity—Indians and non-Indians are both part of humanity. I ask you to serve the sages. Light the lamp of their love in human hearts. This is my order, and I hope you will obey it."

"Swamiji, you have already been doing this," I replied. "Isn't it that just by walking in your footsteps, I will obey you?"

"Yes," he said. "However, the method of presenting the teachings of the sages needs to be changed. When the time comes you will know what to do and how to do it." With this he dismissed me for the night.

A few days later, on the evening of August 11, he taught me a practice he had been promising to teach for eleven years, and afterwards he mentioned in passing that he had decided to make some changes in the Institute's constitution. My mind, however, was filled with the joy of receiving the practice, and his comment did not register. Then on August 15 Swamiji left the Institute for India, stopping in Buffalo, Toronto, New York City, and Moscow on the way. He never came back.

The day he left, Suzanne Grady, secretary of the board, told me that Swamiji had resigned as spiritual head of the Himalayan Institute and appointed me in his place. I was amazed. In the past I had often seen him doing things that made no sense at the time, but this appointment was different—it stirred up a great deal of anxiety in me. Many on the staff were older than I and more experienced in administrative matters. Some had assumed that they would be appointed as his successor, and I knew that desire leads to anger and anger must find a way to express itself. I also remembered Swamiji's often-repeated saying: "The life of a swami is constant torture." Although I was not a swami, I knew that the "son" of a swami was bound to inherit some of that torture, especially the son of a mysterious swami who displayed so many personae, who headed big organizations, and who had such a wide variety of followers. Then I thought: Who am I to think of all these things? Just seventeen years ago I was a speck of dust drifting along the roadside. He picked me up and gave me a place in the inner chamber of his lotus heart. I also remembered that in 1976 he had said, "If you are ready to be happy with pain, only then think of being with me."

At that time I did not know what he meant, and yet I had pleaded, "All I want is to be with you." Remembering this conversation now, it occurred to me that perhaps this appointment would help me understand the meaning of what he had said.

His reassuring voice flashed in my memory: "Then give up all your desires. I will take full responsibility for you. I will make sure that you get what you need and keep what you have achieved." At that, I had placed my head at his feet and he had put his hand on my head, saying, "Rise and promise that you will not involve yourself in astrology, politics, or petty sectarian religions." This memory was a source of peace and strength, and I was convinced that no matter what the situation, he would guide me, just as he always had.

In the interval from September of 1993 through the spring of

1994 there were endless meetings at the Institute and much confusion. Some of the directors resigned, and a few residents left. Some, feeling betrayed, even began to doubt Swamiji and the Institute. At that time Swamiji was usually to be found either in his apartment in Delhi or at the Rishikesh ashram, and I tried to talk to him several times. But he wouldn't accept my calls. Finally, realizing that he did not want to involve himself, I stopped trying to contact him. I knew exactly what to do, but my dilemma was that everyone caught in this confusion was a longtime student of Swamiji's and it was below their standard to listen to me. So I did what I felt was appropriate: said goodbye to those who were leaving, served those who stayed, and welcomed those who came.

Almost a year passed. Never since our first meeting had I gone such a long time without seeing Swamiji. I was missing him, and so were hundreds of his other students. But without his permission I could not go to India to see him, and there was no reason to ask his permission. Then one day I heard that the prime minister of India was going to inaugurate the medical college at the Himalayan Institute Hospital Trust near Dehra Dun, so I wrote Swamiji and asked if I could bring a group to tour the Himalayas at a time that coincided with the ceremony. Swamiji agreed, and ninety people accompanied me. But when we arrived in Rishikesh we learned that there had been a landslide in the mountains and the road leading to our destination, Gangotri, was impassable. Furthermore, because of political unrest the entire region was under curfew and no one was allowed to travel. The prime minister had to cancel his visit.

Our group was confined to a Rishikesh hotel much of the time, but even so these calamities brought us good fortune. The hotel was only a short walk from the ashram, and if we walked along the Ganga we could make our way there without drawing official attention. And during our month-long stay Swamiji taught the *Shvetashvatara Upanishad* every day, sometimes even twice a day. In the States he had never taught a scripture for more than seven days, but here we had the luxury of studying with him for weeks. For the first few days he explained the general content of the Upanishads; then he focused on the *Shvetashvatara*. "Life is a grand ceremony," he told us. "In this

381

ceremony mind, body, and senses are the participants. These participants are always worshipping the Lord of Life, the Divine Light, which resides in this body. Due to ignorance, when the ego begins to claim that it is the boss and everything else is supposed to serve it, problems begin.

"Meditation is the way to lift the curtain of ignorance so that the ego can see that it is in the service of the Divine, not the other way around. Meditation is the core of yoga. Meditation is the core of spiritual discipline. Meditation introduces you to yourself. It makes you become aware of your relationship with the body, senses, mind, and ego. It tells you where you are weak, so you can throw your weaknesses into the fire of yoga. In fact, this Upanishad is one of the most profound scriptures. It unveils the mystery of fire. Here fire is known as 'Rudra'; in tantric literature it is called 'Shakti'; Shaivite texts called it 'Shiva'; yogis call it 'kundalini shakti.' And according to the sages, fire is the Divine Being, the primordial master."

I found Swamiji's speech and actions more mysterious than ever. In the course of his lectures he presented the material in his usual style: straightforward, simple, and down-to-earth. But now and then his talk would suddenly become so esoteric that hardly anyone could grasp his meaning—and then he would abruptly revert to his previous style. While interacting with the students, he was nice to some and abrupt and seemingly irrational with others.

For example, when Gwen Burdick, whom he had entertained with so much love and affection in Honesdale the year before, came to see him, he did not even look at her but continued reading his newspaper instead. She said, "Swamiji, I'm here."

All he said was, "Yes."

She waited awhile and then asked, "Don't you have something to say?"

He replied, "No," and went on reading the newspaper. Finally he looked at her and asked, "What brought you here?"

She asked, "Don't you remember me?"

He said flatly, "No."

Describing the experience later, Gwen said, "It was like talking to a wall." Finally she left in tears, but even then Swamiji paid no attention.

She came to me and asked why he had behaved that way. I told her I didn't know but that perhaps we would understand in the course of time.

That evening when I went to see Swamiji he asked me abruptly whether I had read the *Shvetashvatara Upanishad,* and when I hesitantly said, "Yes," he started to talk about it. "It is an amazing scripture," he told me. "If you know this scripture well, you will be able to swim across the streams of joy and sorrow." He told me that to understand it well, I should first study Shaivite scriptures, especially *Netra Tantra* and *Svachchhanda Tantra.*

Then out of the blue he said, "Everything in the world has come out of one Divine Being, the sacred fire. The sages are the direct manifestation of that fire. No one understands them. No one talks to them. No one walks with them. They live in their own world and yet, driven by intense compassion, they descend and walk among human beings. They are kind and ever-engaged in guiding those who are in search of the Divine Experience. When you have a real desire to see them, they come to you in the flesh. Don't waste your time running here and there: they are always with you; they are your real companions."

383

Then he said, "The people with you have come from so far away. You should take them somewhere. What about Haridwar?"

I nodded and said, "Okay, Swamiji."

Prem Sobte, the ashram manager, arranged for transportation and food for the ninety members of the group, and the next morning we set off in three busloads. It was almost lunchtime when we arrived and made our way to the bank of the Ganga. Some of us began to distribute the lunch boxes, while others took pictures and made videotapes. Such a large group of Westerners soon attracted hundreds of priests, beggars, and shopkeepers, who quickly surrounded us, staring at our food and cameras; an assortment of monkeys and cows joined the crowd.

This was the first time I had taken a group to India, and I had no experience in managing ninety people. After three weeks of virtual house arrest, no one was in the mood to be managed, anyway. My charges quickly dispersed, negotiating with shopkeepers, trying to understand what the beggars were saying, and dealing with a large and aggressive monkey that was demanding his share of the food. Some thought that the monkey was cute and tried to feed him biscuits and chocolate, but the monkey had other ideas. He wanted bananas, and when none were forthcoming, he advanced on us. Our people were frightened, and the more frightened they were, the bolder the monkey became. It was hard to eat, even to sit. We tried to move somewhere else, but the crowd and its leader—the monkey—followed. Finally, a frail old sadhu detached himself from the mob and came forward. He was in silence, and the peaceful aura around his face told me that he was not an ordinary sadhu, and certainly not a beggar. He scolded the monkey by brandishing his walking stick, and the monkey calmed down. Then he told the group in sign language that the monkey would not harm them and there was nothing to fear.

The commotion subsided, but as we ate our lunch the crowd watched us as if we were animals in a zoo. Suddenly a strange-looking person emerged from the crowd—bright red clothing, long beard, bloodshot eyes, long hair, and a bamboo stick. He approached one of the members of our group, shouting, "This is a holy place! Photography is not allowed! These Westerners make fun of us—they take our pictures and sell them in their countries for a high price!" And he tried to grab one of the cameras. I had not seen any signs saying that photography was forbidden, but I told the group not to take any more pictures and not to fight with anyone.

Then the man turned on me, assuming I was a tour guide making lots of money from gullible Westerners. He demanded his share, and when I refused to give him anything he insisted that all our film be destroyed, especially from "the big camera." I told him the big camera was a video camera and did not have a roll of film in it—so he raised his bamboo staff and threatened to destroy the camera. I realized that this was not the time to be kind and loving. Jean-Pierre, an expert in martial arts, was in our group, and I knew that if this strange sadhu raised a hand against me, he would be sorry. So I shouted at the sadhu at the top of my lungs, spoke a few dirty words, and threatened to throw him in the Ganga if he did not leave immediately. He vanished into the crowd.

The old sadhu who had protected us from the monkey came up to me, looked into my eyes, and touched my cheek, and for a split second

I was transported to a blissful state like the one I had experienced when I first recognized Swamiji in the Akbar Hotel. The light I saw in his eyes reminded me of the light in Swamiji's eyes and in the eyes of another master, Swami Sadananda. And from the expression on his face I knew that he and Swamiji were on the same level. In sign language the old sadhu asked me who my teacher was, and when I told him, he paused for a second, turned his face toward Rishikesh, folded his hands, and bowed his head in that direction. He then put his hand on my wife's head, blessed her with a sweet smile, and by pointing to a nearby hut and then to himself and gesturing to us, he invited us to his home.

The hut and small courtyard in front of it were surrounded by a fence of bamboo sticks two feet high. The gate was so small that even a child could step over it, yet the sadhu opened it as if he were opening the door to a palace. He then stepped in and signaled for my wife and me to follow. But just as we were about to enter, a group of beggars and shopkeepers ran toward us and warned us not to go in. It was dangerous, they said. The sadhu indicated that it was all right—he had invited us and we would not be harmed. Now the local people, even more frantic, were shouting, "Don't go in—it's very dangerous! There are cobras! There are evil spirits! Some of you might die, and certainly all of you will be sick and become possessed! It's very dangerous!" The sadhu brandished his stick, warning them off, and we entered the courtyard, which was planted with hundreds of holy basil plants.

Indicating that I had nothing to fear, the old sadhu invited me to enter his hut, and I stepped into the tiny room. Several cobras lay quietly on the floor, so I paid mental homage to them as friends of Shiva, and came back out. We thanked the old sadhu for his kindness and said goodbye.

Then we went on to visit the holy sites in Haridwar, and as we made our way around the town some of the local people told me that the sadhu had arrived only a few months earlier. He had gone to the Ganga, they said, drawn a line around a small area next to the river, and warned people not to disturb him and not to cross that line without his permission. He redrew the line several times each day to make sure it was visible, and the few times someone did cross the line they were immediately confronted by a hissing cobra. The news spread and the

385

sadhu was left in peace—until one of the local toughs stalked down to the riverbank and boldly stepped over the line. At that instant he was picked up by a force which tossed him into the air a few times, slapped his cheeks, and hurled him out of the enclosed area. No one ever bothered that sadhu again. Instead they helped him build his hut and erect a short fence along the boundary line.

For the rest of the day I found myself thinking of this old sadhu and his mysterious behavior. And that evening, as I was massaging Swamiji's feet at the ashram, I told him about the old man. He listened to the whole story and then said, "What happened in Haridwar?" This time I summarized the story. When I had finished, he got up, then sat down and said again, "So it happened in Haridwar? Is he in Haridwar? Did you see him?"

386   When I said, "Yes," he turned his face toward Haridwar, folded his hands, and bowed his head, just as the old sadhu had done.

When I asked who he was, all Swamiji said was, "He is a great adept, an immortal one. I am so grateful to him that he blessed you all."

I went blank and did not know what to say, yet these words slipped from my mouth: "He has been there for the last several months. It is amazing that no one knows him. Strangers think he is a beggar, and the local people think he is a magician who possesses evil powers."

In a serious tone, Swamiji replied, "Who knows whether he ever lived there? It might all be maya."

Everyone in the group had sensed that the encounter with this old sadhu had something of the extraordinary about it, but most of them focused on the fact that he lived with cobras. When they returned to the States in mid-October, however, a few people stayed in India for a while longer, and when they visited Haridwar again, there was no trace of either the sadhu or his hut.

I also stayed behind for a few weeks after the group left. By this time the curfew had been lifted, and work at the hospital site was accelerating. There were more than a thousand construction workers on site, and another few hundred people were employed as doctors, nurses, technicians, administrative and clerical workers, gardeners, and cleaning staff. Swamiji was everywhere. He looked tired and yet joyful.

He was losing weight and people assumed he was doing some special sadhana. But one day one of Swamiji's students from Delhi told me he had asked Swamiji about his health and Swamiji had replied, "It is so hot here. Even the trees and grass lose their sap and become dry." He asked me if I knew what Swamiji meant by that.

Through the years I had learned that Swamiji did not like discouraging comments about his health or his work, so there was no point in asking direct questions about either. But I too was wondering about his health and knew that I had to find a way to cast the question in a positive light if I expected to be told. So one day when the opportunity presented itself, I asked him, "Are you preparing for something where a lighter body is more convenient?"

Swamiji responded in a flash: "The lighter the luggage, the easier the journey. You just wait. There will be hardly anything but bones."

387

"But, Swamiji," I said, "you need to be healthy. You have so much work to do."

"What do I do?" Swamiji asked. "The real doer is someone else. Hard work and remembering God are the two great gifts that life offers." Then he asked me when I was going back to the States. I got the hint: it was time for me to leave India.

A year later, in the fall of 1995, the Institute organized another trip to the Himalayas. This time our main destinations were Dharmsala, the home of the Dalai Lama, and the beautiful valleys of Kulu and Manali. But when we arrived at Shimla, a hill station on the way to these valleys, we learned that the day before a massive landslide had destroyed not only the road but also the hotel in which we were supposed to stay. But while everyone expressed thanks that we had not come a day earlier, my mind was engaged in figuring out if there was a message in this landslide.

To me, this was not a trip but a pilgrimage. I had not mentioned it to anyone, but my main destination was the cave in Manali where Swamiji had spent eleven months before coming to the West, and where he had returned for a few days in 1981 when he was ill and had been miraculously cured. Swamiji had said that this cave had been one of the favorite places of the immortal sage Parashurama, and I had wanted to visit it for years. Now my heart said that perhaps this was not the right time to go there. Instead, we visited Dharmsala and the nearby shrines and then joined Swamiji in Rishikesh.

That year Swamiji did not give any lectures to the tour group. His health had declined, and in addition to a drastic weight loss, he had some kind of skin disorder and was scratching constantly. His symptoms pointed to mercury poisoning, but when samples of his hair were sent to experts in Washington, D.C., this was ruled out. Swamiji was also coughing a lot and bringing up copious amounts of phlegm, and the doctors diagnosed pleurisy. A few weeks later he said to the hospital's medical staff, "I think you people are mistaken. I don't think there is anything wrong with my lungs." The doctors checked again and found his lungs clear. Yet he continued to cough.

By this time Swamiji had moved to an apartment on the hospital campus and visited the ashram in Rishikesh only occasionally. I saw him only two or three times, and on those occasions I either applied an herbal paste to his body, which he said helped relieve the itching, or sat with him quietly. He asked whether I had gone to Manali, and I answered, "Not all the way. I could not reach the cave."

He said, "Because it was not the right time." Then giving me a mischievous look he said, "What's wrong with you? Wherever you want to go, you always end up with a landslide. Last year you could not go to Gangotri because of the landslide. You should do something about it."

When I asked him what I should do, he answered, "You should meditate on your *muladhara* chakra and make it firm. That's where all landslides originate." Then he added something to the practice he had given me in the late summer of 1993.

Shortly afterward I returned to the United States, but my mind kept returning to Swamiji's comment about the landslides. I was able to grasp his meaning only in part, and that only because he had told me I should meditate on the *muladhara* chakra and make it firm. But the incident had intensified my memory of his earlier statement: "There will come a time when no one will be able to understand my actions and speech. That is when I will disappear in the Himalayas and no one will find me." I could not stop fantasizing about a way of finding him if he ever disappeared into that vast mountain range.

Despite his poor health Swamiji continued working as hard as ever in India. His extreme weight loss had everyone worried except him. In administrative matters he still acted like a CEO, but in relation to his personal life he had become like a child. Health professionals as well as non-professionals were giving him advice, and he complied with all of it. Allopathic doctors gave him conventional medicines; he took them. Ayurvedic doctors offered their treatments, which often consisted of medicine containing heavy metals, and he took them. Then came the experts in Yunani medicine, herbalists, and homeopaths, and Swamiji took whatever they gave him. He knew better than to turn his body into a medicine cabinet, yet he did it anyway. Everyone involved felt honored and important to be helping him, and one of his students sent a letter to thousands of Swamiji's students all over the world asking them to undertake a special practice to heal Swamiji. When Swamiji heard about it he remarked to his secretary, Kamal, "How can someone else's practice help me? It's useless."

389

When Kamal asked Swamiji why he didn't help himself, he replied, "It is time."

During this last phase of his life Swamiji no longer had any real privacy. The activities of the hospital, medical college, nursing school, and rural development projects were constantly making headlines. Everyone knew where Swamiji went, what he did there, and what kind of treatment he was receiving. And everyone knew that his health was continuing to deteriorate. Still, those working closely with him tried to mystify even the simplest information about his health.

It was the spring of 1996, and everyone at the Institute in Honesdale was concerned about Swamiji. I began to receive a stream of telephone calls from different parts of the world—each giving a bit of information about his health in the expectation that I would complete the picture for them. My problem was that I had no accurate information. People found this bewildering. They assumed that I would know what was going on. I made several attempts by telephone to learn about Swamiji's health from reliable sources at the hospital campus, but got empty replies: "Swamiji alone knows what he is doing." "You know, he doesn't tell anything to anyone." Then I called Dr. P. N. Chuttani, the director of the Postgraduate Institute and Medical

Research Centre of Chandigarh Medical College. A long-time student and friend of Swamiji's, Dr. Chuttani had been instrumental in setting up the medical college on the hospital campus, and he described Swamiji's medical condition in detail. He told me that he had end-stage cancer. I received similar information from doctors in Bombay.

In the first week of May I came to know that Swamiji had gone to Malaysia for treatment, and I figured that if he was there then he must be staying with either Dr. Mohan Swami or Dr. Ganashan. My guess was right. When I called Dr. Mohan Swami at home, Dr. Ganashan answered the phone, and in the middle of the conversation he said, "Hold on."

The next voice I heard was Swamiji's. We spoke for a minute or two, but from his voice I knew that he was weak and was making an effort to talk to me. I did not want to prolong his discomfort, so I simply asked if I could come and see him. He replied, "Come and see me in India. I'll be reaching there tomorrow."

My wife and I took the next available flight and reached the hospital campus the day after Swamiji returned. As soon as he saw us he said, "People are caught in their own thinking." I did not know the context of the statement and so I did not know what he meant. Then he asked Maithili, one of the students attending him, to give us a milkshake. We had not yet finished it when Swamiji asked, "When are you going back?" This was unprecedented. Always before his first question had been, "When did you come?"

My reply was, "Whenever you say."

Then he asked a series of trivial questions—something he had never done before—ending with, "Where are you staying?"

I said, "Anywhere. I can stay at the ashram or here at the hospital site if there is any space."

He asked, "Where would you like to stay?"

I said, "Wherever you want me to, Swamiji."

He said, "The atmosphere here is too hot. The air is also not moving. You should stay at the ashram. I will take you there."

On the surface, Swamiji's comments made no sense. Dehra Dun, where the hospital is located, is cooler than Rishikesh and the breeze is better. And why had Swamiji said he would take us to the ashram?

Meera and I could easily go by ourselves. We had stayed there often in the past and everyone knew us.

I knew there was something I did not understand, but still I resisted the suggestion. "You rest, Swamiji," I said. "We can go by ourselves."

Swamiji said, "No, no. This way I will get some exercise and fresh air."

He sent for his car. Swamiji sat in the front seat, while Meera and I sat in the back with the guard. When we arrived at the ashram Swamiji told Prem, "Make sure Meera and Panditji are comfortable." Even though Prem had already told him which room he had given us, Swamiji still asked, "Which room are they staying in? Is it comfortable?" In obvious discomfort, Swamiji climbed the stairs to his own rooms, stayed there for a few minutes, then came down again and was driven back to the hospital campus. This seemingly trivial sequence of events was so puzzling that I felt Swamiji was trying to tell me something.

391

We stayed at the ashram but visited Swamiji every day. And each time I saw him he repeated the same question: "Did you see so-and-so?" referring to someone he knew I saw every day. On the third day, when he asked yet again, he added, "Did you visit the hospital and the campus?" So I visited every corner of the hospital building and the surrounding complex of buildings and grounds, hoping my extensive tour would help me understand what Swamiji was trying to tell me. In bits and pieces, I gathered that the person Swamiji was inquiring about had told someone that Swamiji did not like me. In fact, Swamiji's exact words were supposed to have been, "I'm against Panditji."

The next time I saw Swamiji, he asked whether I had visited the hospital and campus. And when I replied that I had, he asked, "So how is everything?"

"Things seem to be fine," I answered. "Except for a radical change in the spiritual standards of our tradition."

"What's that?" he asked.

"So far, the tradition has been that due to his ignorance a student may go against his teacher," I replied, "but not the other way around."

At this, Swamiji said softly, "Thousands of times I have said good things about you to so-and-so. But forgetting all about it, that person remembers only this comment and is broadcasting it for no reason. That is what this world is all about. Give the best of yourself to it, lovingly and selflessly, but do not expect anything from anyone. Be strong and fearless. You don't have time for friends and foes, but only for God."

"But, Swamiji," I protested. "That person knows me well—we have been friends for ages. Without any reason, how can this person suddenly come to dislike me?"

"That person is a robot," he replied.

"But, Swamiji," I said, "so-and-so loves you very much."

"How can a person who was deprived of love as a child love others?" he asked. "Love is spontaneous. It is ever-filled with kindness and compassion. Forgiveness is its nature. Love sees only good qualities in others. One who truly loves cannot hold a grudge against anyone. One blessed with true love does not hate one person to demonstrate love for another. For people like so-and-so, relationships with others are temporary and aimless. In the procession of life you will encounter many such people. Such people deserve as much love as you can give them. But don't be emotional; be strong in heart and clear in mind."

Then he changed the subject and asked, "When are you going back?" During our ten-day stay he had asked this question many times, and when he asked it this time I realized that it was not appropriate for us to linger, even though I wanted to.

As soon as we boarded the plane my mind was flooded with memories of my twenty years with Swamiji. Many of them centered around discussions we had had about death. And during the long flight between Delhi and New York I found myself remembering how he had explained the death and resurrection of the prince of Bhawal, how his master had died voluntarily and then returned again to the same body, and how his grandmaster had transformed himself into a cloud and condensed his consciousness to animate a wooden plate. I remembered Swamiji saying, "Death and birth are but two commas in the long sentence of life. To know life in its fullness, you have to see what lies before and after these commas. You cannot free yourself from the subtle impressions of your past if you have no access to the life that existed before you were born. You cannot free yourself from fear and anxiety if you are not able to comprehend the dimension of life that exists after you die. Those who have access to both the known and unknown aspects of life are the true adepts. Such adepts leave their old body and enter a new one just as an ordinary person takes off an old, tattered garment and puts on a new one."

Sitting there with my eyes closed, it was as if I were in a movie theater, watching Swamiji come to me in the ninth-floor lobby of the Akbar Hotel in New Delhi, taking me to his room, and talking to me. I saw the young man I had been, spending eleven nights in Nehru Park, and on the twelfth receiving Swamiji's blessing: "There will always be a shelter for you, and there will always be food for you. You will not go hungry." I remembered my first Guru Purnima with Swamiji in 1980, when he had vanished from his room and reappeared right in front of me. Hundreds of other experiences replayed themselves in my mind's eye, until finally I came to the events surrounding my father's death. I was deeply absorbed in the thought that masters like Swamiji not only are able to cast off their body, but also are able to guide others in their transition. How is it possible? Then answers from his conversations with me through the years flashed in my mind. And these memories brought forward hundreds of other issues pertaining to karma, rebirth, reincarnation, destiny, God's grace, the role of spiritual practices, freedom of choice, willpower, and the power of habits.

393

There were times during that long flight when I could not contain my thoughts, and so I shared them with my wife. As soon as I had overcome my jet lag, I began writing *From Death to Birth,* and working on it was like reliving my time with Swamiji. The book was half done when I returned to India in early September with another group.

When I saw Swamiji the first thing he said was, "How long are you staying?" I said, "As long as you want." He replied, "Good."

He had lost even more weight and was subsisting on juice and water. When he stood, it looked as if his clothes were hanging on a stick of bamboo—but his bearing was still regal: he walked with his body straight and his head erect. He was no longer monitoring the construction work on the medical college in person, but he still held meetings and issued directives. At such times his speech was extremely precise and subtle, and most people attributed this to his weakness.

But according to my observation, that was only part of the reason. Physically he was weak, but he still had the same indomitable will— his way was the only way.

One day as Meera and I walked into his room we found him reclining on his bed, his face emitting an indescribable aura of joy and peace. He closed his eyes for a moment, then opened them, and gesturing with his head, eyebrows, and eyes, he asked, "Where is the little one?" In those days our nine-year-old daughter was going to school in Mussoorie, an hour and a half from the hospital campus, and would visit Swamiji on holidays. When I told him that she was in school, he said in a booming voice, "You know, she loves me very much. She is part of my heart." We were startled—there was no sign of weakness; he was using the voice he used when lecturing to a large crowd. It was as if he had forgotten for a moment that he was playing the role of a sick man.

Now when Meera and I visited Swamiji, we often simply sat with him. Once in a while he spoke a sentence or two: "Do I have anything which is not already yours?" "I have given you a task. Your life is only for that." "This world is a dream. Don't mistake it for real." One day when Meera and I walked in, we found him with a student named Mahesh. We sat quietly, and after Mahesh had gone Swamiji said, "*Aur bolo* [Say something or ask whatever you wish]." In response to our silence, he said, "You are a child of the tradition. Doubt and fear are not made for you. The sages are always with you. They give their love to all humanity, just as they give it to you. Don't look behind when you have to walk forward."

Then he inquired, "When is the group arriving?" When I told him the date, he asked, "Where are they going this time?"

"They are expecting to go to Uttar Kashi and Gangotri," I replied. "Can they go this time?"

"Why not?" Swamiji asked. "You are doing your practice. There is no reason for a landslide. There are beautiful places in Uttar Kashi. There you must visit the site of Renuka Devi, the mother of sage Parashurama."

A week later the group reached Uttar Kashi. ("Uttar Kashi" means "northern Banaras.") Situated on the bank of the holy Ganga as it runs through the mountains, this village has been the abode of saints and sages for untold ages, and it is famous for its Shiva temple. Peaceful ashrams dot the riverbank and the nearby hills. We wanted to pay our homage to Shiva at the main temple there; when we had planned this tour we decided to stay here for three or four days to acclimate ourselves in preparation for the higher altitudes we would encounter on our journey to Gangotri and Gomukh.

But when Swamiji said we must visit the site of Renuka Devi, our main goal became a visit to the shrine of Mother Renuka. Years ago I had read in the *Skanda Purana:* "If while being there one remembers the deeds of Renuka's life, one attains freedom from present karmic bonds. By having her *darshana,* karmic impurities of seven lifetimes are verily washed off." I had never taken that passage seriously—the scriptures are full of such claims. But now, because of Swamiji's words, this passage became a living proclamation of truth for me. I shared what I knew about Uttar Kashi with the group, telling them stories about the adepts who lived in this region. And I told them how Swamiji had spent three years here in the late 1960s. I was trying to create an atmosphere in which the group would approach the shrine of Mother Renuka in the spirit of pilgrimage.

When we arrived we did not know where the shrine was located, so we asked our tour guide, who asked the local people. It seemed that no one knew. But luckily we met a priest, also the principal of the local Sanskrit school, who had known Swamiji well, and he knew the location of Mother Renuka's shrine. He told us it was on a hilltop six kilometers outside of town and that we could easily reach the base of the hill in our buses. From there he told us it was a thirty-minute trek to the shrine itself. It sounded like an easy trip so we decided to go that afternoon, and the priest arranged for one of his students to come with us as a guide.

As we were having our lunch at the local guesthouse we were joined by a group of Germans who had just returned from Gangotri. They reported that the weather in the area had turned nasty—for the past three days they had been caught in a snowstorm. Once in a while the sun had come out, and at night the melted snow turned into ice. In essence they told us that it was not safe to travel further into the mountains in the direction of Gangotri, and I found myself wondering if for some reason the landslide had been replaced by this unseasonable storm. But we reminded ourselves that on occasions like these it is best to just live in the present, and so we set off for the shrine of Renuka Devi.

At the base of the hill the shopkeepers said it would take us two hours to walk to the shrine. Others, who seemed to be visitors, said it was a minimum of three hours, while the villagers said, "It is just over there. Follow us; we'll take you." Our trek began on the western side of the hill. The sun was bearing directly down on us, and after walking for an hour we found we were still at the foot of the hill. It was hot and muggy and we were almost out of water. There were a few older people in the group; a few more were overweight; and others had diabetes or high blood pressure. I discouraged them from exceeding their capacity and reminded people not to fight their way up but to maintain an attitude of surrender. Eileen Diorio, who had been with Swamiji since the mid-seventies, wanted to continue on even though she was exhausted. She argued that Mother Renuka would give her strength and help her reach the summit. Even if she didn't make it, she said, dying in the vicinity of Mother Renuka's shrine was preferable to being alive elsewhere. So I asked her to walk slowly, rest often, and start descending before sunset. We would catch up with her on our way down.

It took the main group another two hours to reach the summit, and when we did, we found the door of the tiny temple locked. The young man the priest had sent to accompany us had walked twice as fast as we had, and had reached the top almost an hour and a half earlier. He had discovered that the temple priest lived nearby, and said that if a few of us went together to the priest's home he might come and open the door. The priest wasn't there when we reached his home, but his two young daughters brought the key and unlocked the temple.

Then a sadhu who had been sweeping the courtyard asked us to stay outside while he cleaned the temple, and while we waited on the verandah I told the group stories of Mother Renuka, her husband, and their son, Parashurama. I also quoted the *Skanda Purana:* "If while being there one remembers the deeds of Renuka's life, one attains freedom from present karmic bonds. By having her *darshana,* karmic impurities of seven lifetimes are verily washed off." Someone asked if it was possible to see her. I asked what difference it made whether we saw her or not—she is seeing us, and that is enough. Then someone else, Michael Robinson, wanted to know if we could ask Mother Renuka to give us good weather for our trip to Gangotri. Without thinking I said, "Why don't you ask her? There is nothing she cannot give."

By this time the sadhu had finished cleaning the temple. We did not know what to expect—whether there would be a statue, a Shiva lingam, a yantra, or an altar where we could offer our homage. I entered first. Everyone wanted to follow me but there was hardly enough space inside for eight or ten. It was quite dark, and as people crowded in behind me and those left outside stuck their heads in the door, it became even darker.

Then, as our eyes adjusted to the darkness, we saw an old woman standing near a small idol next to the wall. I wondered how she came to be there, and then decided she might be the priest's mother or grandmother. She began reciting something in what sounded like heavily accented Hindi, and it seemed as if she was trying to perform rituals for us. She pointed to a hole in the ground next to the idol, and the young man sent by the priest interpreted her gesture to mean that at the request of Mother Renuka the Ganga had appeared there in the form of a stream and that the water still flows there. The old woman dipped a small vessel in the hole, and it filled with water. She sprinkled that water on us, lit an oil lamp, and then walked across the packed chamber to get incense from the other side, somehow managing to do it without touching anyone. After lighting the incense, she recited some prayers and then tied a thread on each of our wrists, something the priest traditionally does at the end of the ritual worship. This was puzzling and disorienting, for she was tying the threads without touching us, but at the time we attributed our sense of disorientation to our exhaustion, the darkness, the lack of air, and the smoke from the incense. She came out of the temple with us and signaled for those who could not fit inside to come forward so that she could tie the thread around their wrists also.

It was almost sunset. Some of the group rushed to get down the hill before it got too dark, while others lingered to enjoy a few quiet moments or take some pictures. Just then Eileen, whom we had left behind hours earlier, arrived, flushed and sweating profusely. I was happy that she had made it to the top, but worried about how she would get down again in the dark. But the old woman had walked over to her and asked for her right hand so that she could tie the thread. Then, after tying it, she looked at Eileen's flushed face, asked for her left hand, and tied another thread on her left wrist. As she did, Eileen's fatigue dropped away and she was filled with energy. The two looked into each other's eyes, and Eileen said, "May I kiss you?" Although she was speaking in English, the old woman understood and offered her cheek. Eileen bent to kiss her and was immediately bewildered—it was not a human cheek. She had touched the woman's cheek with her lips, and yet she had not.

Eileen bid the woman goodbye and joined the members of the group waiting for her outside the courtyard. She could not contain her excitement. "Did you know that she is not human?" she asked her friends. As soon as she said it, everyone began to reflect on their own experiences. All had several in common: the woman had appeared in the temple out of the blue, she had walked from one side of the jammed temple chamber to the other without touching or crowding anyone, and she had tied the thread on their wrists without touching anyone. Everyone in the group began to compare how they had felt in her presence, especially when she had tied the thread on their wrists. But the most tangible proof that something extraordinary had just taken place was that Eileen, who was stout and middle-aged, had become as agile as a teenager. She had no trouble with the long walk down the hill in the gathering darkness. In fact, it seemed as if everyone had a new set of eyes as they made their way back to the buses.

The next day we began our journey to Gangotri, and as we wended our way deeper into the mountains we could see snow and sleet falling everywhere except right on the road where we were driving. When we looked down the road we had just traveled, the bad weather seemed to close in behind us. But except for a few rain showers, our buses encountered no bad weather. From Gangotri we trekked to Gomukh glacier, and there was sunshine everywhere.

Throughout the rest of the trip everyone talked about these things, but I tried to avoid their conversations. I did not want to fuel anyone's imagination or add my own interpretation of the events we had just witnessed. Those who had taken the old woman's picture were curious to see if she would be visible when the photos were developed, and when we returned to Rishikesh they took their film to be processed immediately. To everyone's astonishment the old woman was clearly visible—but in some photos her sari had a colored border, and in others it had no border at all; in some photos the sari was pure white, in others it was light blue. Now everyone was free of doubt: this had been a divine occurrence.

When I went to see Swamiji a few days later, he asked, "Did you visit her?" I said "Yes," and he was quiet for a moment.

Then he said, "She is the Divine Mother, all-pervading, without name and form. The great souls like Parashurama and Ganesha dwell in her. She is eternal and so are her blessed children, the sages. I am a faithful servant to those who have surrendered themselves at her feet."

399

By this time Swamiji had become extremely weak; he could speak only with great effort. And as he was almost always attended by those who took care of him, opportunities for conversations of this nature were rare. But in these few sentences he had poured out the entire bible of the tradition of the Himalayan sages. I wanted to be alone somewhere to reflect on what he had said and assimilate what he meant. Next to the building housing Swamiji's apartment was the building housing the Department of Combined Therapy, and there I found an empty room on the second floor and locked myself away for a couple of hours. Sitting there, I realized that Swamiji had just explained who he is, who the sages are, who the Divine Mother is, what the sages' relationship with the Divine Mother is, and what the tradition's obligation is to those who have surrendered themselves at her feet.

Absorbed in contemplation, I began to remember some experiences I'd had with Swamiji that revealed his relationship with the Divine. In the early 1980s I was fortunate enough to read some of the letters he had written between 1956 and 1975 to Dr. Agnihotri, his beloved friend and disciple. In one of those he had drawn a picture of the Divine Mother as she had appeared to him. At that time I could not comprehend the spirit of the drawing, and I did not understand the meaning of the letter either. I thought Swamiji was simply writing it in a mystical style. But in the light of the few sentences he had just uttered I saw him as a sage inebriated with divine love. And in this light all his other identities—scientist, researcher, philosopher, yogi, poet, author, humanitarian, and the founder and head of a multi-national organization—were mere shadows of his true identity: the blessed child of the Divine Mother.

My contemplation also brought forward an incident from 1980. Swamiji had been dictating a letter in response to one he had received from an astrologer in New Delhi who was closely related to Swamiji's biological family. The astrologer had written to warn of a calamity which, due to the placement of planets and stars, was soon to befall Swamiji. Now Swamiji's reply to this astrologer came back to me with a new clarity. In essence he had written that once the Divine Mother had bestowed her unconditional love and protection on him, placing him under the safety of her feet, he no longer had a reason to protect himself from the movements of the planets and stars. As he was dictating this reply there had been a light in his eyes that did not seem to be of this world, and I now realized that a few minutes earlier Swamiji had confirmed that the light shining in him was indeed not of this world.

This realization pulled me back to a conversation I'd had with Swamiji in the mid-1980s. It was one of those Sunday mornings when he was scheduled to speak, and I was walking to the lecture, wishing that he would talk about something other than his usual stuff: "Be practical, don't be emotional, be nice to yourself, and take care of your duties . . . ." I was thinking that if he asked me beforehand, "What's my topic today?" (as he often did), I would trick him. I would say "The Divine Mother, the guiding light." When I reached the Institute's main building I discovered that Swamiji was still in his room. He was putting on his shawl when I entered.

I touched his feet, and he said, "How do I look?"

I replied, "You look beautiful, Swamiji." Then I went on: "Swamiji, I want to tell you that I have just achieved a great *siddhi*." When he asked what it was, I replied, "Now I can read anyone's mind and can predict the immediate future. In fact, I can tell exactly what you are going to say in your lecture today."

He smiled and said, "Okay, tell me."

I said, "You'll walk to the stage in your regal style, go to the podium, and while looking at the audience you will bow your head and say [and here I began to imitate his speaking style], 'I pray to the Divinity in you. How are you today? Are you comfortable? Do you like the food here at the Institute? If you have any problem, please tell Kevin or Dr. Clarke.' Then very gracefully you will walk to the blackboard, and while looking at the audience you will say, 'A human being is not body alone, not mind alone. A human being is a breathing being too.' Then you will draw two circles on the board and say, 'Here is the body, and here is the mind. Between these two there is something called breath,' while you connect the circles with arrows."

I was still in the flow of my playlet when Swamiji grinned and roared, "*Badmash* [rascal]! You are making fun of your guru?"

"No, Swamiji," I replied. "But all these years this is the only thing I am hearing. Is this the only thing yoga and spirituality are about? Isn't there something more to it?"

"Then you tell me, what is yoga? What else should I be teaching?"

I said, "What's the use of catching hold of the nose, breathing left and right, and concentrating on the breath, if just by thinking of the beautiful toes of the Divine Mother one can become absorbed in her and find oneself in the consummate state that renders the joy of samadhi tasteless?"

As I said this, Swamiji's eyes closed and his head began to sway in a gentle circle. He sank down on a nearby chair, and it seemed as if he had entered a world that was unreachable by the ordinary mind. There he stayed for the next five minutes. When he opened his eyes he said gently, "Promise that from today, you will not remind me of her. For if you do so I will not be able to function, and my master has given me a task that I must accomplish before this body falls apart."

That experience touched me deeply. Although he spoke about the Divine Mother from time to time after that, he never said enough to convey the depth of his relationship with her.

401

While I was remembering these experiences and others like them, almost two hours had elapsed. Now I realized that my wife must be wondering what I was doing. It was getting late and we needed to return to the ashram. At the time I was completing the book *From Death to Birth*. At least that had been my plan. But my conversation with Swamiji had stirred up so many emotions that for the next few days I was unable to concentrate on my writing.

My mind kept returning to the words Swamiji had uttered a few days before, as well as other references he had made to the Divine Mother in the past twenty years. From time to time I went to the ashram's tiny library and paged through *Living with the Himalayan Masters* and *Love Whispers;* I also went for long, solitary walks along the Ganga and adjacent canals downriver from the ashram. I had read all of Swamiji's books thoroughly, especially these two. Now, looking at them again, I was amazed. In some passages he had stated openly who he was and what his relationship with the Divine Mother was. And yet my mind had barely registered these passages. For example, he had written in *Love Whispers:* "When I was seven years of age, I suddenly felt a thundering shock that transported me to a different realm of reality that I had not been aware of. Terrified, I approached my master, and he said, 'There dawns something higher—something exquisite, implicitly wondrous, and unexplainable—so do not talk. Lay your hand on your mouth, and do not allow the secret to come out of the chamber of your heart, for anything that comes from the heart to the mouth becomes impure. Therefore, let it remain in the heart of hearts.'"

Addressing the Mother, Swamiji had also written, "O silent Divinity, Thou art a majestic queen among women, a flame of light in the dark chamber of my being. Why hast Thou forsaken me when I need Thee in manifestation? Nothing mundane—no beauty, no charms, no temptations—delights me. I tried once and twice to find fulfillment in the temporal and failed. Thy revelation to me provides great power and freshness to my mind and heart. Thou hast given me glorious spirit to work day and night. That is how I function."

Now, walking along the riverbank, I remembered something that happened when *Love Whispers* was about to go to press. Swamiji was leaning back on his couch one evening with his eyes closed. He was not sleeping, yet he was not aware of this world. I sat quietly for a few minutes, then left. When he saw me the next morning he said, "Come; I'll show you something." And when I went to his room he showed me a poem he had written the night before. It read:

> *Child am I of a sage of the mountain.*
> *Free spirit am I; light walks by my side.*
> *Fearless live I above glacial fountain,*
> *In seclusion of Himalayan cavern reside.*

> *With snowy weather beating around me,*
> *Ascending the peaks of the mountains I go.*
> *No one talks with me, no one walks with me,*
> *As I cross streams and tramp glacial snow.*

> *I roam in the mountains that hark to the skies,*
> *And of silence have made me a friend.*
> *My Love whispers to me with silent replies.*
> *And guided by thee I ascend.*

When I asked Swamiji what this meant, he replied, "I slipped into the future. This is the reality of the future." Then he said, "Don't feel bad. Read the last stanza."

> *Offering my life at Thy holy feet,*
> *Loving all—selfless and complete.*

As I read the final couplet, he said, "I love you and I love those who have surrendered themselves at her holy feet. Safeguard the secret by sealing your lips. Service is the way to be with me."

For the next few weeks I lived more in the world of reverie than in the world of events. In the world of events, I occupied myself with completing *From Death to Birth*, visiting the hospital campus, and catching glimpses of Swamiji from a distance. On November 10 I completed the practice that he had given me on August 11, 1993, before he left the

403

Institute in Honesdale. The rules of the tradition required that I conclude it with a fire offering, and Prem Sobte, the ashram manager, made all the arrangements for this special practice at the bank of the Ganga. The offering I began that evening stretched well into the early morning hours of the eleventh. And when I offered the final oblation, the area behind the sacred fire just above the Ganga was lit with the effulgence of a gathering of sages. Swamiji was among them.

After the sun came up my wife and I went to see Swamiji. With his glance Swamiji asked us to sit down, and after a few minutes of silence I asked Mahesh, who attended Swamiji, if we could have a few private moments with him.

When he had gone, Swamiji said, "The Mother is all-pervading. She is eternal and so are her children, the sages. Following her wishes, my master emerges from her and is reabsorbed into her. I am simply an extension of him. My master is the creator of my destiny. He decides when I come and when I go. Now he needs someone there to disturb the monotony of his samadhi. I must go."

He was leaving—I was trying to comprehend that as my sinking heart cried, "What is left here in this world for me?"

His heart heard mine, for his next words were, "Serve the sages. Light the lamp of their love in human hearts. That is how you offer your life at her holy feet. Be selfless. Be fearless. When the time comes, walk out from here as though you never were here to begin with."

"I completed the practice today," I told him. "Three years ago, you taught me the final step but asked me not to practice it without your permission. Today may I have permission to practice it?"

"Yes," he said. And with a mysterious smile he spoke his last words to me: "Start the practice. One day I will take you to our ancestral cave."

Mahesh returned. My wife and I placed our heads at Swamiji's feet, and concealing his gift of sorrow and joy, we left the room.

Two days later, on November 13, Swamiji ascended to join his master, the Sage from the Highest Peak.

404

glossary

AGHORA ~ The most peaceful, beautiful, and benign form of Shiva; in present-day India, however, this word is used to denote a dirty and ugly form of Shiva, a usage which has no basis in the scriptures.

AGNI SARA ~ A yogic technique to fan the fire at the navel center.

ARYA SAMAJ ~ A particular sect within Hinduism that was founded by Swami Dayananda Saraswati in the nineteenth century.

ATMAN ~ The center of pure consciousness; the self; the soul.

AYURVEDA ~ The ancient Indian medical science that promotes a long, healthy life.

BALA TRIPURA ~ The child aspect of the Divine Mother known as Tripura or Sri Vidya; a special three-syllable mantra, which according to the scriptures is supposed to remain secret.

BANDHAS ~ Special techniques of hatha yoga consisting of postures and breathing exercises; in English, such practices are roughly translated as "locks." Also, bondage, especially when referring to karmic bondage, which aspirants try to overcome by committing themselves to meditation and inner purification.

BHAKTI ~ Love and devotion; the path of total surrender and faith.

BHASTRIKA ~ Bellows breathing; a kind of pranayama involving forceful inhalation and exhalation by activating the lower abdominal muscles.

BINDU BHEDANA ~ Piercing the subtle knot at the eyebrow center.

BRAHMACHARYA ~ Practice leading to the realization of Brahman; often used synonymously with celibacy.

BRAHMA JAGARANA ~ A practice "to stay awake in the night while contemplating the highest truth."

BRAHMA NADI ~ The innermost energy channel.

BRAHMA RISHI ~ The highest-caliber sage.

DARSHANA ~ "Glimpse"; the direct vision of the invisible, absolute reality; revelation; system of philosophy.

DEVA DASI ~ "Female servant of the divine"; a woman from a particular group in Indian society who served the temples by performing daily housekeeping chores and giving ceremonial music and dance performances.

DEVA ~ Divine being.

DHARMA ~ The higher principles of life that help individuals and society to live peacefully; the values that are the foundation of a healthy society; in modern times, the word is used to indicate both sectarian religion and the philosophy of life.

DHUNI ~ Sacred fire; ceremonial fire; the fire that ascetics make as part of their practice.

DURGA MANTRA ~ A mantra devoted to the goddess Durga, who is usually shown riding a lion and carrying weapons of war.

DURGA SAPTASHATI ~ A scripture consisting of seven hundred mantras dedicated to propitiating the goddess Durga.

GARHWALIS ~ People from the Garhwal region of the Himalayas.

GAYATRI MANTRA ~ The most sacred of the Vedic mantras, which every devout Hindu is supposed to learn and practice as a part of daily meditation.

GURUBHAI ~ Brother disciple; a disciple of one's guru.

407

GURU CHAKRA ~ The center above the eyebrow center; the center of consciousness where, according to yogis, one attains the glimpse of the inner guru, the primordial master.

GURU DAKSHINA ~ Love offering a student makes to the teacher upon receiving initiation.

GURUDEVA ~ *Guru* means "one who dispels the darkness of ignorance"; *deva* means "bright being"; *gurudeva* means "divine being; the bright being that dispels the darkness of ignorance"; a term used for addressing one's spiritual teacher with reverence.

GURU MANTRA ~ The mantra a disciple receives from a teacher during formal initiation.

GURU PURNIMA ~ The day of the full moon dedicated to honoring the tradition; it normally falls in the month of July.

HARIJAN ~ "Man of God"; the name of a magazine published by Mahatma Gandhi's ashram.

HATHA YOGA ~ The school that aims to balance solar and lunar, masculine and feminine energies by means of postures, breathing techniques, cleansing practices, mudras, and meditation.

JAPA ~ The repetition of a mantra.

KABIR PANTHI ~ A sadhu associated with the tradition of Saint Kabir.

KARMA ~ "Action"; in the yogic tradition it refers to the law of action and reaction.

KARMA YOGA ~ The yoga of action; selfless service.

KARNA PISHACHINI ~ A tantric goddess who supposedly resides in the ears of a tantric who invokes her; when invoked, she whispers the answer to questions asked by others into the ear of the tantric practitioner.

KRIYA ~ Any of various yogic purification practices.

KULA DEVI ~ Family deity.

KUMBHA MELA ~ A grand spiritual festival held every twelve years in four different cities in India: the grandest of these is held in Allahabad, attracting millions of people from India and abroad.

KUNDA ~ The sacred fireplace.

KUNDALINI ~ "Coiled-up energy"; the dormant potential energy in all living beings; the spiritual energy that yogis attempt to awaken.

LAGHU SAMADHI ~ Spiritual absorption lasting for a short period; a meditative state in which a yogi suspends prana and leaves the body, returning to the same body shortly afterward.

MAHA KALA ~ The devourer of time; the presiding deity of all the shrines in Ujjain; also known as the destroyer of death.

MAHAVIDYAS ~ The exalted paths of tantra sadhana.

MAHIKARI ~ A Japanese spiritual organization founded by Okadasan; it has its headquarters in Tokuyama.

MANAS ~ Mind; specifically, the state of mind that contains the element of doubt and uncertainty.

MALA ~ Beads used in mantra recitation; rosary beads.

MAYA ~ That which makes one perceive oneself as limited; the veil of illusion.

MOKSHA ~ Liberation; freedom from the bondage of karma.

MUDRA ~ A yogic gesture; various yogic mudras that, combined with asanas and bandhas (locks), are practiced as prerequisites for awakening kundalini.

MUKTI ~ The same as *moksha*; liberation; freedom from the bondage of karma.

MULADHARA ~ The first, most basic center of consciousness; according to kundalini yoga, it is located at the perineum.

NADIS ~ Energy channels; the pathways of the pranic force.

NAGA SADHU ~ A sadhu who wears little or no clothes.

NAVA RATRI ~ An annual nine-day celebration in honor of the Divine Mother.

NAVARNA MANTRA ∼ The nine-syllable mantra dedicated to the Divine Mother Durga.

PANCHAGNI SADHANA ∼ A practice that entails completely surrounding oneself with five fires: the fire in all four directions and the Sun above.

PARA-KAYA PRAVESHA ∼ An advanced yogic technique for leaving one's body and entering the same or another body at will.

PRAKRIT ∼ One of the ancient languages of India in which the Jain scriptures are written.

PRANA ∼ Vital energy; subtle energy; the life-force that holds the body and mind together.

PRANAYAMA ∼ Expansion of, or voluntary control over, the pranic force; the system of breathing exercises.

PURANAS ∼ The group of scriptures compiled by sage Vyasa.

PURNA AHUTI ∼ Final offering; normally it is made by offering oblations to the fire.

RAJA YOGA ∼ "The royal path"; The eightfold path as described by Patanjali in the *Yoga Sutra*.

RAMANUJACHARYA ORDER ∼ A spiritual and philosophical tradition founded by Ramanuja, a saint from south India in the twelfth century; according to this tradition, God is both absolute and immanent—simultaneously with and without attributes.

RUDRA ∼ The most compassionate Divine Being, who sheds tears upon seeing the pain and misery in the world; the most valiant form of Shiva, who is always adept at destroying ignorance.

RUDRAKSHA MALA ～ A rosary made of seeds of the rudraksha plant.

SABAR MANTRA ～ A non-traditional mantra, usually in a language other than Sanskrit.

SADHANA ～ Spiritual practice.

SAMADHI ～ A state of tranquility; spiritual absorption; a balanced state of mind. Also, the burial ground of a saint.

SAMAYA AGNI ～ Peaceful, radiant fire, as opposed to the destructive fire of Rudra.

411

SAMSKARAS ～ The subtle impressions of the past; karmic impressions stored in the unconscious mind.

SAMVARTA AGNI ～ The destructive fire of Rudra, as opposed to the peaceful, radiant fire of samaya.

SAMYAMA ～ Inner transformation through concentration, meditation, and samadhi.

SANATANA DHARMA ～ The eternal teachings outlined in the Vedas.

SANDHYA BHASHA ～ "Twilight language"; the mystical language of the yogis.

SANKALPA SHAKTI ～ The power of will and self-determination.

SANNYASA ～ Renunciation; the path of non-attachment; the monastic life.

SANNYASA DHARMA ～ Rules and laws governing monastic life.

SANNYASI(N) ~ One who has taken the vows of sannyasa.

SATSANGA ~ Being in the company of saints.

SHAIVITE ~ Pertaining to the philosophy and practices of the experience of Shiva, the pure consciousness within.

SHAKTI ~ Power; the intrinsic creative energy of consciousness.

SHAKTI PATA ~ The direct transmission of spiritual energy.

SHAKTI SADHANA ~ The practice leading to the experience of the Divine Mother.

SHATA CHANDI ~ The practice of reciting the scripture *Durga Saptashati,* which consists of seven hundred mantras dedicated to propitiating the goddess Durga.

SHAT KARMA ~ A set of six specific tantric practices.

SHIVA ~ Pure consciousness, existence, and bliss; also refers to Shiva as a god.

SHIVA BALI ~ A tantric practice consisting of mantra japa, recitation of a specific set of prayers, and the ceremonial offering of food to the goddess. The practitioners of this discipline view female jackals, wolves, and hyenas as the manifestation of the motherly aspect of the Divine.

SHIVA LINGAM ~ An oval-shaped stone symbolizing Shiva, the nameless and formless God.

SHIVA SVARODAYA ~ *Shiva* means "consciousness"; *svara* means "melody, music, ripple, wave"; *udaya* means "rise, manifestation." A science that describes how the wave of life arises from the primordial pool of consciousness.

SIDDHA ~ An accomplished master.

SIDDHI ~ Extraordinary powers; yogic accomplishments; the ability to exercise one's power of will and determination.

SRI CHAKRA ~ The chakra of the Divine Mother Sri; the chakra of supreme beauty and bliss; the chakra of the Most Auspicious One.

SRI VIDYA ~ The most auspicious wisdom; the most beautiful and blissful form of the Divine Mother; the most esoteric tantric practice.

SRI YANTRA ~ Sri Vidya in geometrical form; the highest yantra, which according to tantrics is a complete map of the microcosm and the macrocosm; another name for Sri Chakra.

413

SURYA VIJÑANA ~ "The science of the sun." The solar science; the mystical knowledge of the sun; also, the practices pertaining to the navel center.

SUSHUMNA ~ The central channel in the subtle body.

SVADHISHTHANA ~ "Her own abode"; the second chakra, located at the pelvic center.

TANTRA ~ The philosophy and practice that aims at experiencing the union of Shakti and Shiva.

TAPAS ~ "Heat, glow"; austerities; practices that help one shine.

THERAVADA ~ "The doctrine of the elders"; refers to the most ancient philosophy and practice of Buddhism.

TIKA ~ Dot; a ceremonial or ornamental dot on the forehead.

TRATAKA ~ Gazing; one of the cleansing practices described in hatha yoga.

UPANISHADS ~ A set of yogic and Vedantic scriptures that are supposed to be studied under the guidance of a teacher.

VAIRAGI ORDER ~ A group of sadhus whose practices center around non-attachment.

VAIRAGYA ~ Non-attachment; the core practice of aspirants belonging to the monastic order.

VAJROLI KRIYA ~ One of the cleansing techniques described in hatha yoga texts, an advanced form of which uses mercury internally.

VEDANTA ~ The highest wisdom described in the Vedas; a system of philosophy that expounds the theory of non-dualism.

VEDAS ~ The world's most ancient revealed scriptures; they consist of thousands of mantras.

VIDYA ~ Knowledge; spiritual science; also refers to the absolute truth in the form of the goddess.

VIRAJA HOMA ~ A special type of fire offering, which according to the scriptures brings inner purification; one of the special practices performed when an aspirant takes a vow of renunciation.

VIRAT RUPA ~ The cosmic form of the Divine; the Divine manifesting in the form of the universe.

VISHWA HINDU PARISHAD ~ "International Hindu Assembly"; India's largest Hindu organization, popularly known as VHP.

YAJUR VEDA ~ One of the four Vedas.

YANTRA ~ A geometrical figure used as the locus for worshipping tantric deities or for meditation in tantric practices.

YOGA NIDRA ~ Yogic sleep; sleepless sleep; a practice whereby the aspirant learns how to give complete rest to body and mind without falling asleep.

YUNANI ~ A system of medicine developed by Greeks and Persians that is still practiced in India.

index

425

about PANDIT RAJMANI TIGUNAIT, Ph.D.

Pandit Rajmani Tigunait, Ph.D., is a specialist in Vedic and tantric studies, and is a lifelong practitioner of yoga and meditation. He holds a doctorate in Sanskrit from the University of Allahabad in India, and a doctorate in Oriental Studies from the University of Pennsylvania. Pandit Tigunait is the Spiritual Head of the Himalayan International Institute of Yoga Science and Philosophy, and successor of Sri Swami Rama of the Himalayas.

Pandit Tigunait has been living in the United States and teaching meditation and spirituality in the U.S. and abroad for the past two decades. He is a leading practitioner and instructor of yoga's sister science, Ayurveda, and is an expert in all branches of Indian philosophy. A regular contributor to *Yoga International* magazine, Pandit Tigunait is the author of eleven books.

the HIMALAYAN INSTITUTE

The main building of the Institute headquarters, near Honesdale, Pennsylvania.

FOUNDED IN 1971 by Swami Rama, the Himalayan Institute has been dedicated to helping people grow physically, mentally, and spiritually by combining the best knowledge of both the East and the West.

Our international headquarters is located on a beautiful 400-acre campus in the rolling hills of the Pocono Mountains of northeastern Pennsylvania. The atmosphere here is one to foster growth, increased inner awareness, and calm. Our grounds provide a wonderfully peaceful and healthy setting for our seminars and extended programs. Students from around the world join us here to attend programs in such diverse areas as hatha yoga, meditation, stress reduction, Ayurveda, nutrition, Eastern philosophy, psychology, and other subjects. Whether the programs are for weekend meditation retreats, week-long seminars on spirituality, months-long residential programs, or holistic health services, the attempt here is to provide an environment of gentle inner progress. We invite you to join with us in the ongoing process of personal growth and development.

The Institute is a nonprofit organization. Your membership in the Institute helps to support its programs. Please call or write for information on becoming a member.

PROGRAMS, SERVICES *and* FACILITIES

Institute programs share an emphasis on conscious holistic living and personal self-development, including:

- ▶ Special weekend or extended seminars to teach skills and techniques for increasing your ability to be healthy and enjoy life
- ▶ Meditation retreats and advanced meditation and philosophical instruction
- ▶ Vegetarian cooking and nutritional training
- ▶ Hatha yoga workshops
- ▶ Hatha yoga teachers training
- ▶ Residential programs for self-development
- ▶ Holistic health services, and Ayurvedic Rejuvenation and Pancha Karma Programs through the Institute's Center for Health and Healing.

A Quarterly Guide to Programs and Other Offerings is free within the USA. To request a copy, or for further information, call 800-822-4547 or 570-253-5551, fax 570-253-9078, email bqinfo@HimalayanInstitute.org, write the Himalayan Institute, RR 1 Box 1127, Honesdale, PA 18431-9706 USA, or visit our website at www.HimalayanInstitute.org.

the HIMALAYAN INSTITUTE PRESS

The Himalayan Institute Press has long been regarded as "The Resource for Holistic Living." We publish dozens of titles, as well as audio and video tapes, that offer practical methods for living harmoniously and achieving inner balance. Our approach addresses the whole person—body, mind, and spirit—integrating the latest scientific knowledge with ancient healing and self-development techniques.

As such, we offer a wide array of titles on physical and psychological health and well-being, spiritual growth through meditation and other yogic practices, as well as translations of yogic scriptures.

Our yoga accessories include the Japa Kit for meditation practice, the Neti™ Pot, the ideal tool for sinus and allergy sufferers, and The Breath Pillow,™ a unique tool for learning health-supportive diaphragmatic breathing.

Subscriptions are available to a bimonthly magazine, *Yoga International,* which offers thought-provoking articles on all aspects of meditation and yoga, including yoga's sister science, Ayurveda.

For a free catalog call 800-822-4547 or 570-253-5551, email hibooks@HimalayanInstitute.org, fax 570-253-6360, write the Himalayan Institute Press, RR 1 Box 1129, Honesdale, PA 18431-9709, USA, or visit our website at www.HimalayanInstitute.org.